I WONDER...
IF YOU CAN FALL IN LOVE
AS SILENTLY AS THIS SNOW IS FALLING.

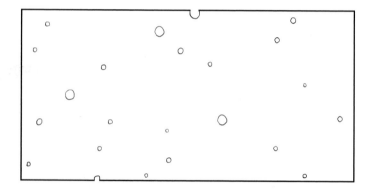

FALLING OUT OF A CLOUDY SKY,
CHANGING THE COLOR OF THE WORLD BELOW.

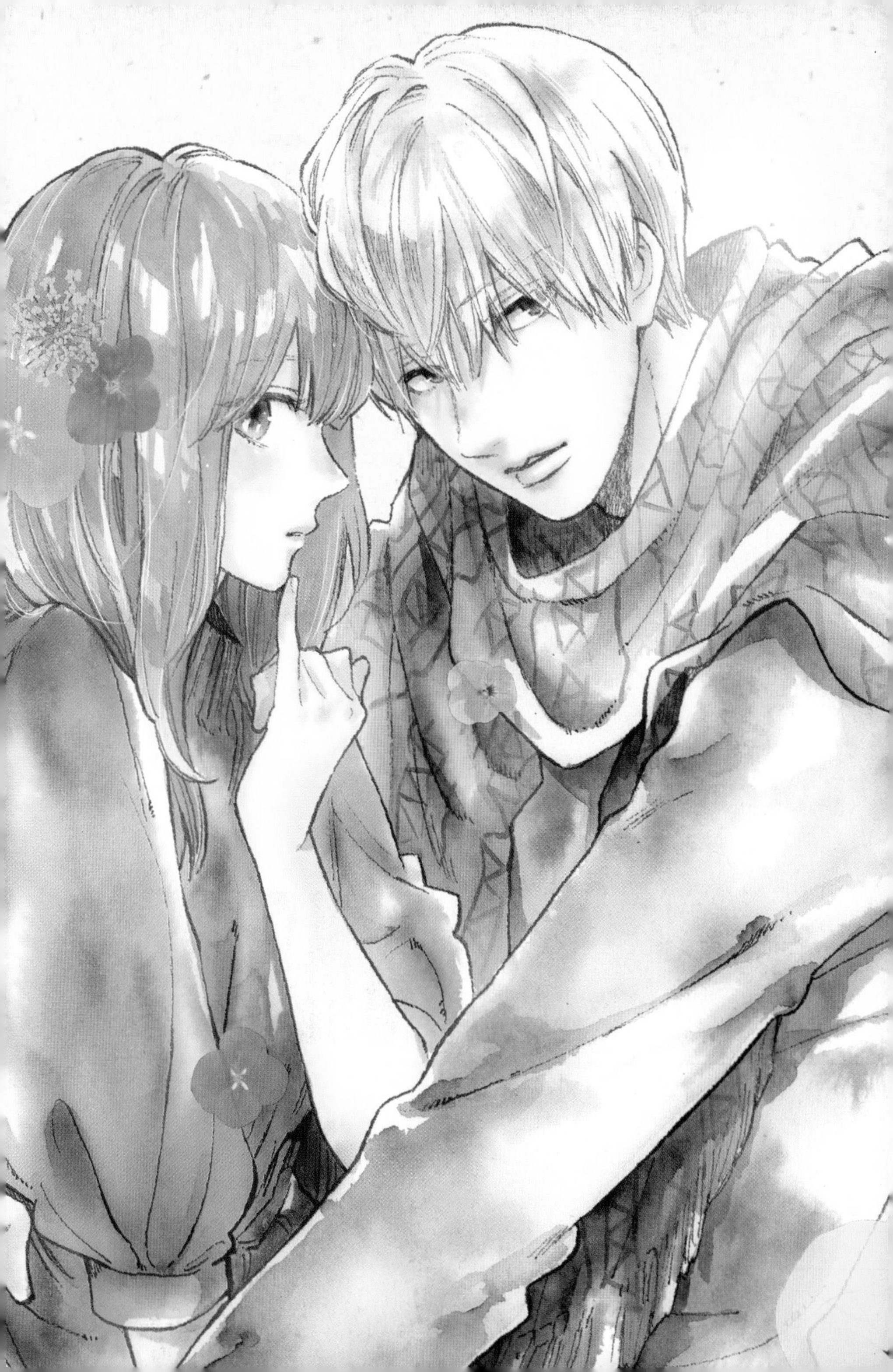

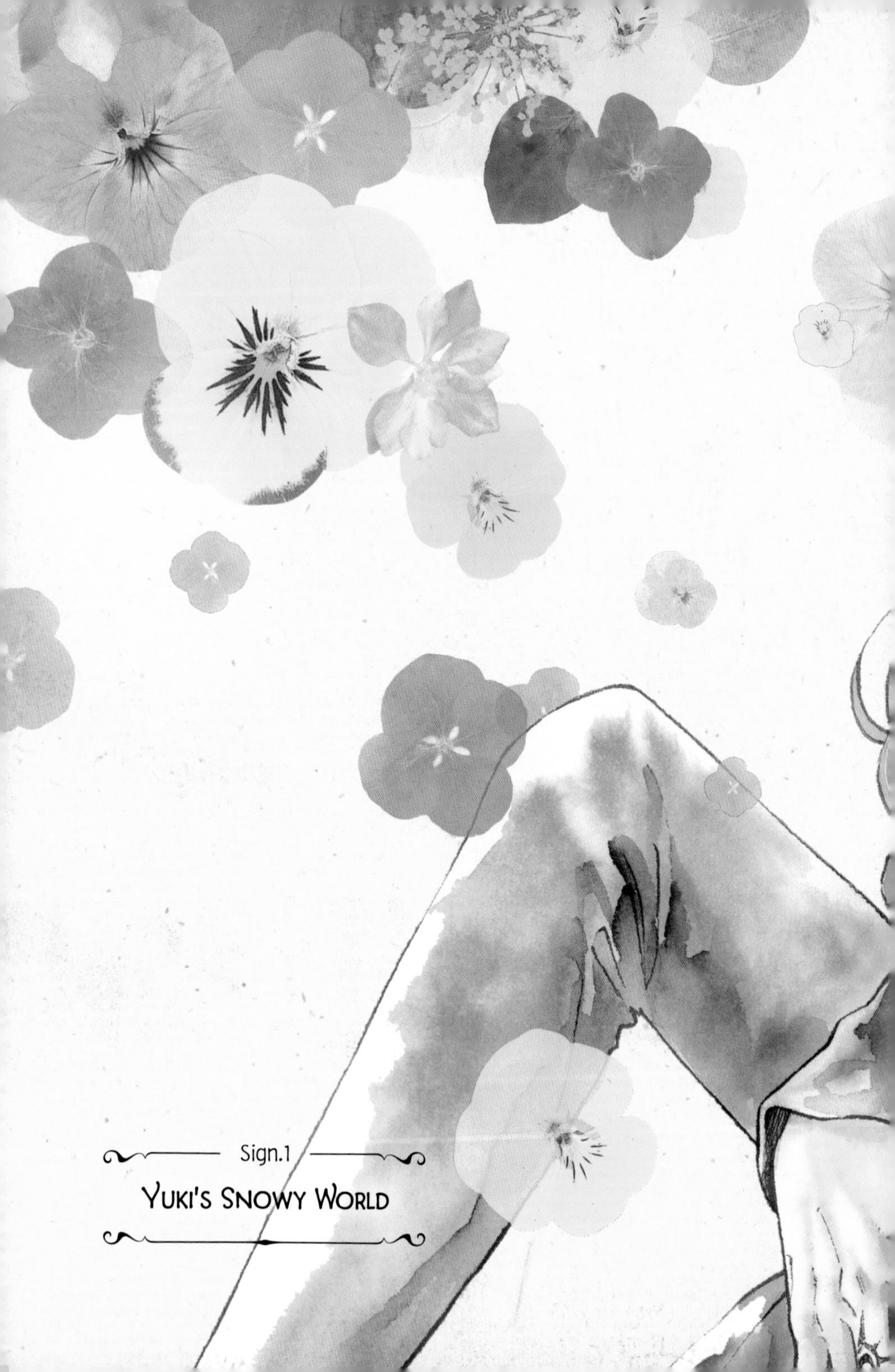
Sign.1
Yuki's Snowy World

Hello, and nice to meet you.
This is volume 1 of *A Sign of Affection.*
In Japan, it's running in
Kodansha's *Dessert* magazine.
The publisher has changed, and the
story itself has faced all sorts of
obstacles, but I'm still working hard
to create a shojo manga that
seamlessly incorporates
sign language.
Thank you for your support!

suu Morishita

A SIGN OF AFFECTION

suu Morishita

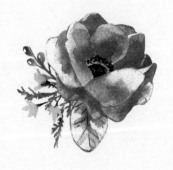

CONTENTS

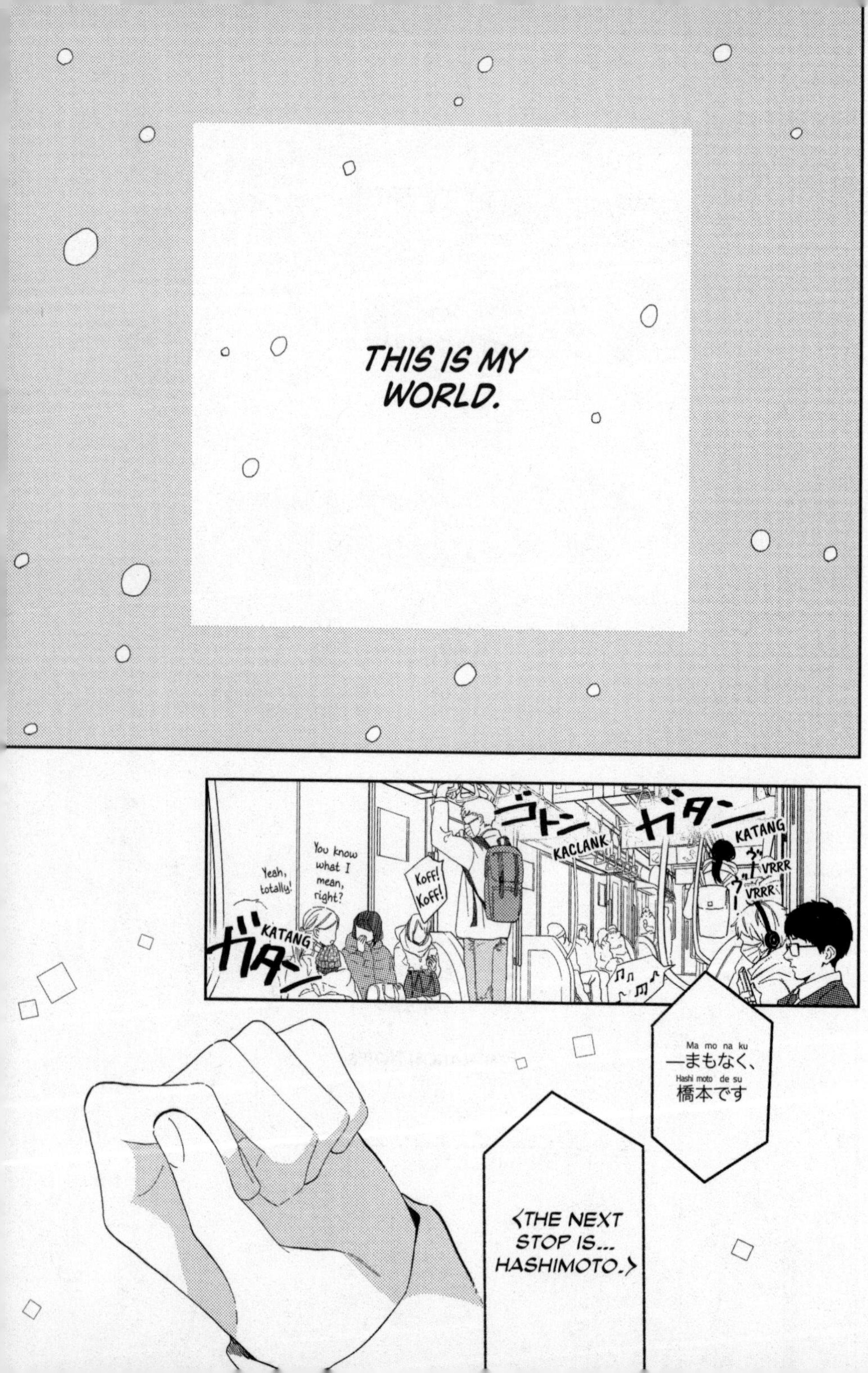
THIS IS MY WORLD.
ガタン KATANG
ヴー VRRR
ヴー VRRR
ゴトン KACLANK
Koff! Koff!
You know what I mean, right?
Yeah, totally!
ガタン KATANG
Ma mo na ku —まもなく、 Hashi moto de su 橋本です
<THE NEXT STOP IS... HASHIMOTO.>

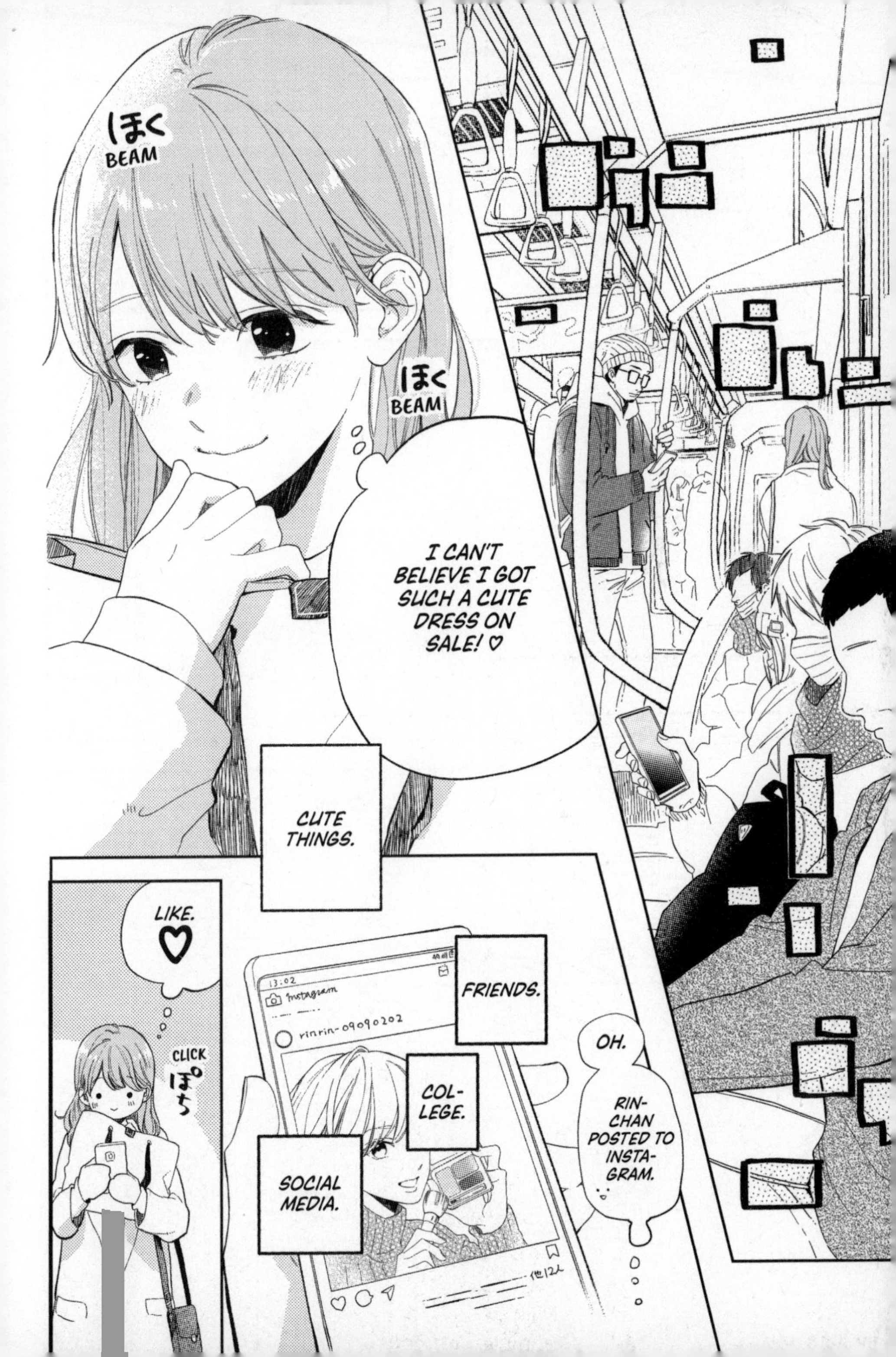
ほく
BEAM
ほく
BEAM
I CAN'T BELIEVE I GOT SUCH A CUTE DRESS ON SALE! ♡
CUTE THINGS.
OH.
RIN-CHAN POSTED TO INSTA-GRAM.
13:02
Instagram
rinrin-09090202
他12人
FRIENDS.
COL-LEGE.
SOCIAL MEDIA.
LIKE. ♡
CLICK
ぽち

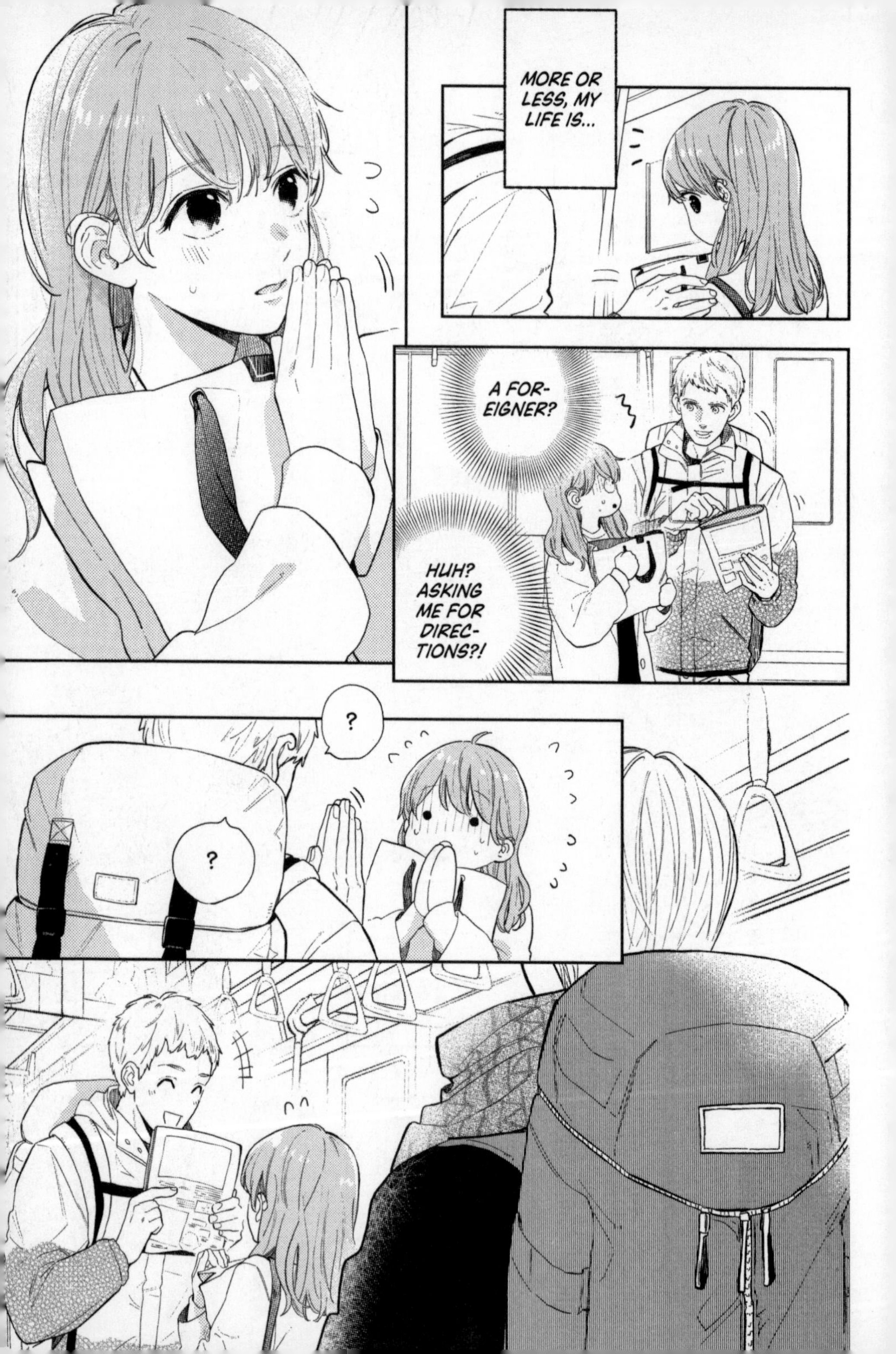
MORE OR LESS, MY LIFE IS...
A FOR-EIGNER?
HUH? ASKING ME FOR DIREC-TIONS?!
?
?

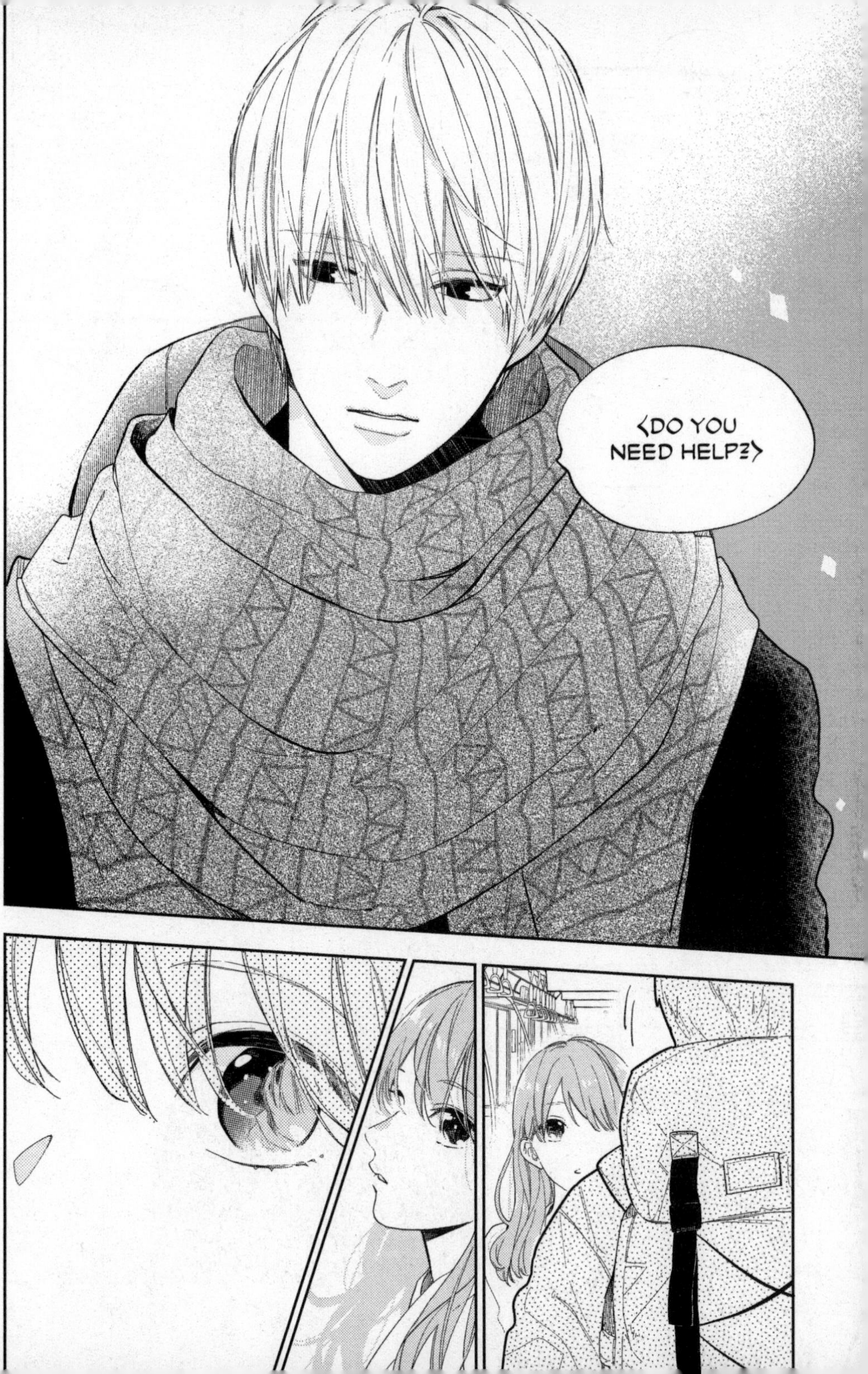
<DO YOU NEED HELP?>

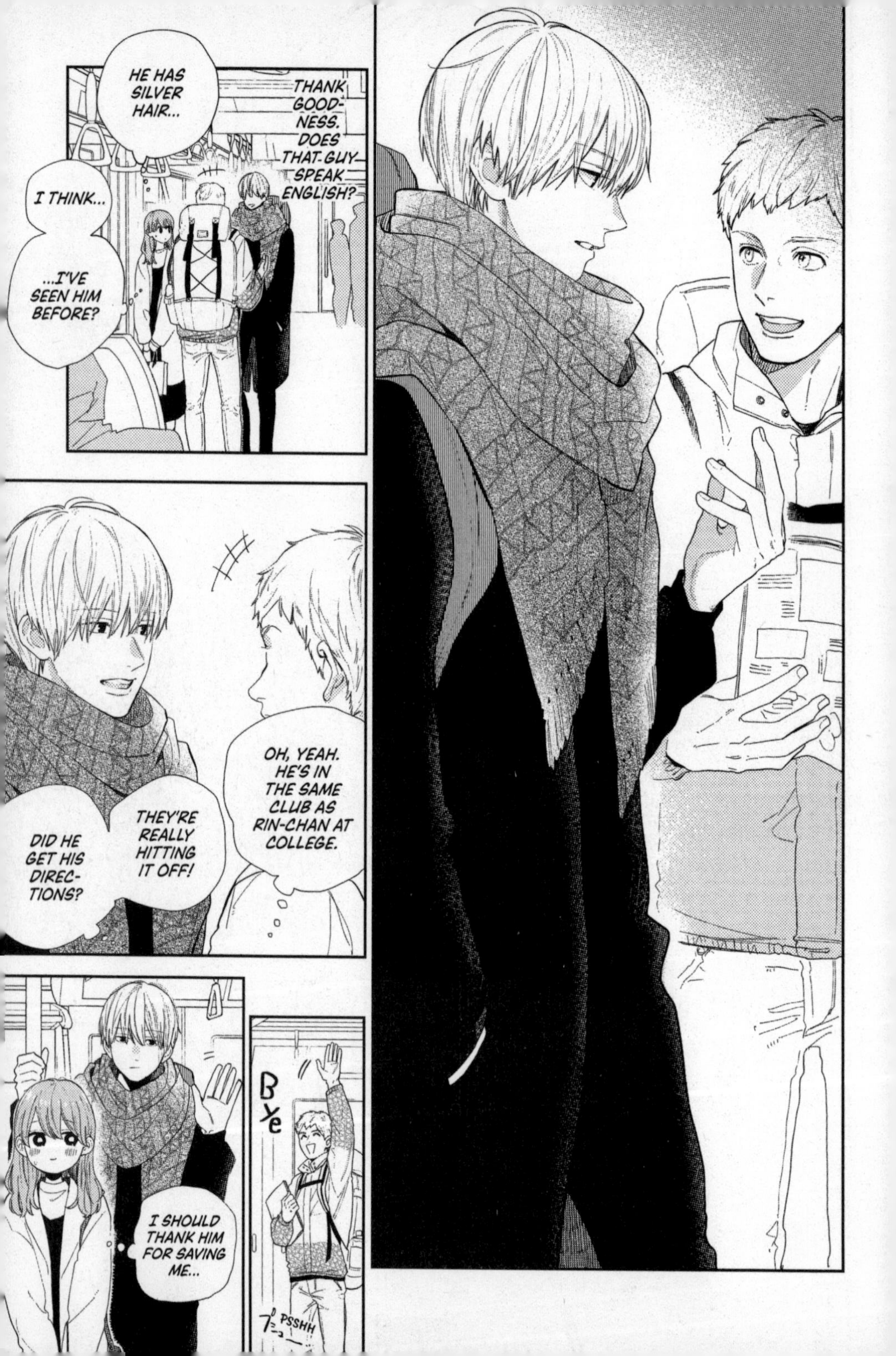
THANK GOODNESS. DOES THAT GUY SPEAK ENGLISH?
HE HAS SILVER HAIR...
I THINK...
...I'VE SEEN HIM BEFORE?
OH, YEAH. HE'S IN THE SAME CLUB AS RIN-CHAN AT COLLEGE.
THEY'RE REALLY HITTING IT OFF!
DID HE GET HIS DIRECTIONS?
Bye
PSSHH
I SHOULD THANK HIM FOR SAVING ME...

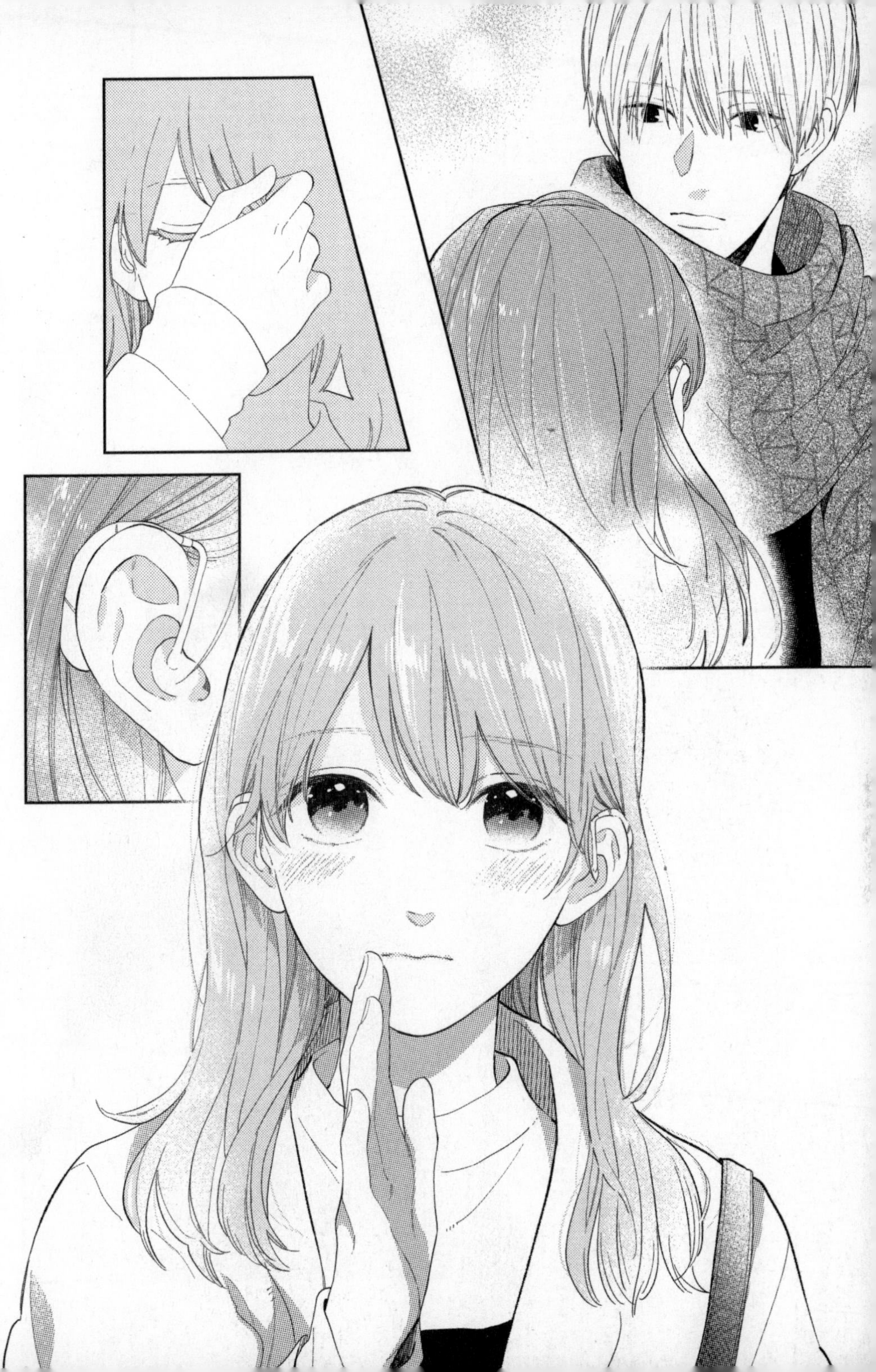

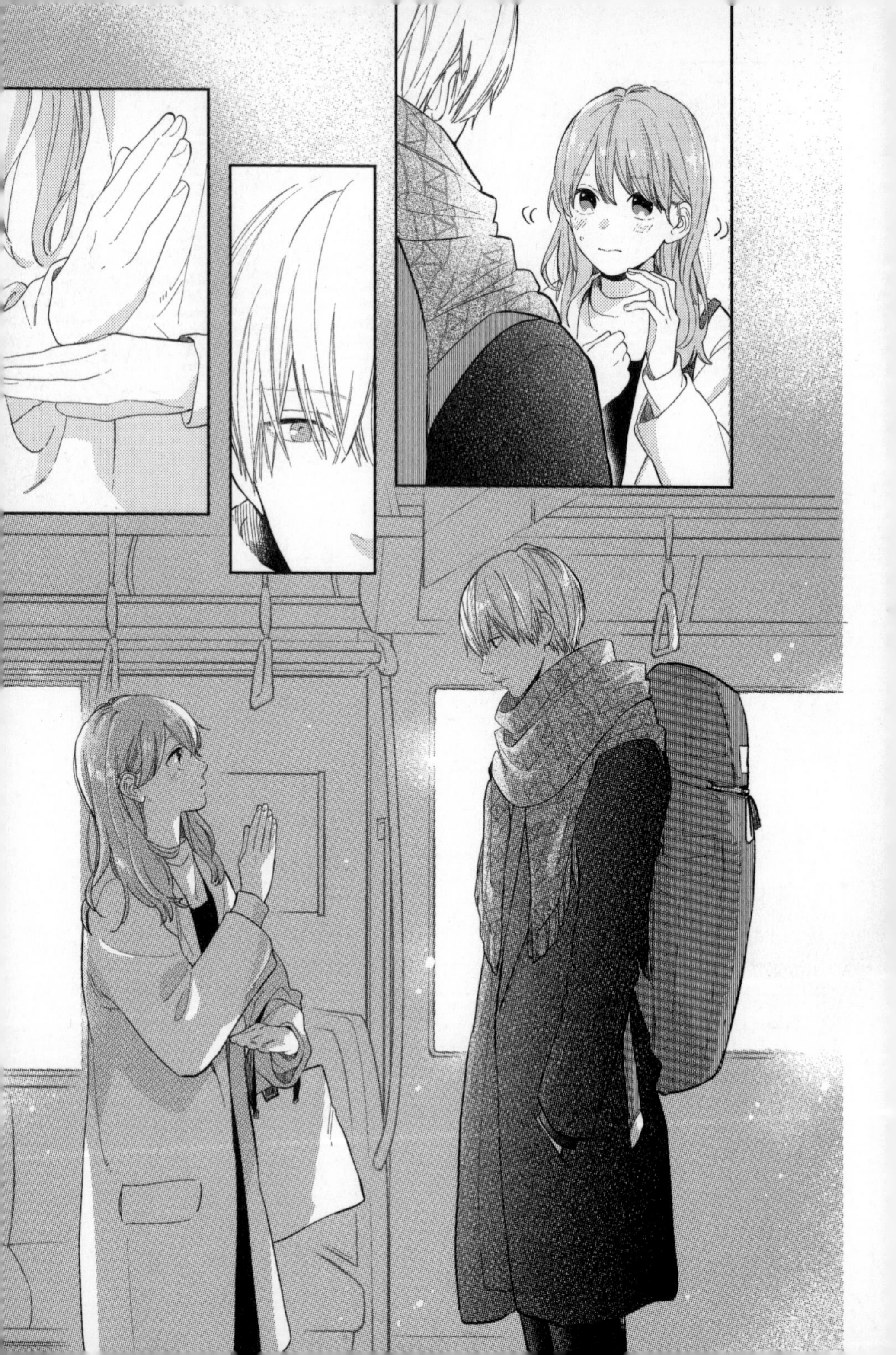

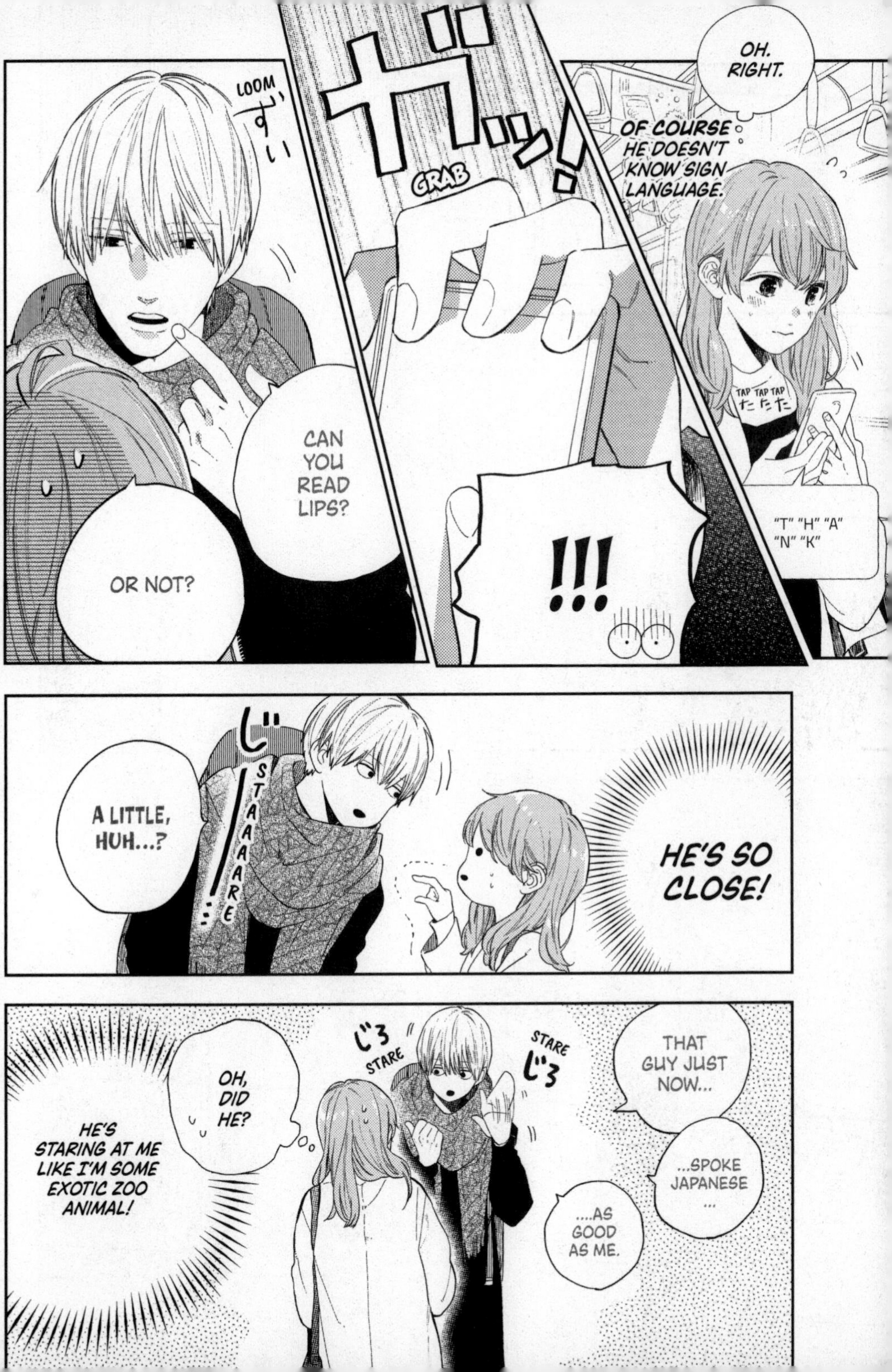
OH. RIGHT.
OF COURSE HE DOESN'T KNOW SIGN LANGUAGE.
TAP TAP TAP たたた
"T" "H" "A" "N" "K"
ガッ!
GRAB
!!!
LOOM すい
CAN YOU READ LIPS?
OR NOT?
HE'S SO CLOSE!
じ STAAAAARE
A LITTLE, HUH...?
THAT GUY JUST NOW...
...SPOKE JAPANESE ...
...AS GOOD AS ME.
STARE じろ
じろ STARE
OH, DID HE?
HE'S STARING AT ME LIKE I'M SOME EXOTIC ZOO ANIMAL!

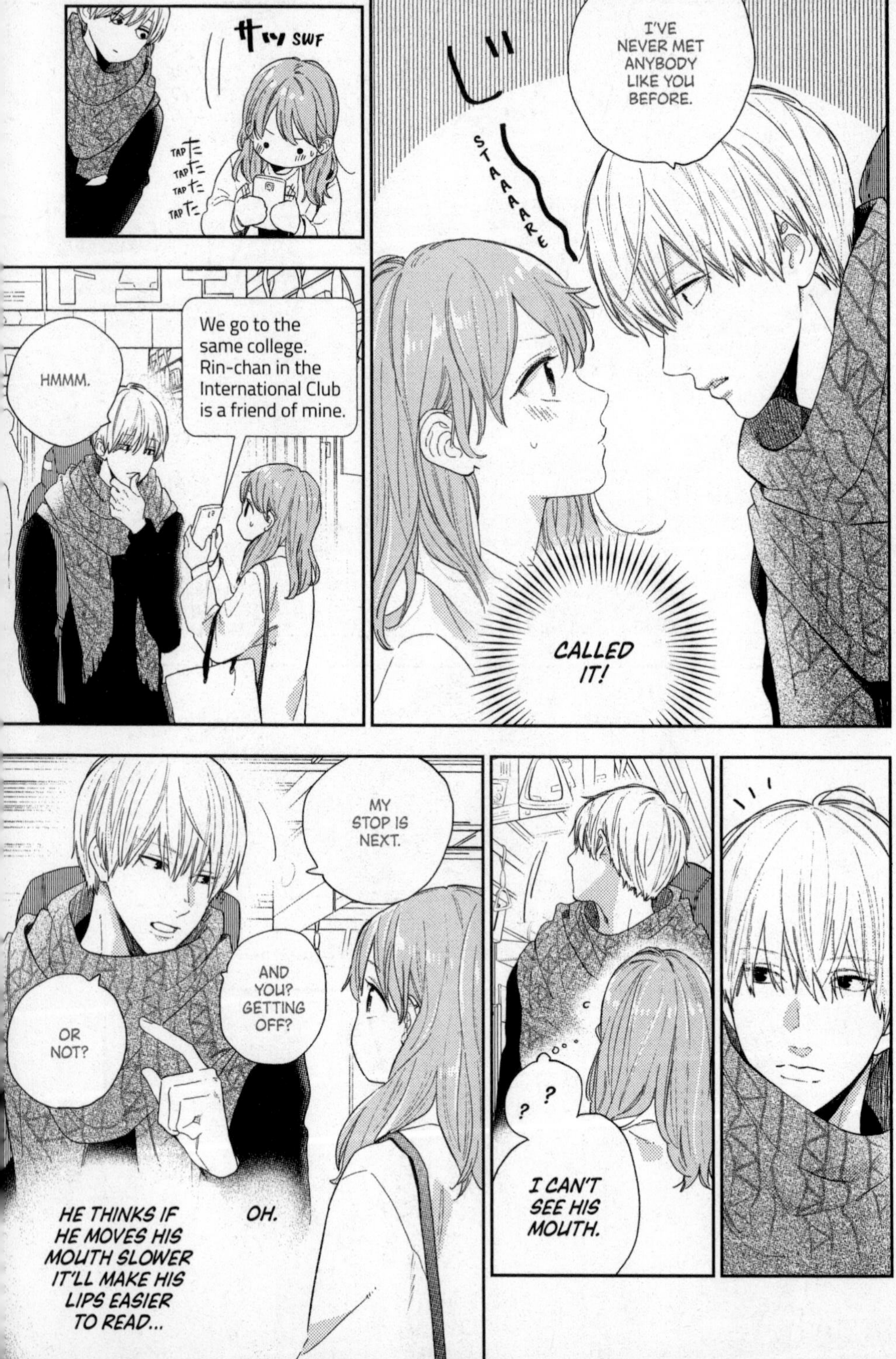
STAAAARE
I'VE NEVER MET ANYBODY LIKE YOU BEFORE.
CALLED IT!
SWF
TAP
TAP
TAP
TAP
We go to the same college. Rin-chan in the International Club is a friend of mine.
HMMM.
I CAN'T SEE HIS MOUTH.
? ?
MY STOP IS NEXT.
AND YOU? GETTING OFF?
OR NOT?
OH.
HE THINKS IF HE MOVES HIS MOUTH SLOWER IT'LL MAKE HIS LIPS EASIER TO READ...

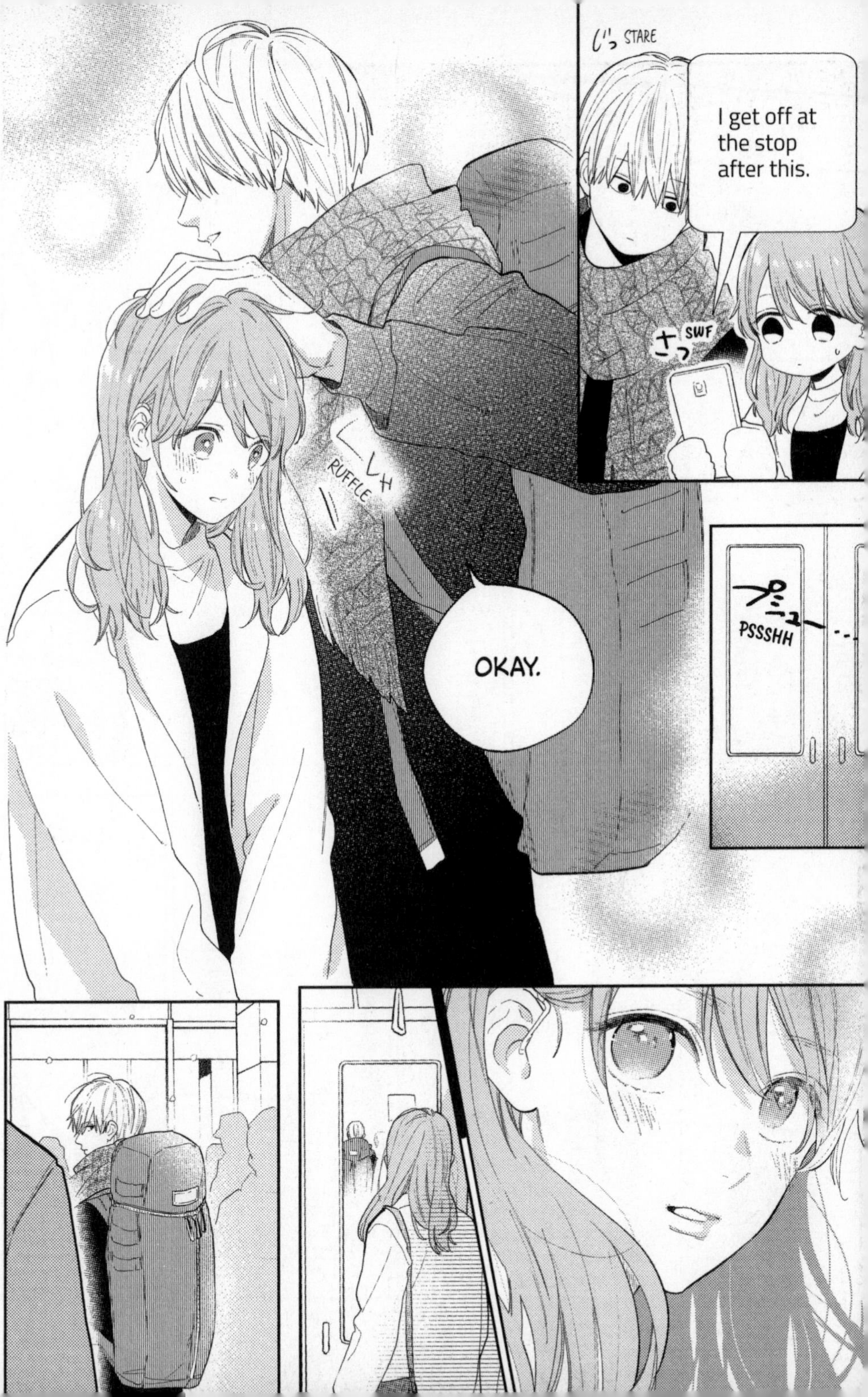
じっ STARE
I get off at the stop after this.
さっ SWF
しゃ RUFFLE
OKAY.
プシュー PSSSHH

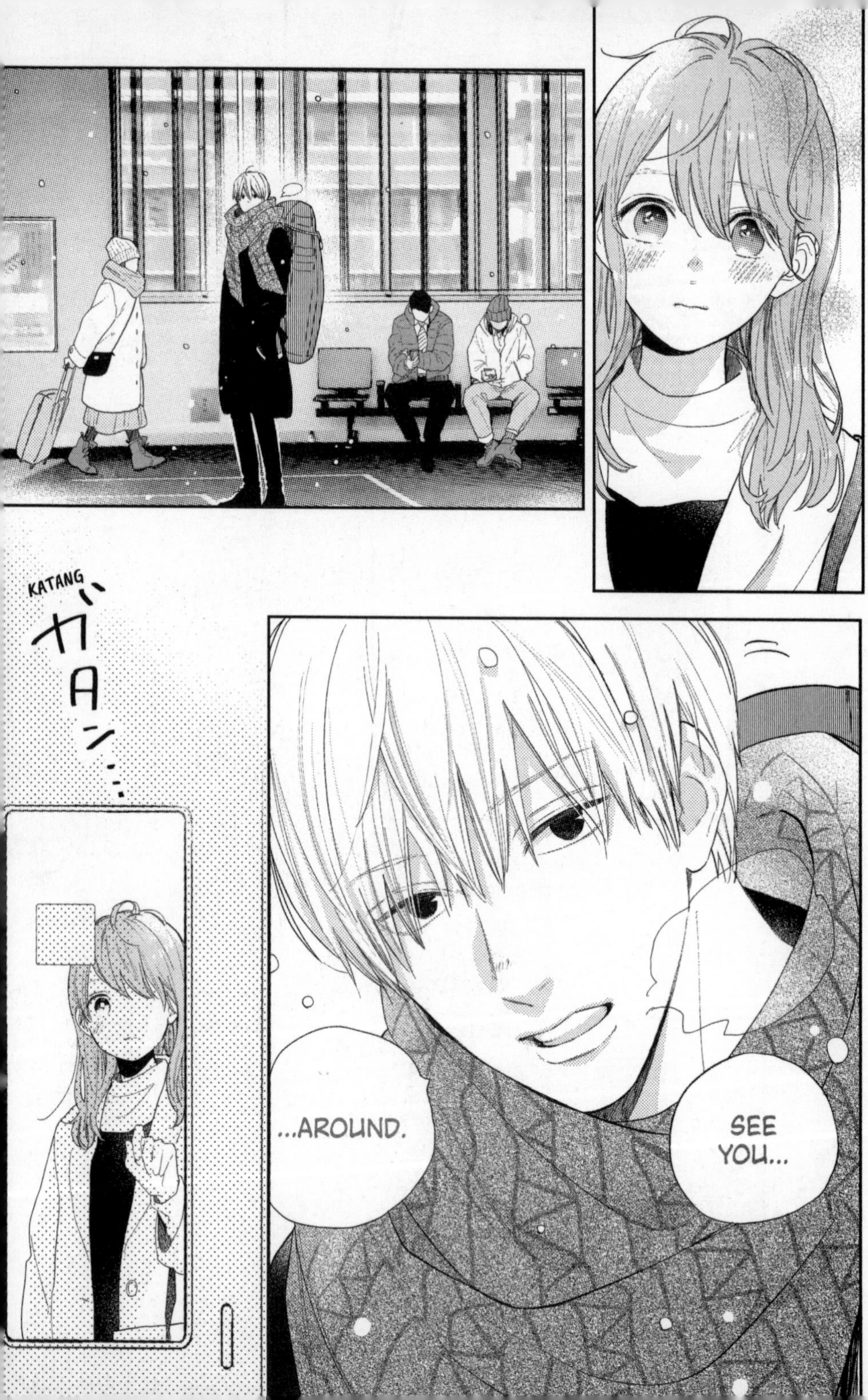
KATANG
SEE YOU...
...AROUND.

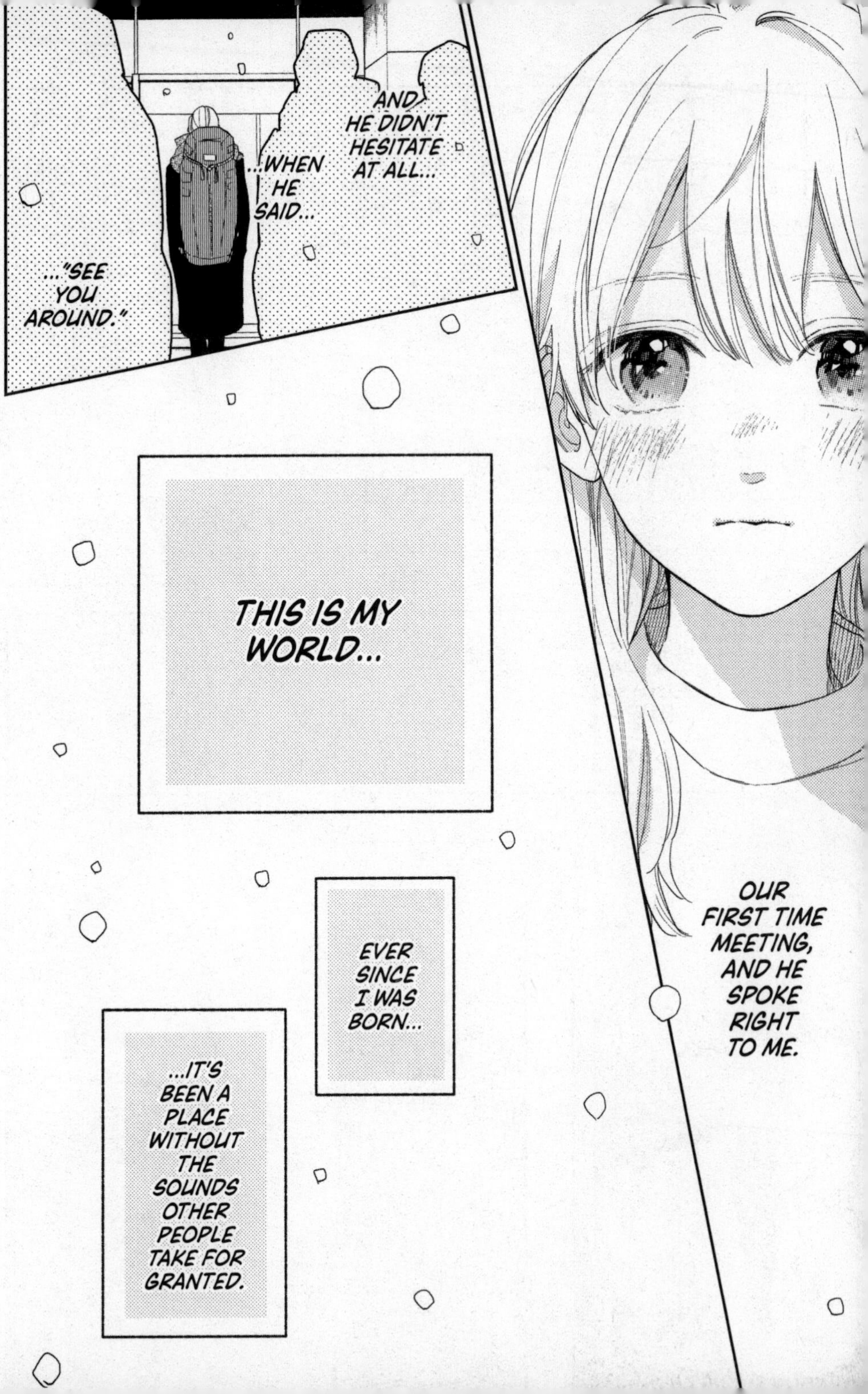
AND HE DIDN'T HESITATE AT ALL...
...WHEN HE SAID...
..."SEE YOU AROUND."
OUR FIRST TIME MEETING, AND HE SPOKE RIGHT TO ME.
THIS IS MY WORLD...
EVER SINCE I WAS BORN...
...IT'S BEEN A PLACE WITHOUT THE SOUNDS OTHER PEOPLE TAKE FOR GRANTED.

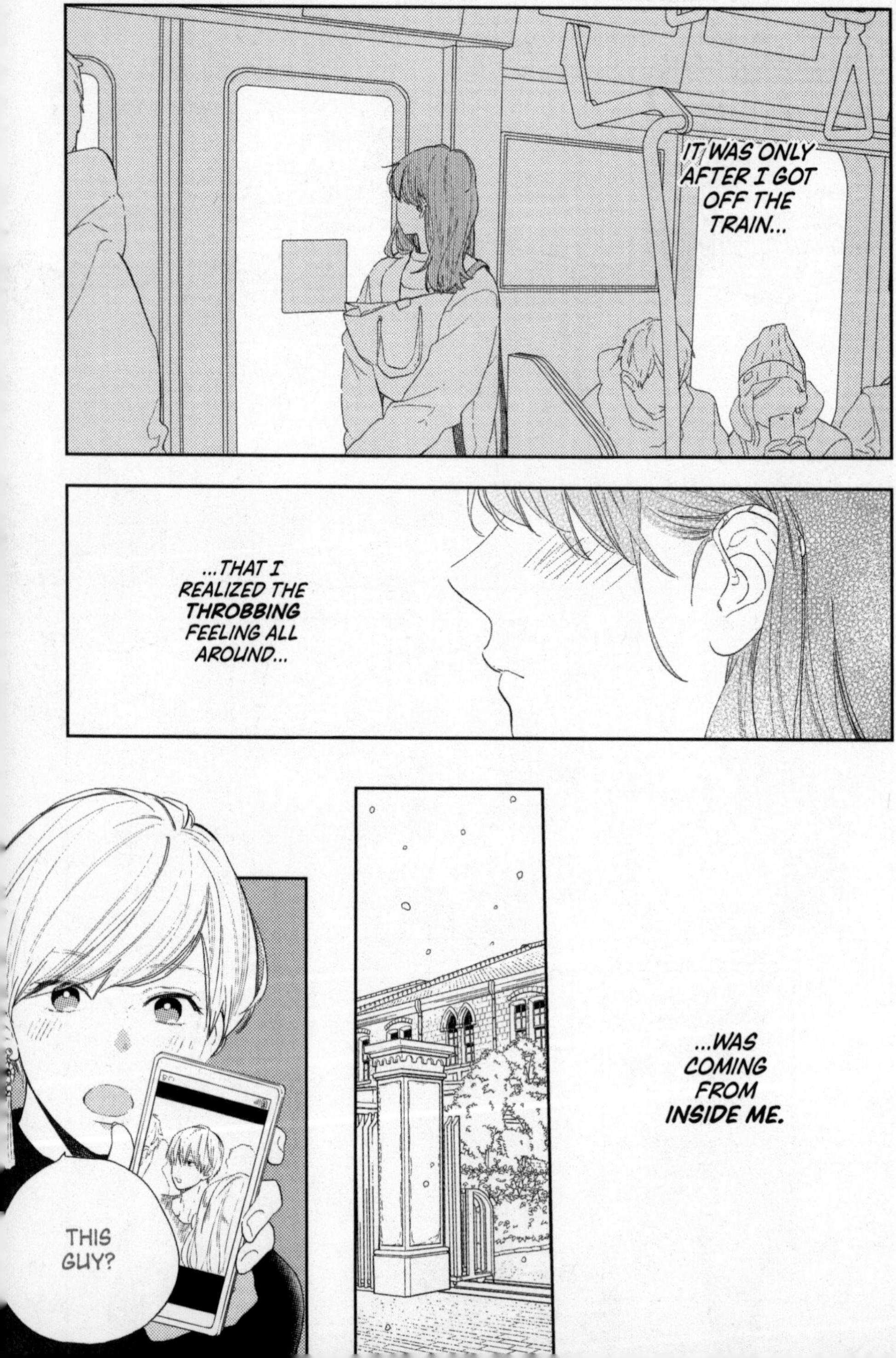
IT WAS ONLY AFTER I GOT OFF THE TRAIN...
...THAT I REALIZED THE THROBBING FEELING ALL AROUND...
...WAS COMING FROM INSIDE ME.
THIS GUY?

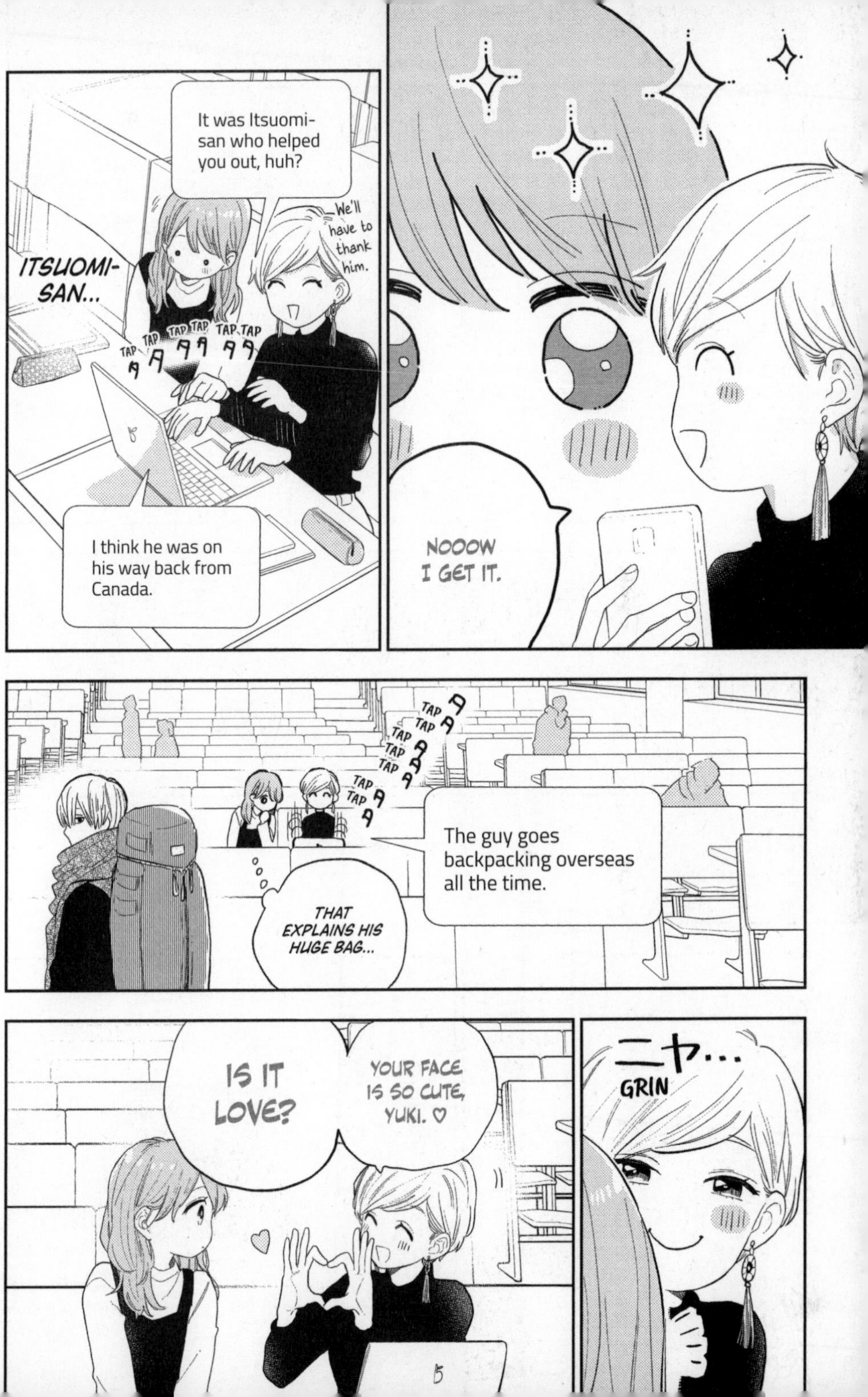
NOOOW I GET IT.
It was Itsuomi-san who helped you out, huh?
We'll have to thank him.
ITSUOMI-SAN...
TAP TAP TAP TAP TAP TAP
I think he was on his way back from Canada.
TAP TAP TAP TAP TAP TAP TAP
The guy goes backpacking overseas all the time.
THAT EXPLAINS HIS HUGE BAG...
ニヤ…
GRIN
YOUR FACE IS SO CUTE, YUKI. ♡
IS IT LOVE?

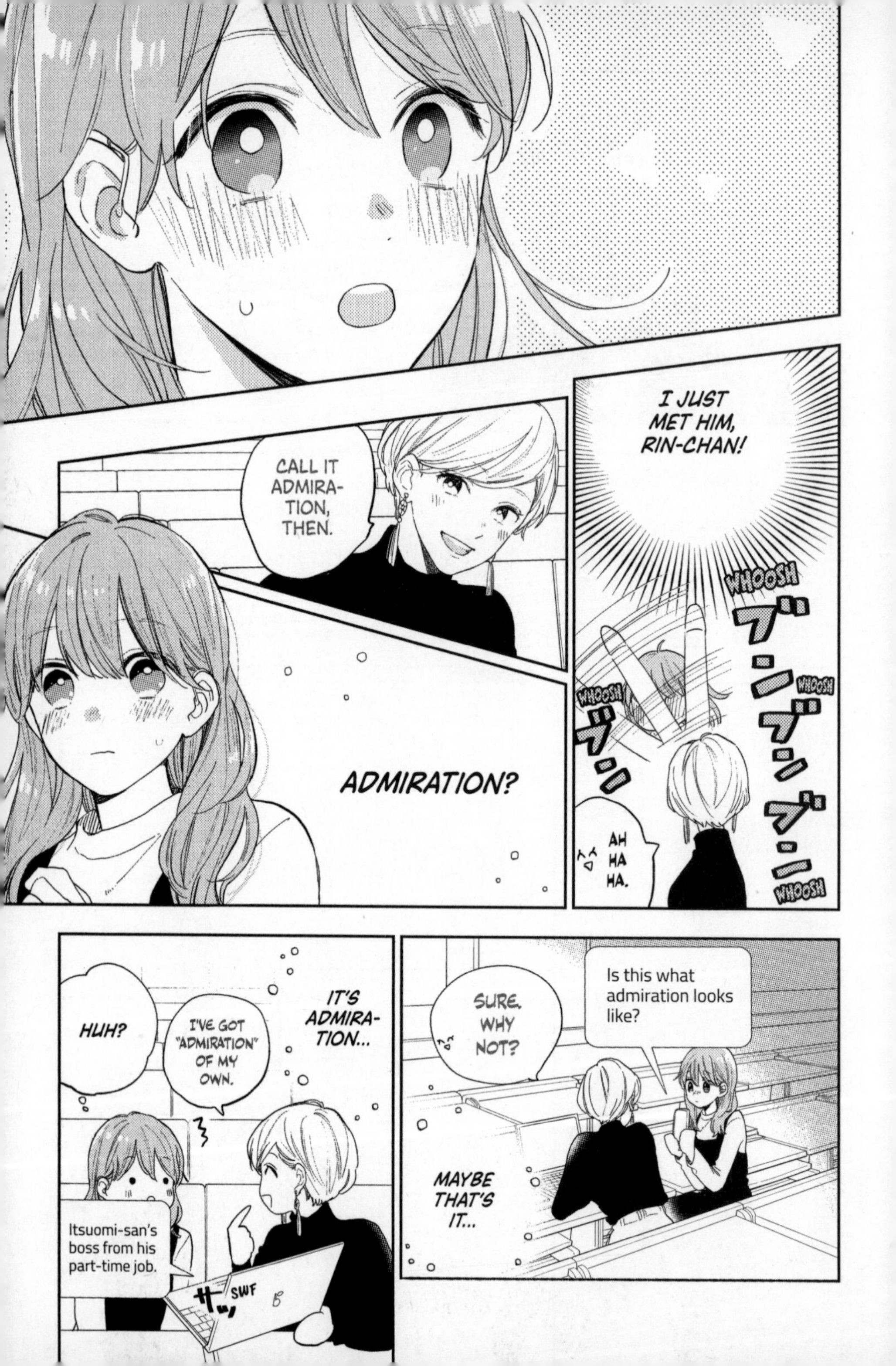
I JUST MET HIM, RIN-CHAN!
WHOOSH
WHOOSH
WHOOSH
WHOOSH
AH HA HA.
CALL IT ADMIRA-TION, THEN.
ADMIRATION?
Is this what admiration looks like?
SURE. WHY NOT?
MAYBE THAT'S IT...
IT'S ADMIRA-TION...
I'VE GOT "ADMIRATION" OF MY OWN.
HUH?
Itsuomi-san's boss from his part-time job.
SWF

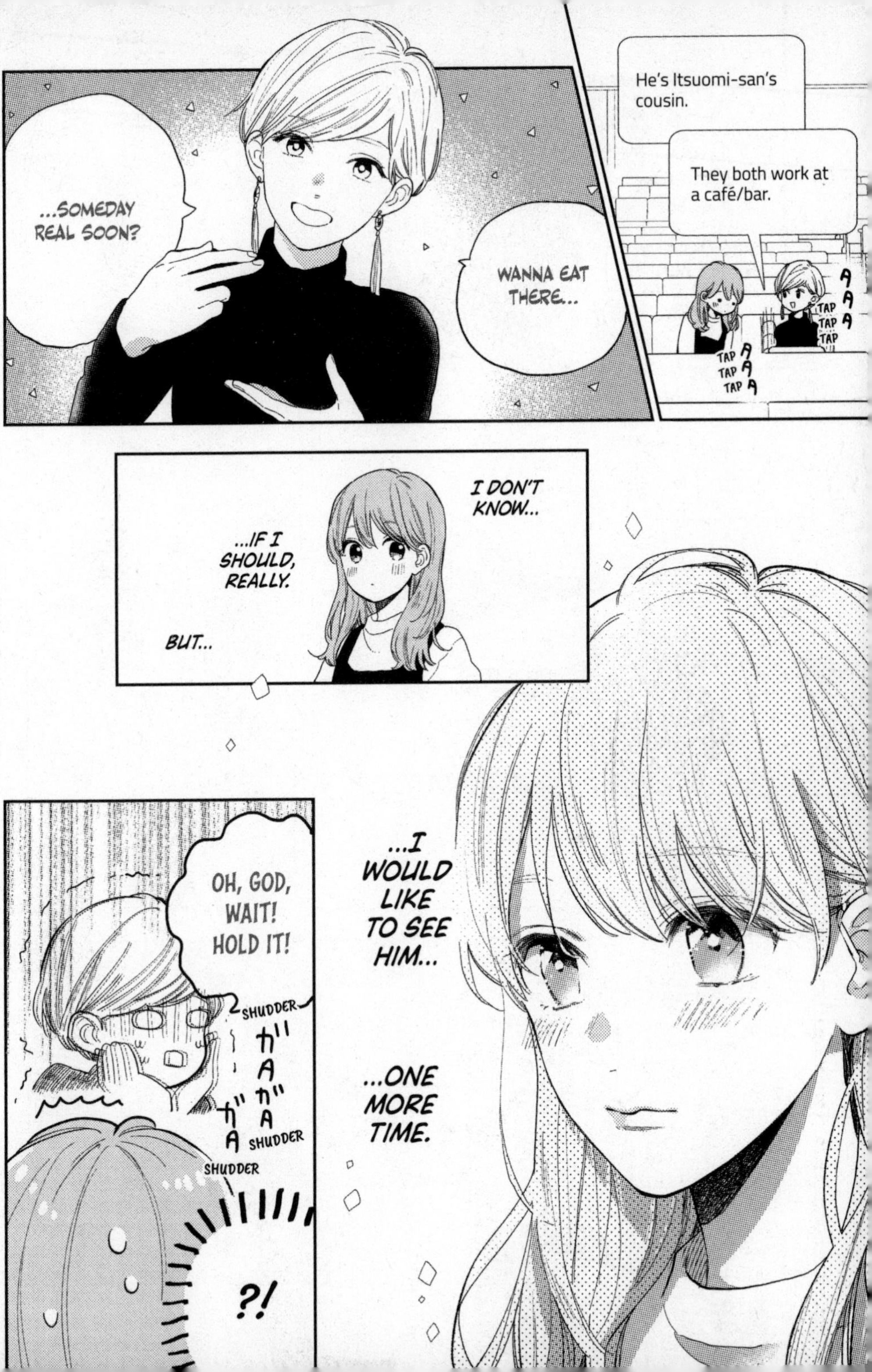
He's Itsuomi-san's cousin.
They both work at a café/bar.
TAP TAP TAP
TAP TAP TAP
WANNA EAT THERE...
...SOMEDAY REAL SOON?
I DON'T KNOW...
...IF I SHOULD, REALLY.
BUT...
...I WOULD LIKE TO SEE HIM...
...ONE MORE TIME.
OH, GOD, WAIT! HOLD IT!
SHUDDER
SHUDDER
SHUDDER
?!

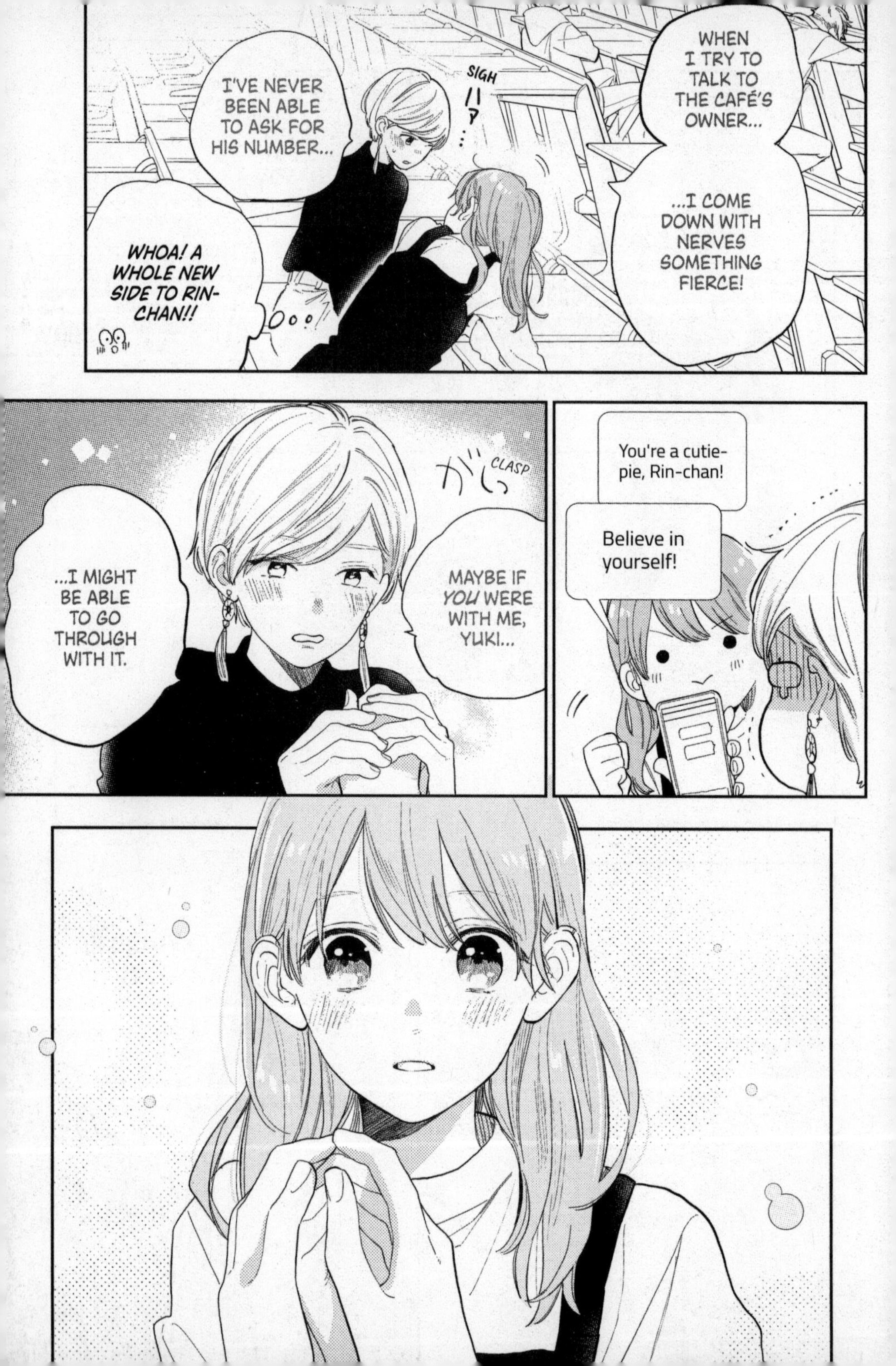
WHEN I TRY TO TALK TO THE CAFÉ'S OWNER...
...I COME DOWN WITH NERVES SOMETHING FIERCE!
SIGH
ハァ…
I'VE NEVER BEEN ABLE TO ASK FOR HIS NUMBER...
WHOA! A WHOLE NEW SIDE TO RIN-CHAN!!
You're a cutie-pie, Rin-chan!
Believe in yourself!
がしっ
CLASP
MAYBE IF YOU WERE WITH ME, YUKI...
...I MIGHT BE ABLE TO GO THROUGH WITH IT.

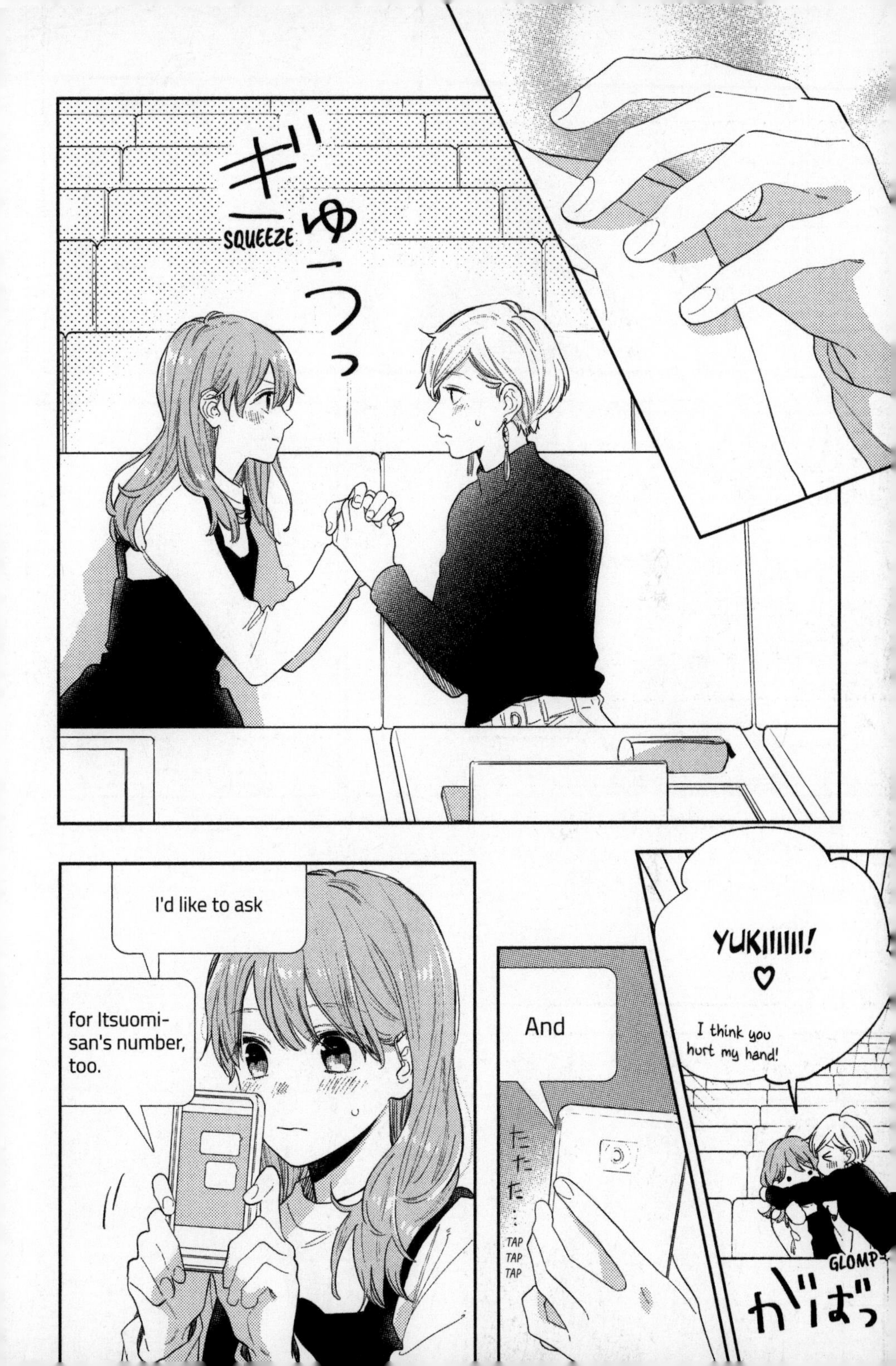
ギューっ
SQUEEZE
YUKIIIIIII! ♡
I think you hurt my hand!
がばっ
GLOMP
And
たたた…
TAP TAP TAP
I'd like to ask
for Itsuomi-san's number, too.

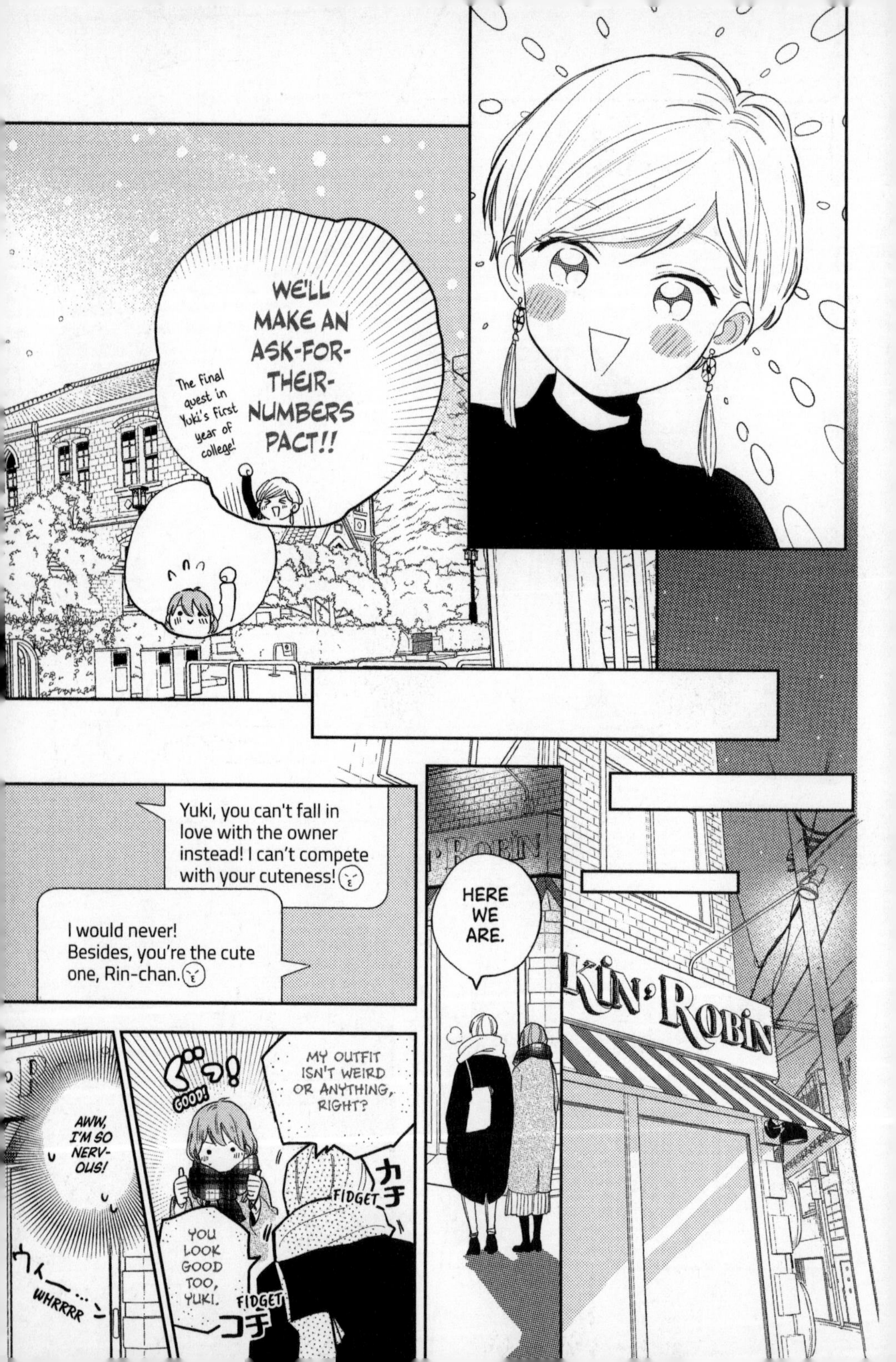

WE'LL MAKE AN ASK-FOR-THEIR-NUMBERS PACT!!
The final quest in Yuki's first year of college!
HERE WE ARE.
ROBIN
Yuki, you can't fall in love with the owner instead! I can't compete with your cuteness!
I would never! Besides, you're the cute one, Rin-chan.
MY OUTFIT ISN'T WEIRD OR ANYTHING, RIGHT?
FIDGET
YOU LOOK GOOD TOO, YUKI.
FIDGET
GOOD!
AWW, I'M SO NERVOUS!
WHRRRR

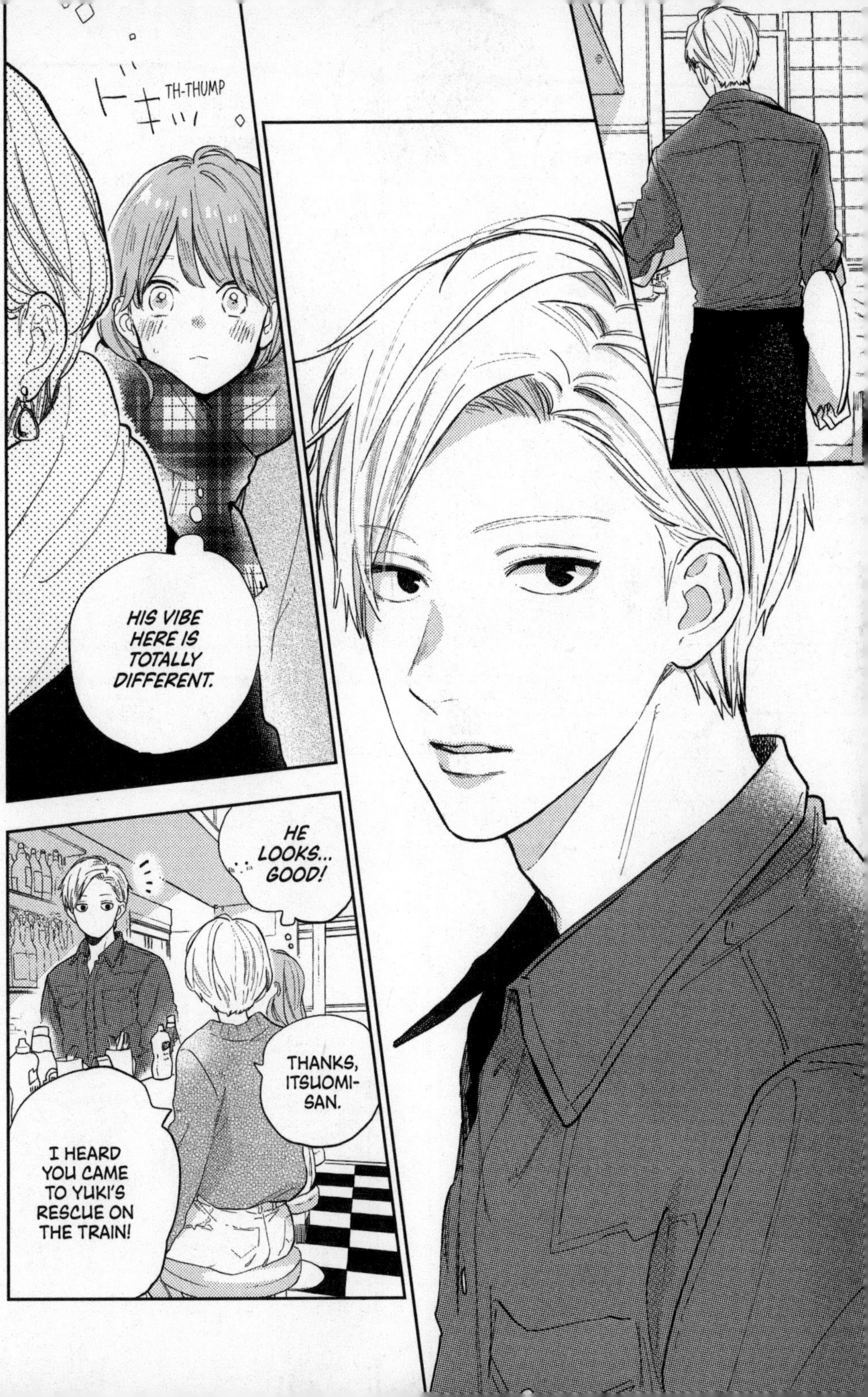
TH-THUMP
HIS VIBE HERE IS TOTALLY DIFFERENT.
HE LOOKS... GOOD!
THANKS, ITSUOMI-SAN.
I HEARD YOU CAME TO YUKI'S RESCUE ON THE TRAIN!

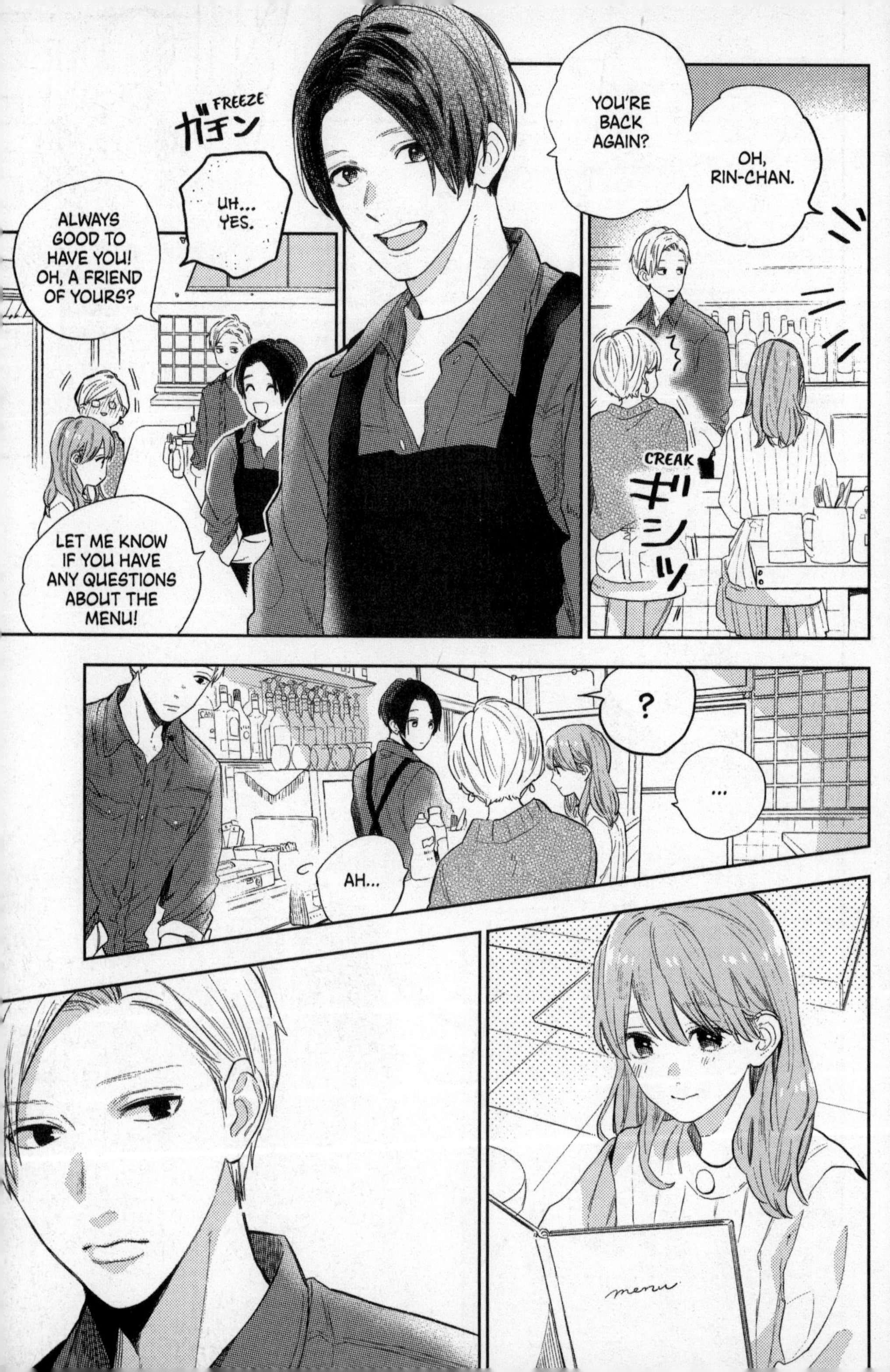
OH, RIN-CHAN.
YOU'RE BACK AGAIN?
CREAK
ギシッ
ALWAYS GOOD TO HAVE YOU! OH, A FRIEND OF YOURS?
UH... YES.
FREEZE
ガチン
LET ME KNOW IF YOU HAVE ANY QUESTIONS ABOUT THE MENU!
?
...
AH...
menu

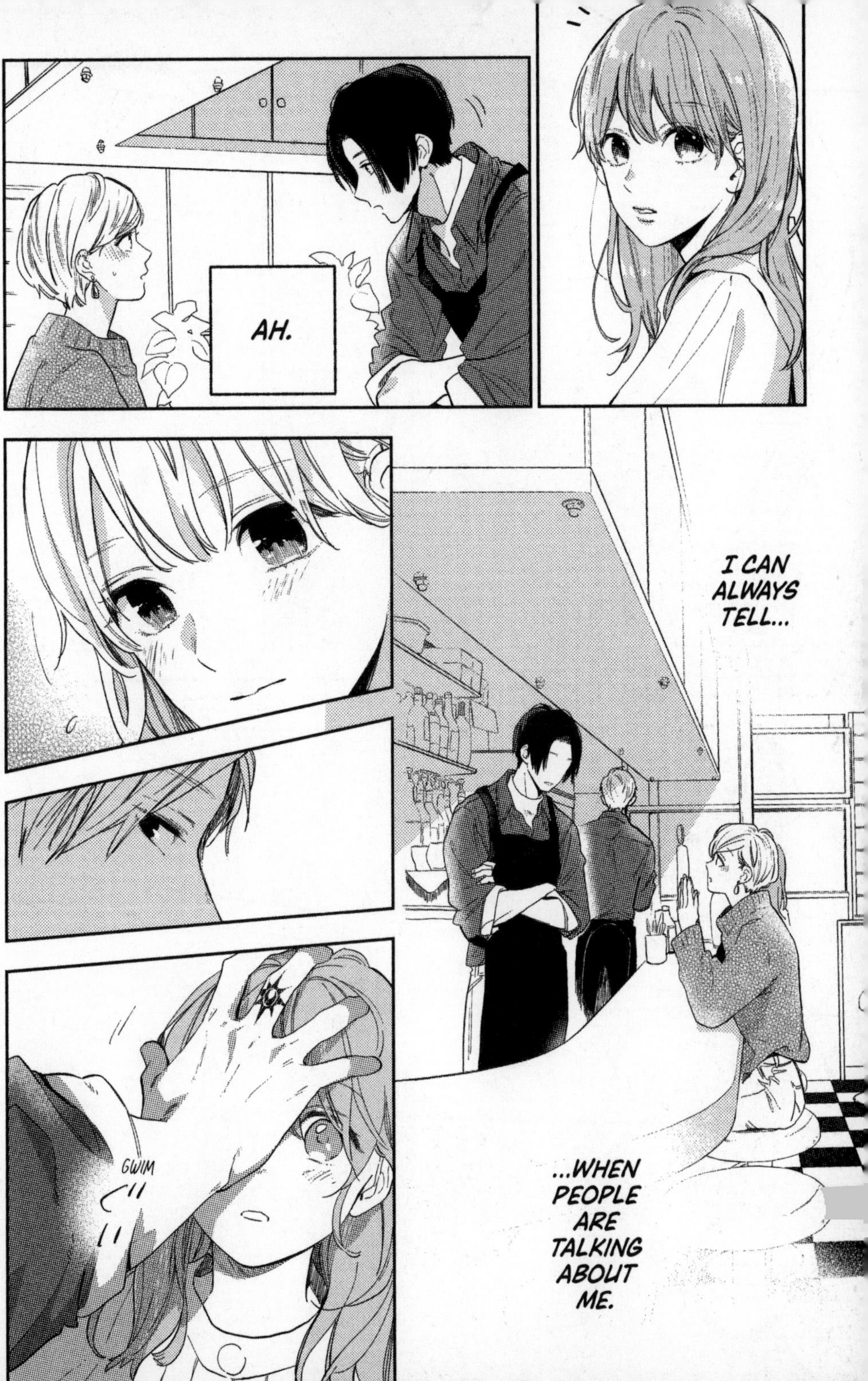
AH.
I CAN ALWAYS TELL...
...WHEN PEOPLE ARE TALKING ABOUT ME.
GWIM

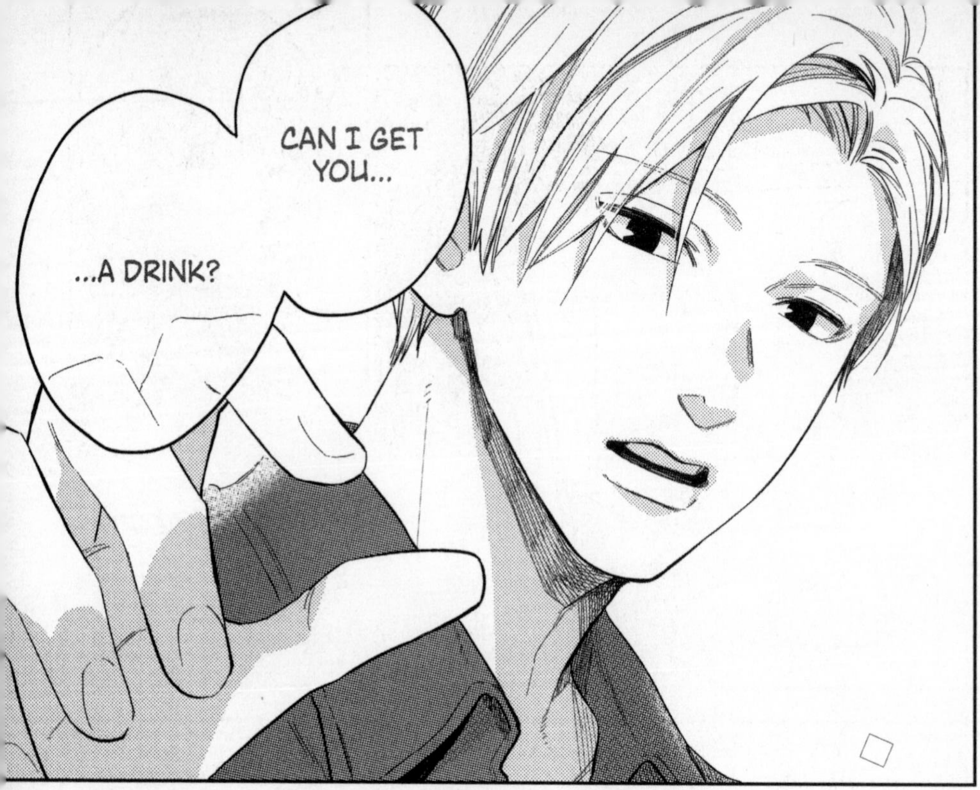
CAN I GET YOU...
...A DRINK?
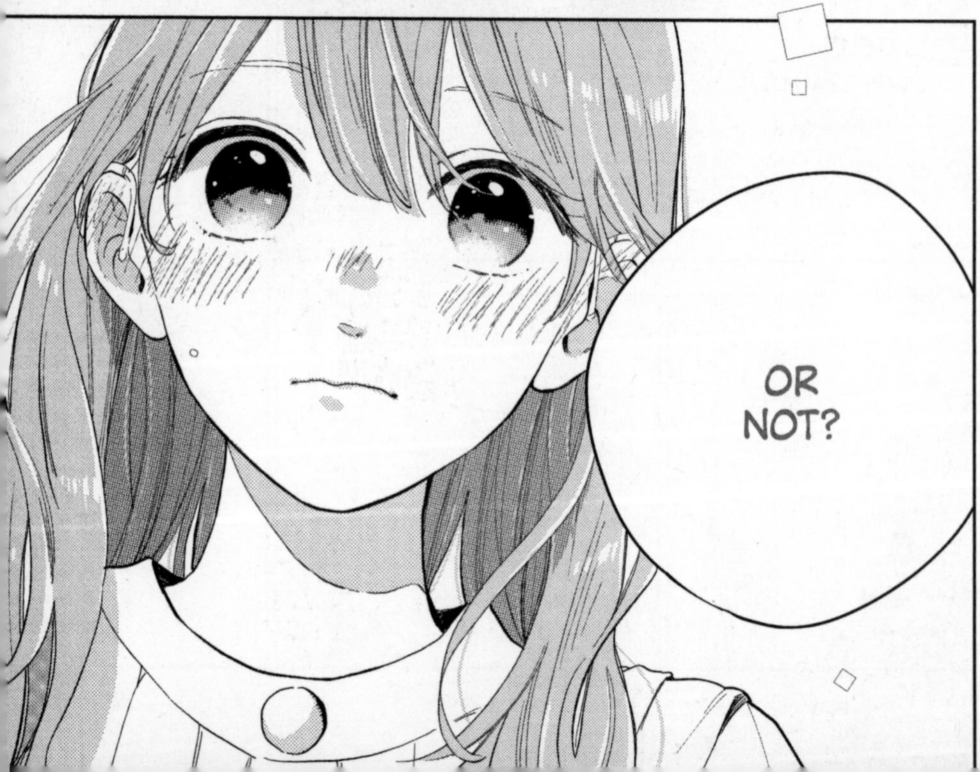
OR NOT?

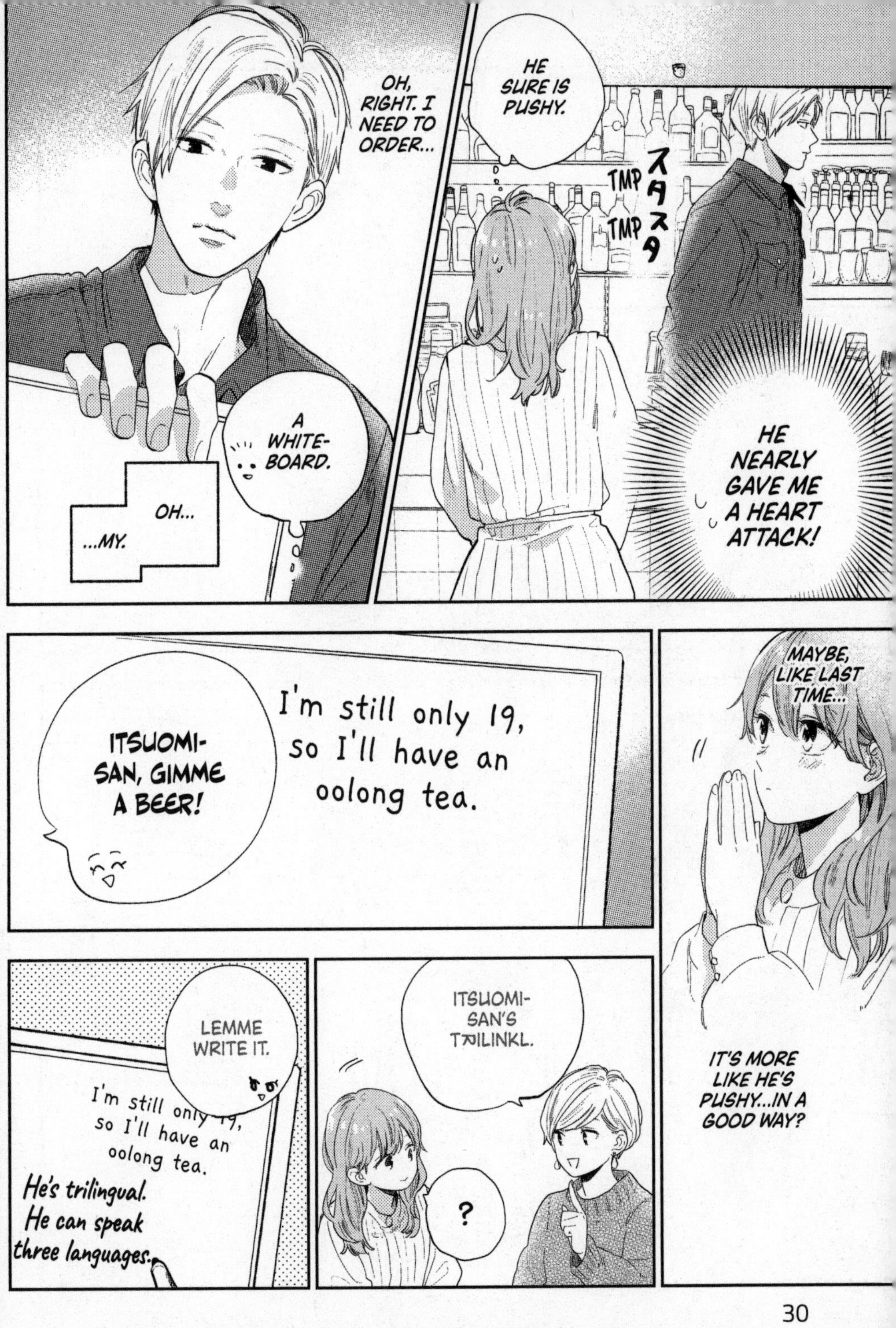
HE SURE IS PUSHY.
TMP TMP
スタスタ
HE NEARLY GAVE ME A HEART ATTACK!
OH, RIGHT. I NEED TO ORDER...
A WHITE-BOARD.
OH...
...MY.
MAYBE, LIKE LAST TIME...
IT'S MORE LIKE HE'S PUSHY...IN A GOOD WAY?
ITSUOMI-SAN, GIMME A BEER!
I'm still only 19, so I'll have an oolong tea.
ITSUOMI-SAN'S TЯILINKL.
?
LEMME WRITE IT.
I'm still only 19, so I'll have an oolong tea.
He's trilingual. He can speak three languages.

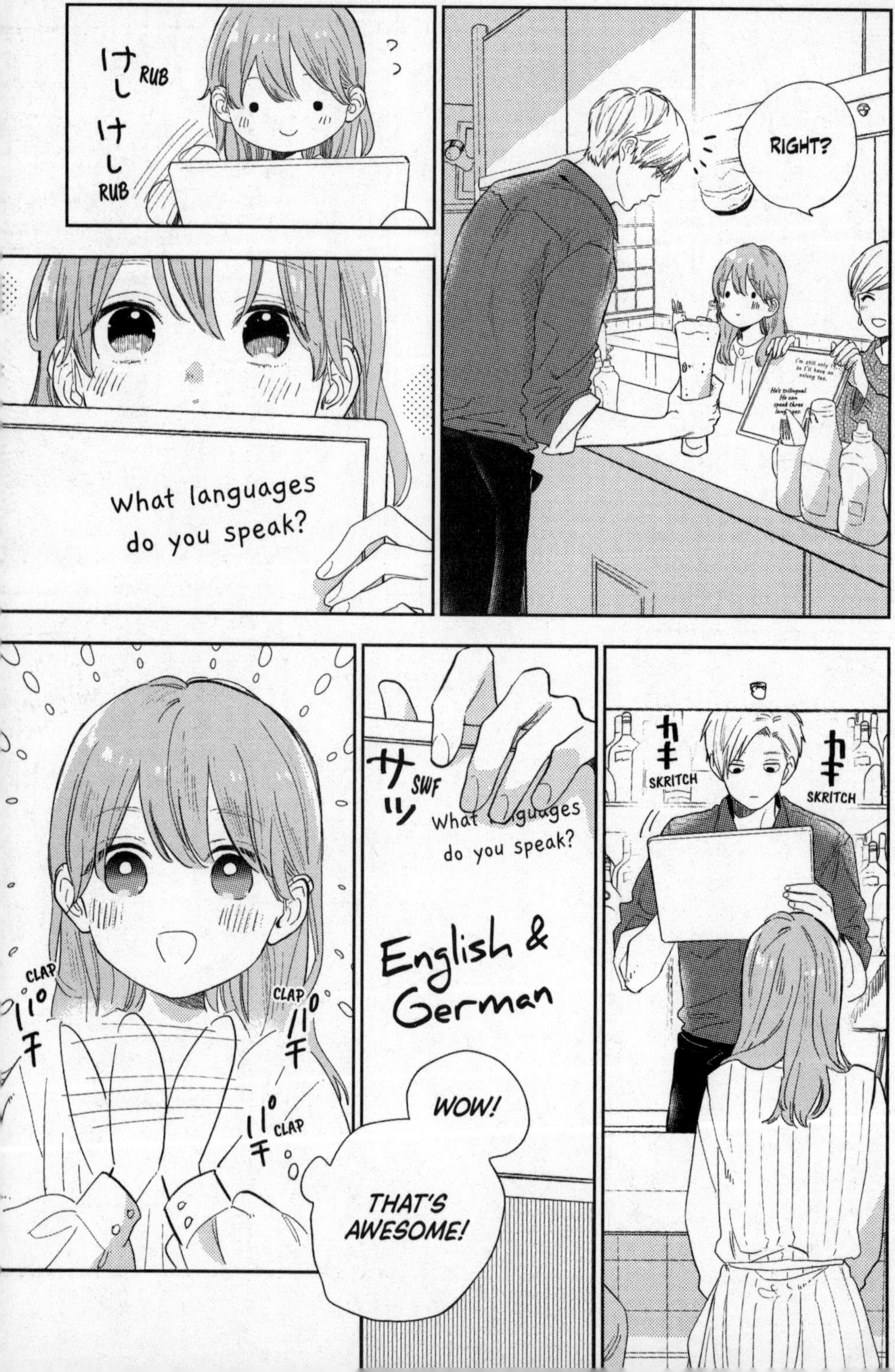
RIGHT?
I'm still only
So I'll have an oolong tea.
He's trilingual. He can speak three
けしけし RUB RUB
What languages do you speak?
カキ SKRITCH
カキ SKRITCH
サッ SWF
What l guages do you speak?
English & German
WOW!
THAT'S AWESOME!
パチ CLAP
パチ CLAP
パチ CLAP

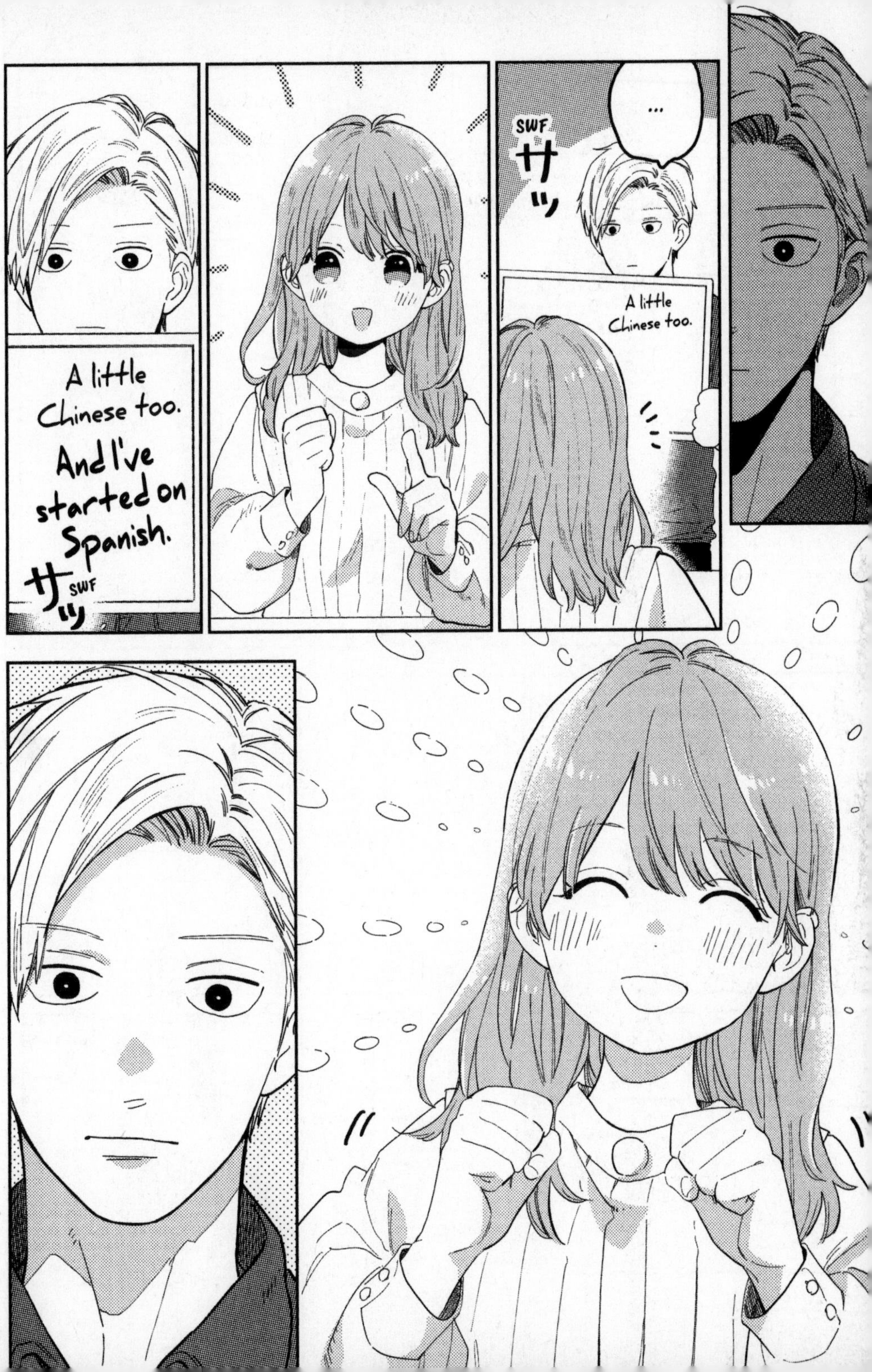
…
SWF
サッ
A little Chinese too.
A little Chinese too.
And I've started on Spanish.
サッ
SWF

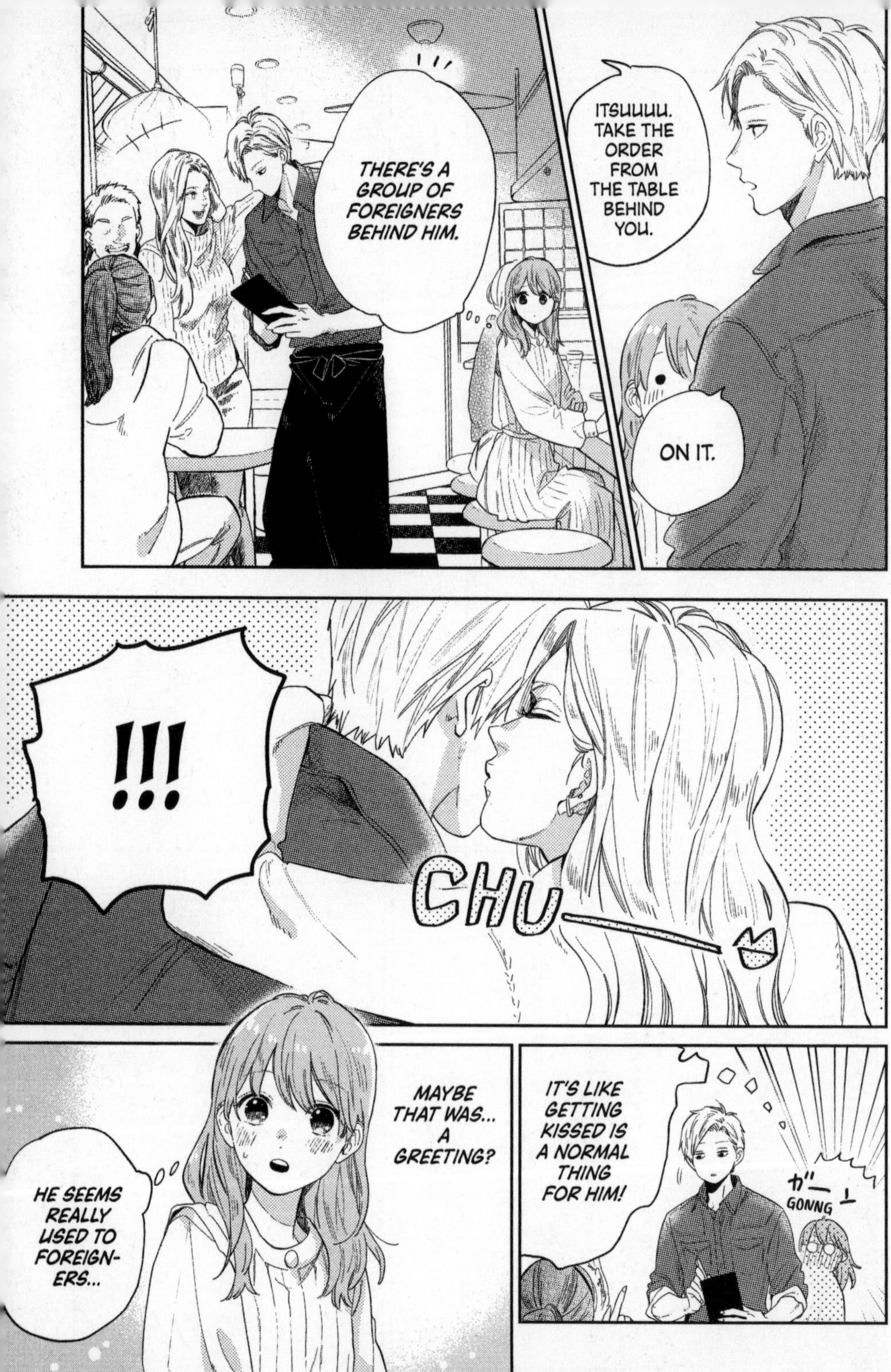
ITSUUUU. TAKE THE ORDER FROM THE TABLE BEHIND YOU.
ON IT.
THERE'S A GROUP OF FOREIGNERS BEHIND HIM.
!!!
CHU—
IT'S LIKE GETTING KISSED IS A NORMAL THING FOR HIM!
ガー
GONNG
MAYBE THAT WAS... A GREETING?
HE SEEMS REALLY USED TO FOREIGN-ERS...

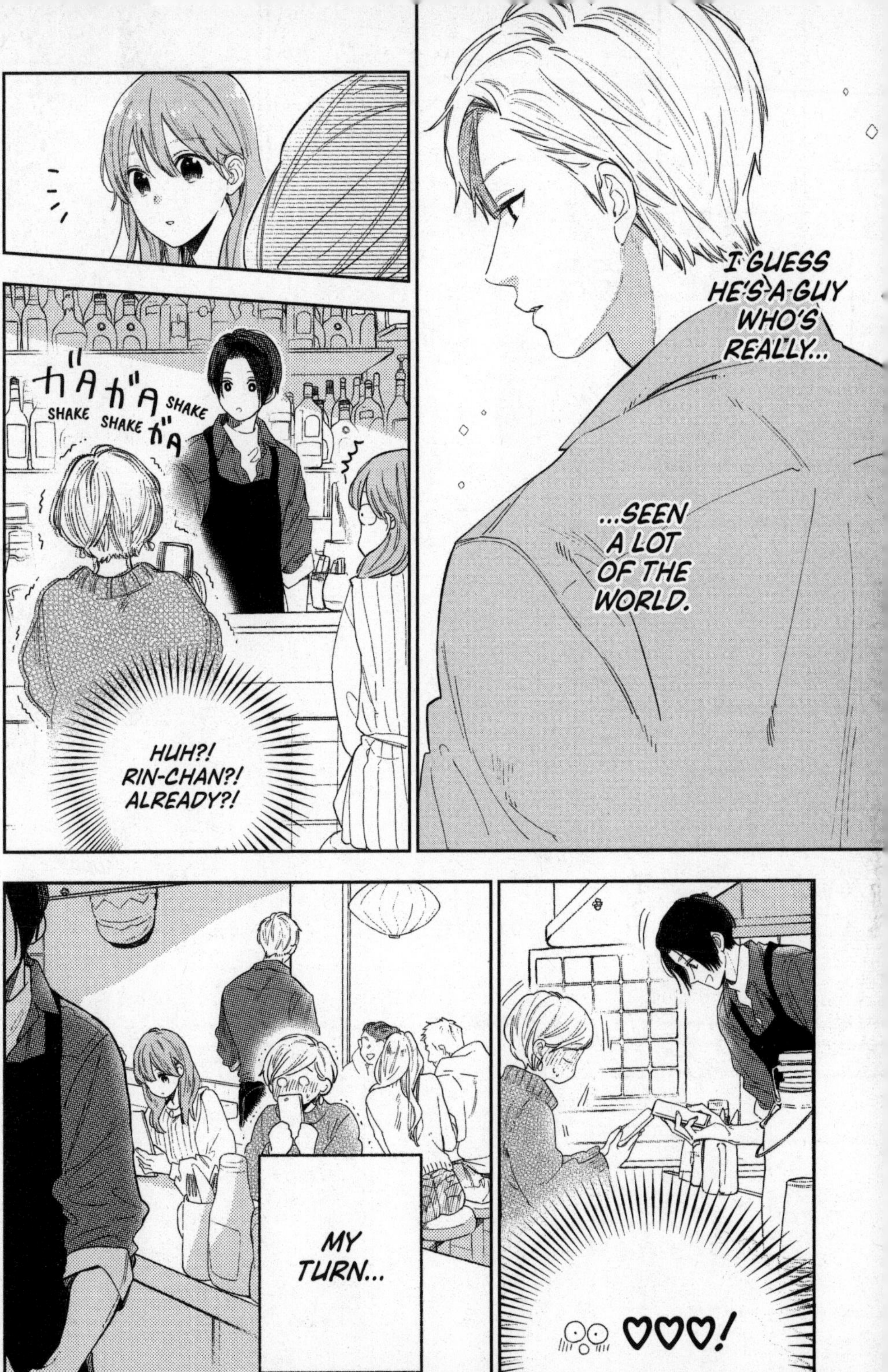
I GUESS HE'S A GUY WHO'S REALLY...
...SEEN A LOT OF THE WORLD.
ガタガタ
SHAKE
SHAKE
ガタ
SHAKE
HUH?! RIN-CHAN?! ALREADY?!
♡♡♡!
MY TURN...

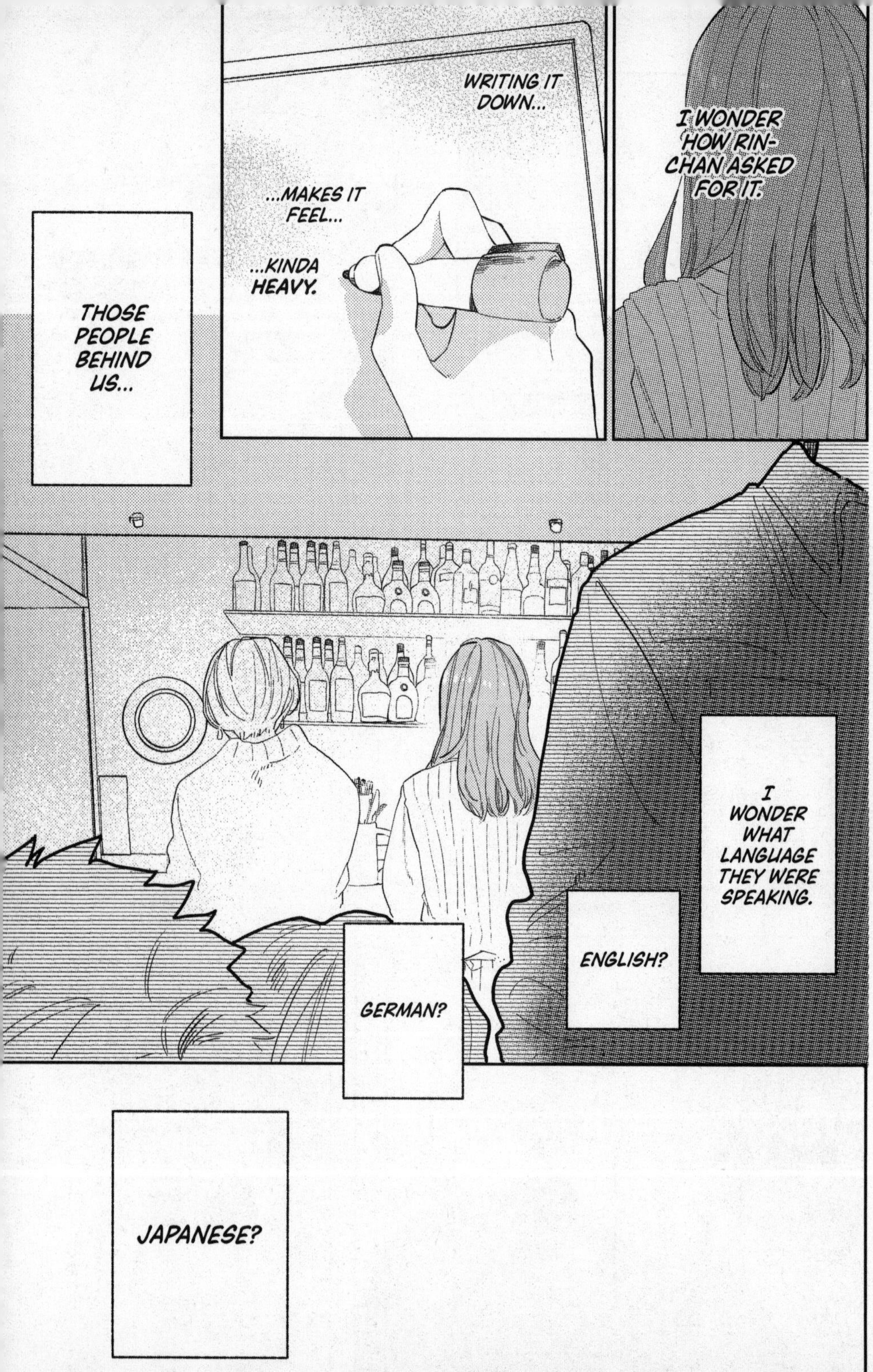
I WONDER HOW RIN-CHAN ASKED FOR IT.
WRITING IT DOWN...
...MAKES IT FEEL...
...KINDA HEAVY.
THOSE PEOPLE BEHIND US...
I WONDER WHAT LANGUAGE THEY WERE SPEAKING.
ENGLISH?
GERMAN?
JAPANESE?

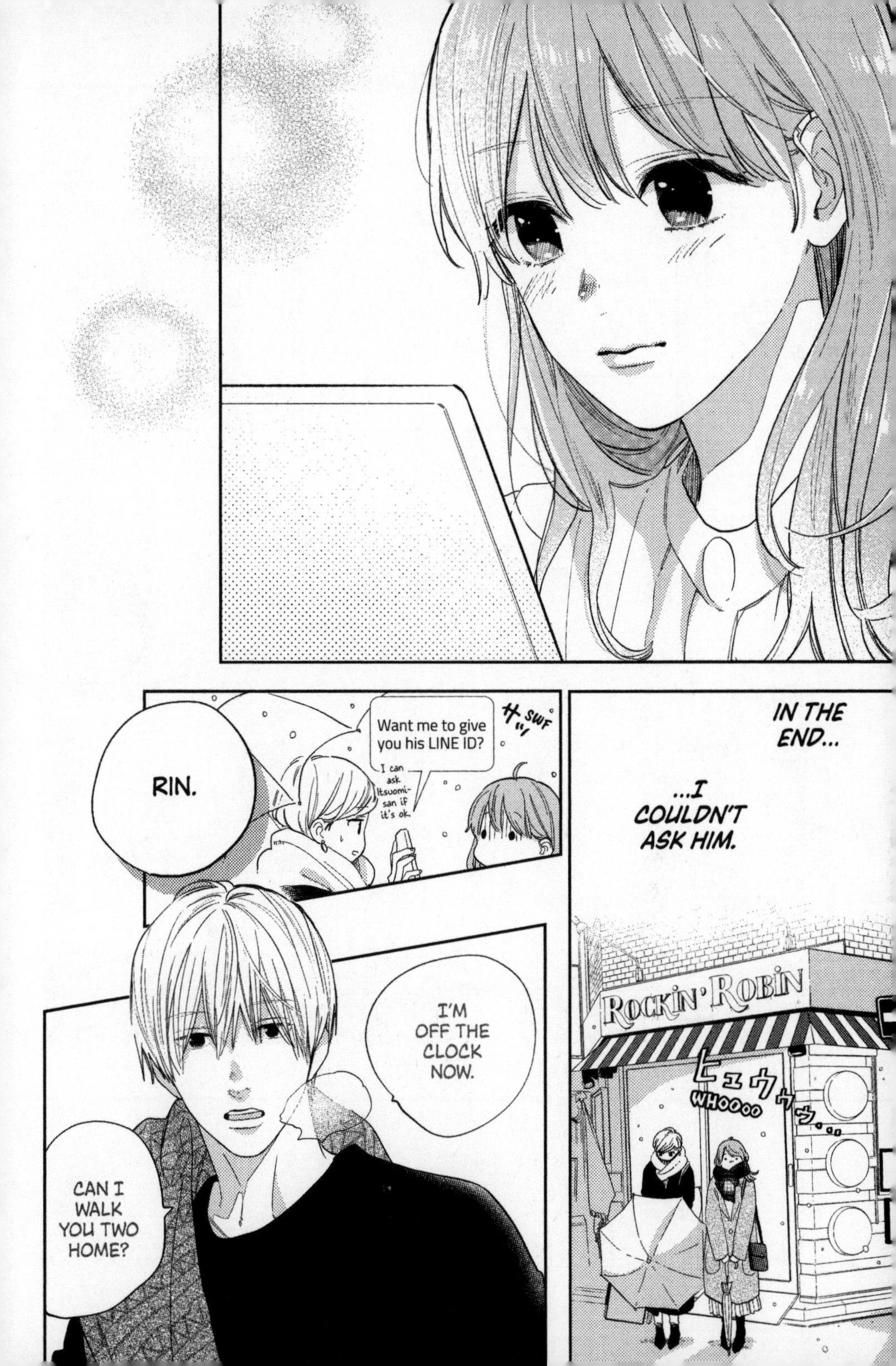
IN THE END...
...I COULDN'T ASK HIM.
ROCKIN' ROBIN
ヒュウウゥ...
WHOOOO
Want me to give you his LINE ID?
I can ask Itsuomi-san if it's ok.
サッ SWF
RIN.
I'M OFF THE CLOCK NOW.
CAN I WALK YOU TWO HOME?

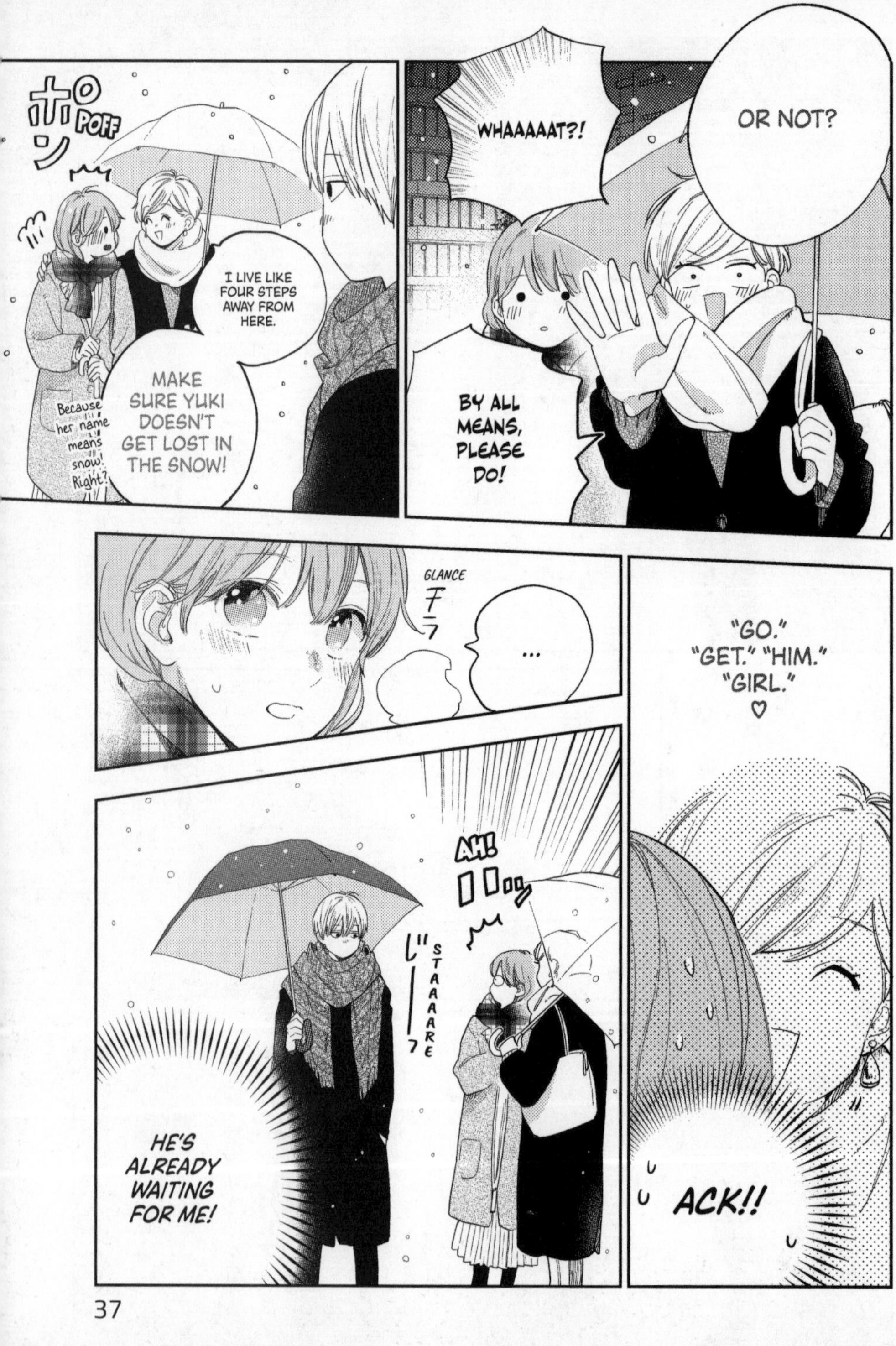
OR NOT?
WHAAAAAT?!
BY ALL MEANS, PLEASE DO!
POFF
I LIVE LIKE FOUR STEPS AWAY FROM HERE.
MAKE SURE YUKI DOESN'T GET LOST IN THE SNOW!
Because her name means snow! Right?
"GO." "GET." "HIM." "GIRL." ♡
ACK!!
GLANCE
...
AH!
STAAAAARE
HE'S ALREADY WAITING FOR ME!

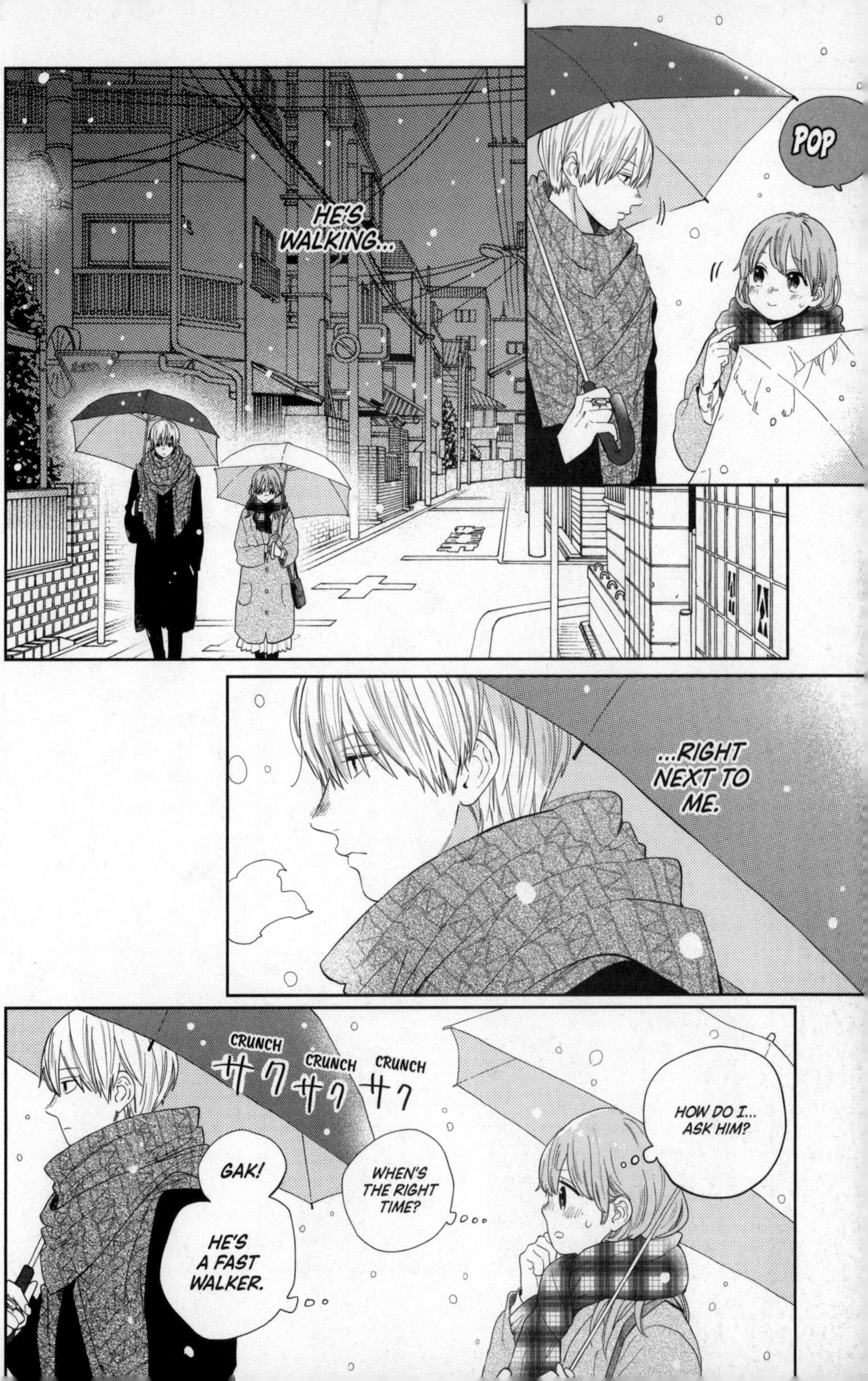
POP
HE'S WALKING...
...RIGHT NEXT TO ME.
HOW DO I... ASK HIM?
サクサクサク
CRUNCH CRUNCH CRUNCH
WHEN'S THE RIGHT TIME?
GAK!
HE'S A FAST WALKER.

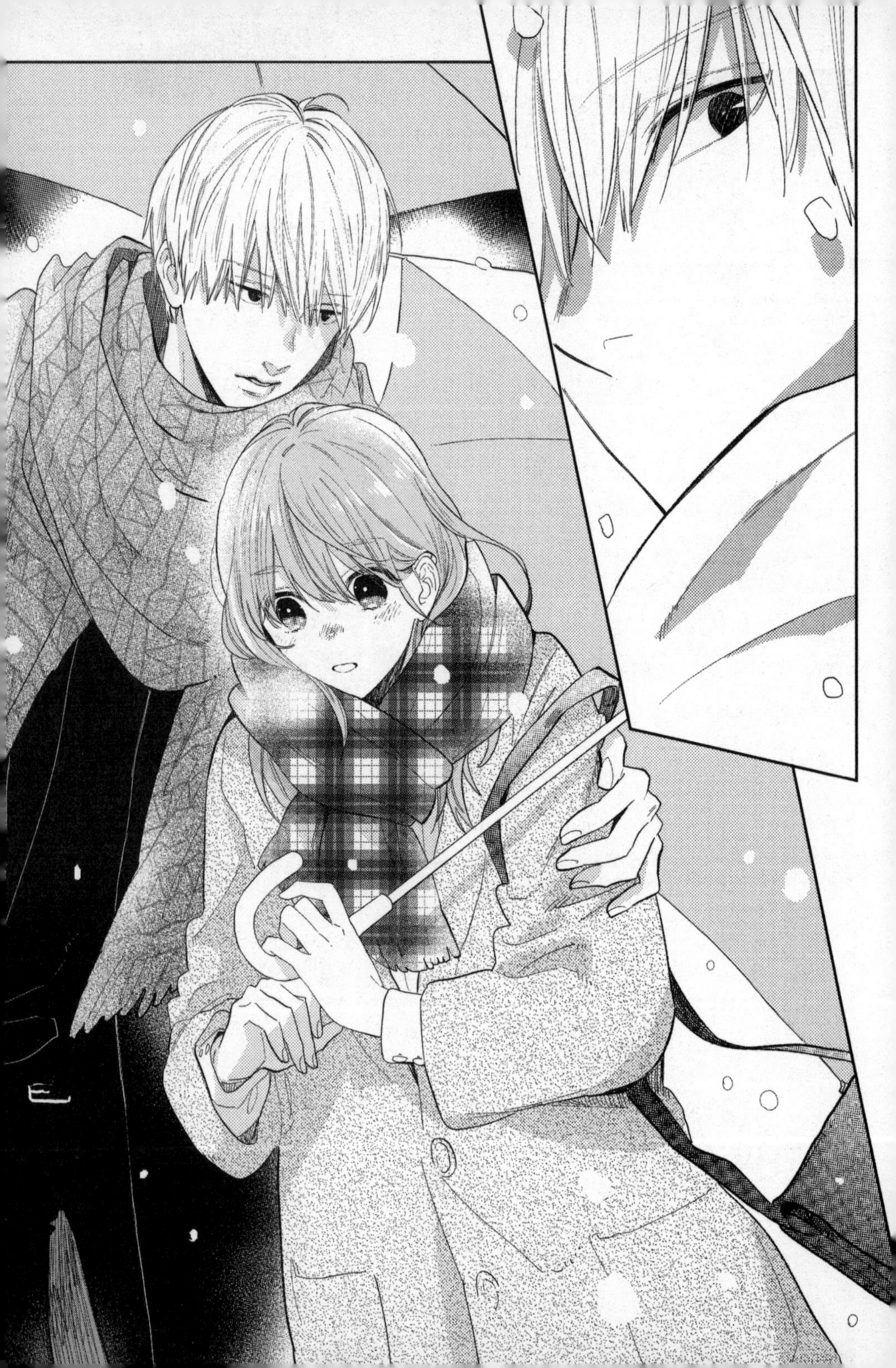

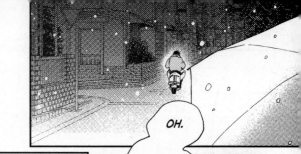

OH.

IT WAS A
MOTORBIKE.

GRIMP

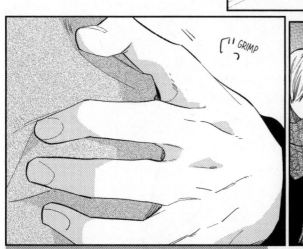

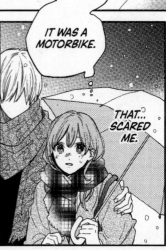

THAT...
SCARED
ME.

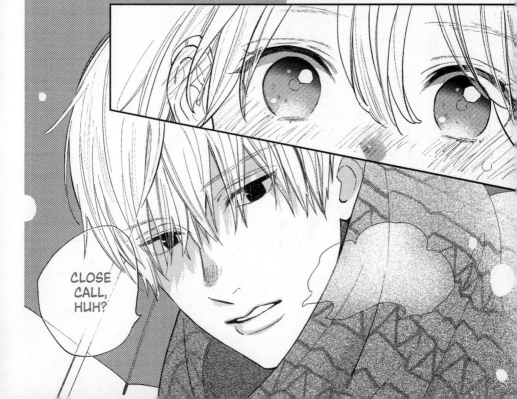

CLOSE
CALL,
HUH?

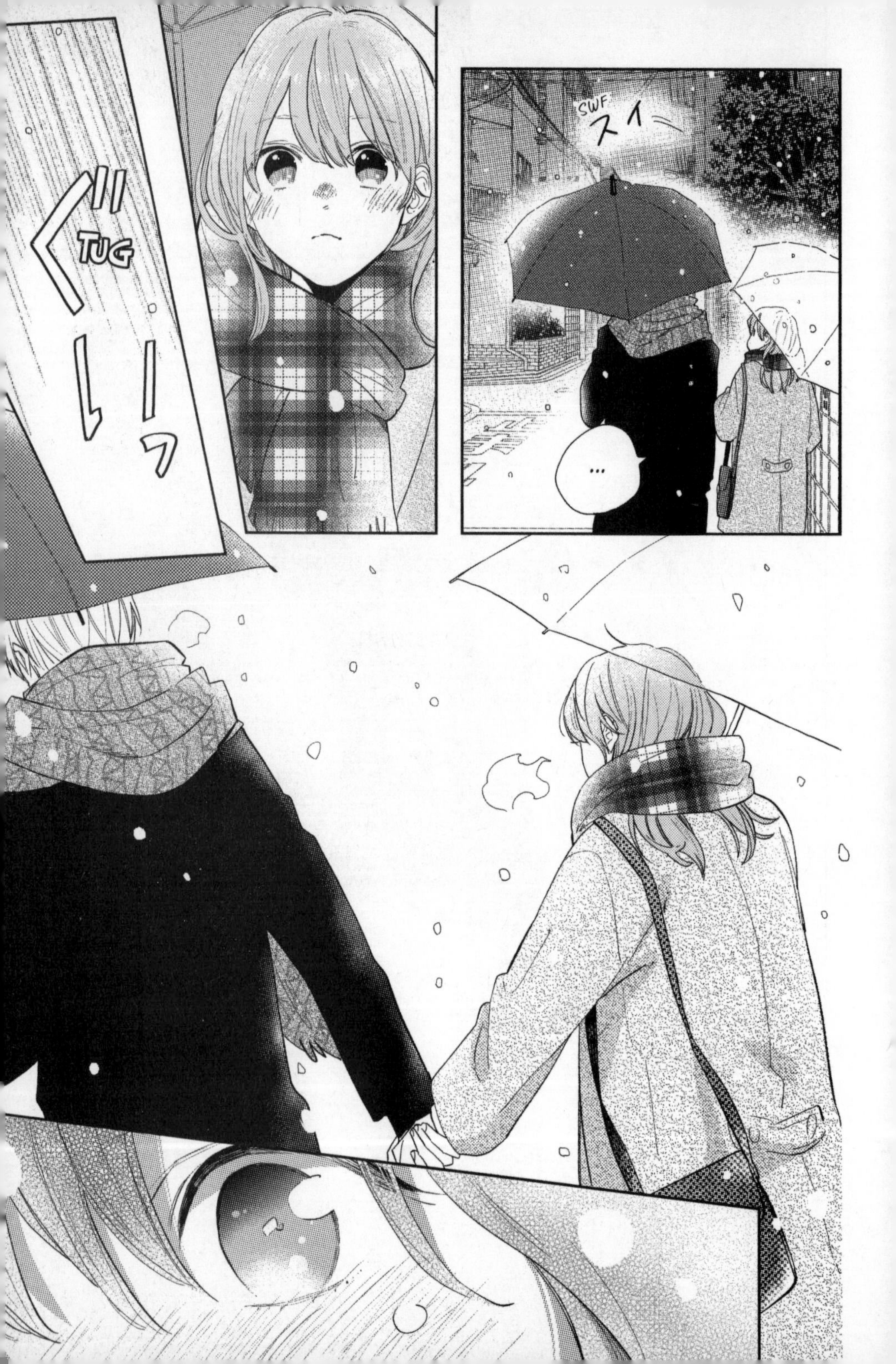
SWF
スイ
...
TUG

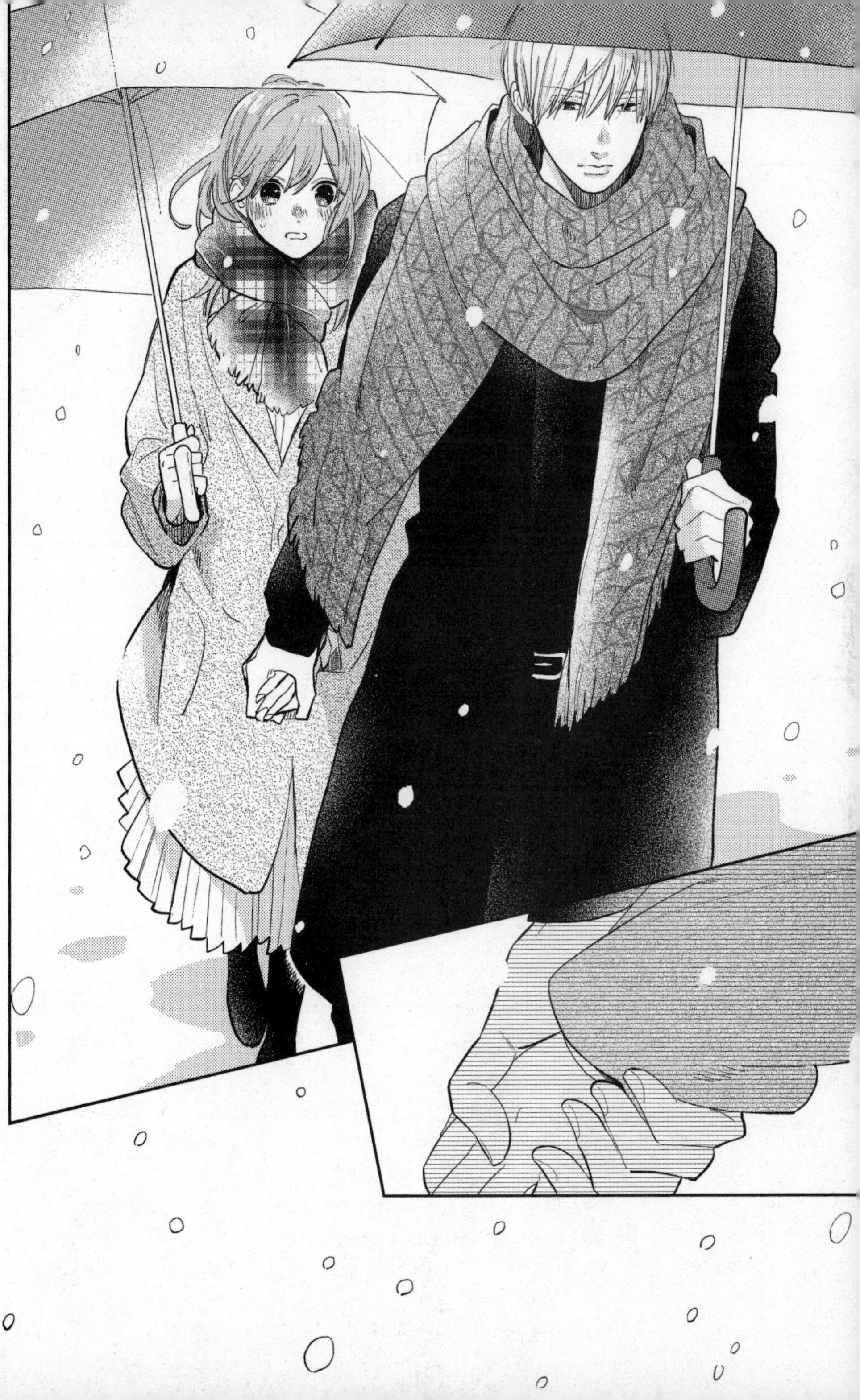

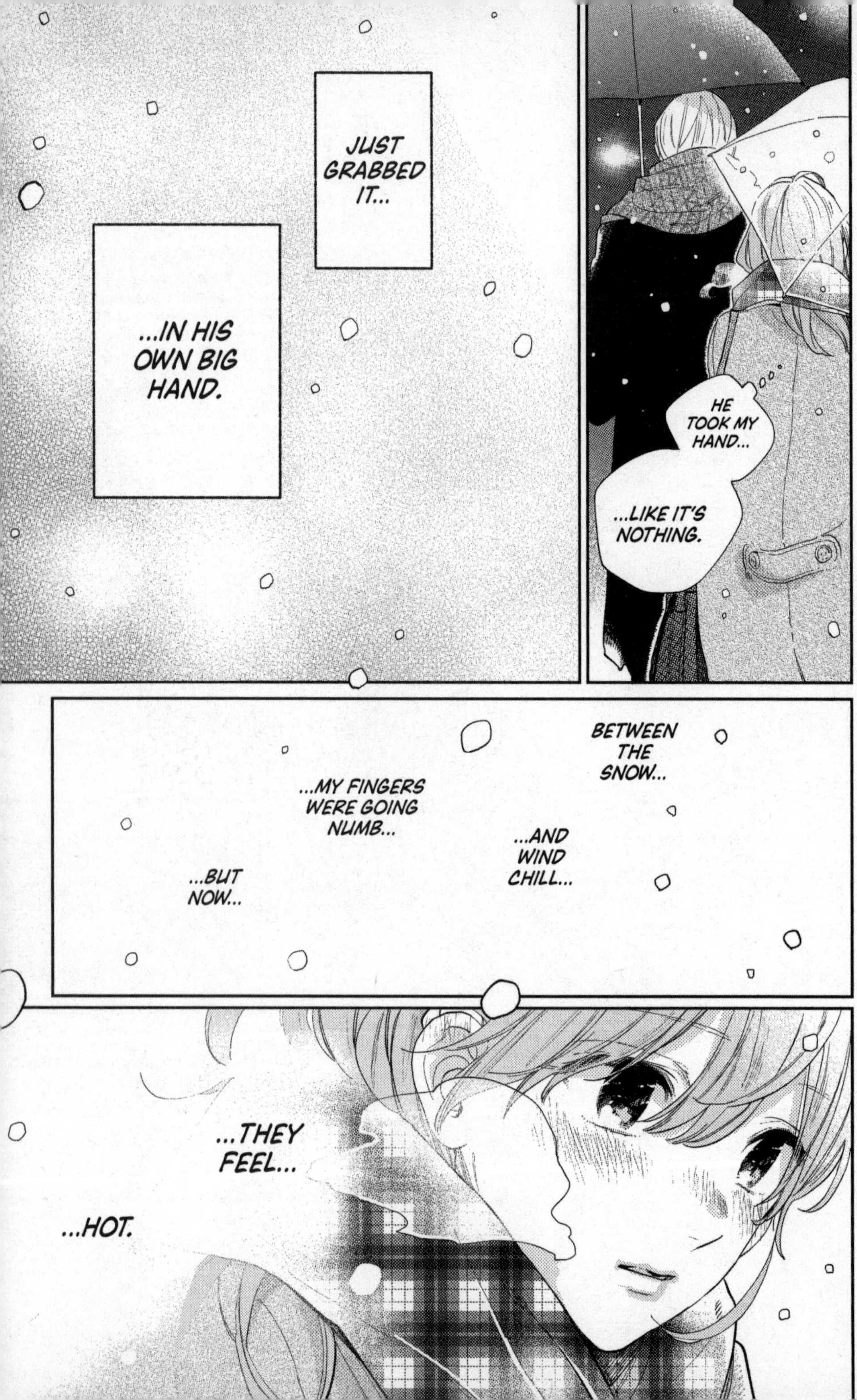
HE TOOK MY HAND...
...LIKE IT'S NOTHING.
JUST GRABBED IT...
...IN HIS OWN BIG HAND.
BETWEEN THE SNOW...
...AND WIND CHILL...
...MY FINGERS WERE GOING NUMB...
...BUT NOW...
...THEY FEEL...
...HOT.

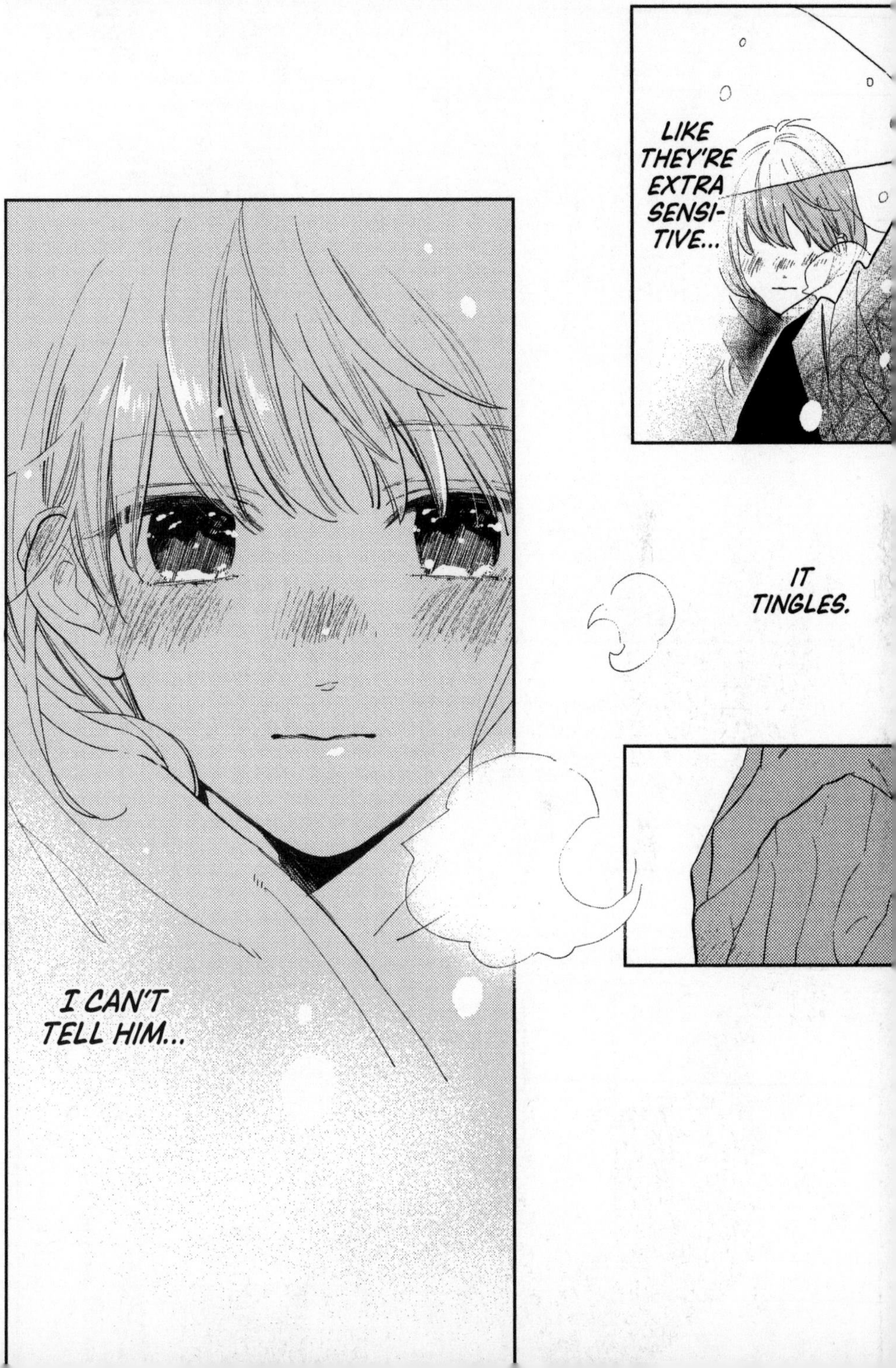
LIKE THEY'RE EXTRA SENSI-TIVE...
IT TINGLES.
I CAN'T TELL HIM...

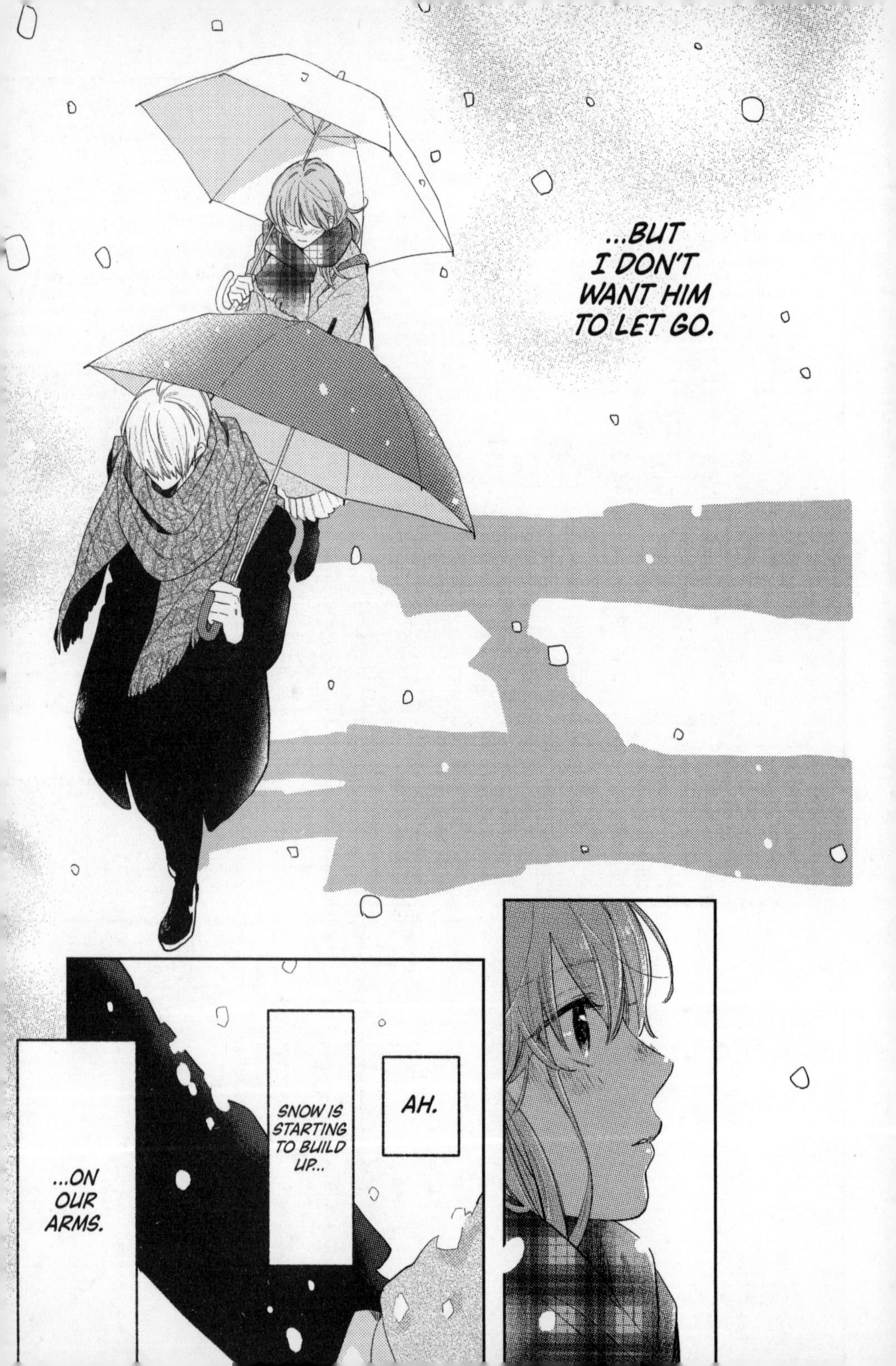
...BUT I DON'T WANT HIM TO LET GO.
AH.
SNOW IS STARTING TO BUILD UP...
...ON OUR ARMS.

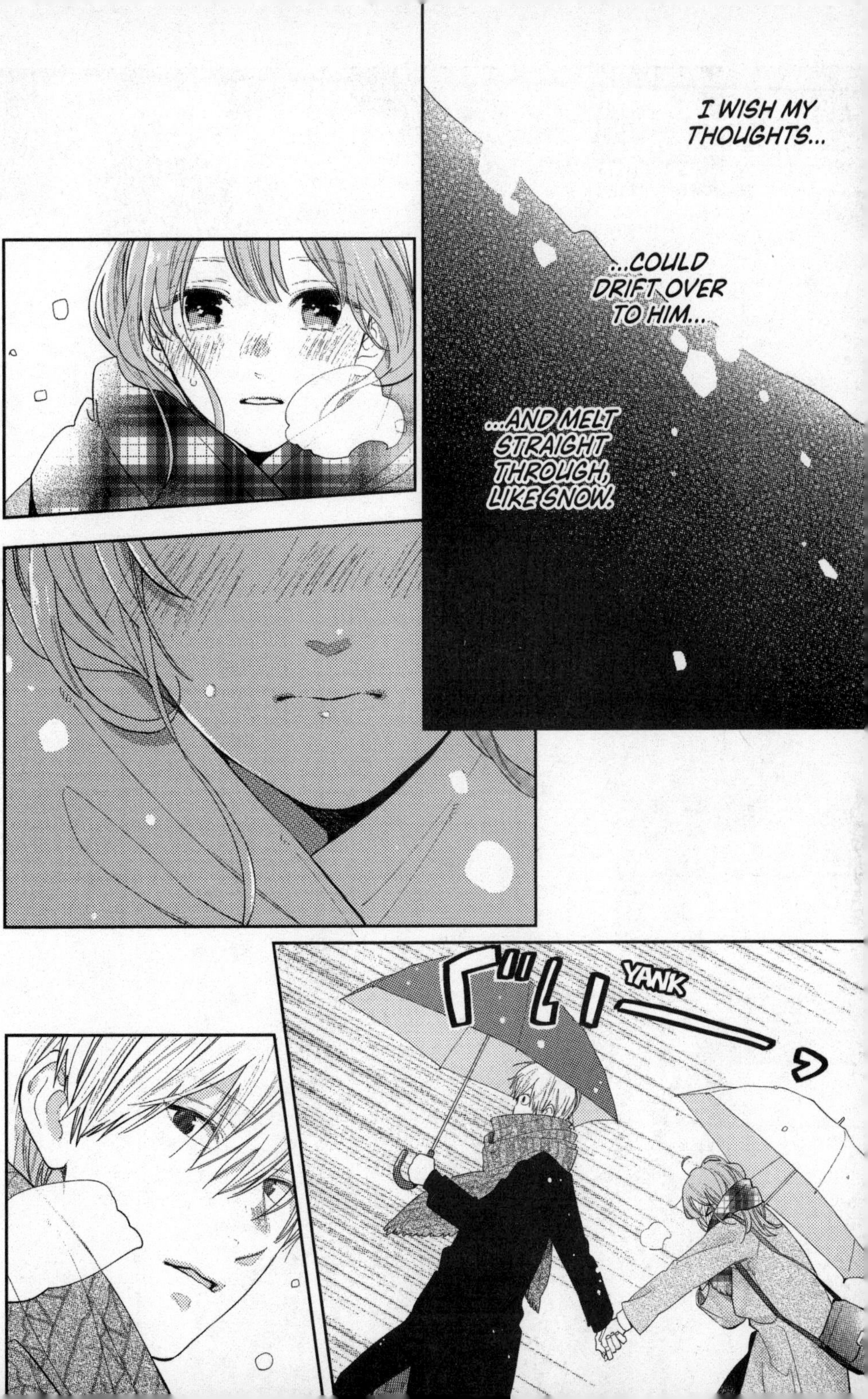
I WISH MY THOUGHTS...
...COULD DRIFT OVER TO HIM...
...AND MELT STRAIGHT THROUGH, LIKE SNOW.
YANK

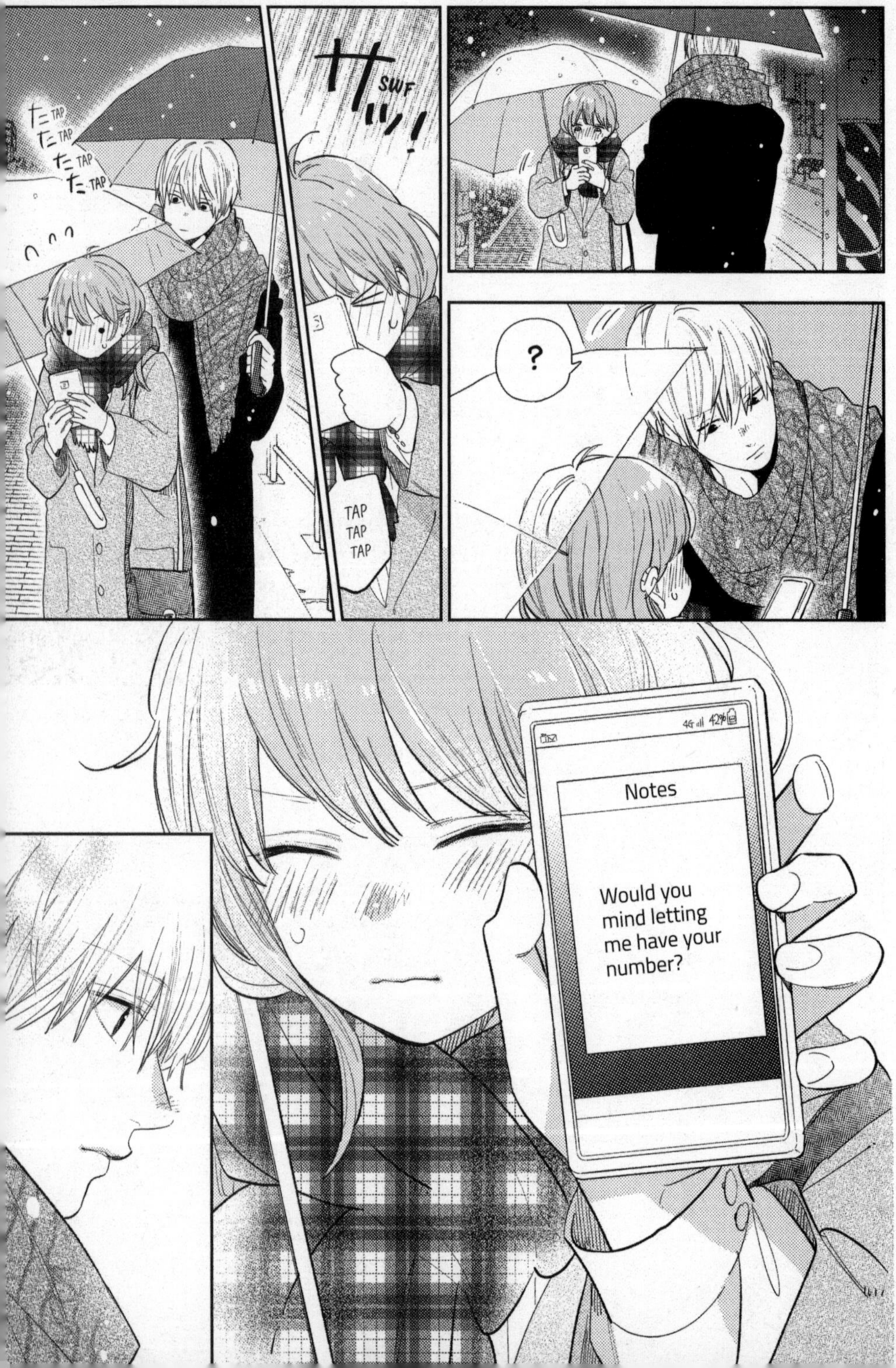
?
ササッ!
SWF
TAP TAP TAP
た TAP
た TAP
た TAP
た TAP
Notes
Would you mind letting me have your number?

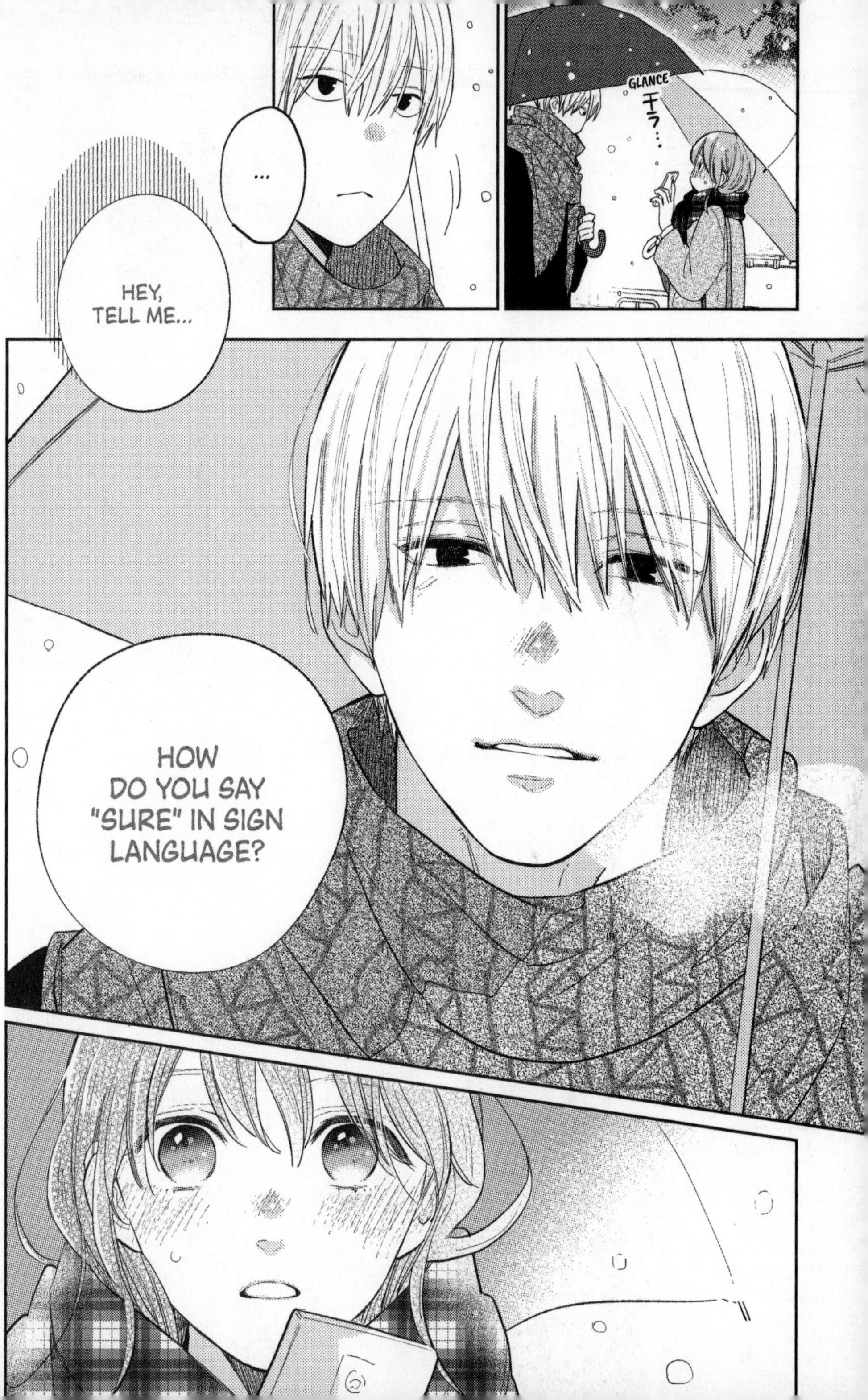
GLANCE
チラ…
...
HEY, TELL ME...
HOW DO YOU SAY "SURE" IN SIGN LANGUAGE?

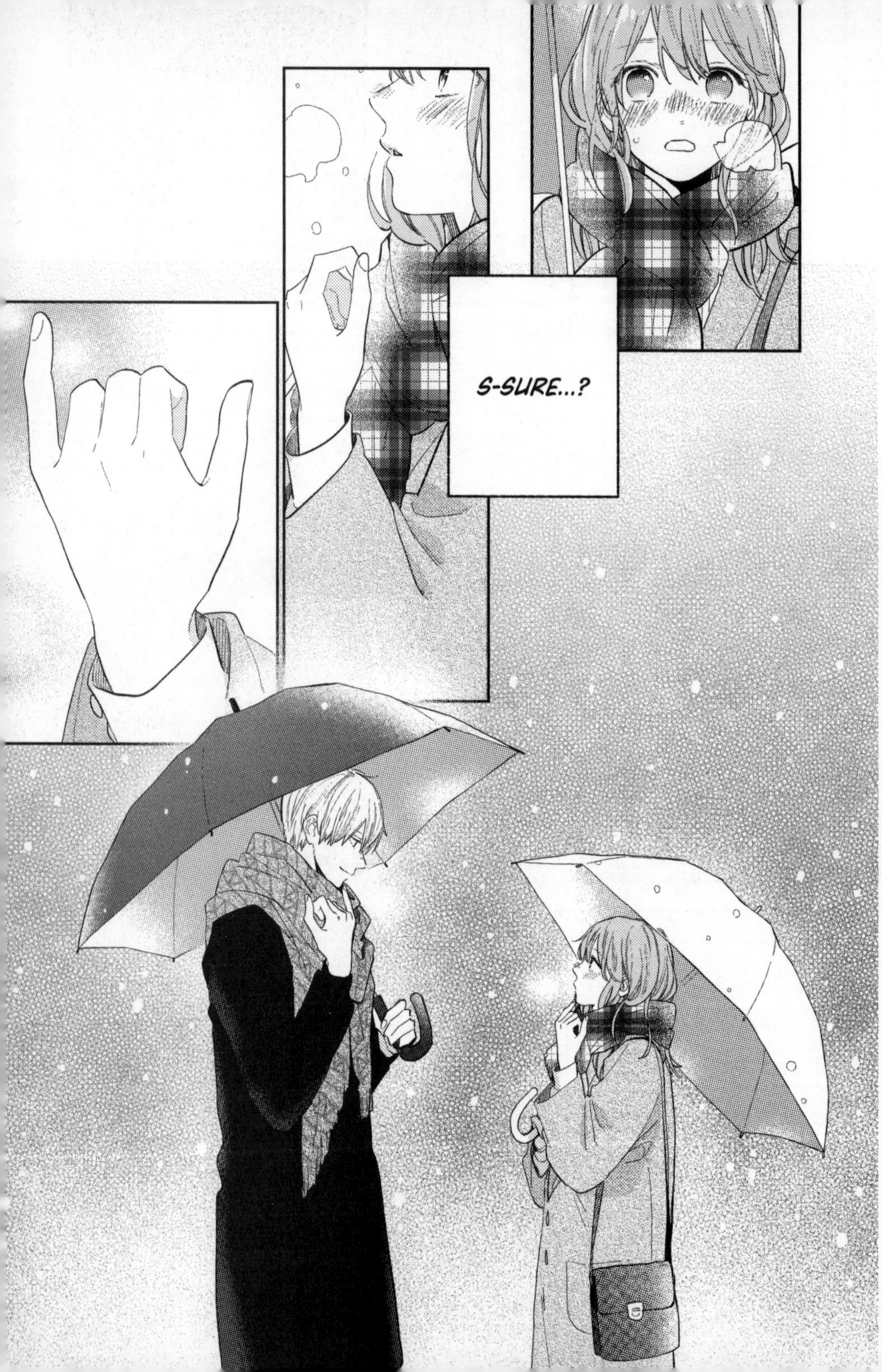
S-SURE...?

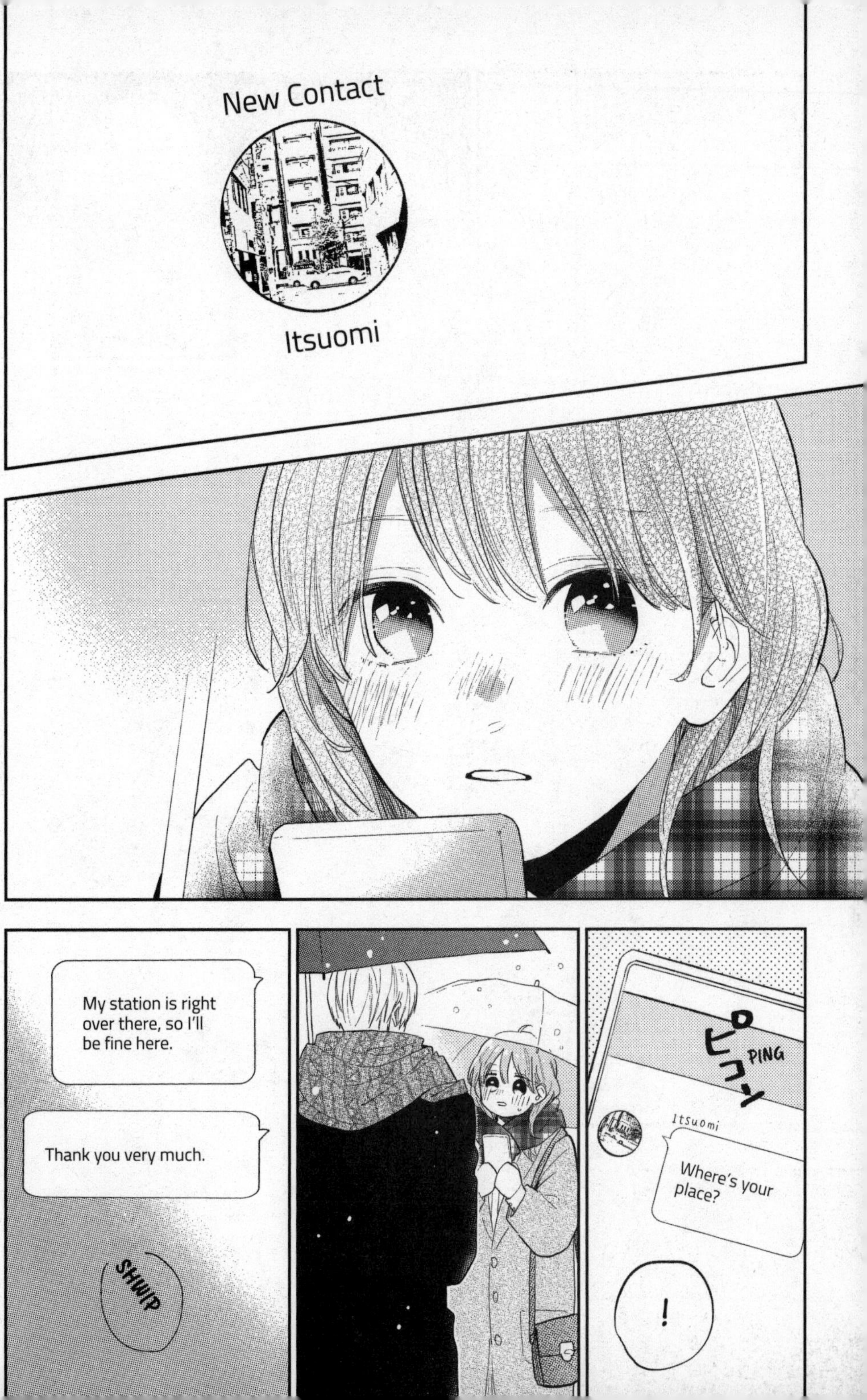
New Contact
Itsuomi
ピコン
PING
Itsuomi
Where's your place?
!
My station is right over there, so I'll be fine here.
Thank you very much.
SHWIP

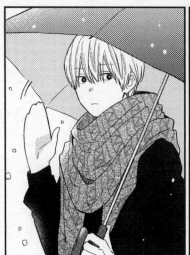

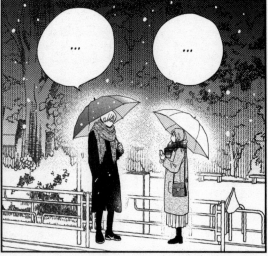

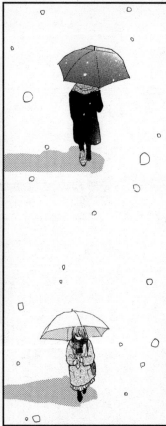

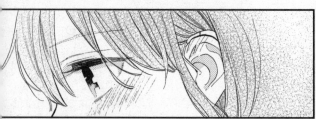

Thank you very much.

Do you mind if I ask you a question?

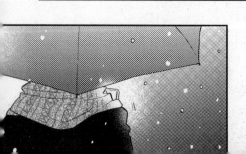

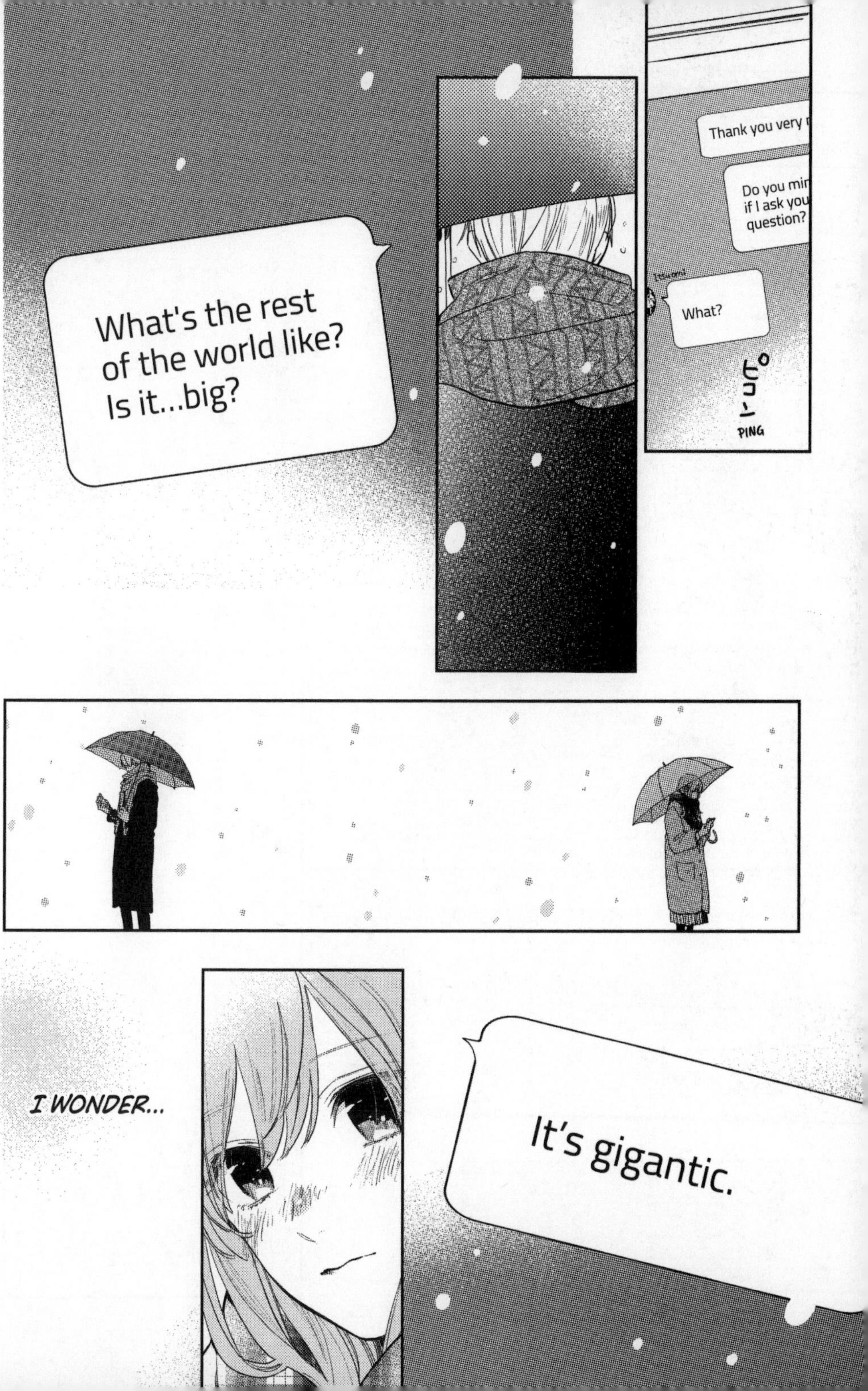
Thank you very
Do you mi if I ask you question?
What?
PING
What's the rest of the world like? Is it...big?
It's gigantic.
I WONDER...

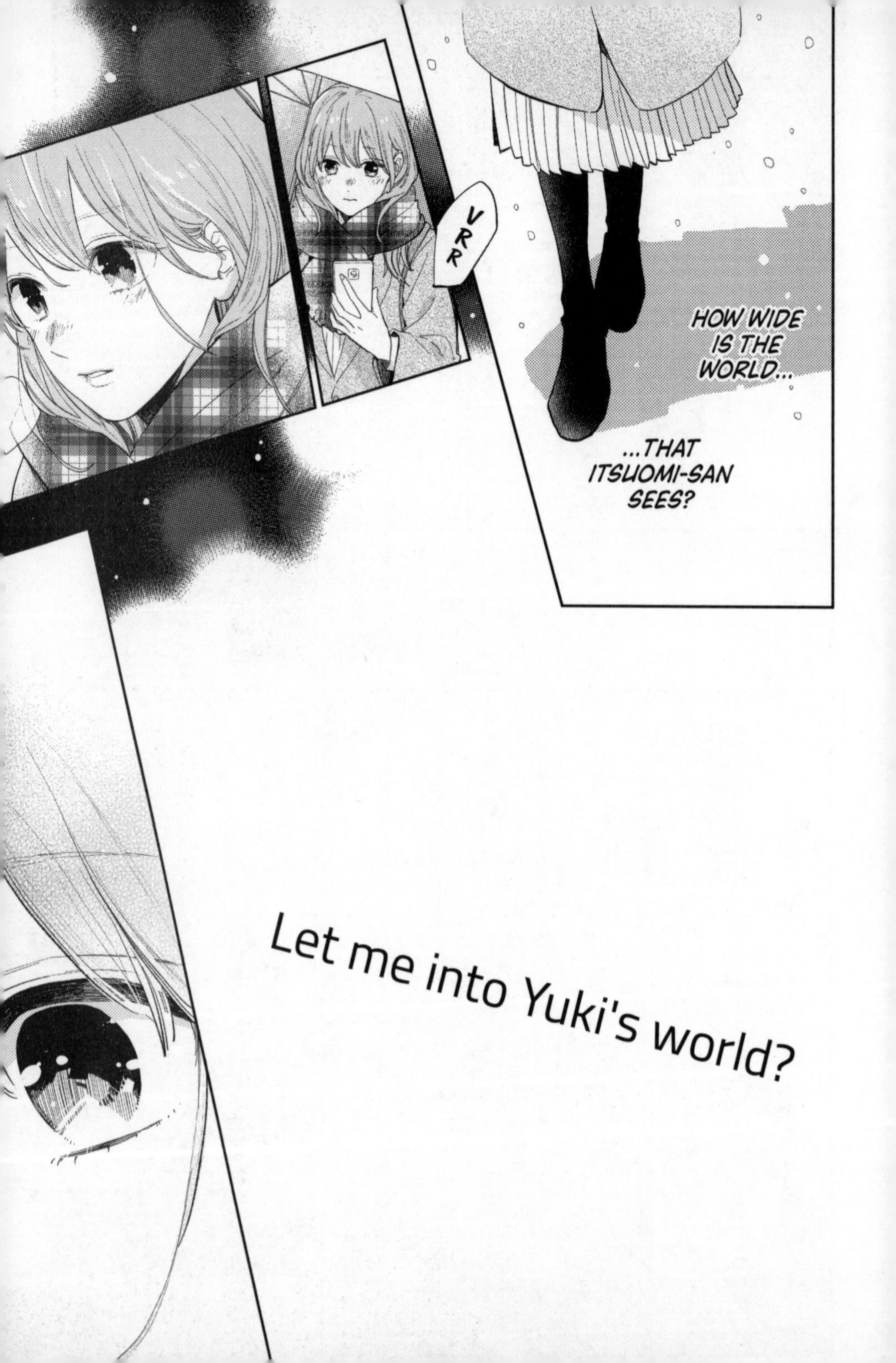
HOW WIDE IS THE WORLD...
...THAT ITSUOMI-SAN SEES?
VRR
Let me into Yuki's world?

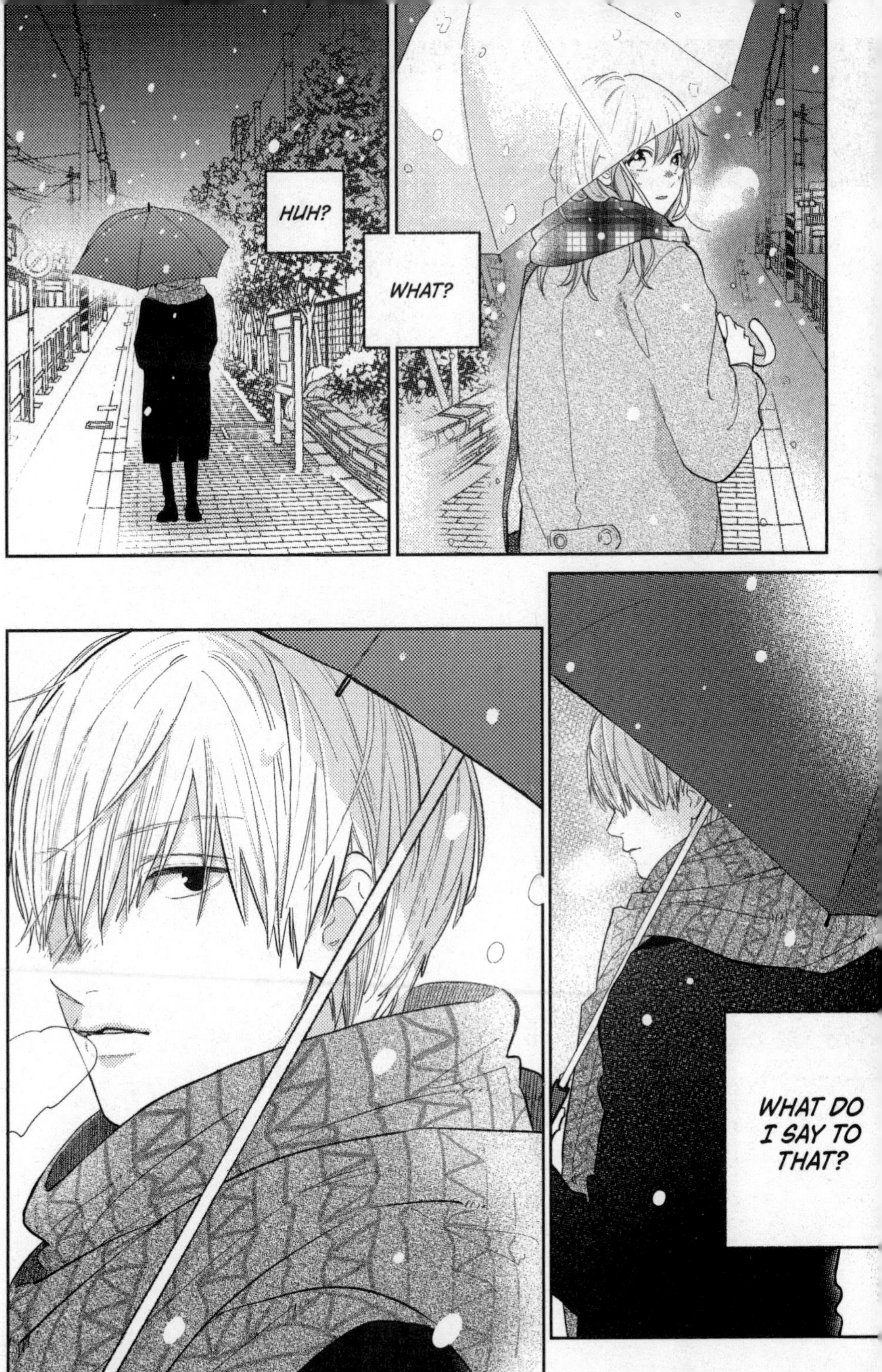
HUH?
WHAT?
WHAT DO I SAY TO THAT?

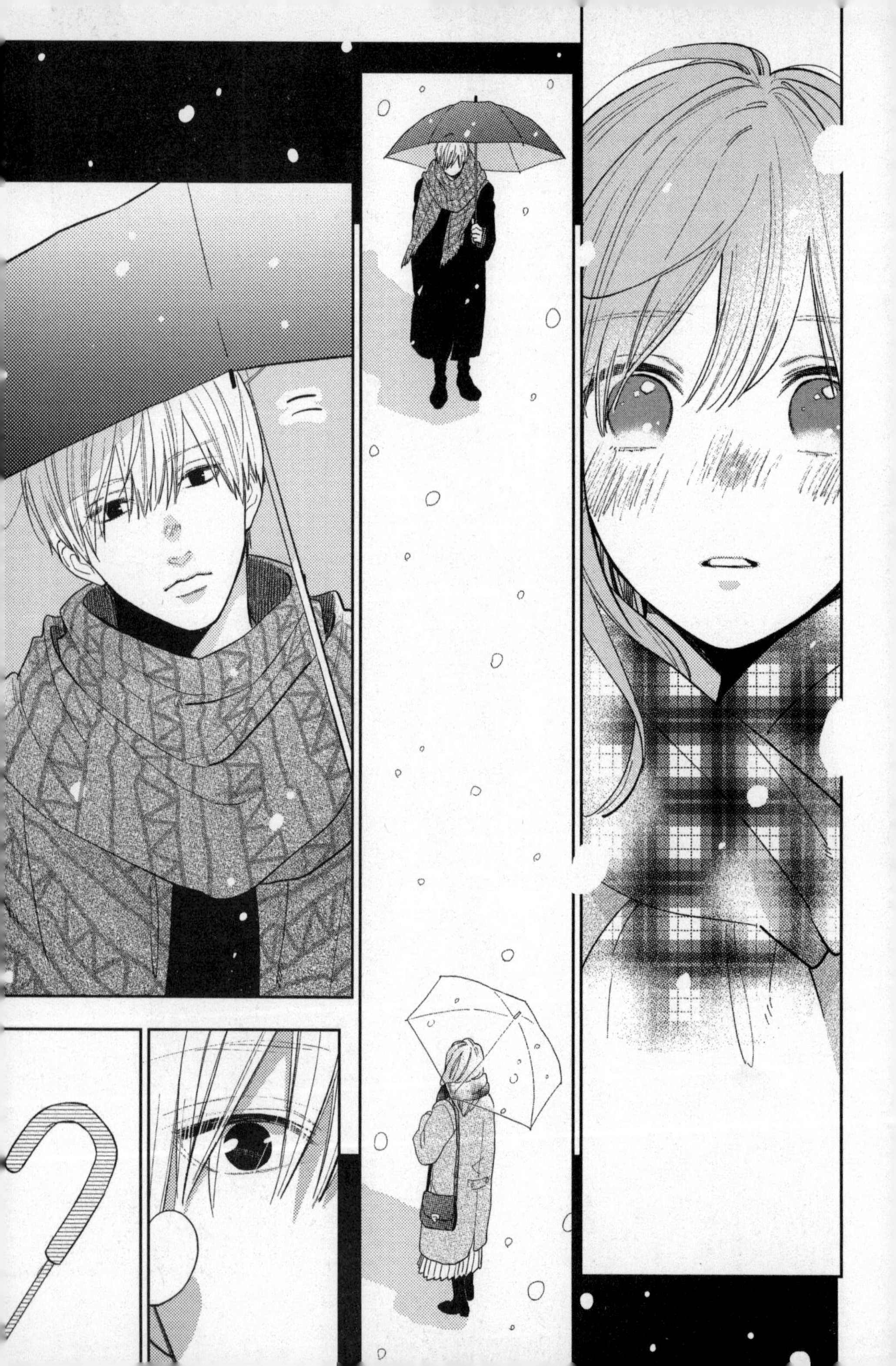

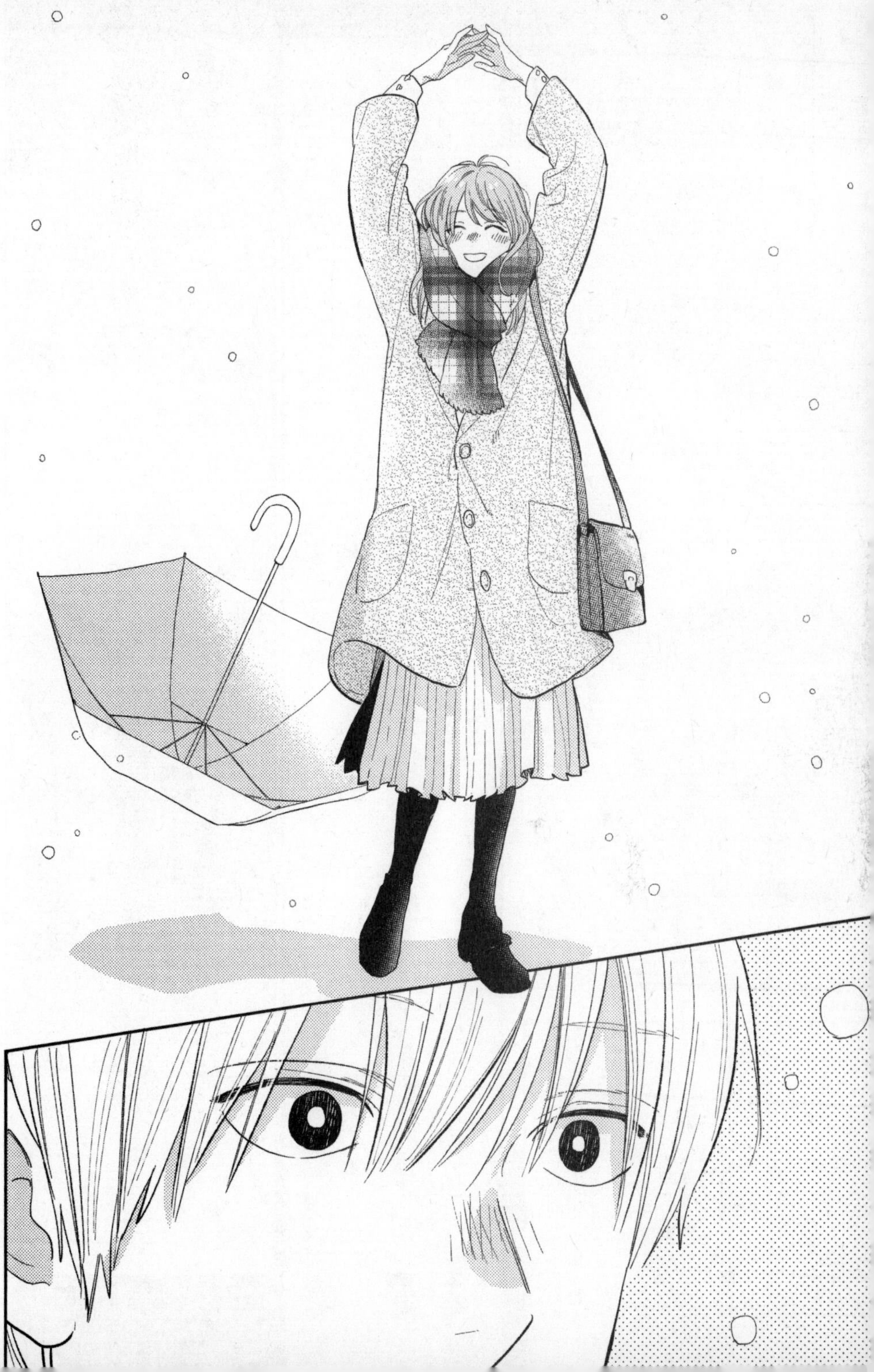

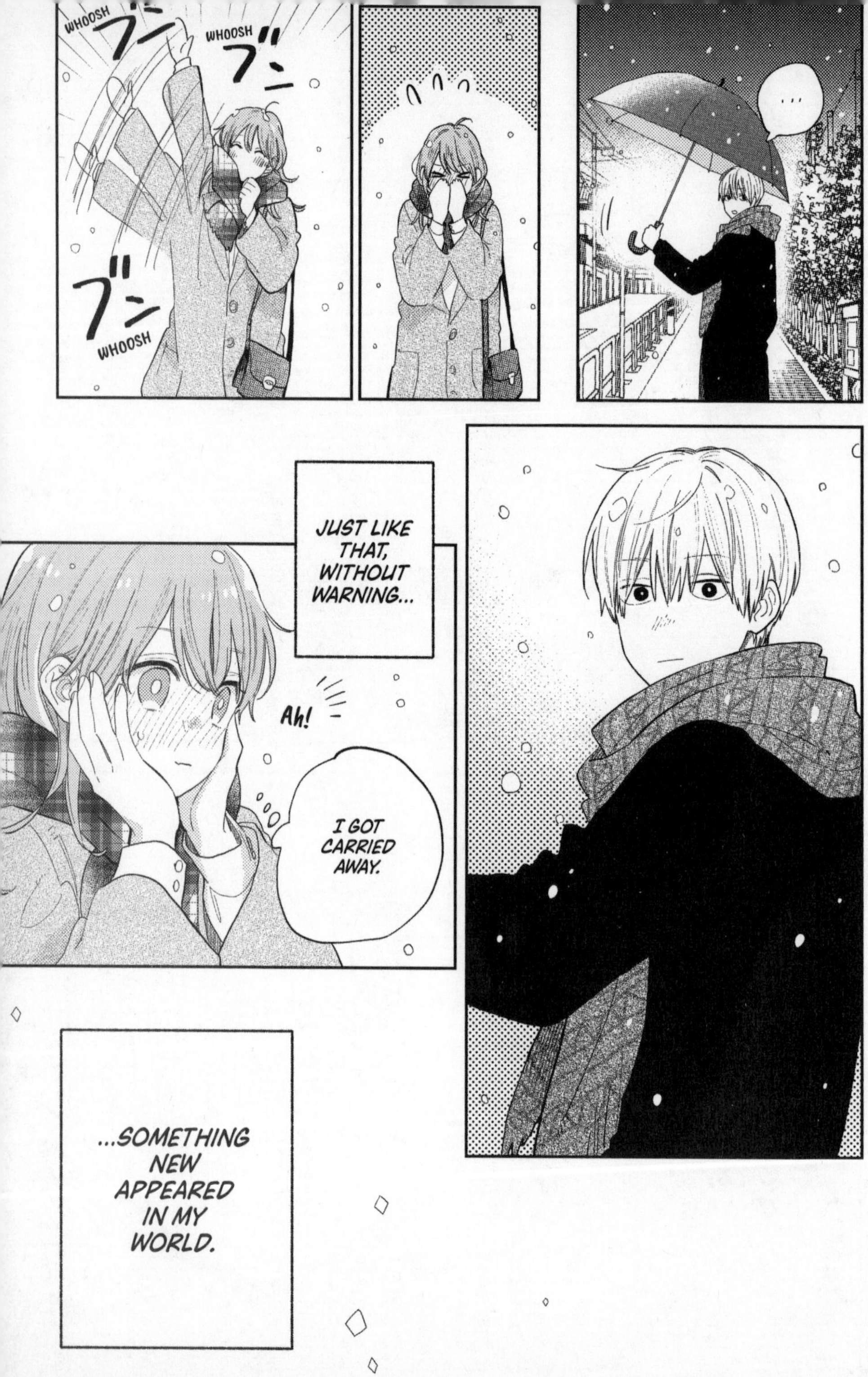
...
ブン
WHOOSH
ブン
WHOOSH
ブン
WHOOSH
JUST LIKE THAT, WITHOUT WARNING...
Ah!
I GOT CARRIED AWAY.
...SOMETHING NEW APPEARED IN MY WORLD.

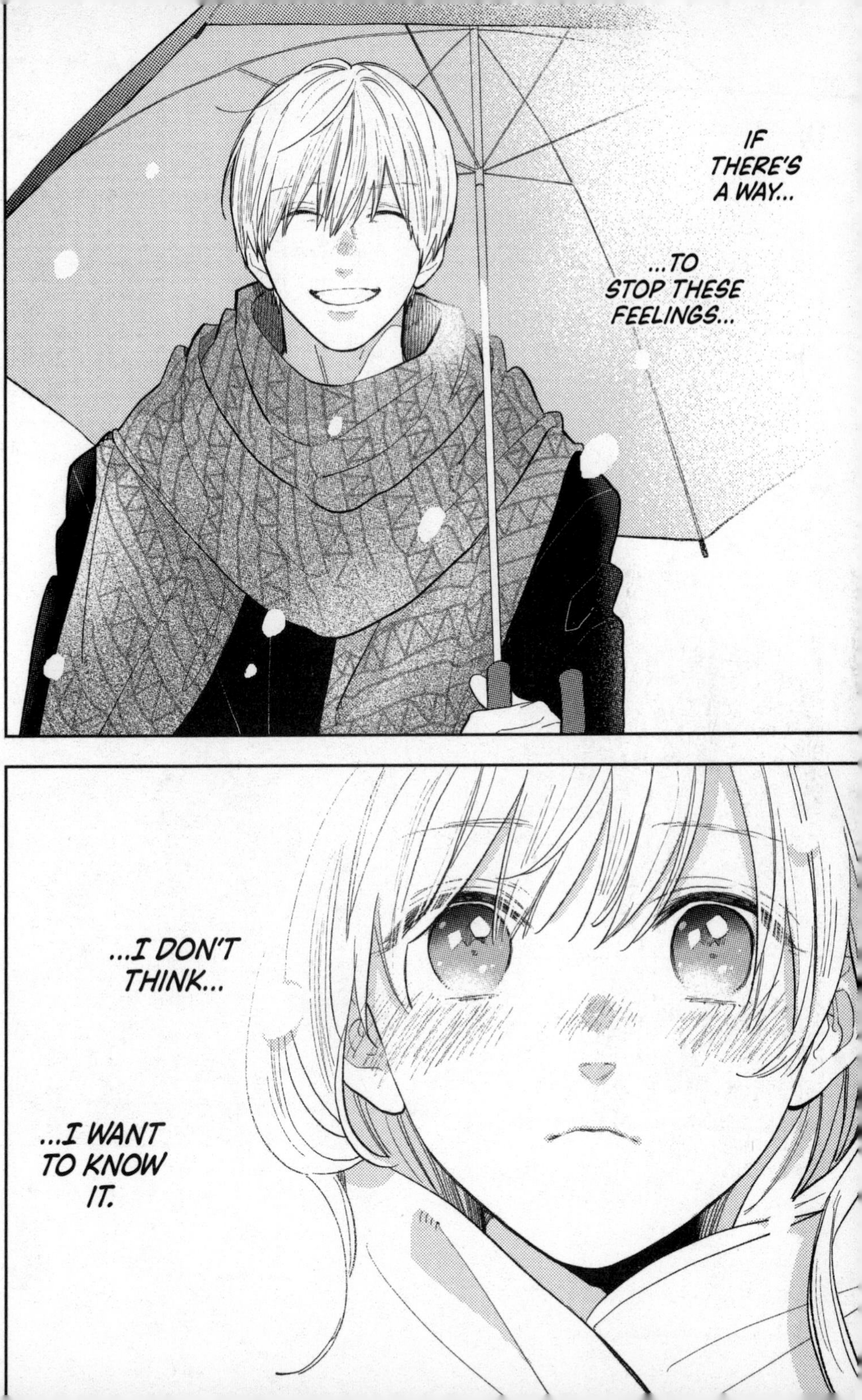
IF THERE'S A WAY...
...TO STOP THESE FEELINGS...
...I DON'T THINK...
...I WANT TO KNOW IT.

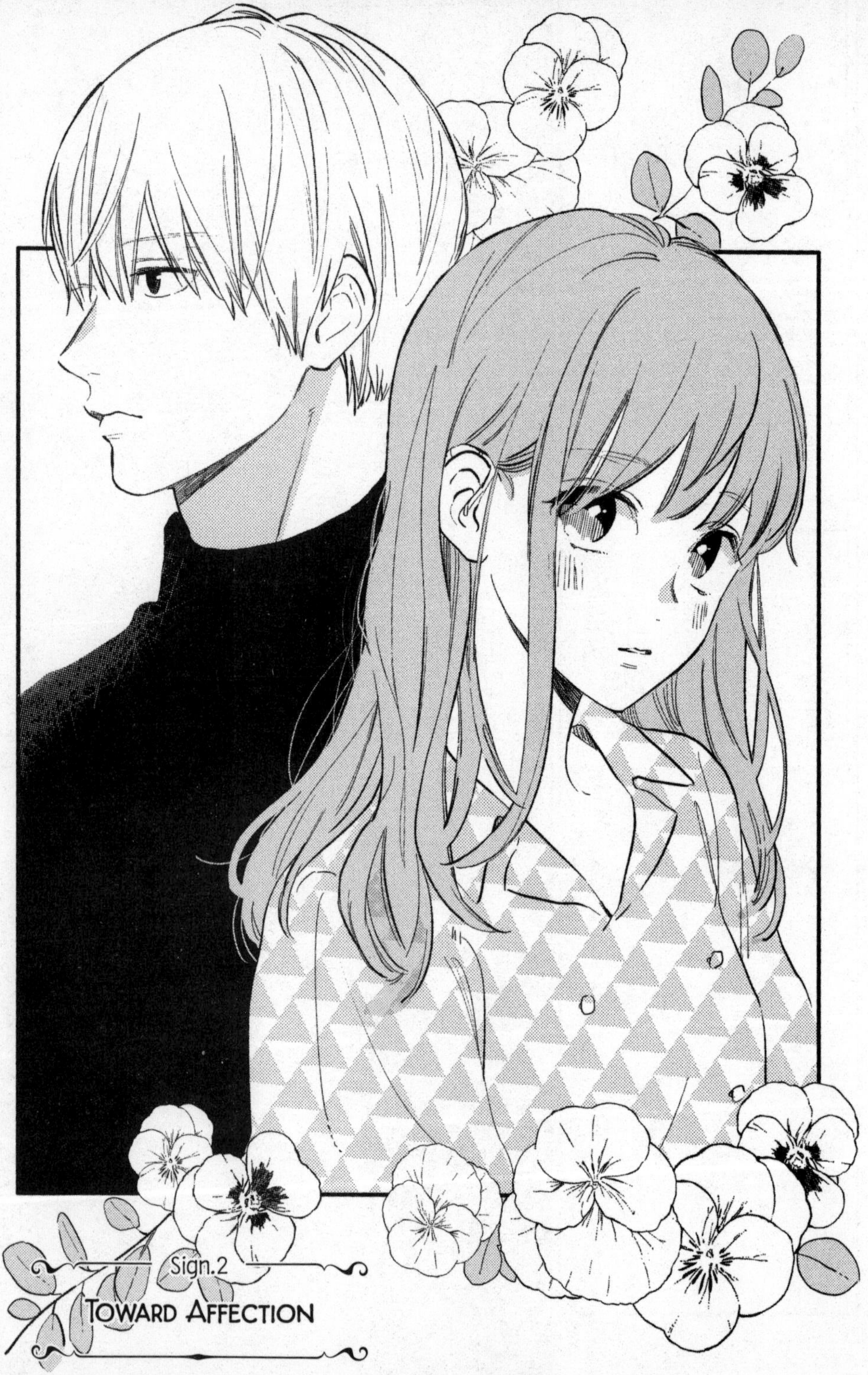
Sign.2
Toward Affection

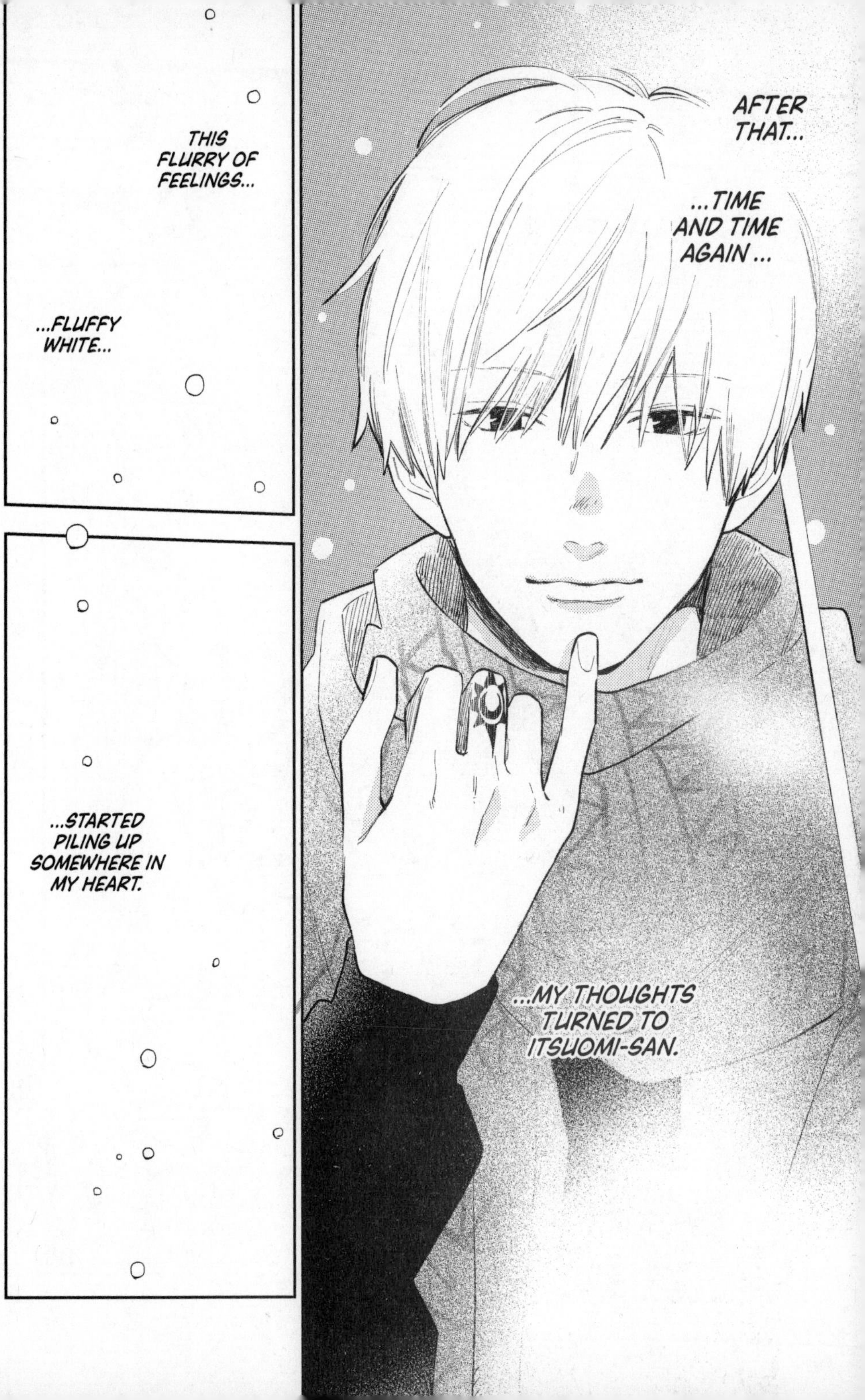
AFTER THAT...
...TIME AND TIME AGAIN ...
...MY THOUGHTS TURNED TO ITSUOMI-SAN.
THIS FLURRY OF FEELINGS...
...FLUFFY WHITE...
...STARTED PILING UP SOMEWHERE IN MY HEART.

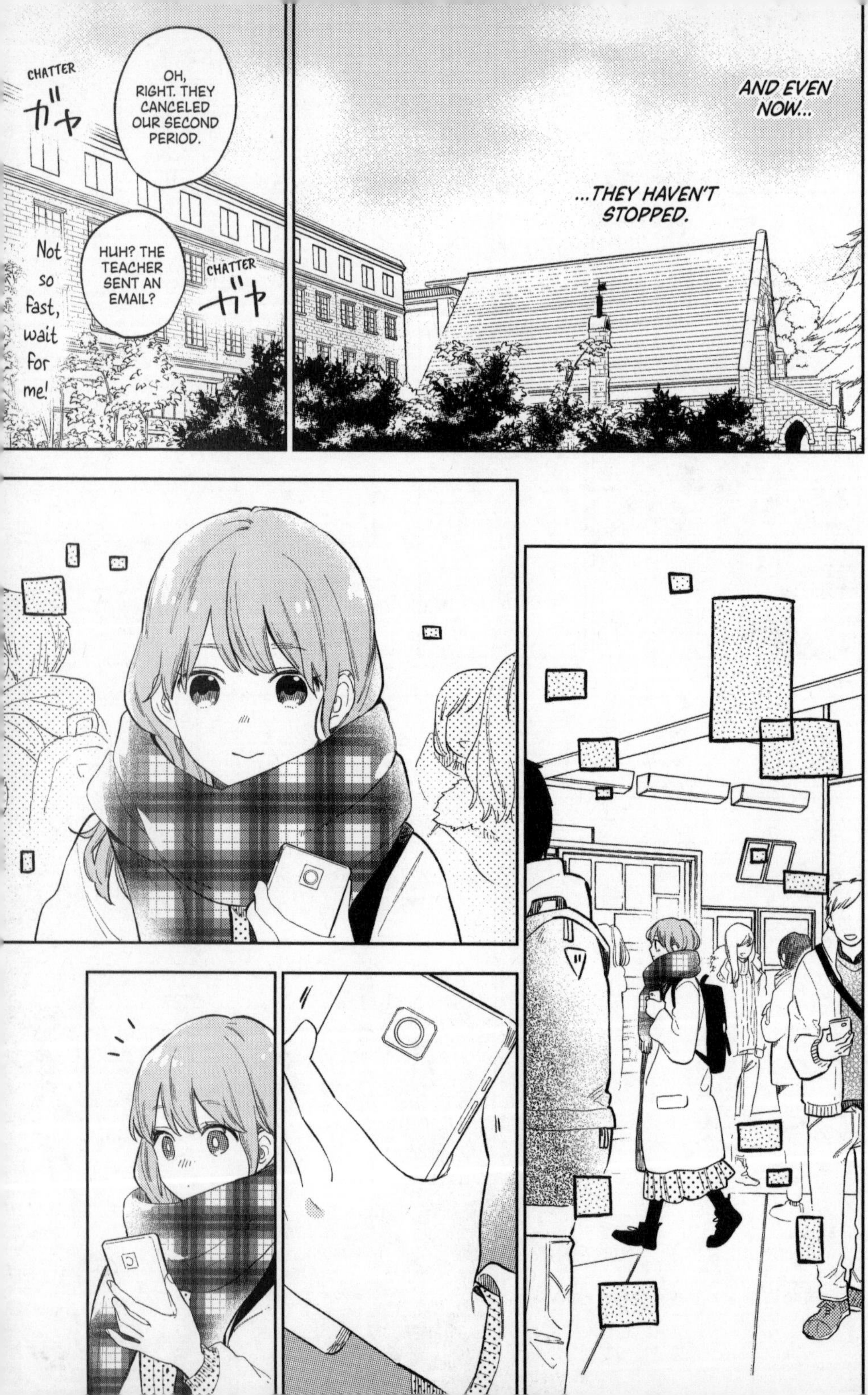
AND EVEN NOW...
...THEY HAVEN'T STOPPED.
CHATTER
ガヤ
OH, RIGHT. THEY CANCELED OUR SECOND PERIOD.
HUH? THE TEACHER SENT AN EMAIL?
CHATTER
ガヤ
Not so fast, wait for me!

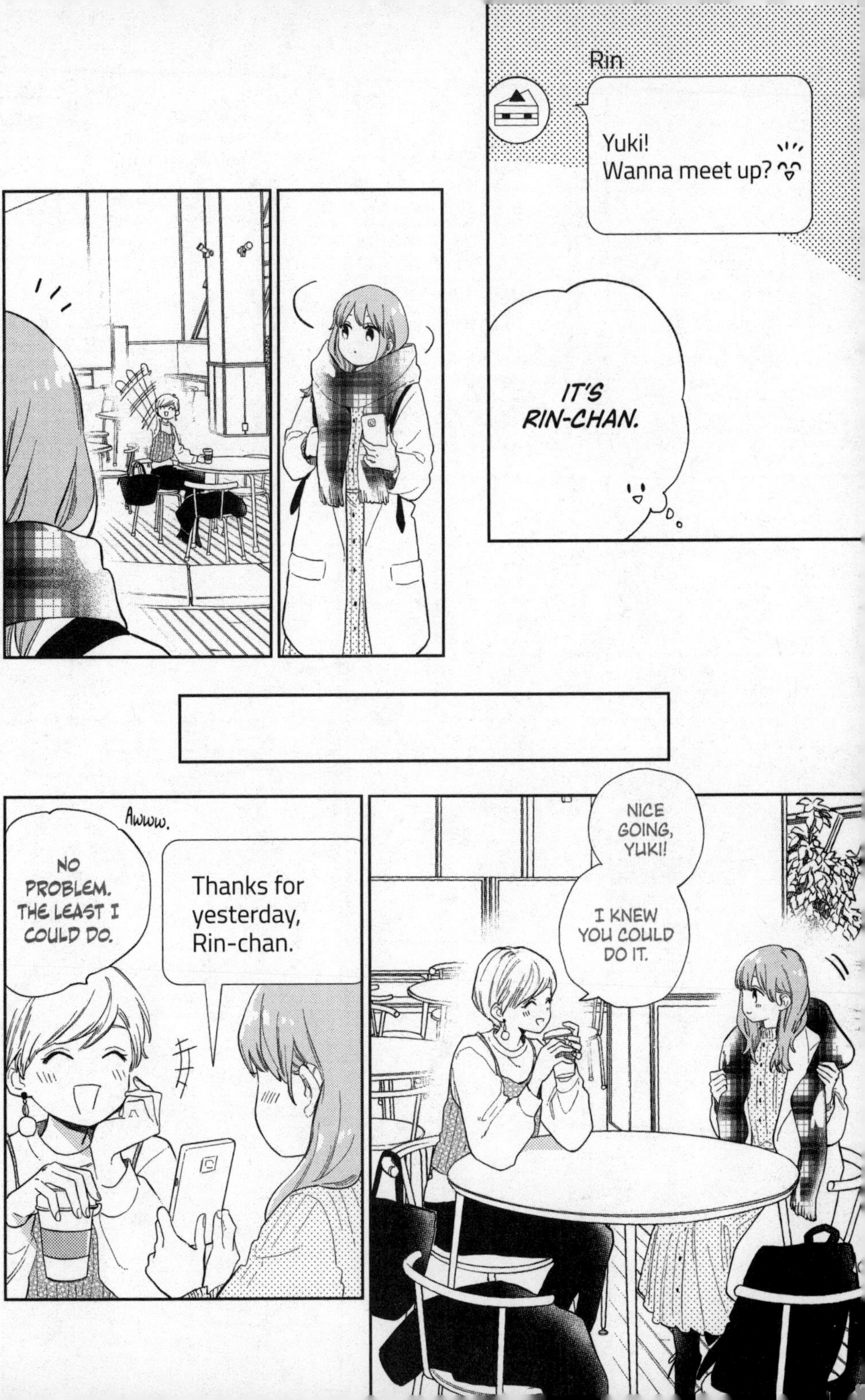
Rin
Yuki! Wanna meet up?
IT'S RIN-CHAN.
NICE GOING, YUKI!
I KNEW YOU COULD DO IT.
Thanks for yesterday, Rin-chan.
Awww.
NO PROBLEM. THE LEAST I COULD DO.

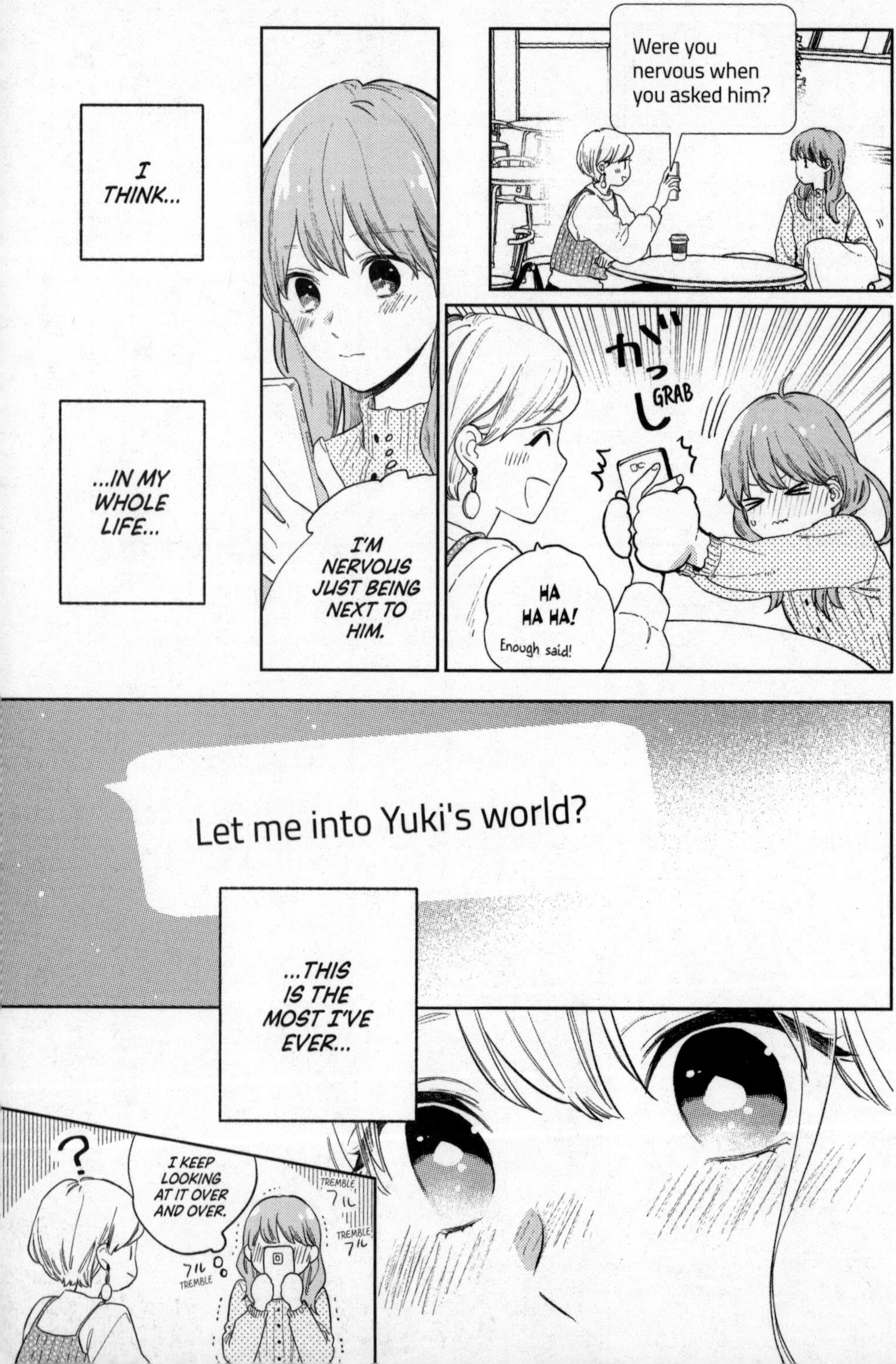
Were you nervous when you asked him?
がっし GRAB
HA HA HA!
Enough said!
I'M NERVOUS JUST BEING NEXT TO HIM.
I THINK...
...IN MY WHOLE LIFE...
Let me into Yuki's world?
...THIS IS THE MOST I'VE EVER...
?
I KEEP LOOKING AT IT OVER AND OVER.
フル TREMBLE
フル TREMBLE
フル TREMBLE

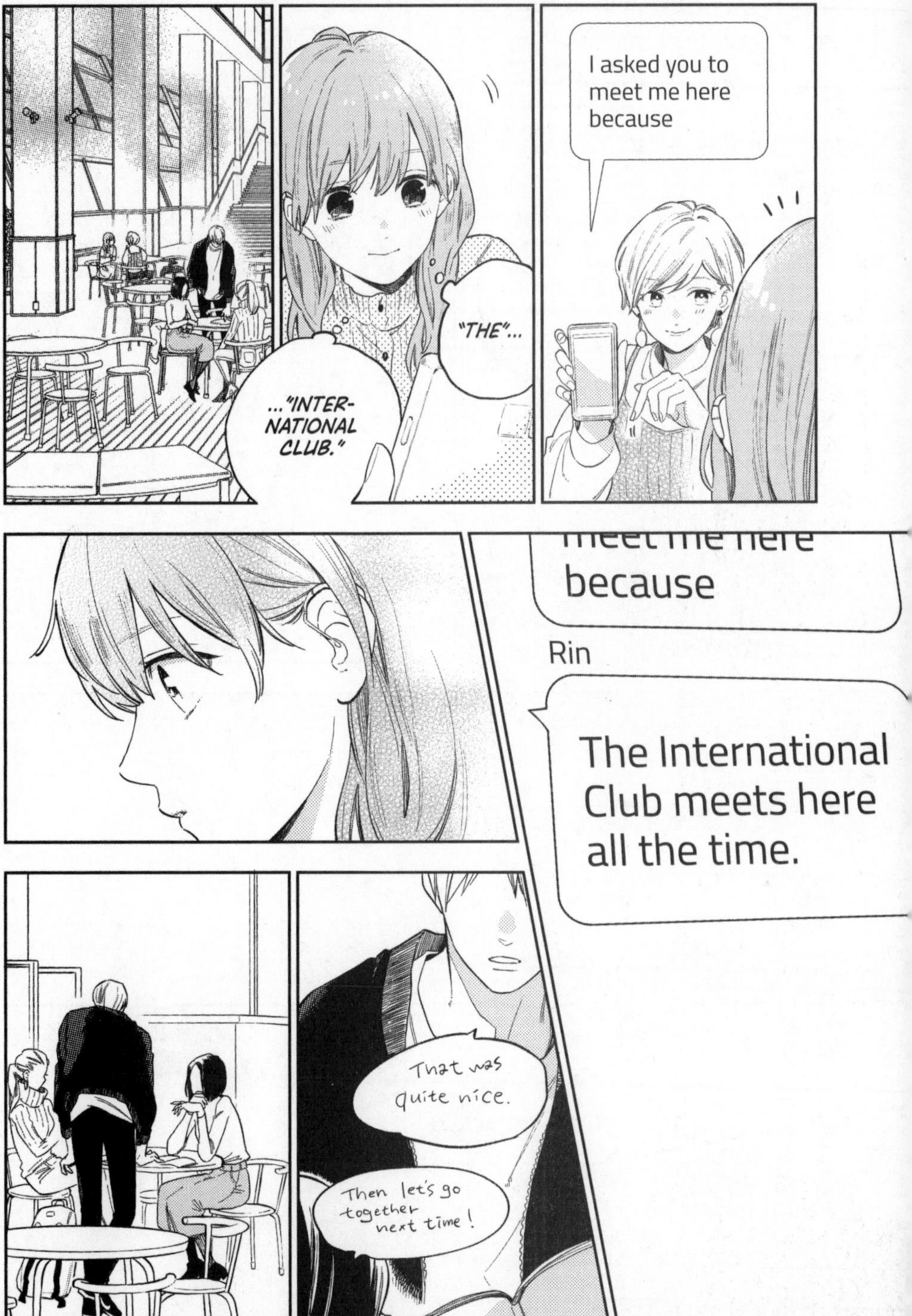
I asked you to meet me here because
"THE"...
..."INTER-NATIONAL CLUB."
meet me here because
Rin
The International Club meets here all the time.
That was quite nice.
Then let's go together next time!

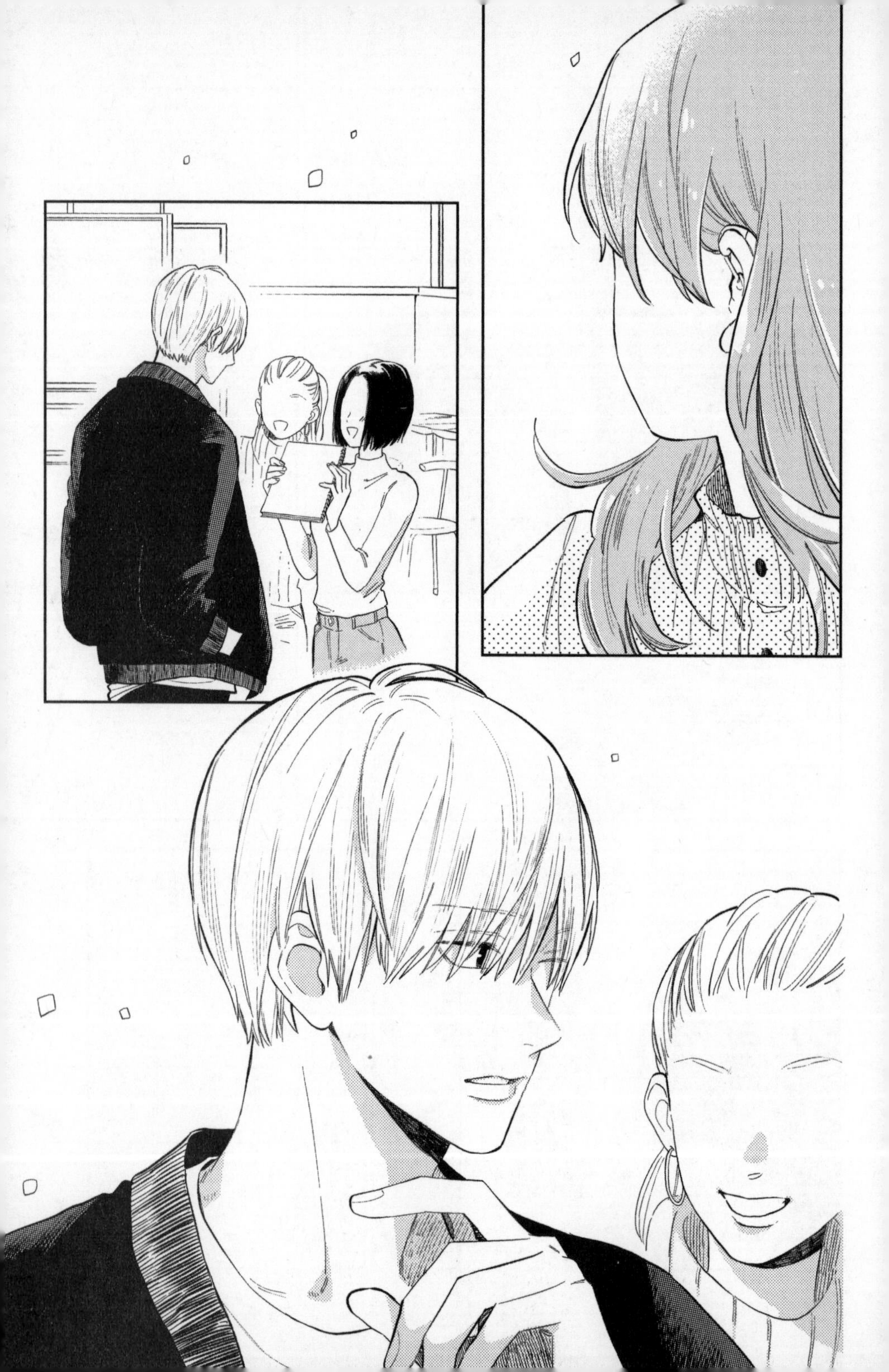

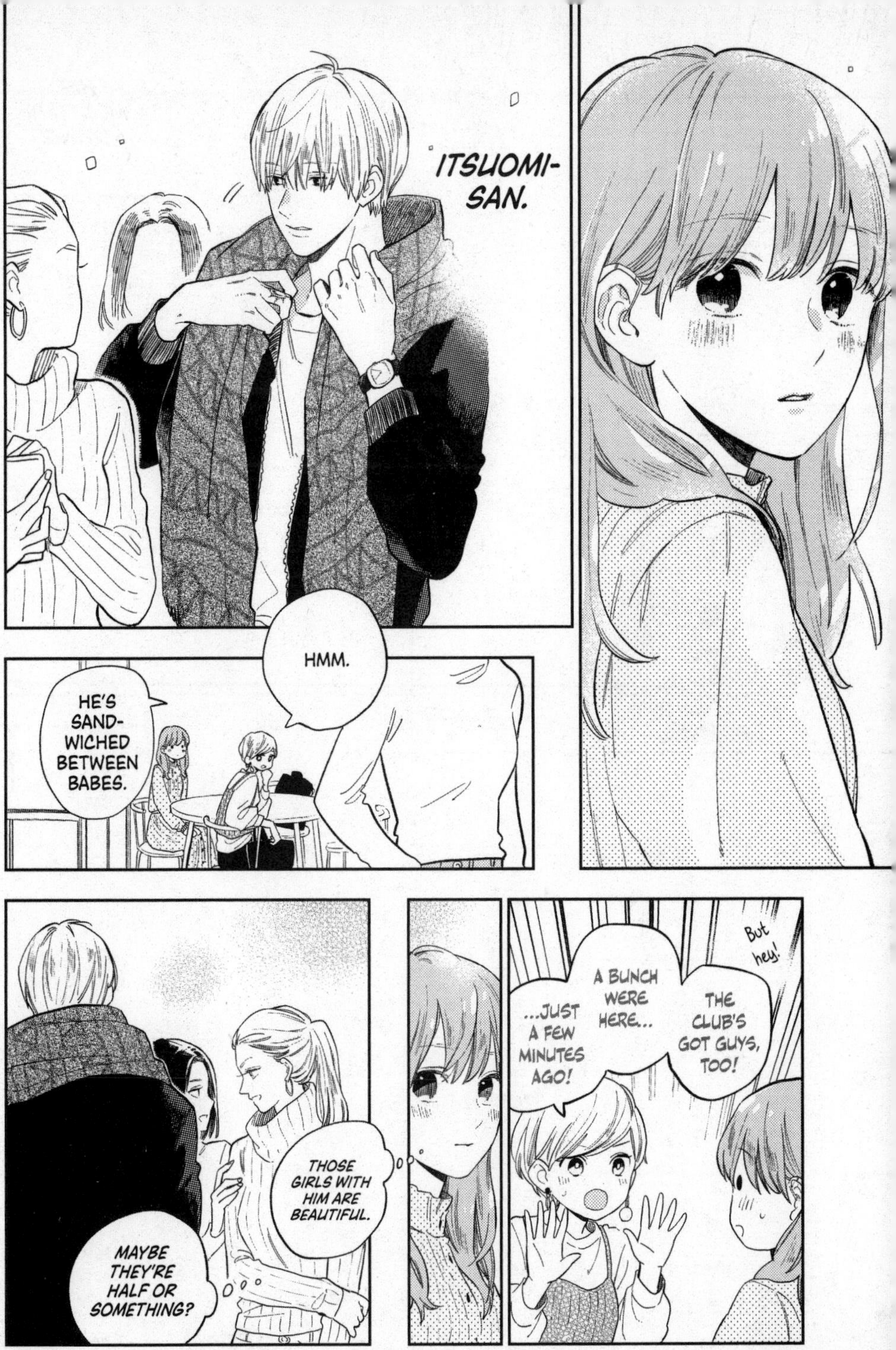
ITSUOMI-SAN.
HMM.
HE'S SAND-WICHED BETWEEN BABES.
But hey!
THE CLUB'S GOT GUYS, TOO!
A BUNCH WERE HERE...
...JUST A FEW MINUTES AGO!
THOSE GIRLS WITH HIM ARE BEAUTIFUL.
MAYBE THEY'RE HALF OR SOMETHING?

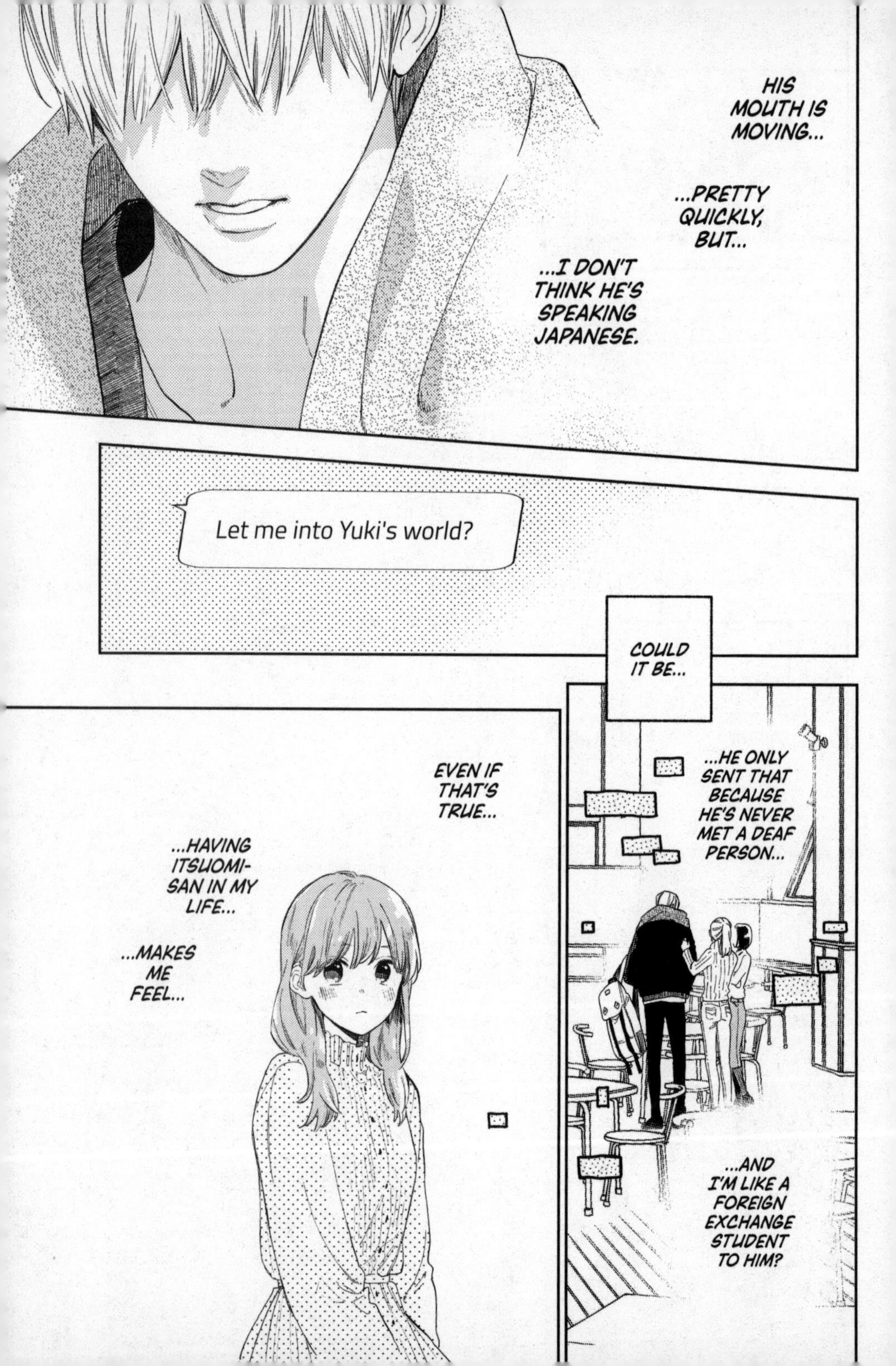
HIS MOUTH IS MOVING...
...PRETTY QUICKLY, BUT...
...I DON'T THINK HE'S SPEAKING JAPANESE.
Let me into Yuki's world?
COULD IT BE...
...HE ONLY SENT THAT BECAUSE HE'S NEVER MET A DEAF PERSON...
...AND I'M LIKE A FOREIGN EXCHANGE STUDENT TO HIM?
EVEN IF THAT'S TRUE...
...HAVING ITSUOMI-SAN IN MY LIFE...
...MAKES ME FEEL...

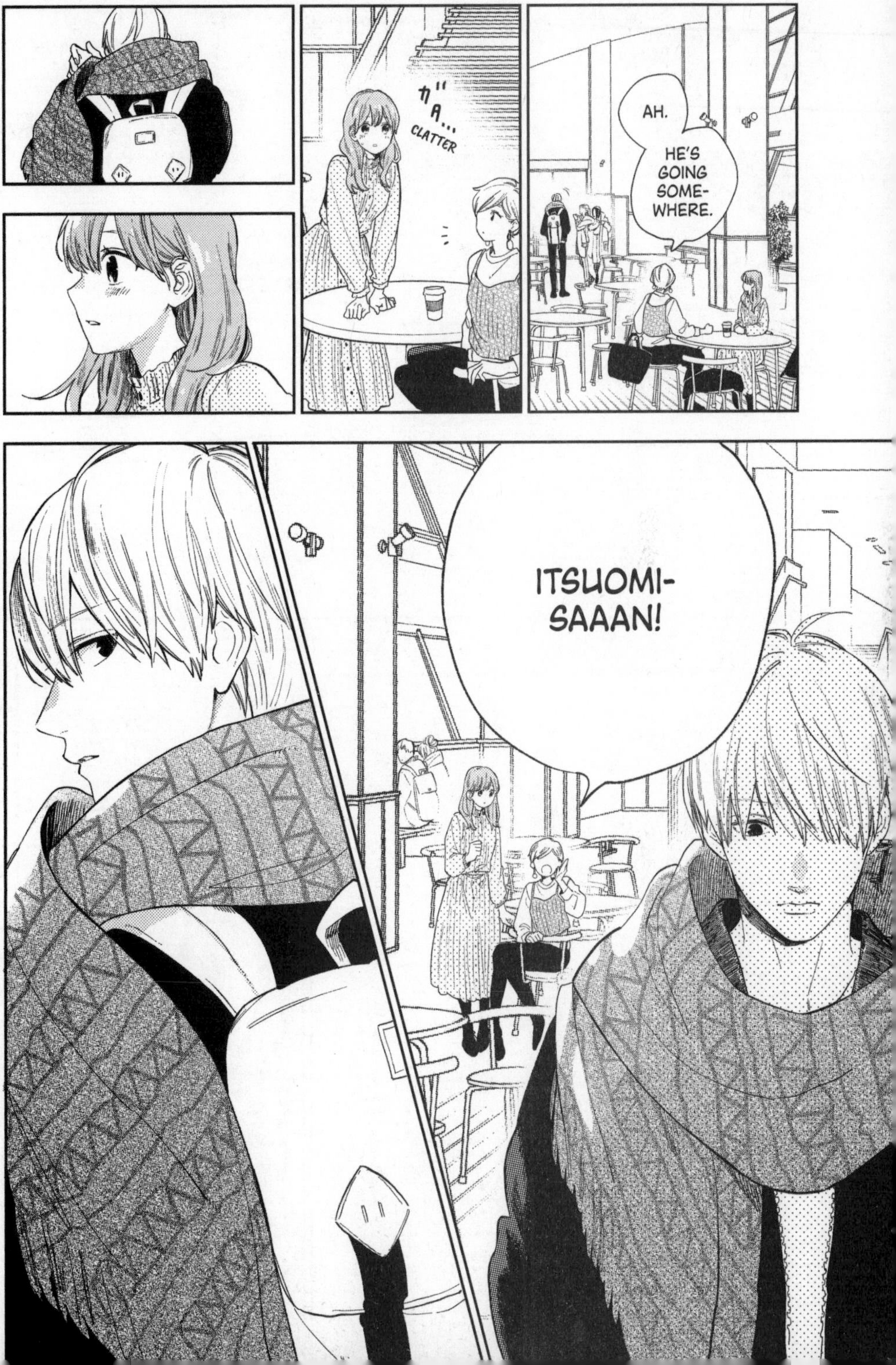
AH.
HE'S GOING SOME-WHERE.
ガ A...
CLATTER
ITSUOMI-SAAAN!

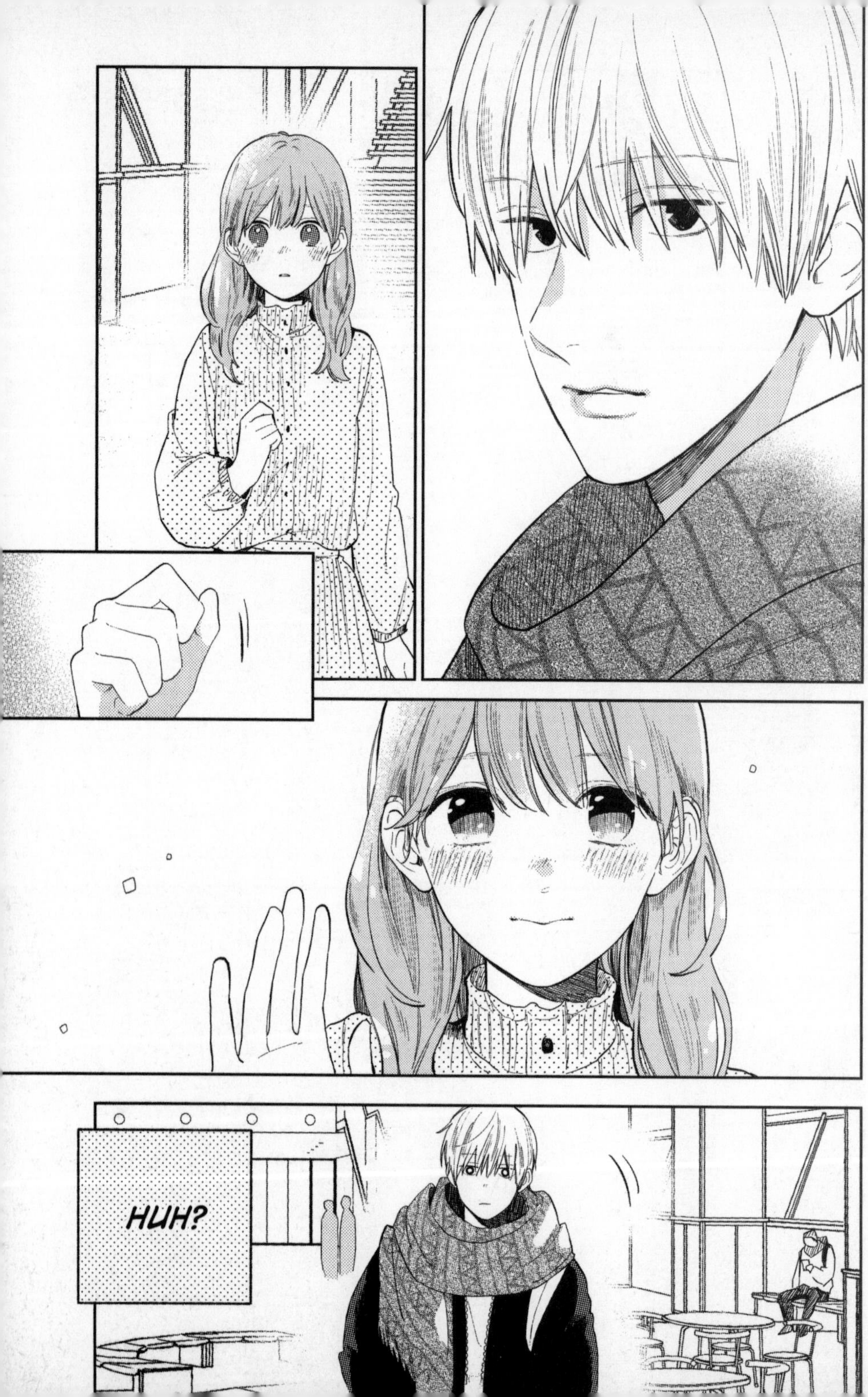
HUH?

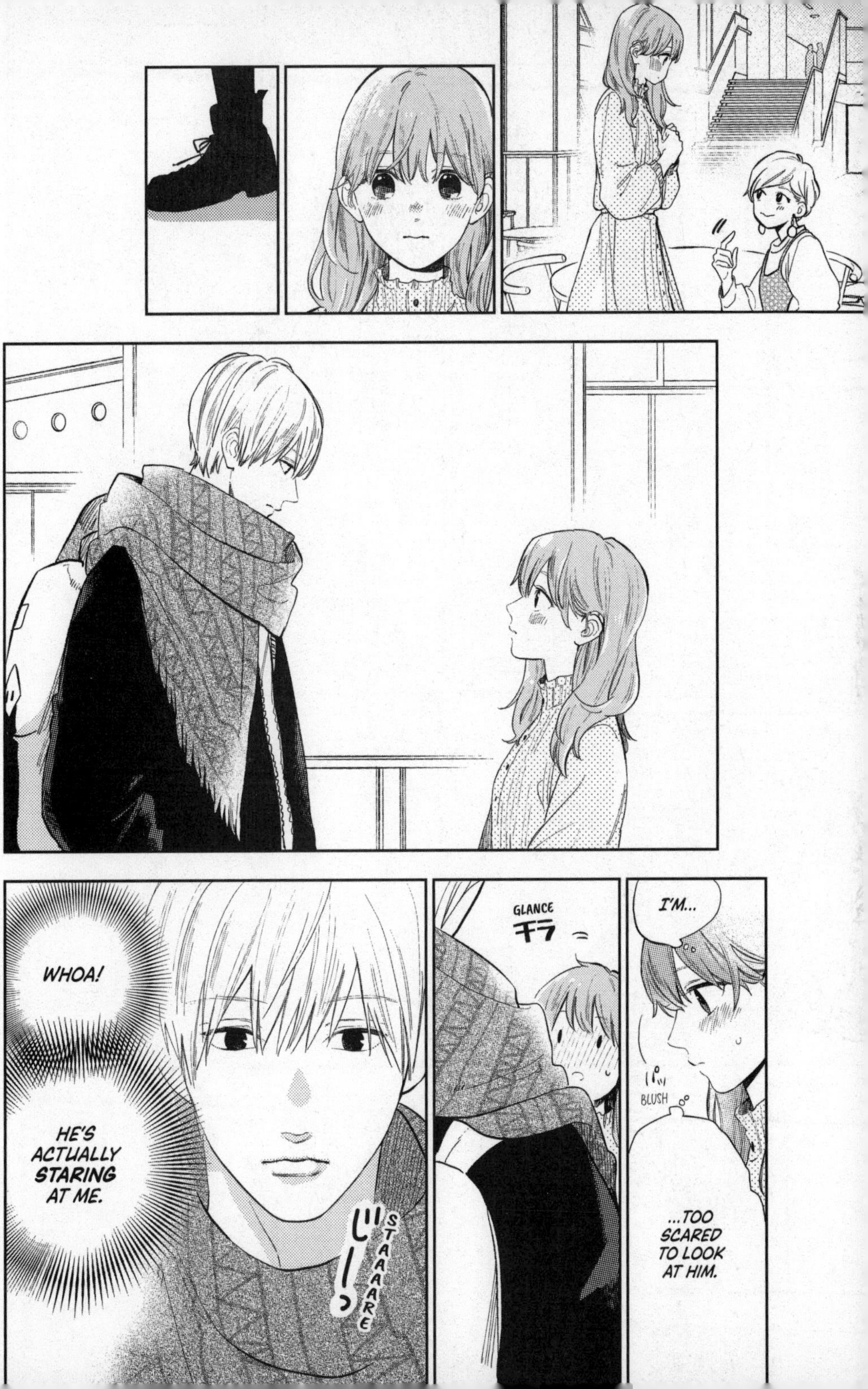
I'M...
パッ
BLUSH
...TOO SCARED TO LOOK AT HIM.
GLANCE
チラ
WHOA!
HE'S ACTUALLY STARING AT ME.
じーっ
STAAAARE

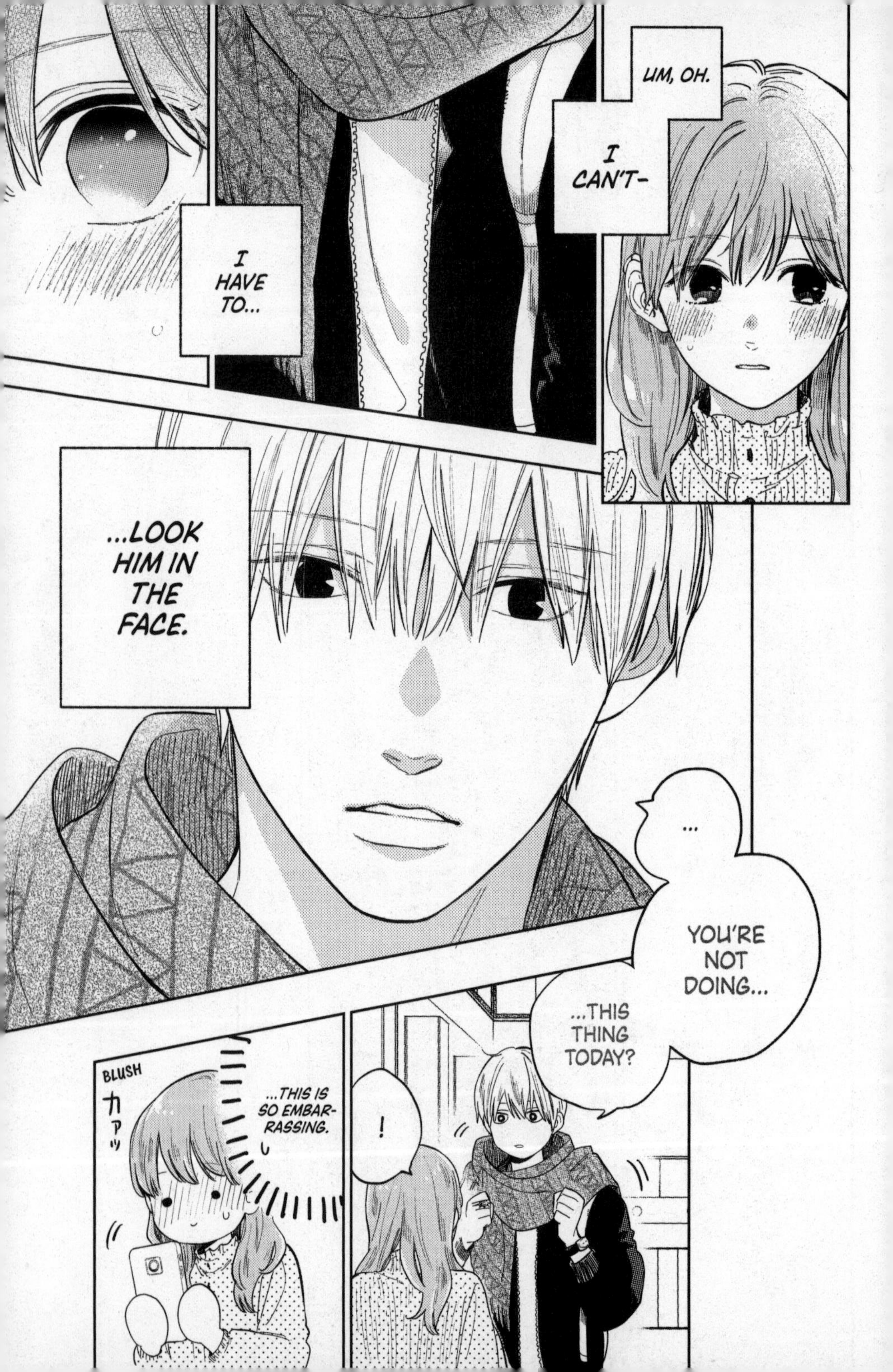
UM, OH.
I CAN'T-
I HAVE TO...
...LOOK HIM IN THE FACE.
...
YOU'RE NOT DOING...
...THIS THING TODAY?
!
BLUSH
カァッ
...THIS IS SO EMBARRASSING.

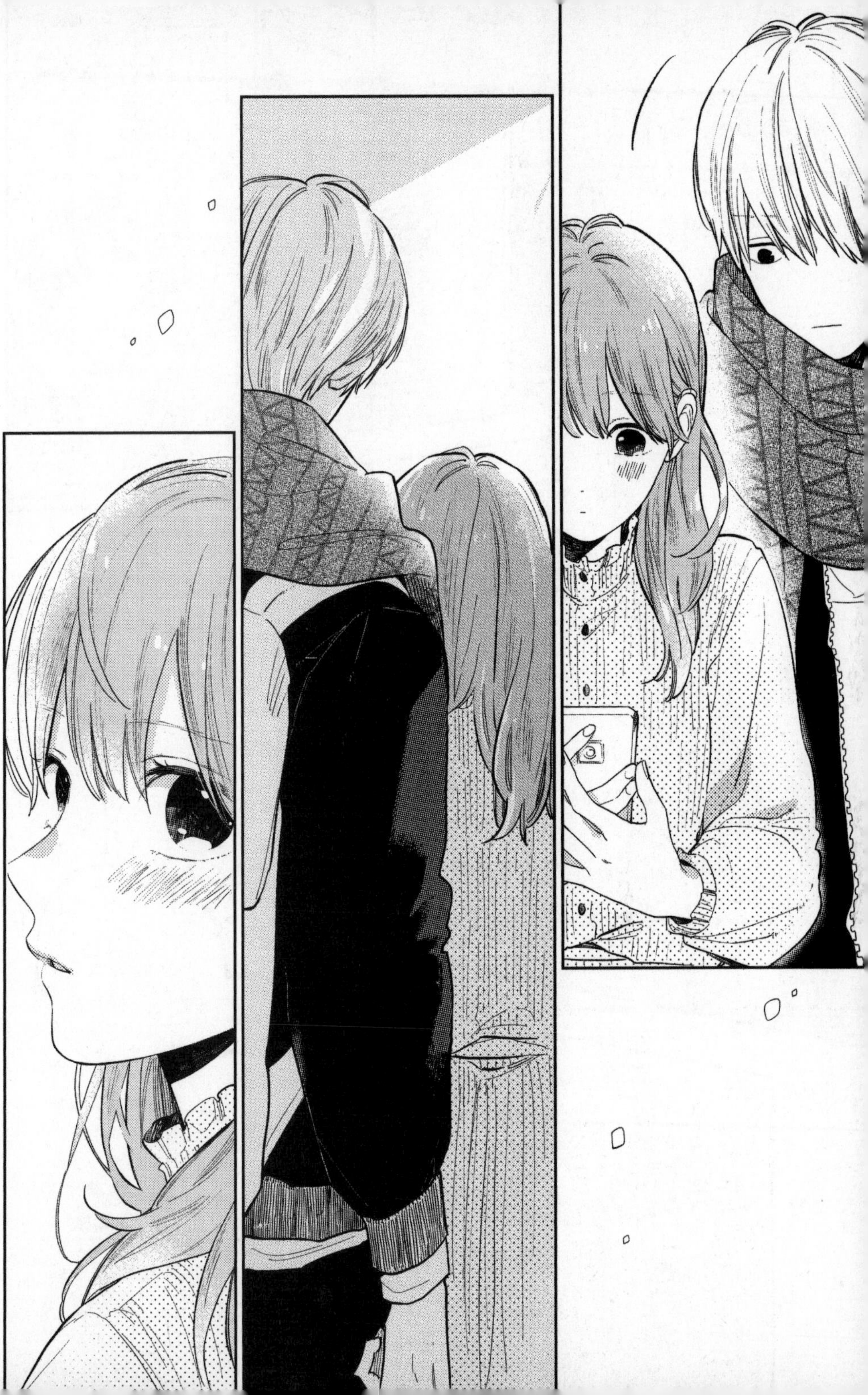

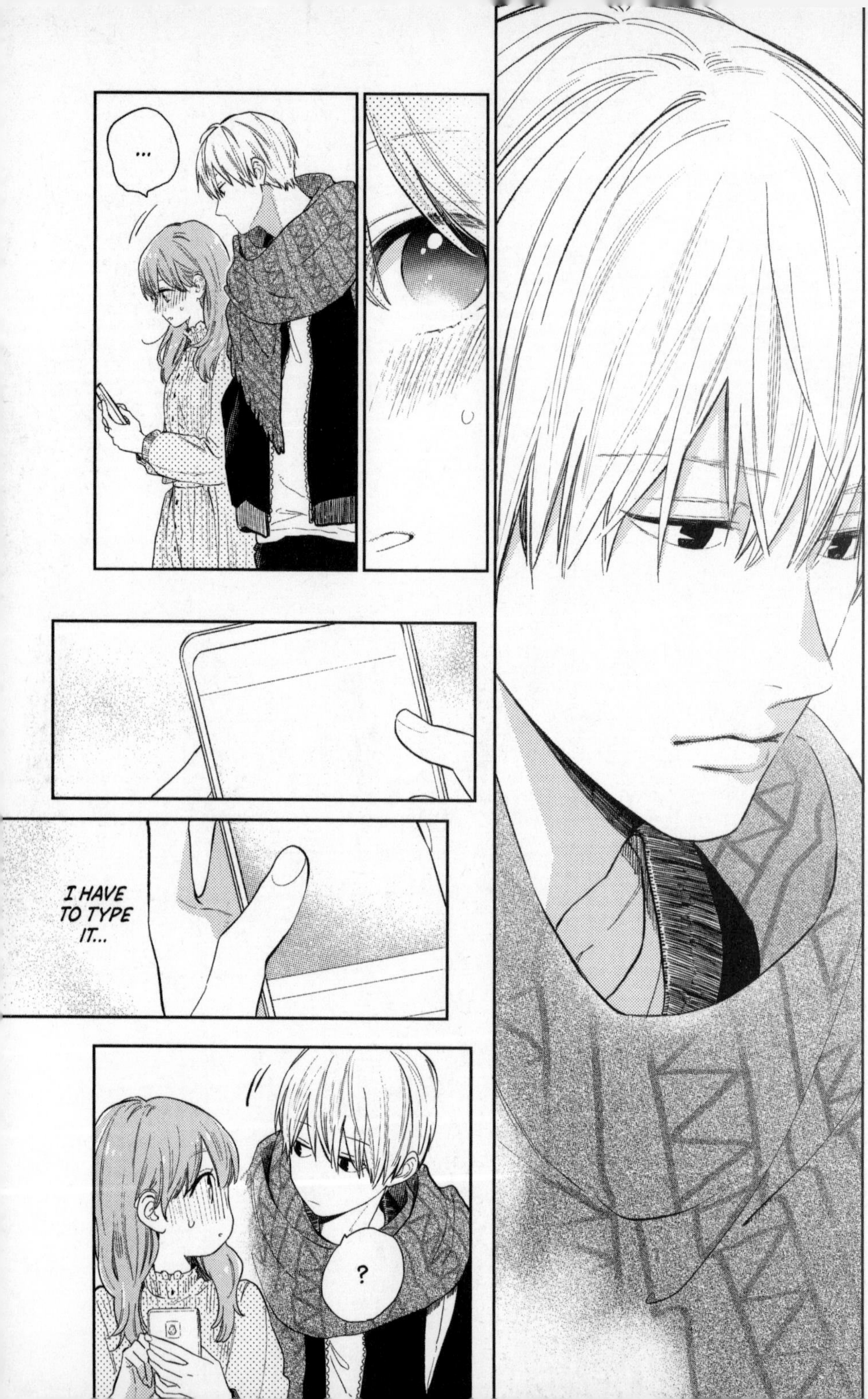
...
I HAVE TO TYPE IT...
?

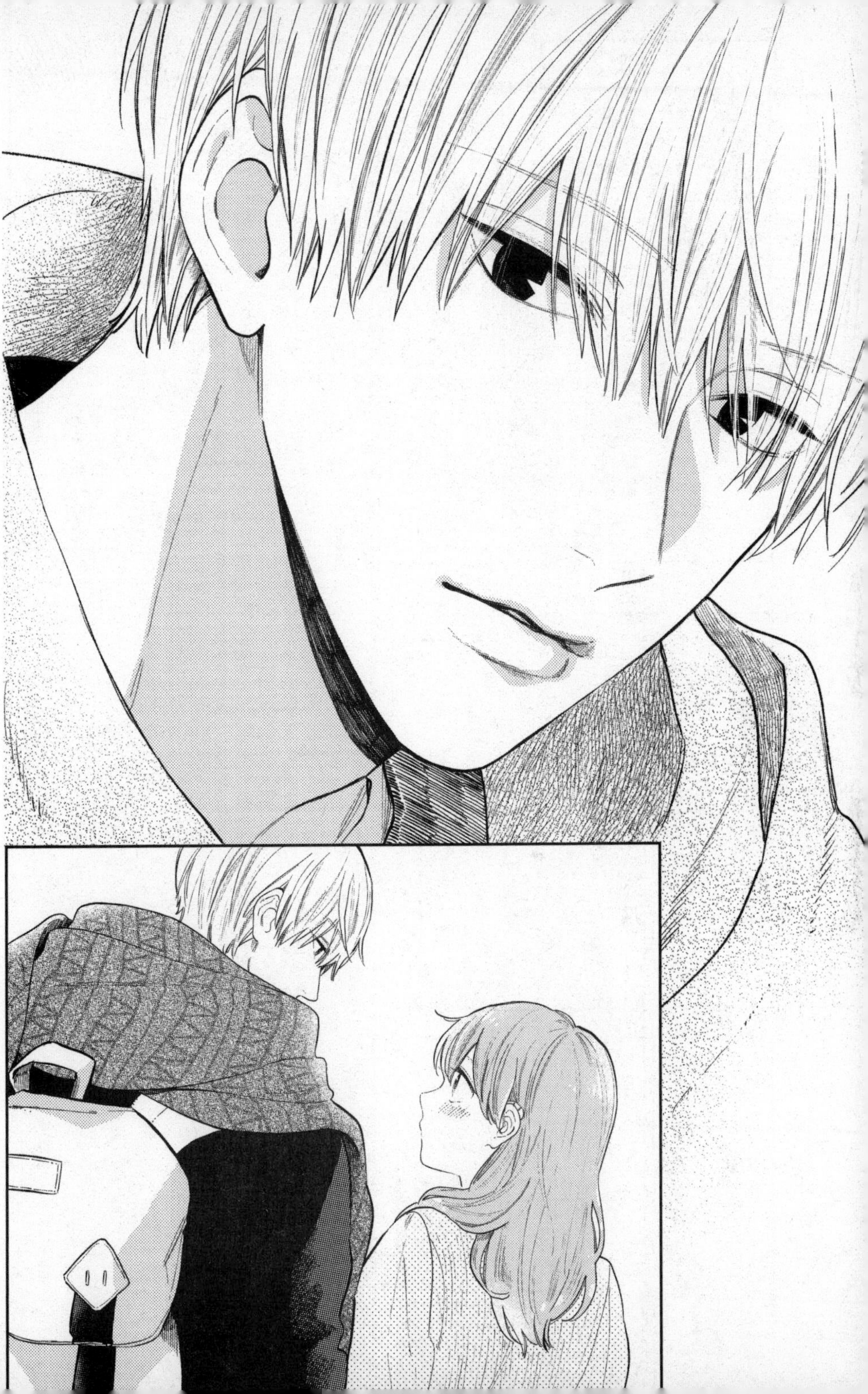

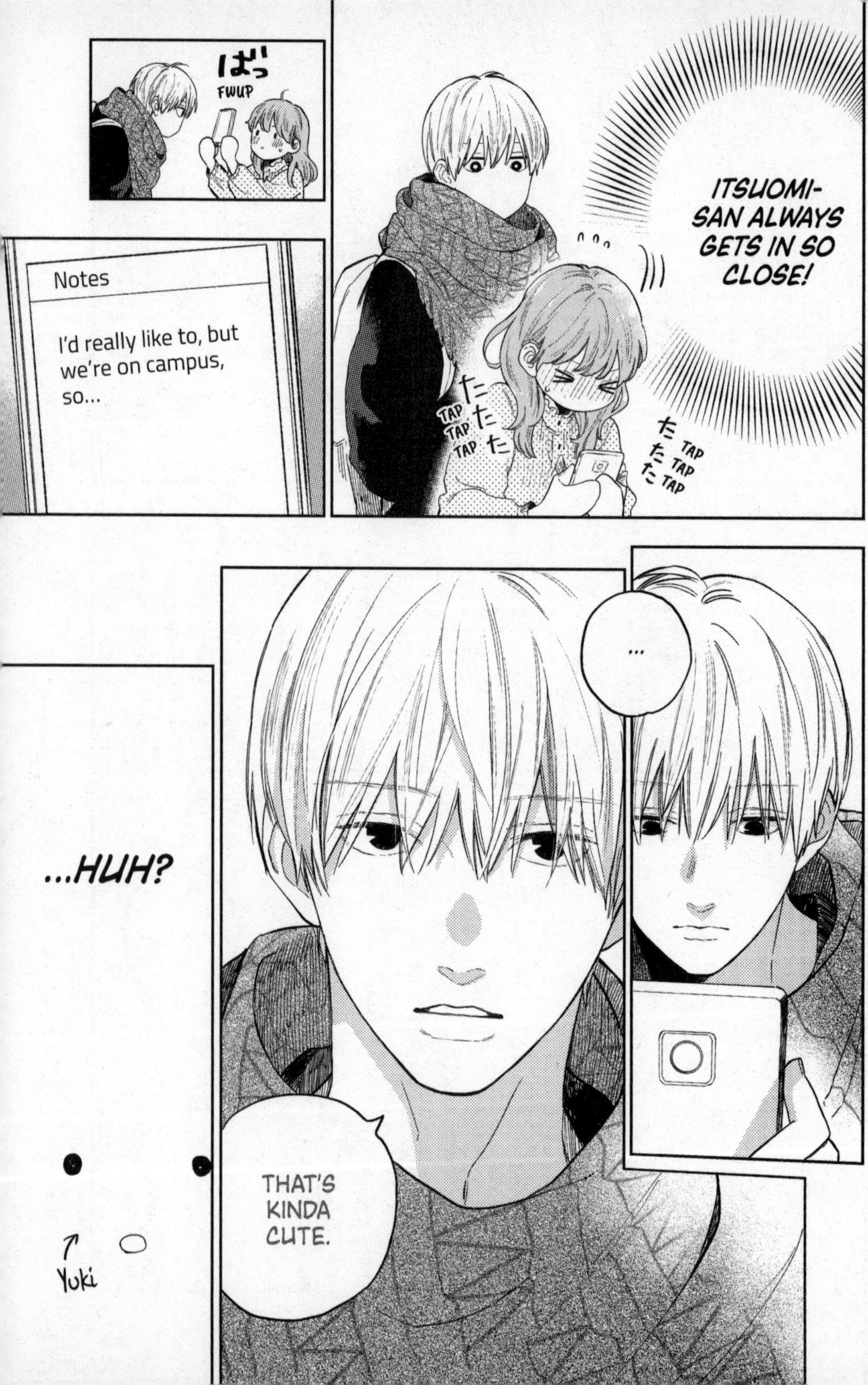
ITSUOMI-SAN ALWAYS GETS IN SO CLOSE!
たたた TAP TAP TAP
たたた TAP TAP TAP
ぱっ
FWUP
Notes
I'd really like to, but we're on campus, so...
...
THAT'S KINDA CUTE.
...HUH?
Yuki

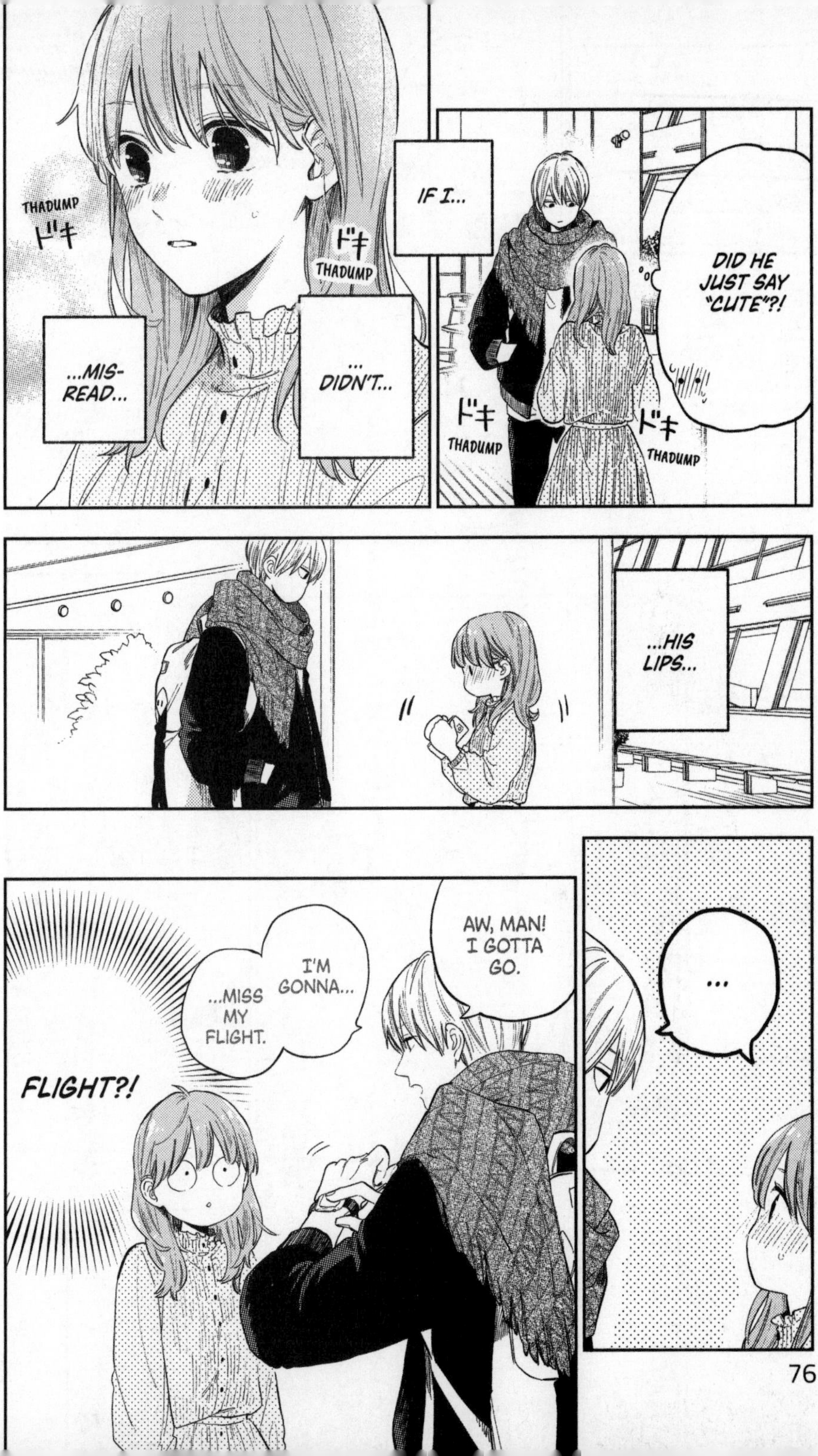
DID HE JUST SAY "CUTE"?!
IF I...
ドキ THADUMP
ドキ THADUMP
ドキ THADUMP
THADUMP ドキ
... DIDN'T...
...MIS-READ...
...HIS LIPS...
...
AW, MAN! I GOTTA GO.
I'M GONNA...
...MISS MY FLIGHT.
FLIGHT?!

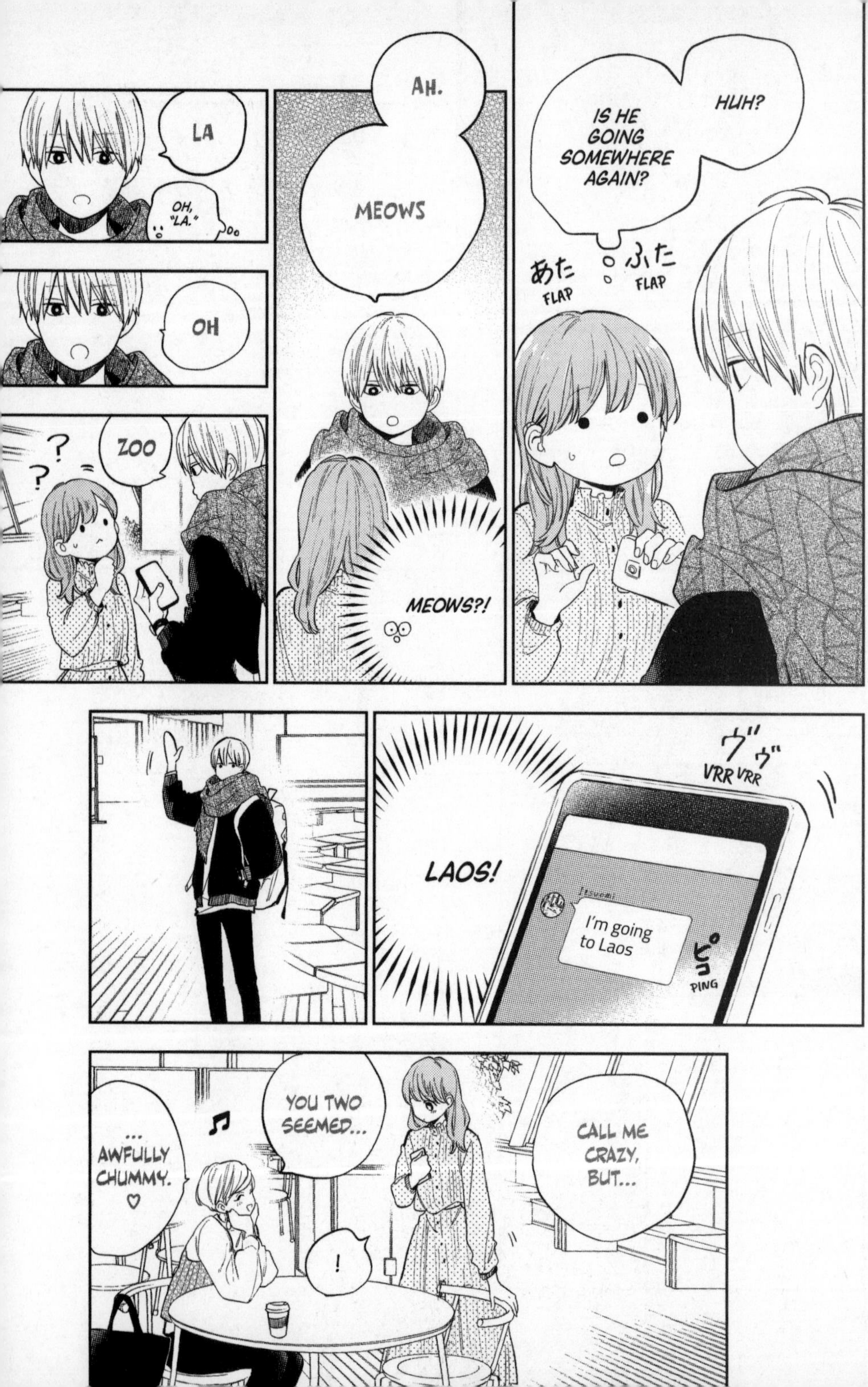
HUH?
IS HE GOING SOMEWHERE AGAIN?
あた FLAP
ふた FLAP
AH.
MEOWS
MEOWS?!
LA
OH, "LA."
OH
ZOO
ヴヴ VRR VRR
LAOS!
I'm going to Laos
ピコ PING
CALL ME CRAZY, BUT...
YOU TWO SEEMED...
... AWFULLY CHUMMY. ♡
!

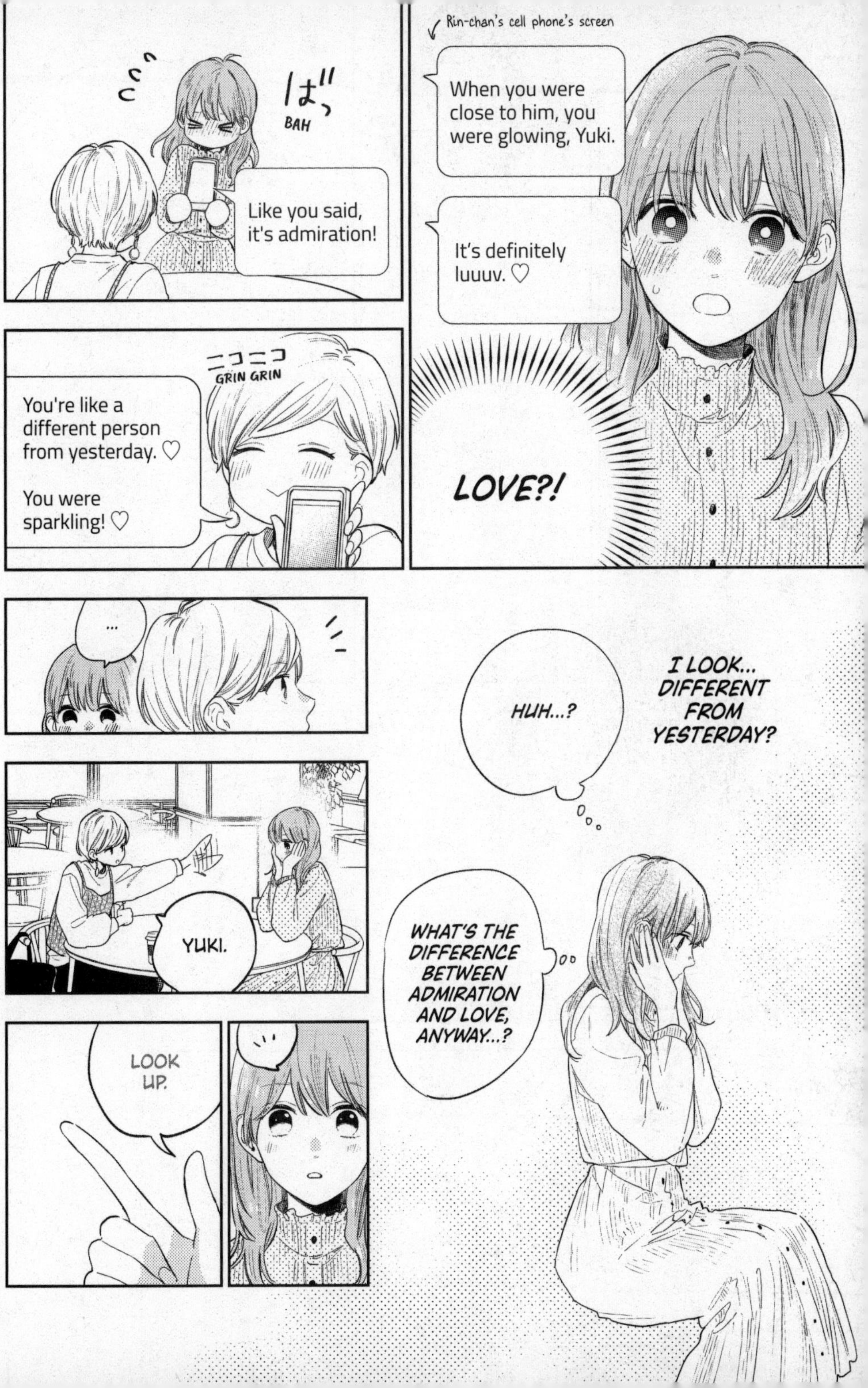
Rin-chan's cell phone screen
When you were close to him, you were glowing, Yuki.
It's definitely luuuv. ♡
LOVE?!
ぱっ
BAH
Like you said, it's admiration!
ニコニコ
GRIN GRIN
You're like a different person from yesterday. ♡
You were sparkling! ♡
HUH...?
I LOOK... DIFFERENT FROM YESTERDAY?
WHAT'S THE DIFFERENCE BETWEEN ADMIRATION AND LOVE, ANYWAY...?
...
YUKI.
LOOK UP.

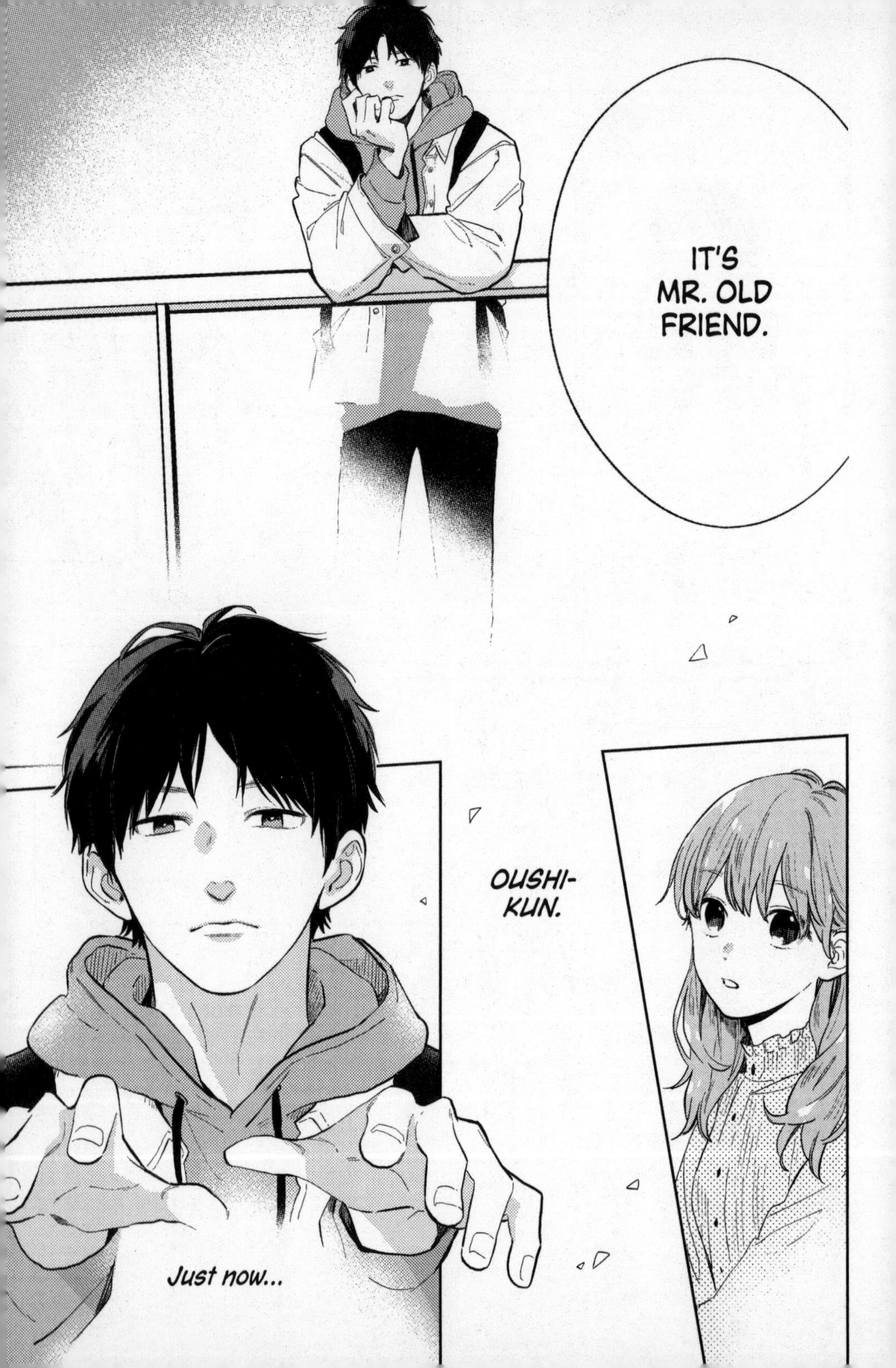
IT'S MR. OLD FRIEND.
OUSHI-KUN.
Just now...

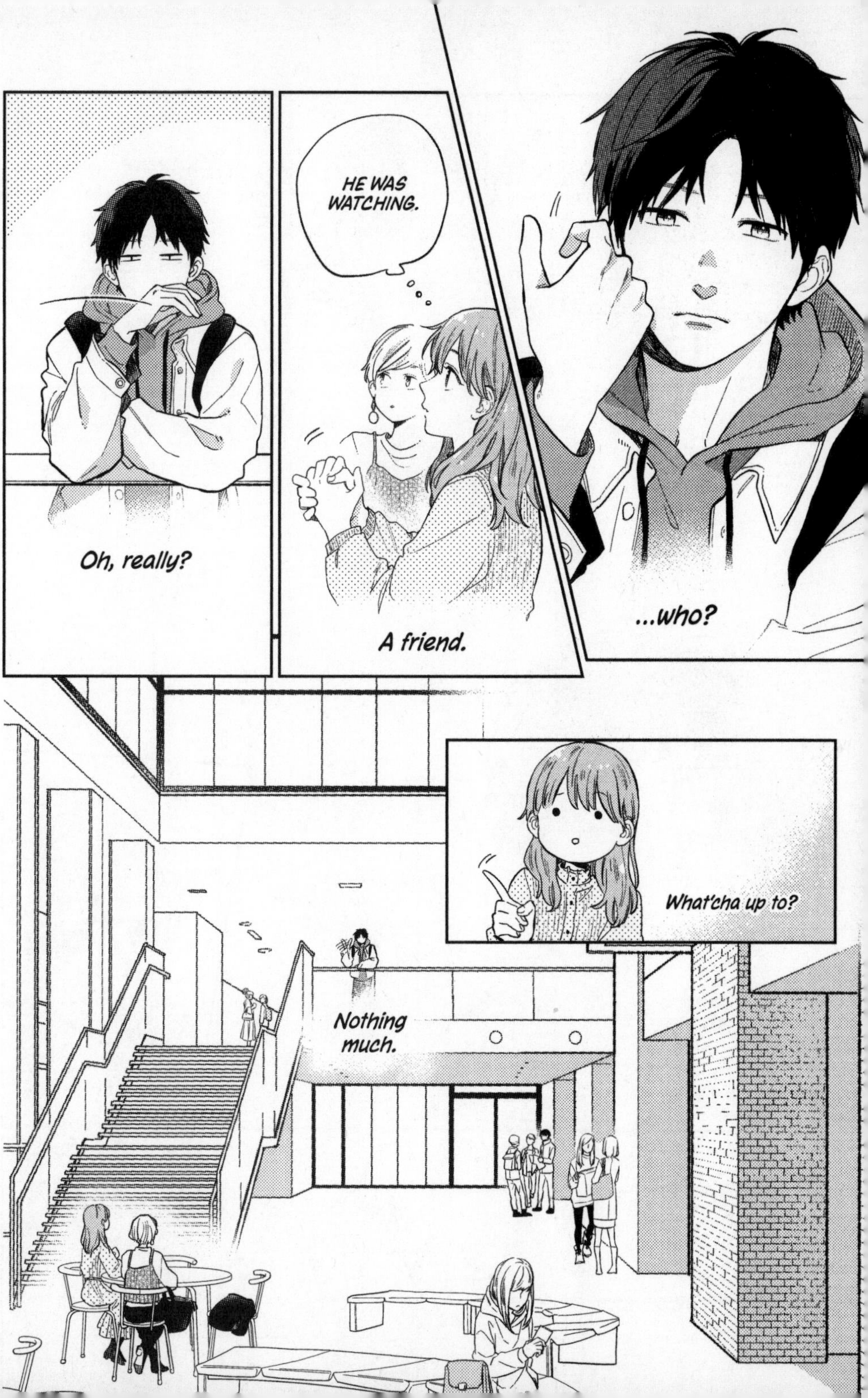
...who?
HE WAS WATCHING.
A friend.
Oh, really?
What'cha up to?
Nothing much.

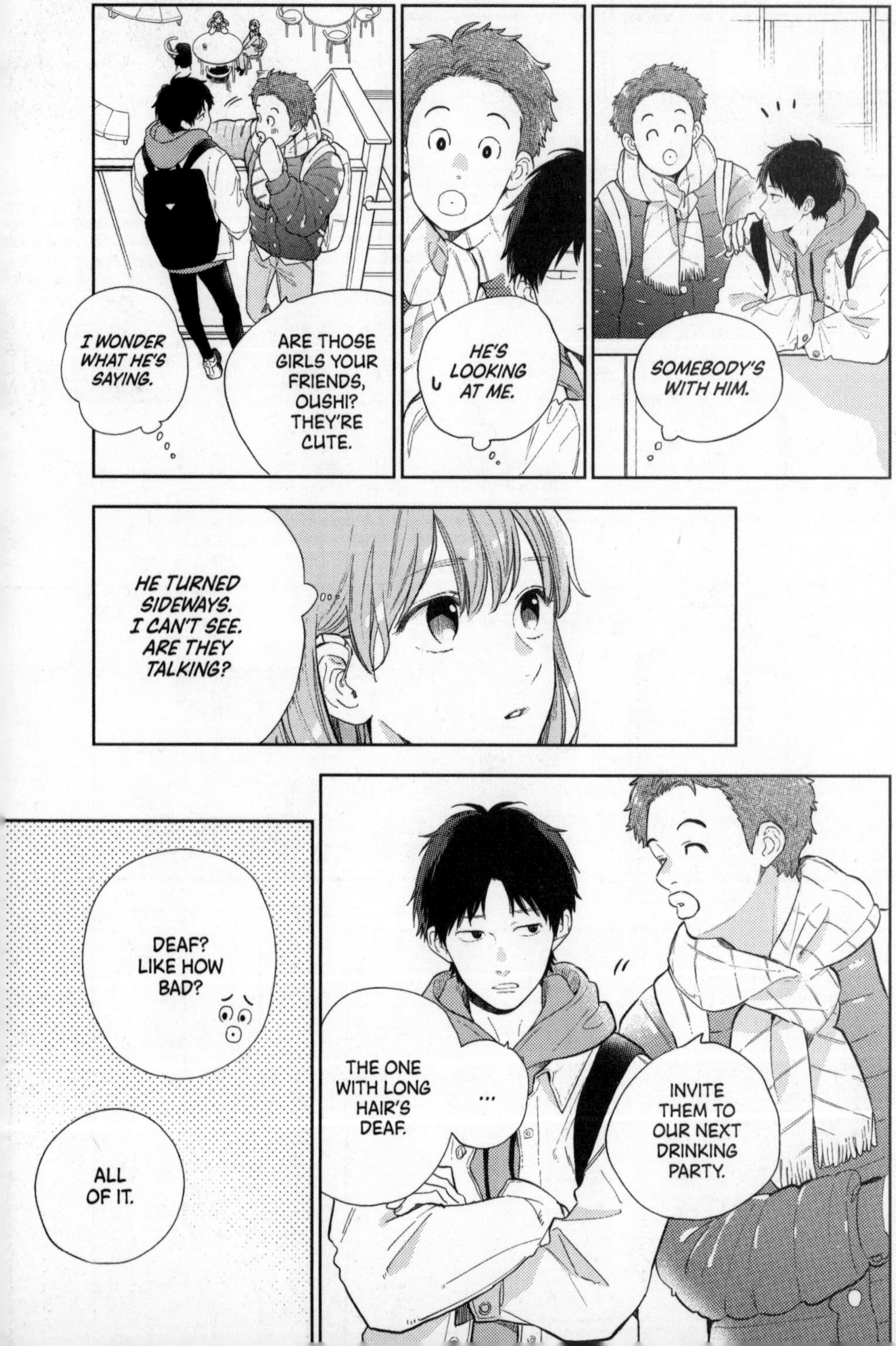
SOMEBODY'S WITH HIM.
HE'S LOOKING AT ME.
ARE THOSE GIRLS YOUR FRIENDS, OUSHI? THEY'RE CUTE.
I WONDER WHAT HE'S SAYING.
HE TURNED SIDEWAYS. I CAN'T SEE. ARE THEY TALKING?
INVITE THEM TO OUR NEXT DRINKING PARTY.
...
THE ONE WITH LONG HAIR'S DEAF.
DEAF? LIKE HOW BAD?
ALL OF IT.

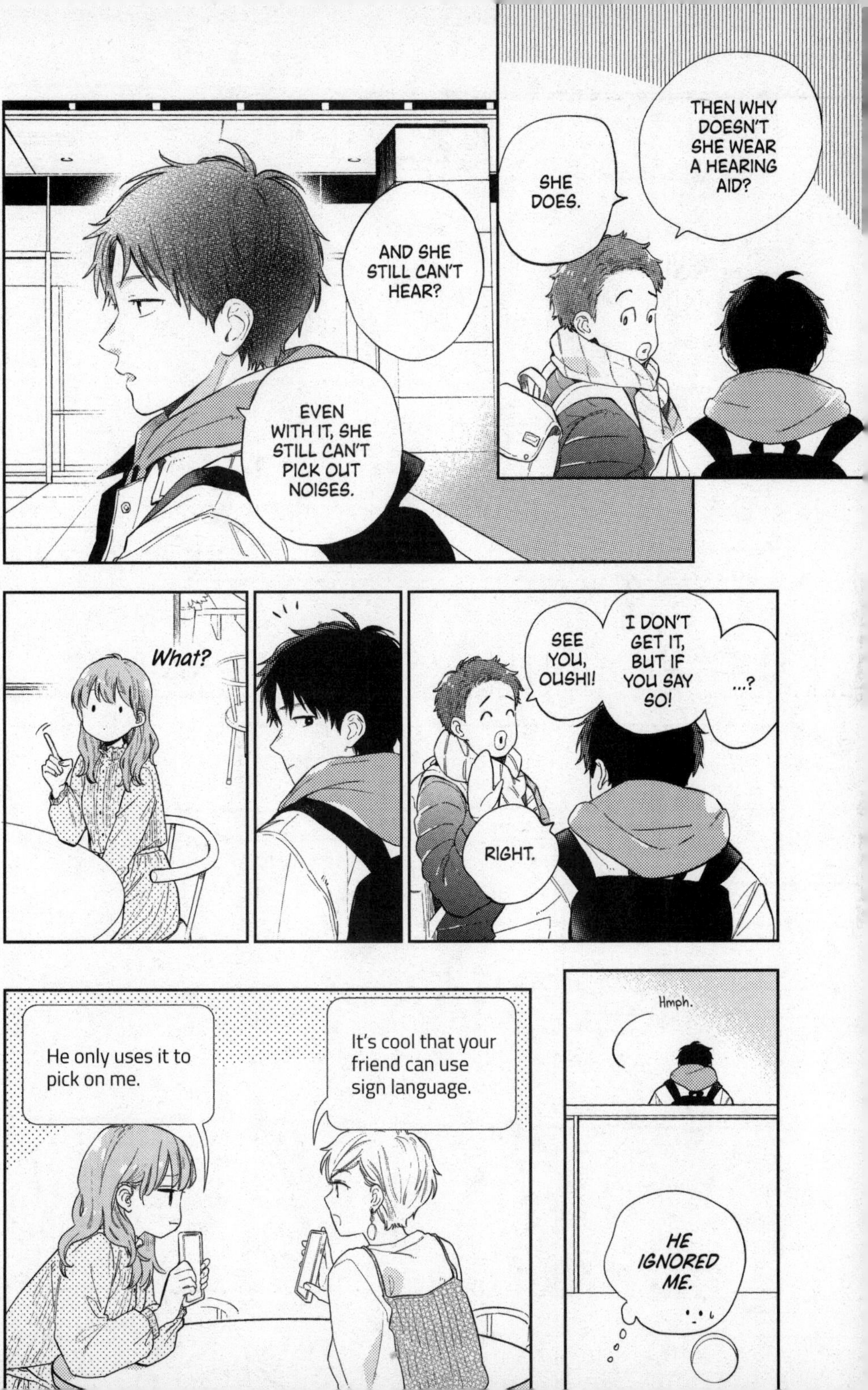
THEN WHY DOESN'T SHE WEAR A HEARING AID?
SHE DOES.
AND SHE STILL CAN'T HEAR?
EVEN WITH IT, SHE STILL CAN'T PICK OUT NOISES.
I DON'T GET IT, BUT IF YOU SAY SO!
SEE YOU, OUSHI!
...?
RIGHT.
What?
Hmph.
HE IGNORED ME.
It's cool that your friend can use sign language.
He only uses it to pick on me.

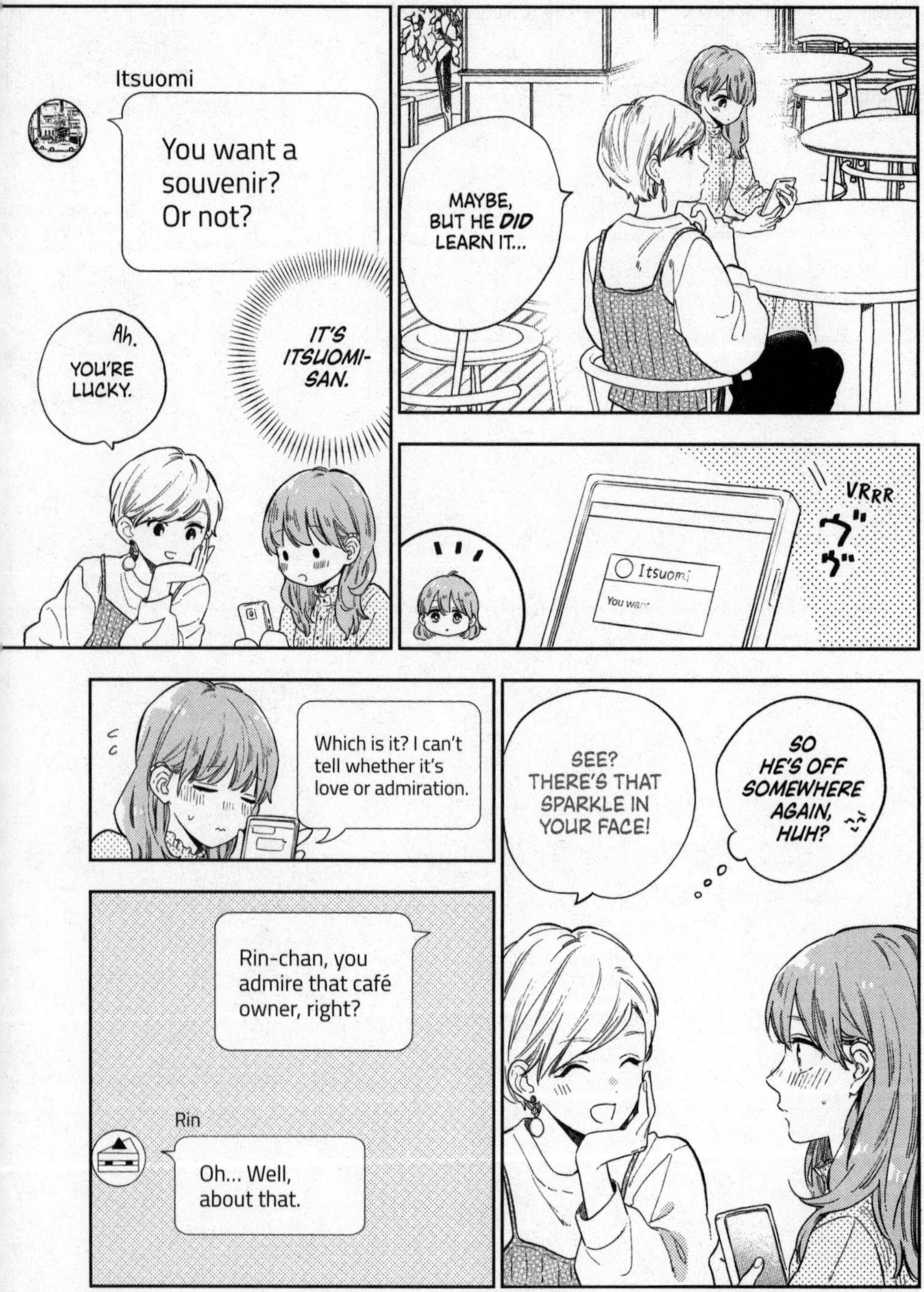
MAYBE, BUT HE *DID* LEARN IT...
VRRR
ヴ
ヴ
Itsuomi
You want
Itsuomi
You want a souvenir? Or not?
IT'S ITSUOMI-SAN.
Ah.
YOU'RE LUCKY.
SO HE'S OFF SOMEWHERE AGAIN, HUH?
SEE? THERE'S THAT SPARKLE IN YOUR FACE!
Which is it? I can't tell whether it's love or admiration.
Rin-chan, you admire that café owner, right?
Rin
Oh... Well, about that.

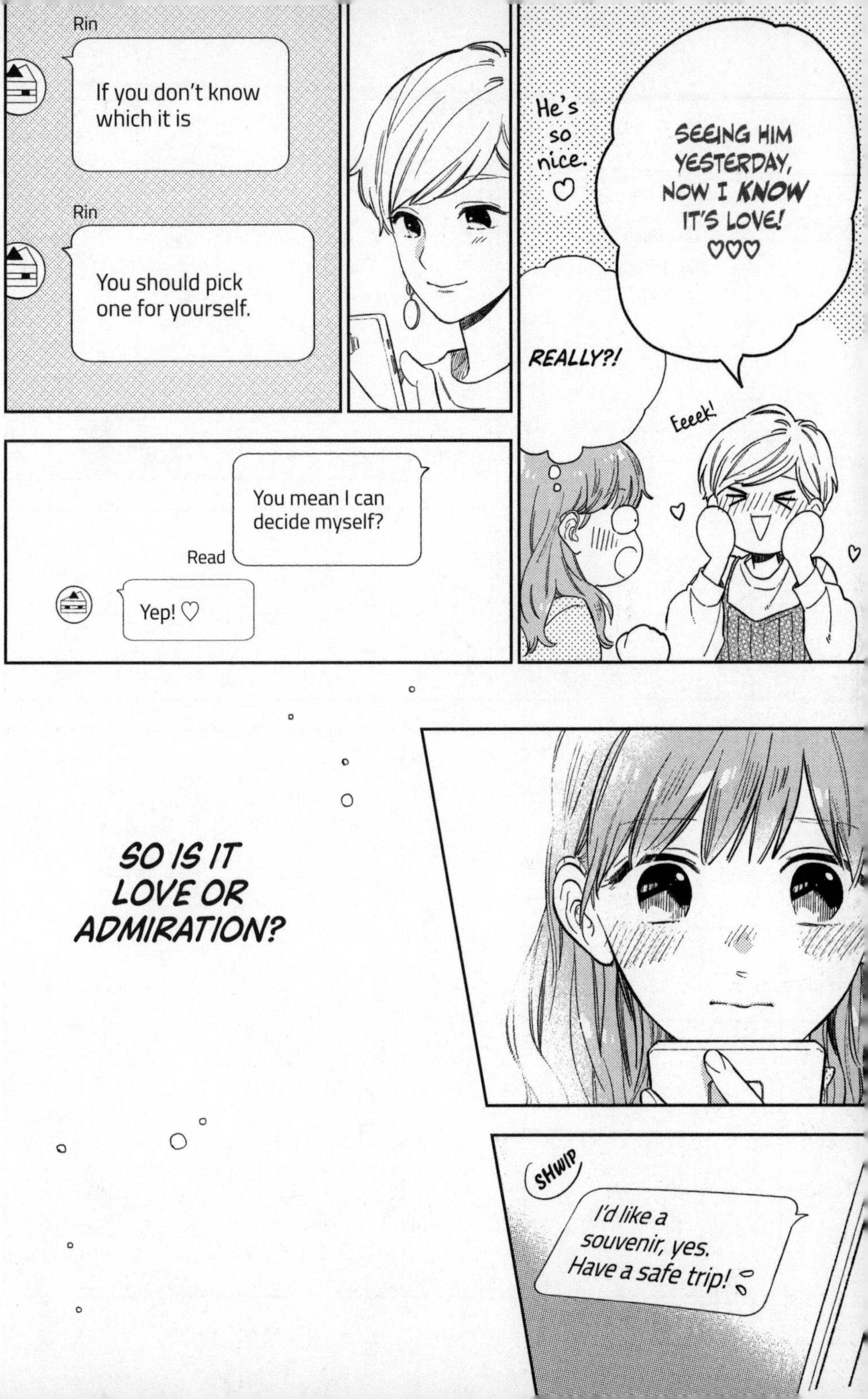
He's so nice. ♡
SEEING HIM YESTERDAY, NOW I KNOW IT'S LOVE! ♡♡♡
REALLY?!
Eeeek!
Rin
If you don't know which it is
Rin
You should pick one for yourself.
You mean I can decide myself?
Read
Yep! ♡
SO IS IT LOVE OR ADMIRATION?
SHWIP
I'd like a souvenir, yes. Have a safe trip!

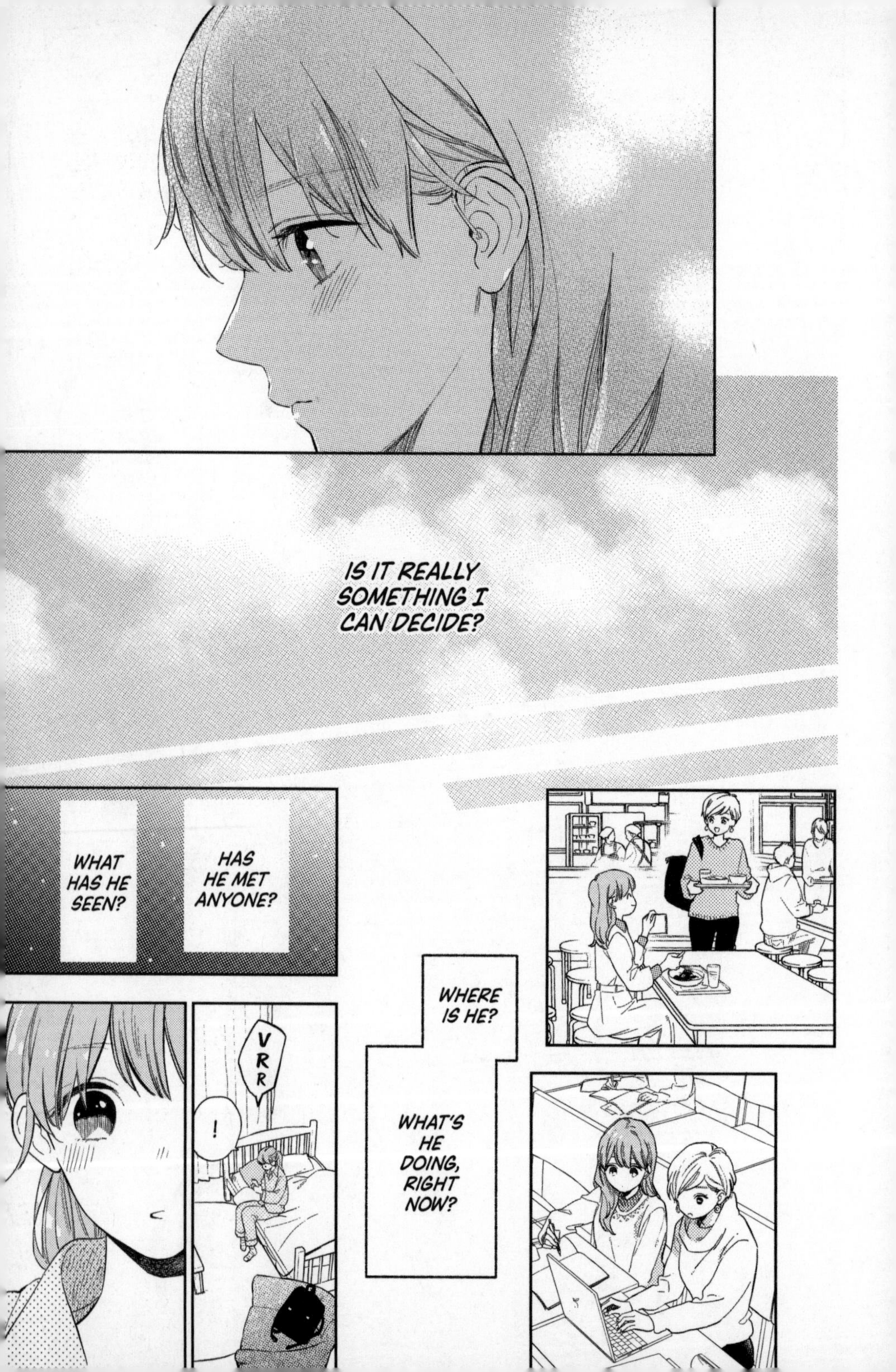
IS IT REALLY SOMETHING I CAN DECIDE?
HAS HE MET ANYONE?
WHAT HAS HE SEEN?
WHERE IS HE?
WHAT'S HE DOING, RIGHT NOW?
VRR
!

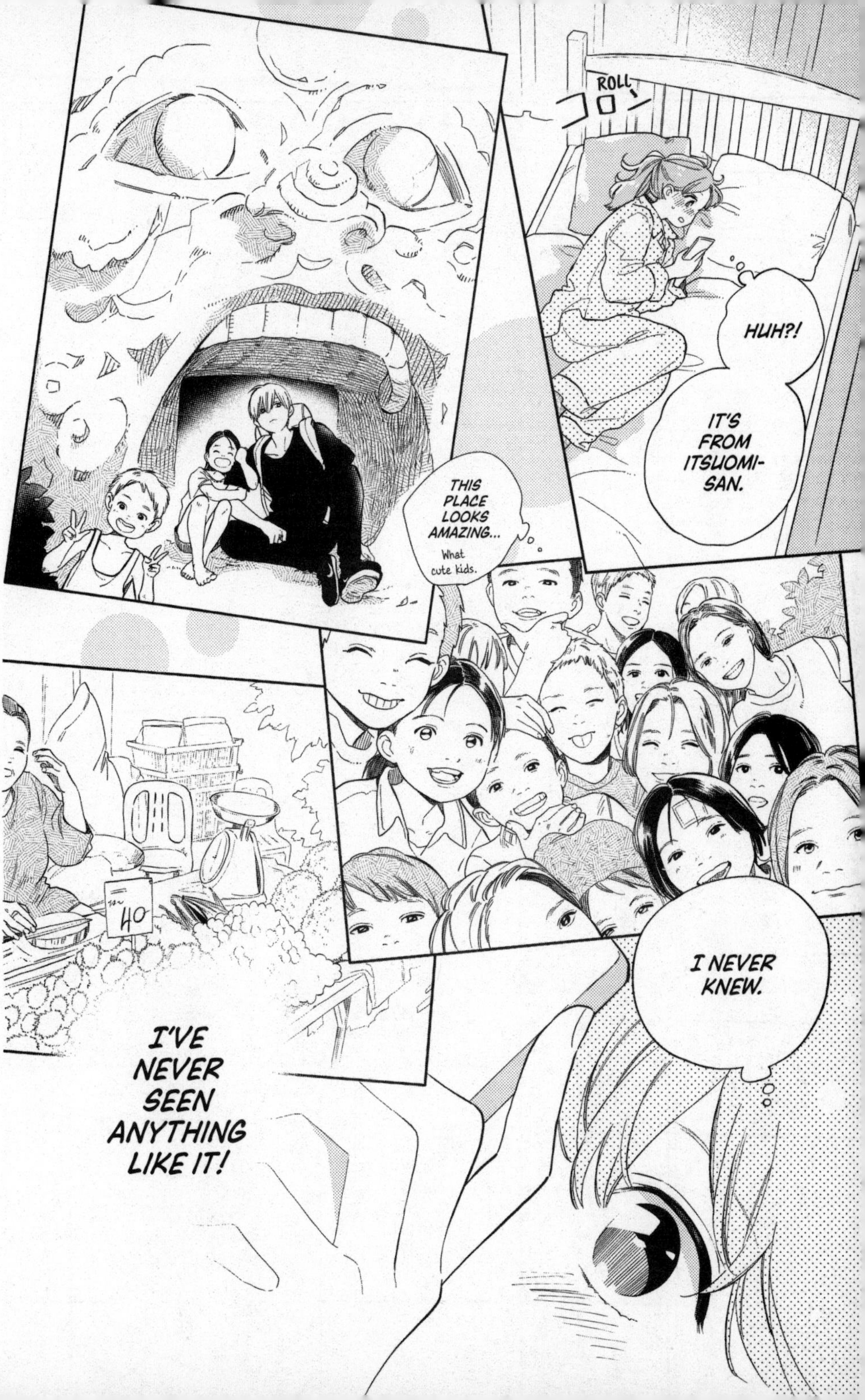
ROLL
コロン
HUH?!
IT'S FROM ITSUOMI-SAN.
THIS PLACE LOOKS AMAZING...
What cute kids.
40
I NEVER KNEW.
I'VE NEVER SEEN ANYTHING LIKE IT!

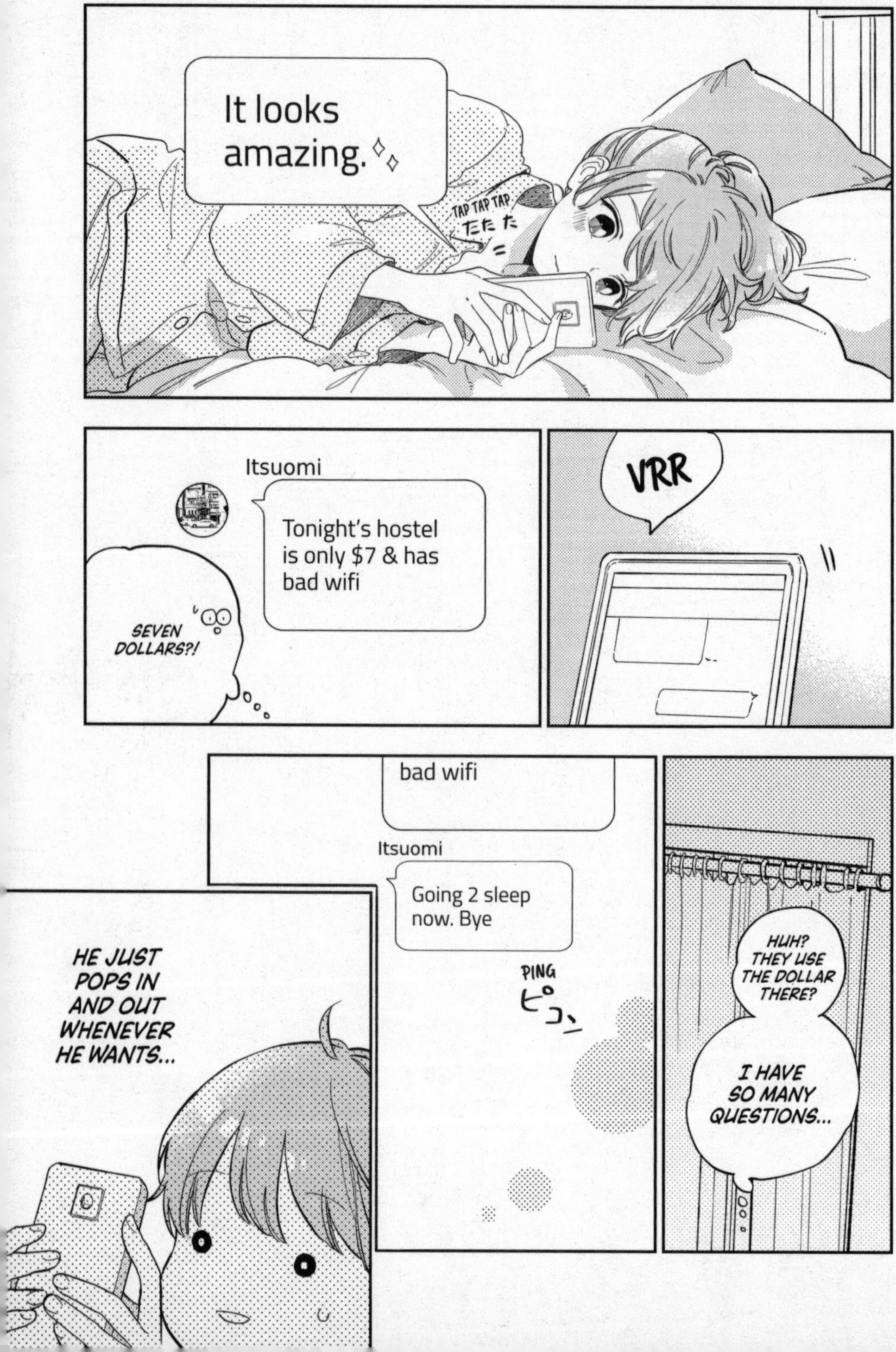
It looks amazing.
TAP TAP TAP
たたた
VRR
Itsuomi
Tonight's hostel is only $7 & has bad wifi
SEVEN DOLLARS?!
HUH? THEY USE THE DOLLAR THERE?
I HAVE SO MANY QUESTIONS...
bad wifi
Itsuomi
Going 2 sleep now. Bye
PING
ピコン
HE JUST POPS IN AND OUT WHENEVER HE WANTS...

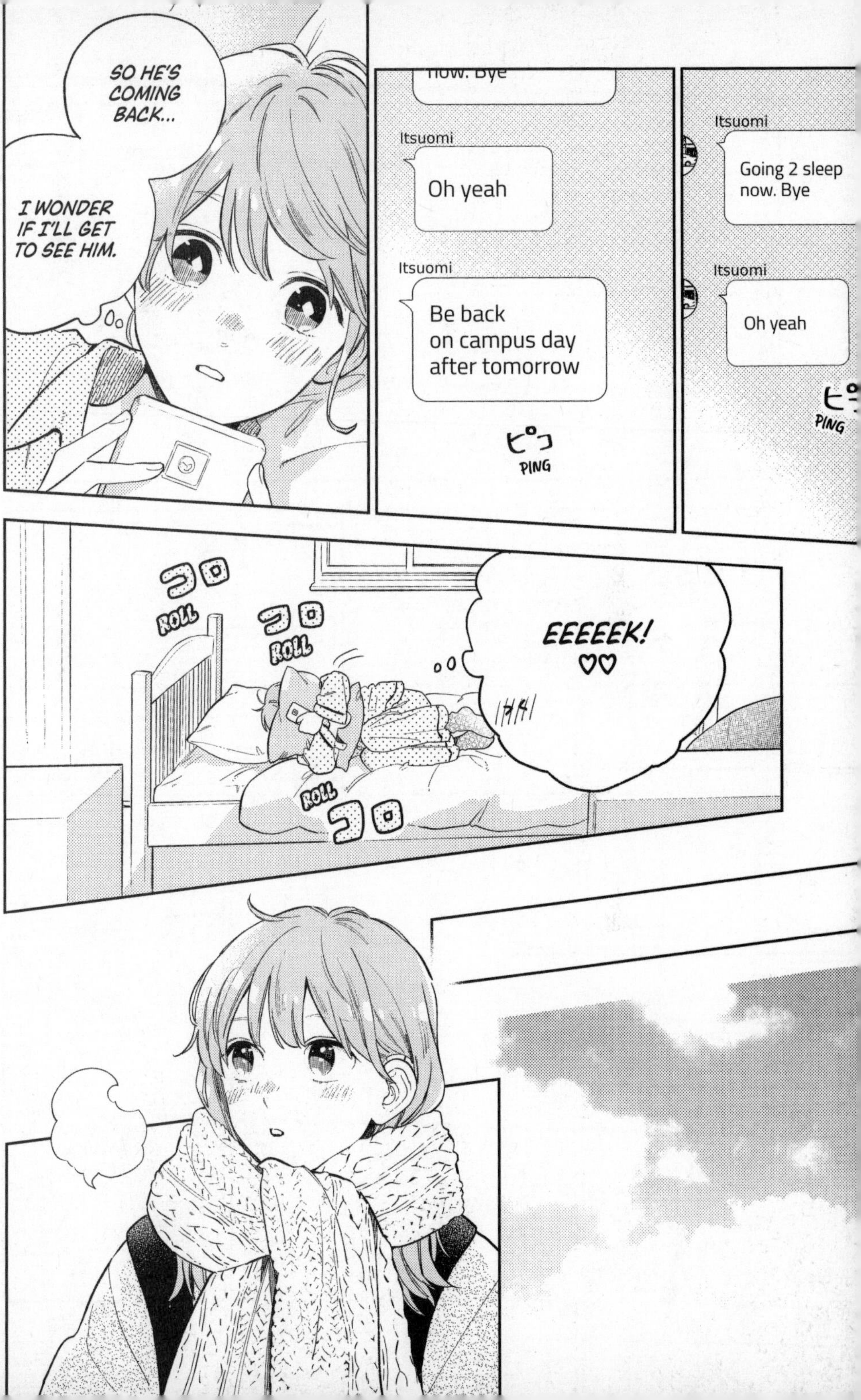
Itsuomi
Going 2 sleep now. Bye
Itsuomi
Oh yeah
PING
now. Bye
Itsuomi
Oh yeah
Itsuomi
Be back on campus day after tomorrow
ピコ
PING
SO HE'S COMING BACK...
I WONDER IF I'LL GET TO SEE HIM.
EEEEEK! ♡♡
コロ
ROLL
コロ
ROLL
ROLL
コロ

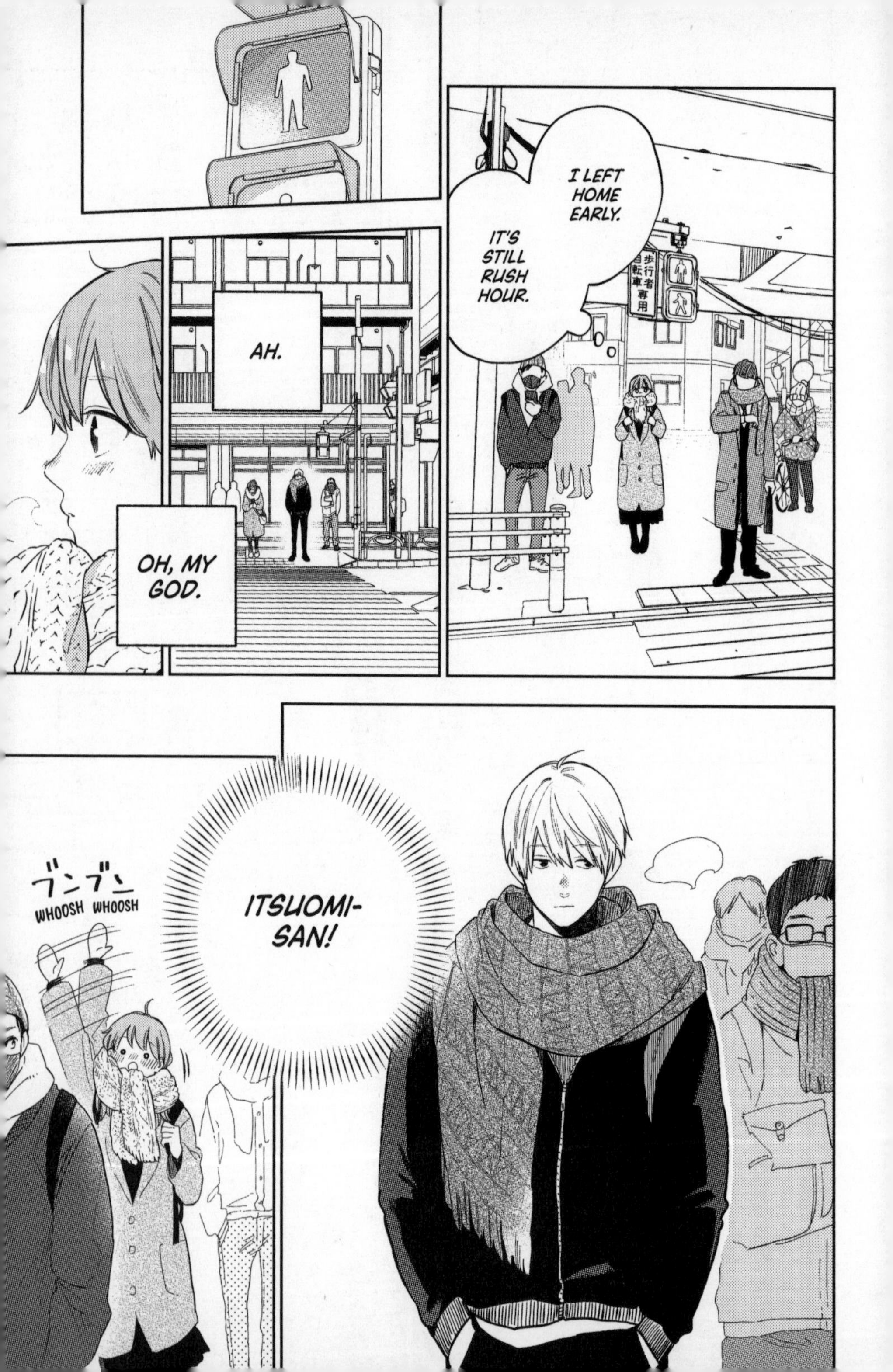
I LEFT HOME EARLY.
IT'S STILL RUSH HOUR.
歩行者自転車専用
AH.
OH, MY GOD.
ITSUOMI-SAN!
ブンブン
WHOOSH WHOOSH

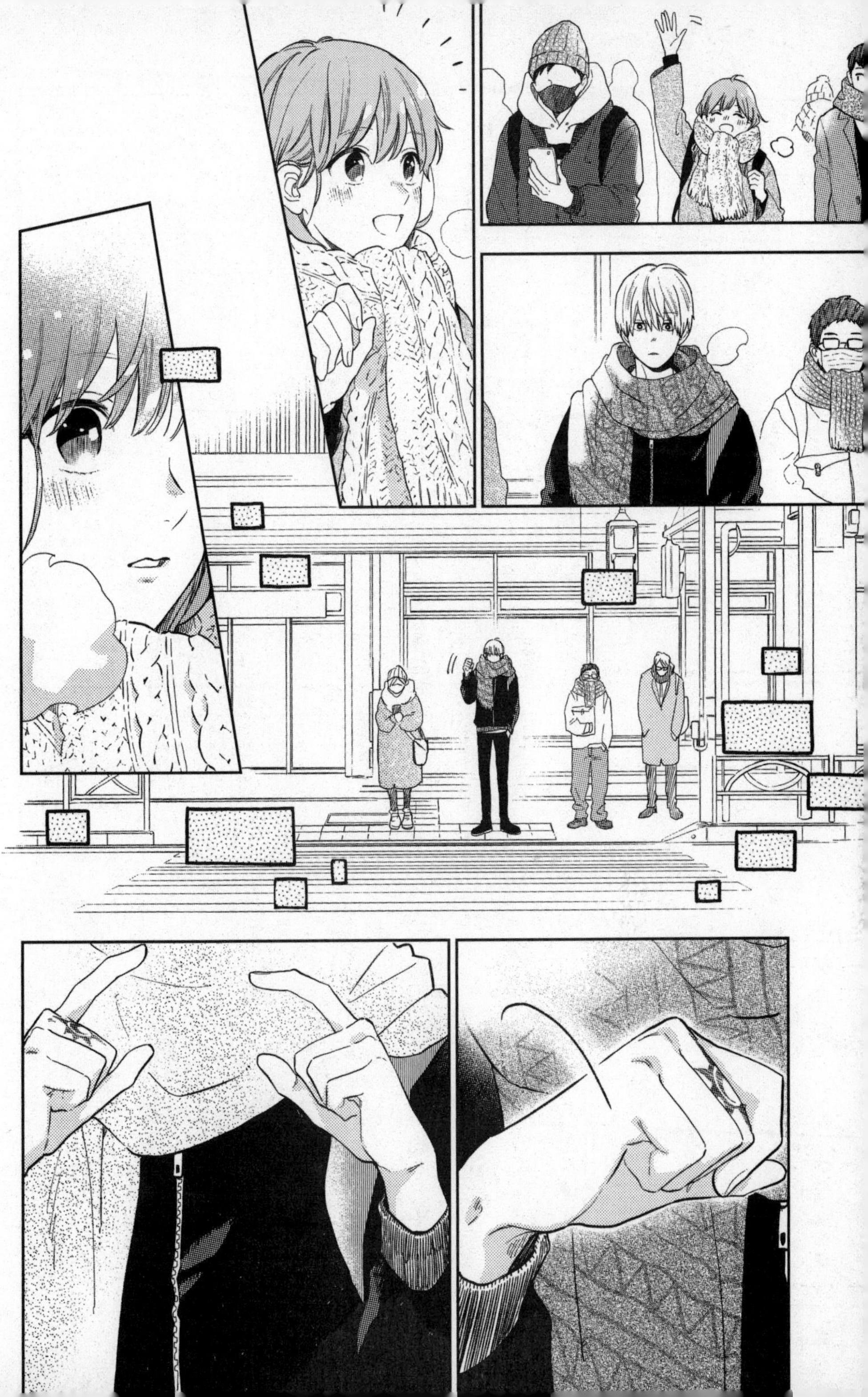

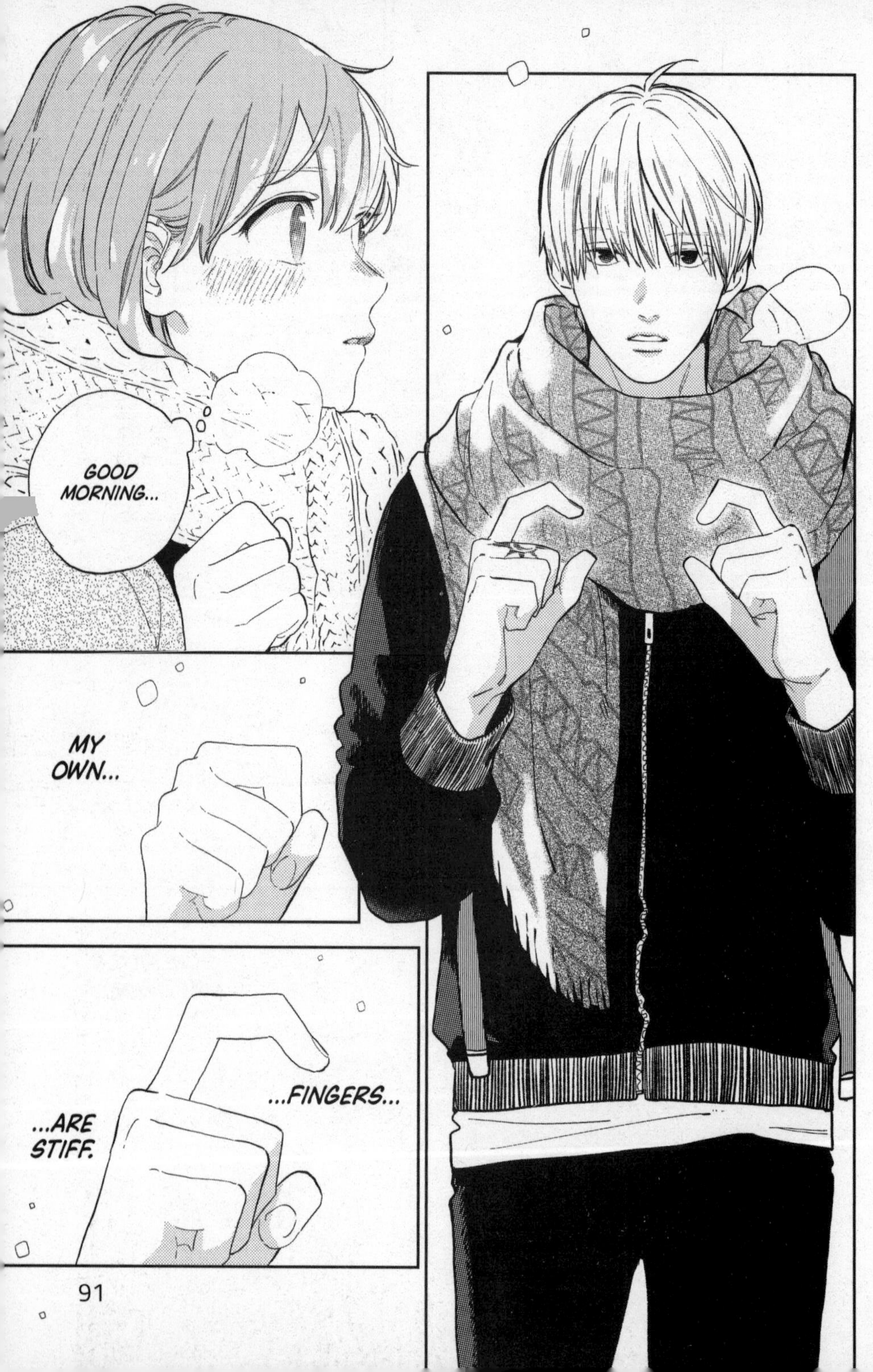
GOOD MORNING...
MY OWN...
...FINGERS...
...ARE STIFF.

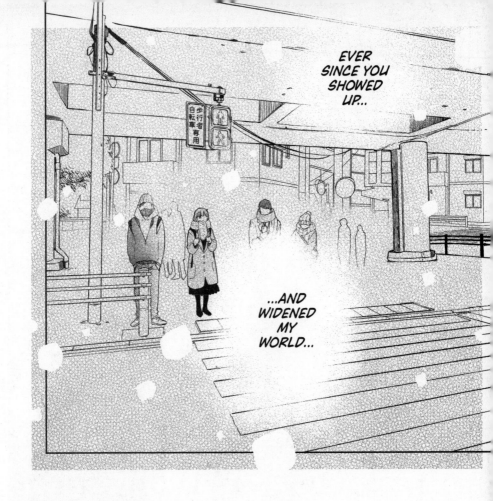

EVER SINCE YOU SHOWED UP...

...AND WIDENED MY WORLD...

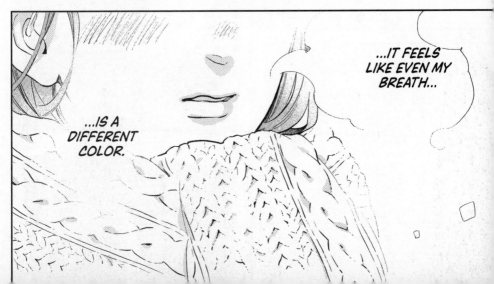

...IT FEELS LIKE EVEN MY BREATH...

...IS A DIFFERENT COLOR.

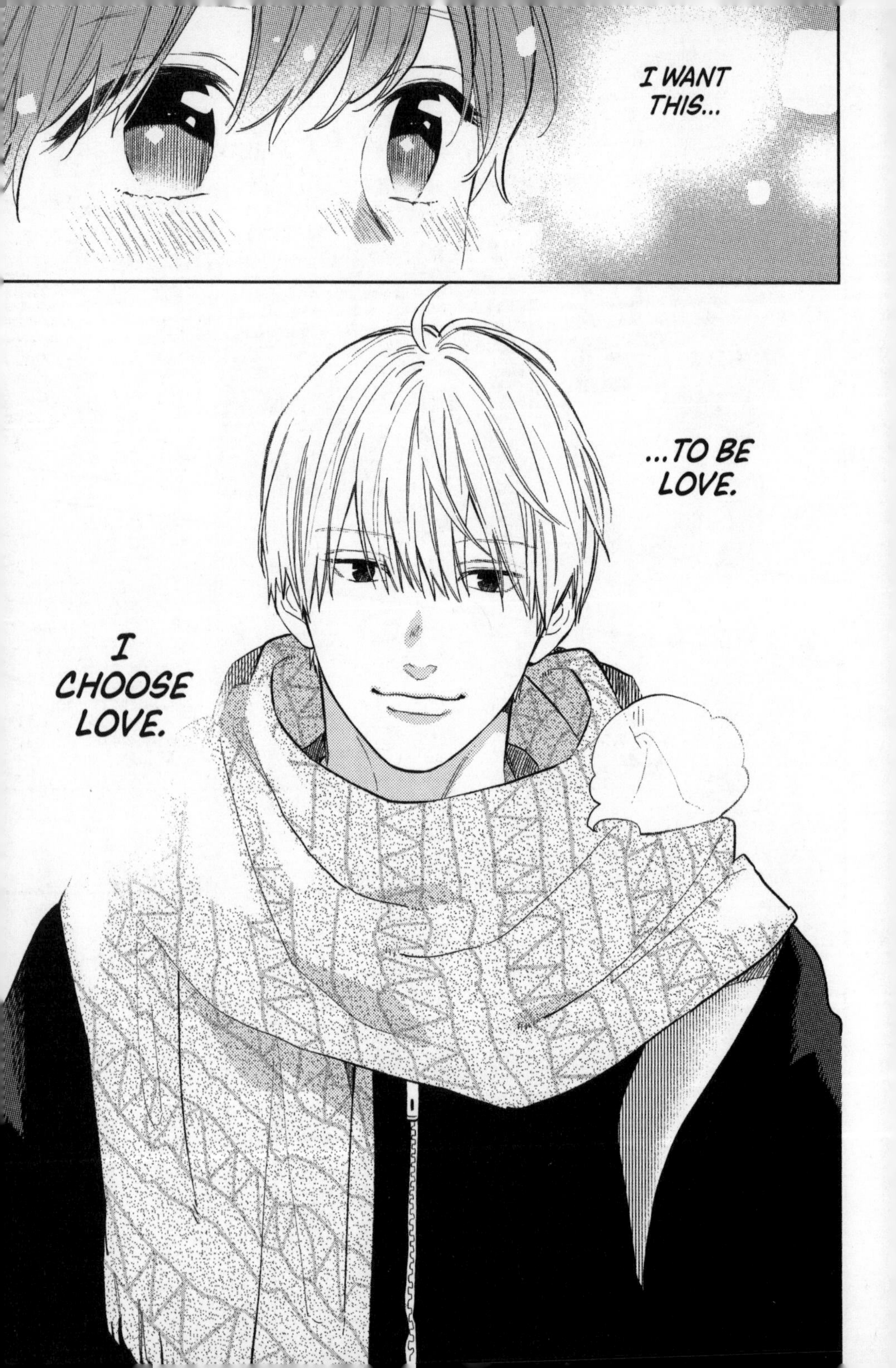
I WANT THIS...
...TO BE LOVE.
I CHOOSE LOVE.

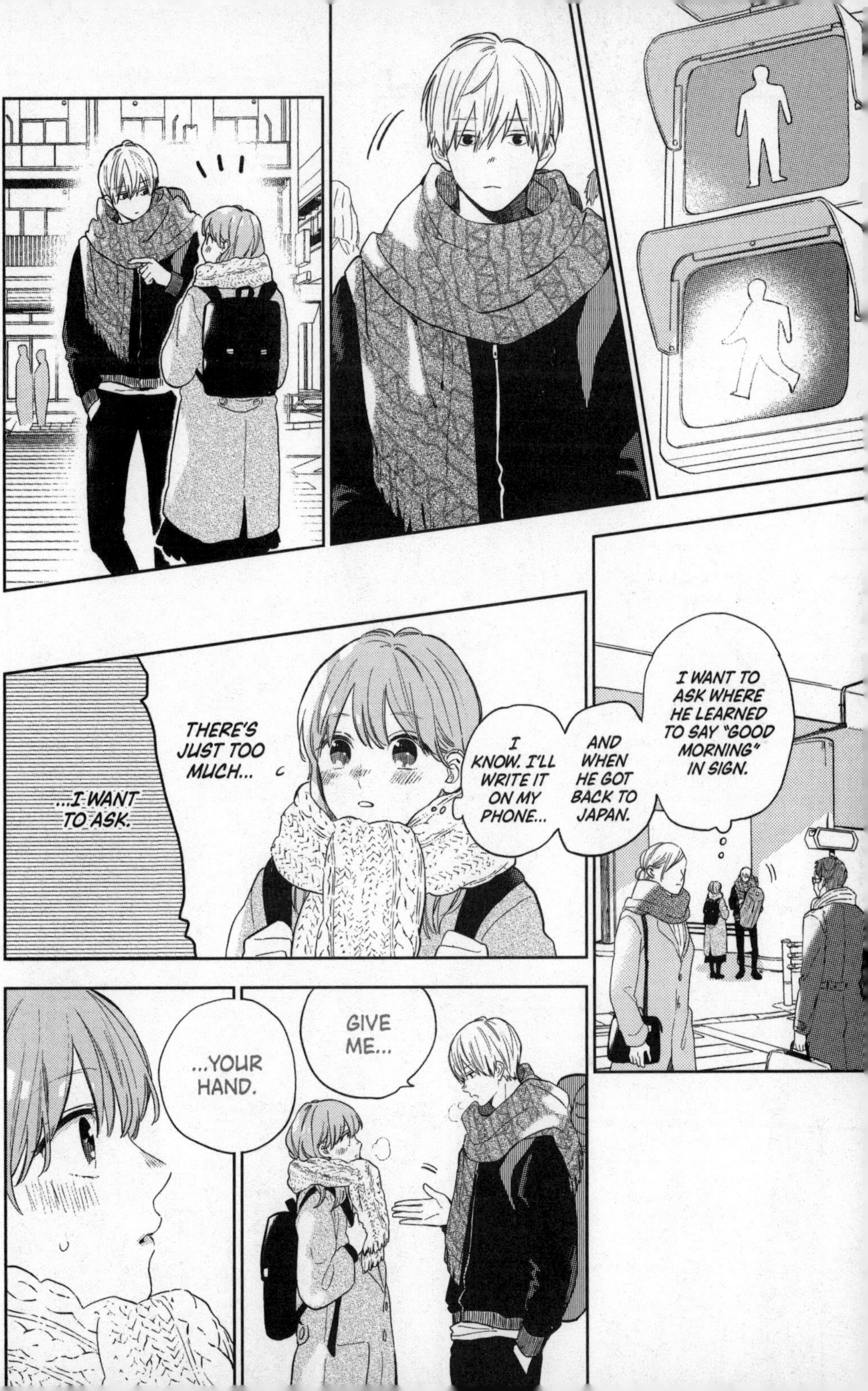
I WANT TO ASK WHERE HE LEARNED TO SAY "GOOD MORNING" IN SIGN.
AND WHEN HE GOT BACK TO JAPAN.
I KNOW. I'LL WRITE IT ON MY PHONE...
THERE'S JUST TOO MUCH...
...I WANT TO ASK.
GIVE ME...
...YOUR HAND.

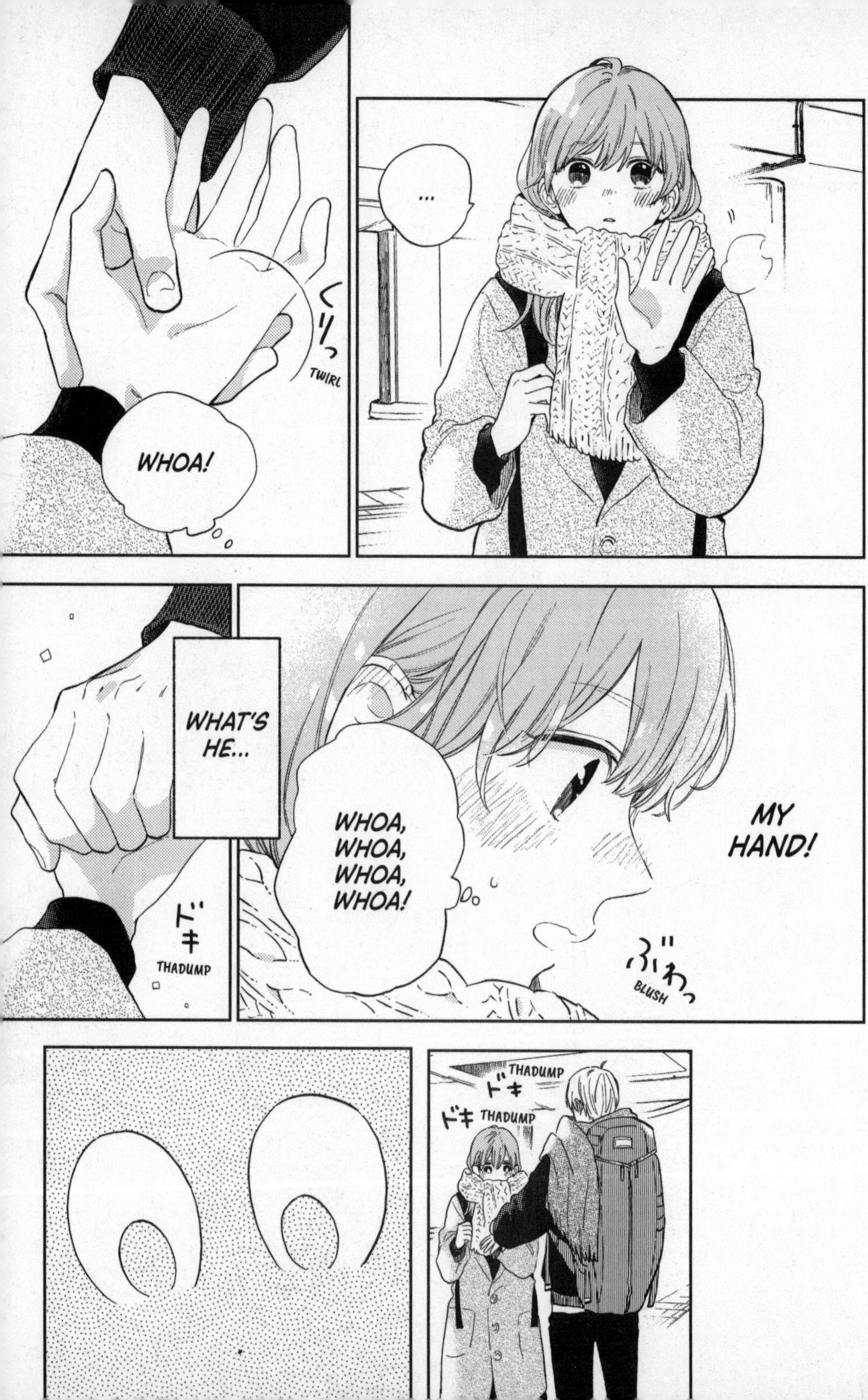
...
くりっ
TWIRL
WHOA!
MY HAND!
WHOA, WHOA, WHOA, WHOA!
ぶわっ
BLUSH
WHAT'S HE...
ドキ
THADUMP
ドキ
THADUMP
ドキ
THADUMP

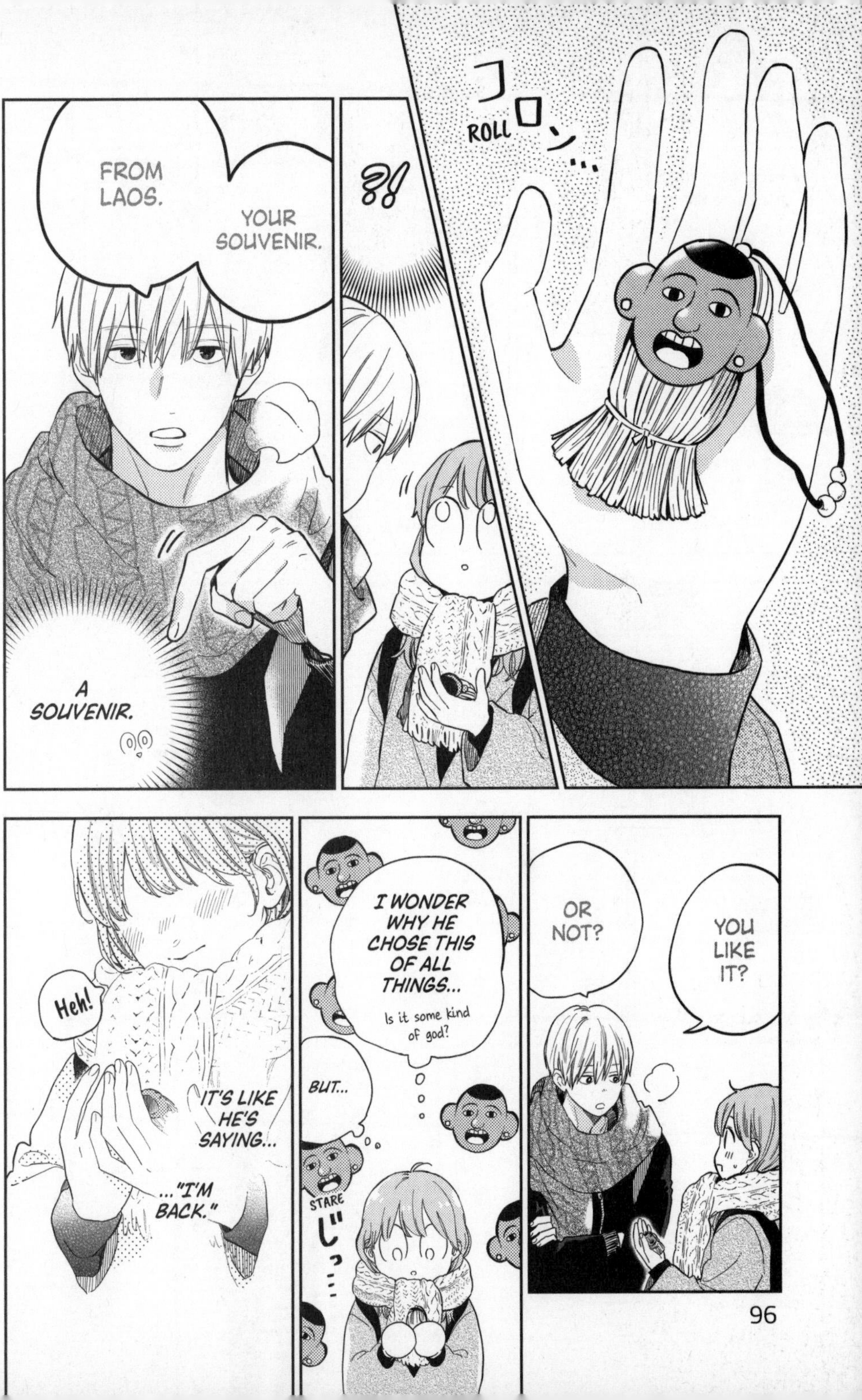
ROLL
コロン…
?!
YOUR SOUVENIR.
FROM LAOS.
A SOUVENIR.
YOU LIKE IT?
OR NOT?
I WONDER WHY HE CHOSE THIS OF ALL THINGS...
Is it some kind of god?
BUT...
STARE
じっ…
Heh!
IT'S LIKE HE'S SAYING...
..."I'M BACK."

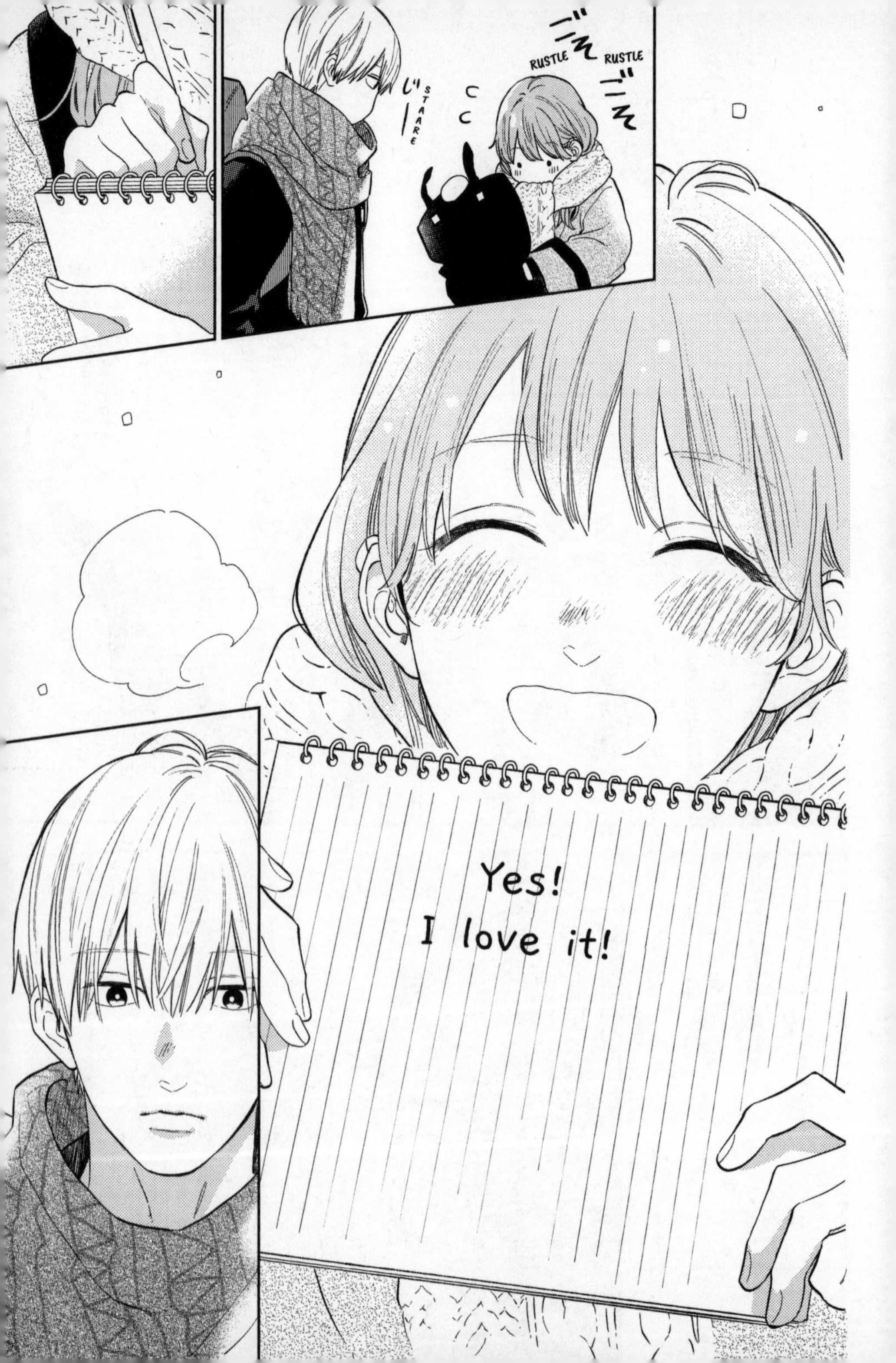
RUSTLE
RUSTLE
STAARE
Yes!
I love it!

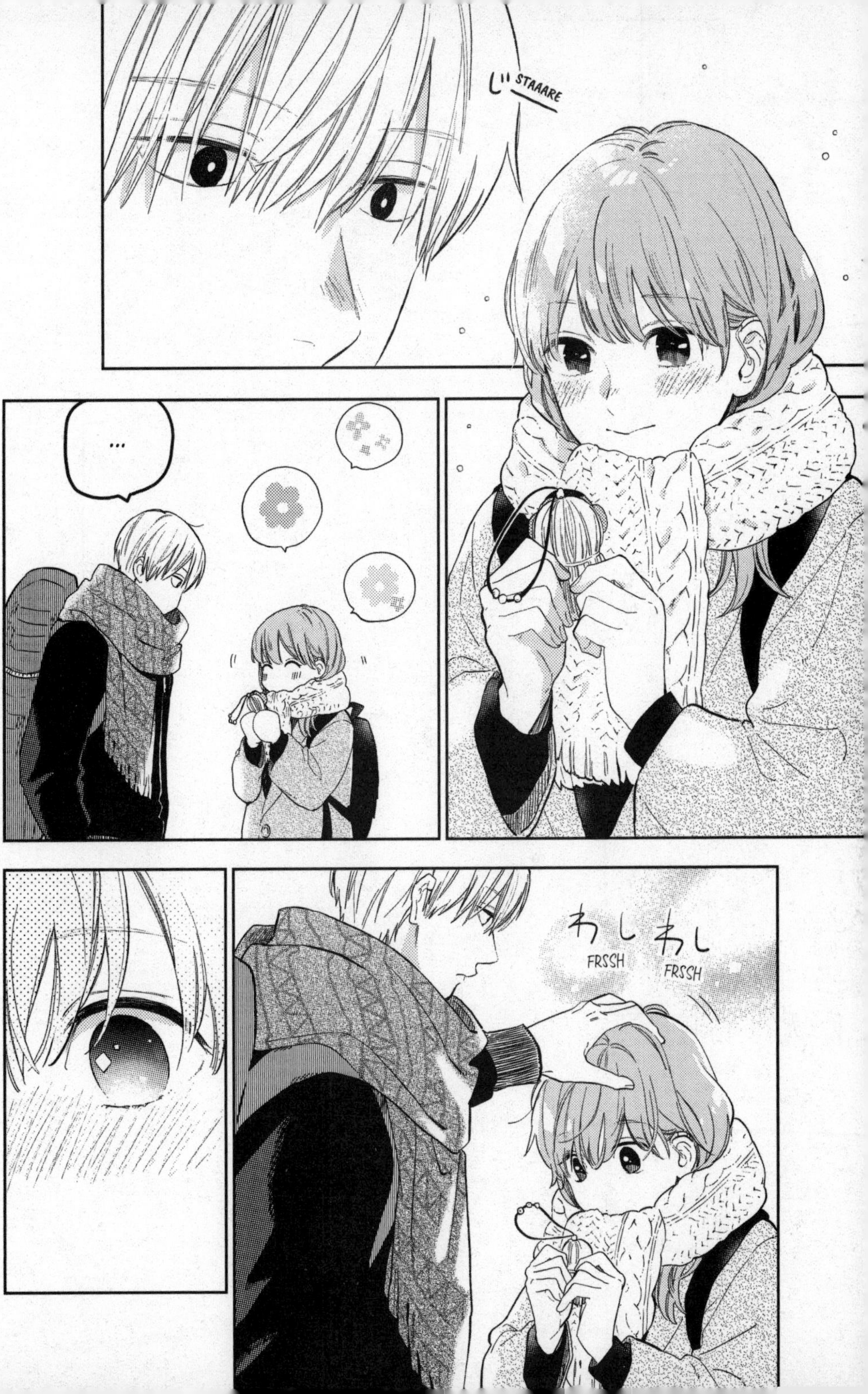
じー
STAARE
...
わしわし
FRSSH FRSSH

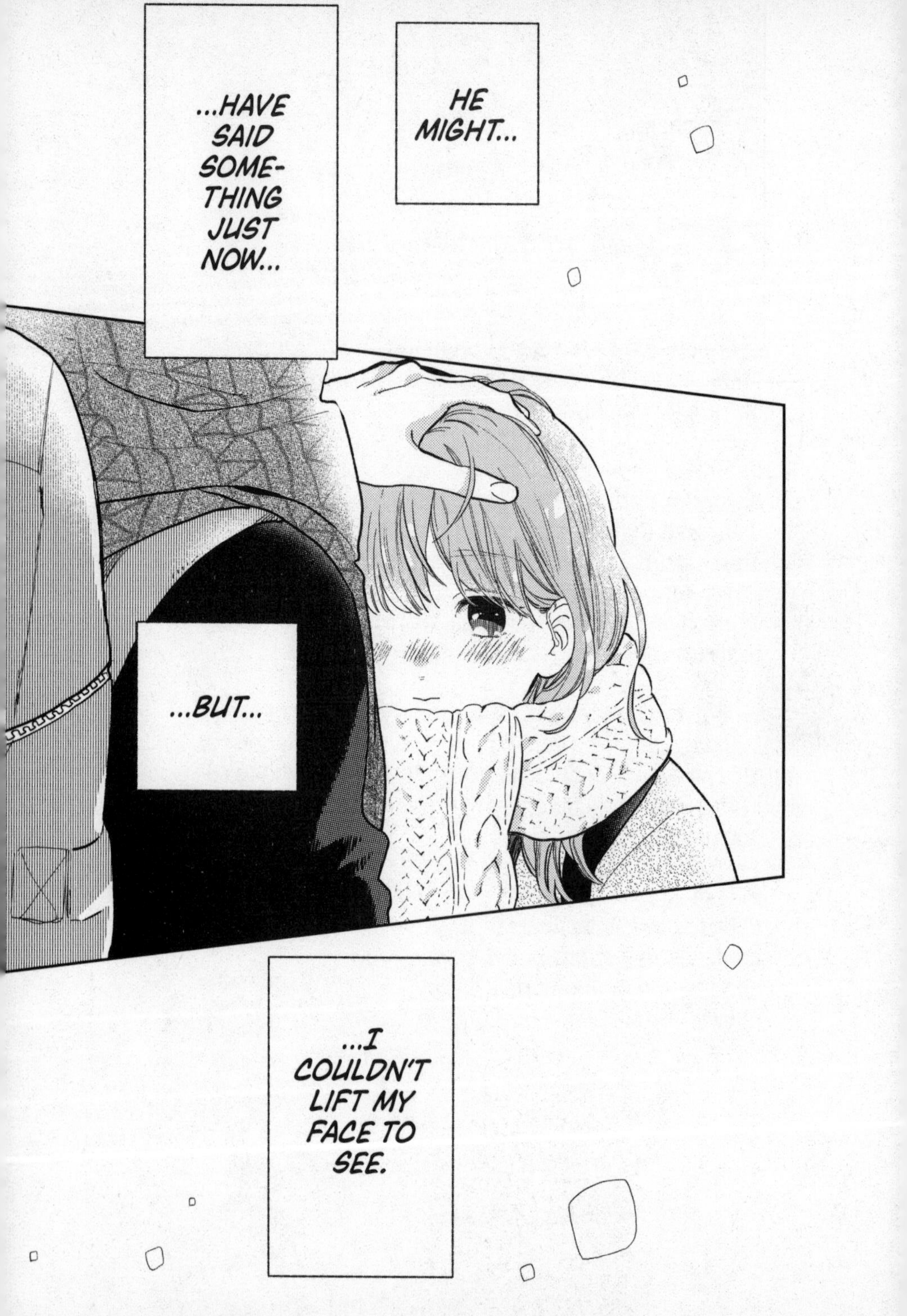
HE MIGHT...
...HAVE SAID SOME-THING JUST NOW...
...BUT...
...I COULDN'T LIFT MY FACE TO SEE.

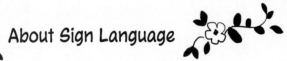

About Sign Language

In Japan, Japanese Sign Language and *Nihongo taiou shuwa,* or "signed Japanese," feature different grammar systems.

In Signed Japanese, each gesture is meant to match a word or phrase, in order, in a Japanese sentence. Japanese Sign Language features its own unique grammar. This makes it richly expressive, like any other natural language. Japanese signs include facial expressions, eye movements, and other visual cues that are vital to correct communication.

With every generation, new idioms come into the language, and the vocabulary grows. My collaborator Yuki Miyazaki-chan, who consults on the signs used in this manga, is teaching me Signed Japanese, which she uses in her daily life.

Please keep in mind that when sign language is depicted in small panels in this comic, some words get left out. I hope you can enjoy the manga anyway.

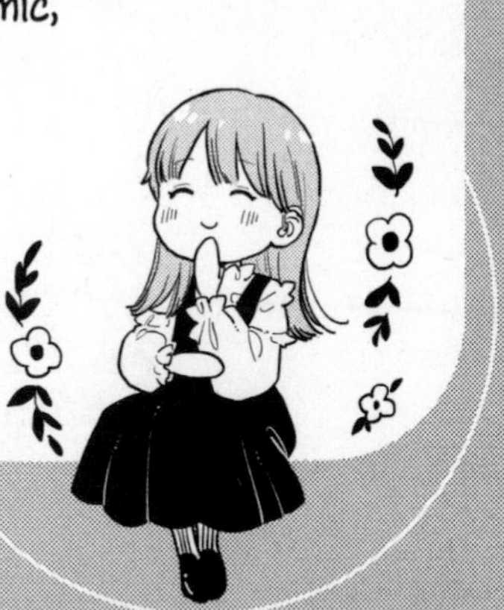

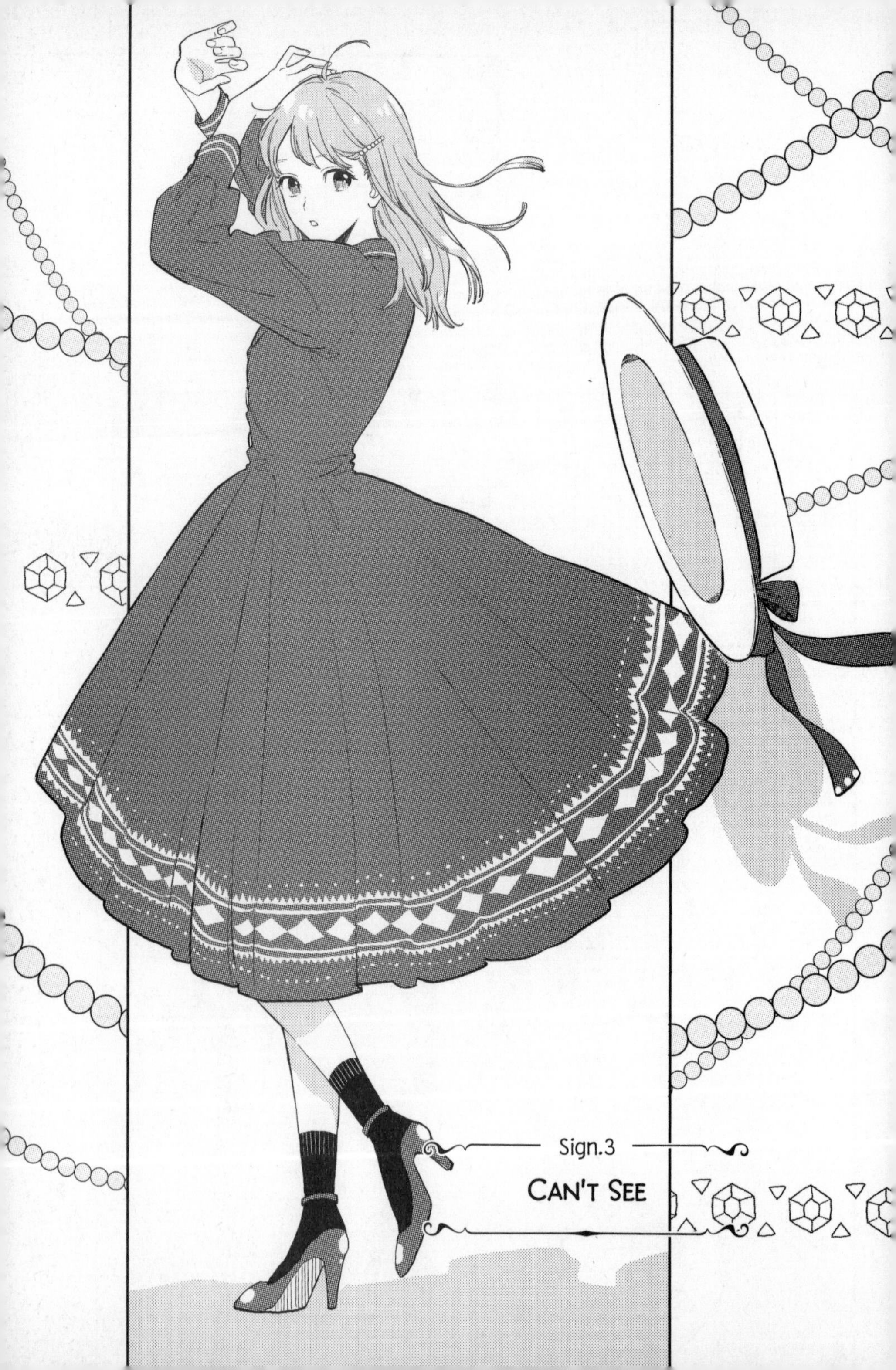
Sign.3
CAN'T SEE

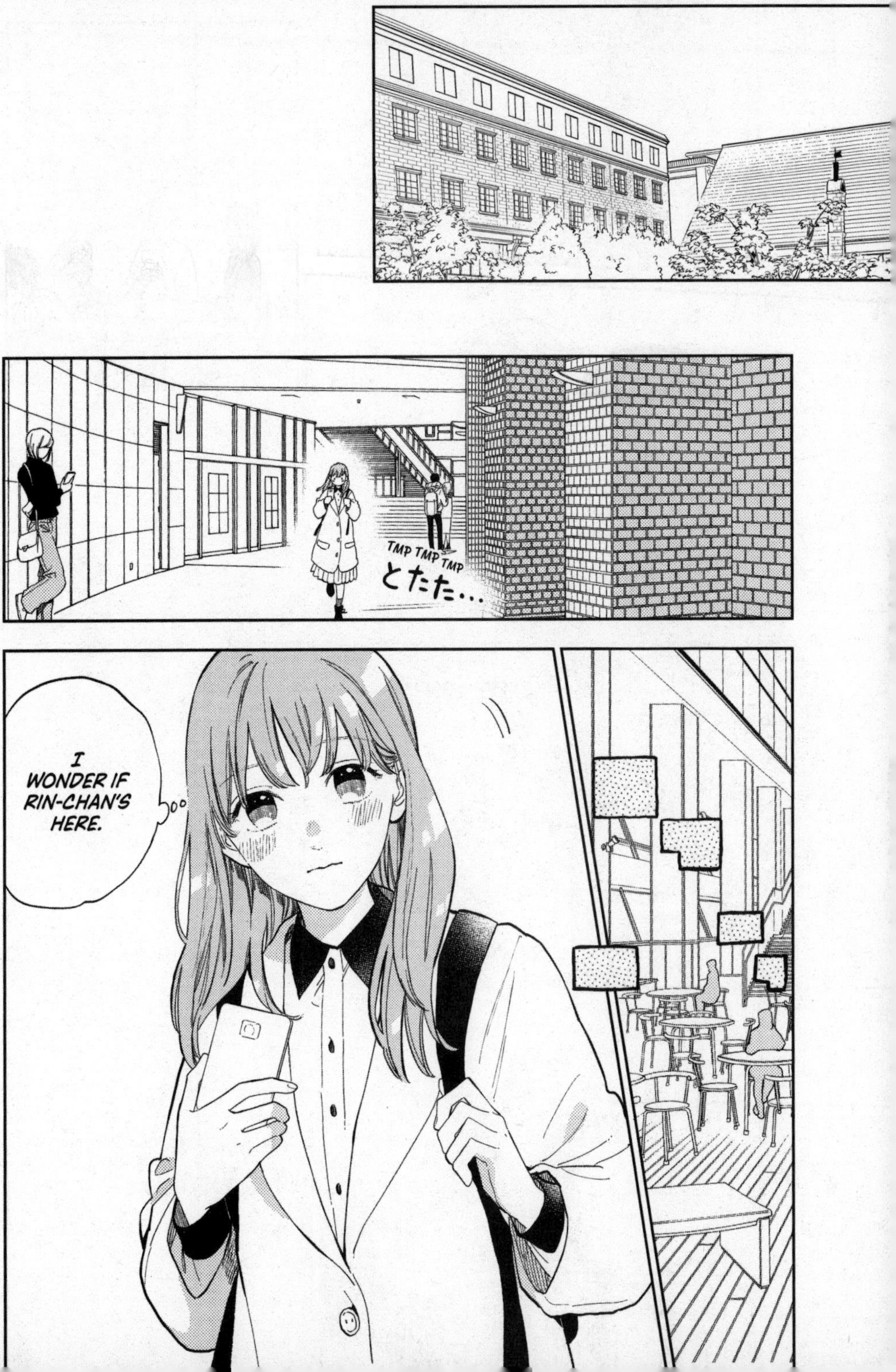
TMP TMP TMP
とたた…
I WONDER IF RIN-CHAN'S HERE.

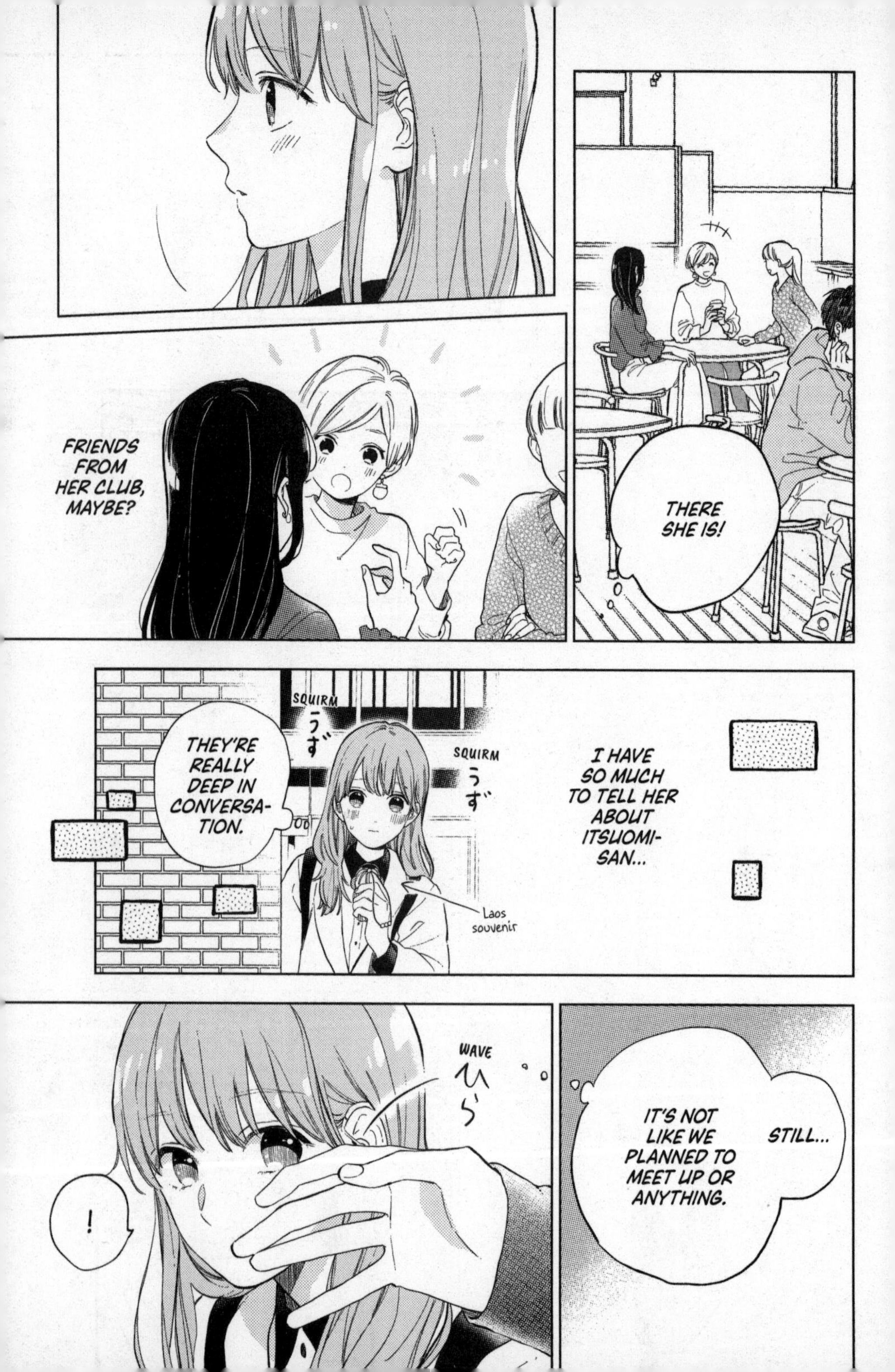
THERE SHE IS!
FRIENDS FROM HER CLUB, MAYBE?
I HAVE SO MUCH TO TELL HER ABOUT ITSUOMI-SAN...
SQUIRM
うず
SQUIRM
うず
THEY'RE REALLY DEEP IN CONVERSA-TION.
Laos souvenir
IT'S NOT LIKE WE PLANNED TO MEET UP OR ANYTHING.
STILL...
WAVE
ひら
!

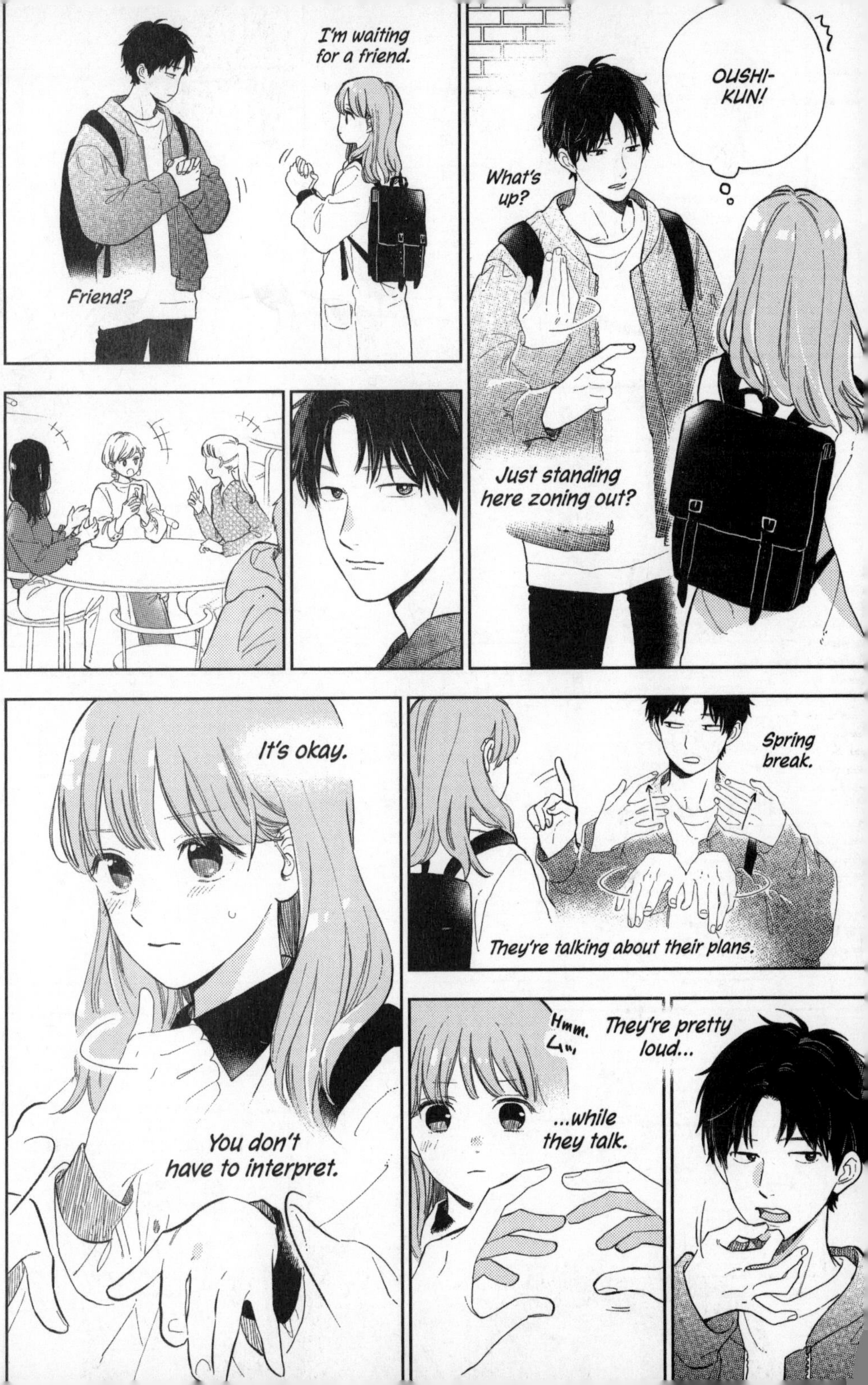
OUSHI-KUN!
What's up?
Just standing here zoning out?
I'm waiting for a friend.
Friend?
Spring break.
They're talking about their plans.
They're pretty loud...
Hmm.
...while they talk.
It's okay.
You don't have to interpret.

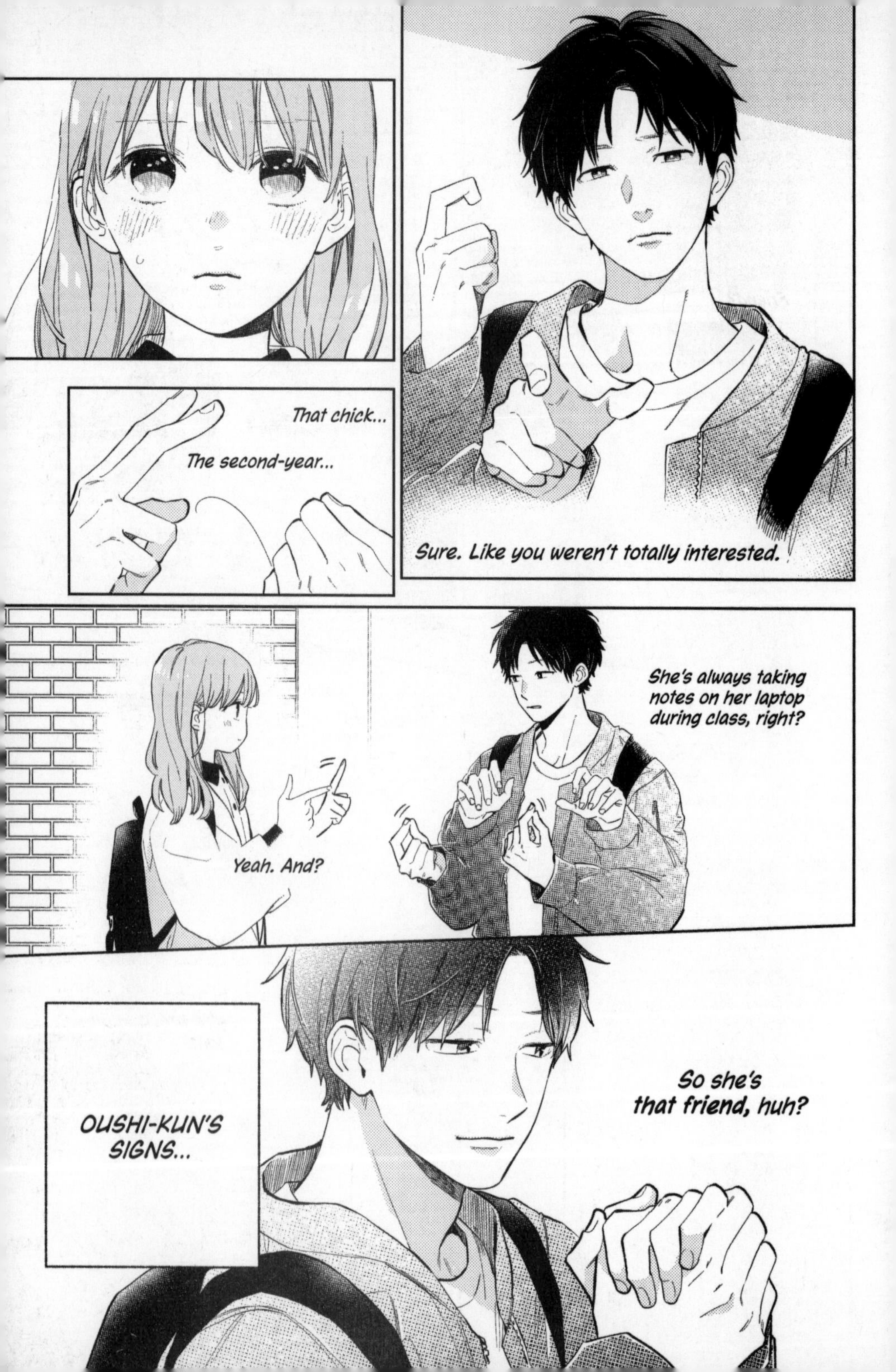
Sure. Like you weren't totally interested.
That chick...
The second-year...
She's always taking notes on her laptop during class, right?
Yeah. And?
So she's that friend, huh?
OUSHI-KUN'S SIGNS...

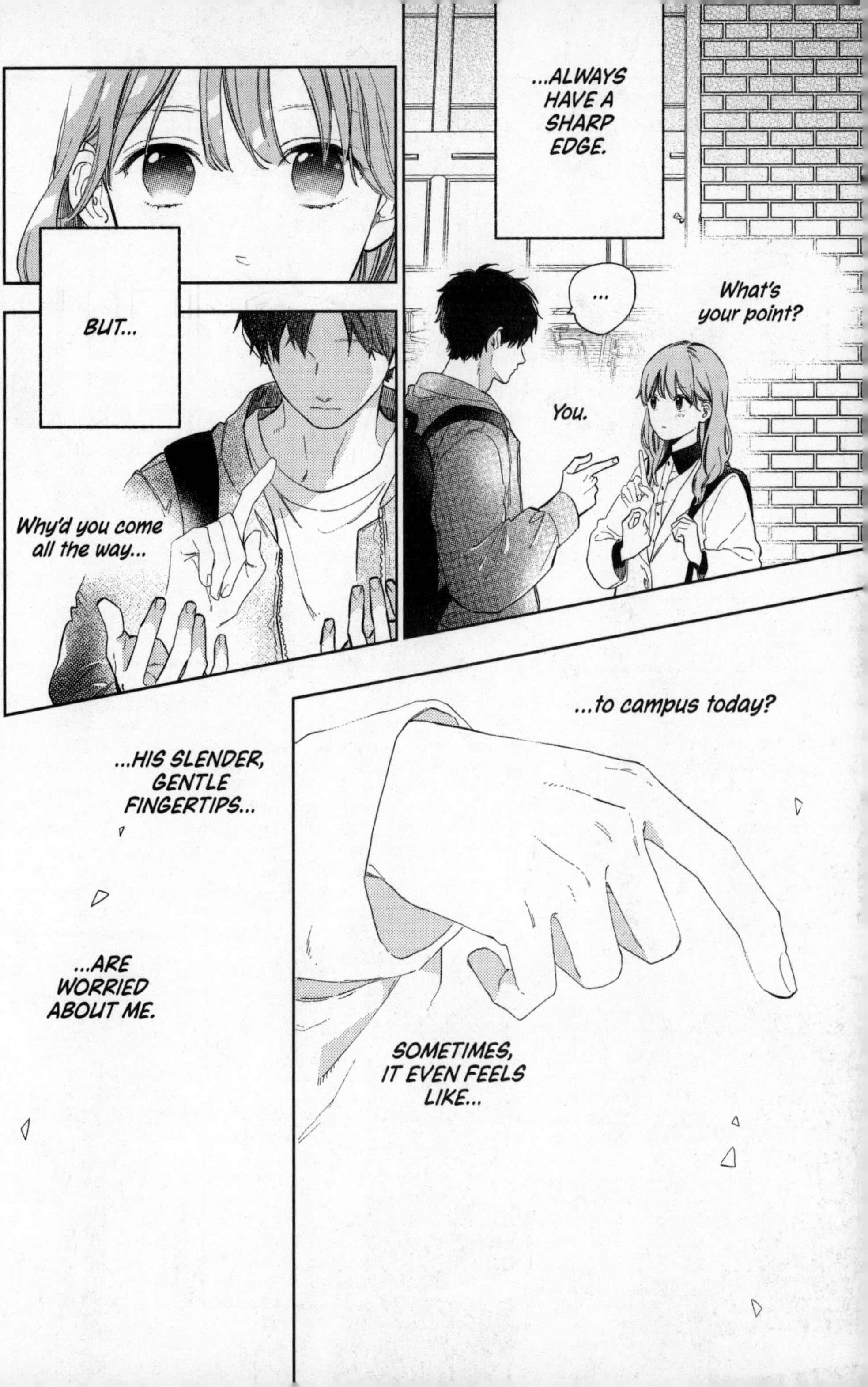
...ALWAYS HAVE A SHARP EDGE.
What's your point?
...
You.
BUT...
Why'd you come all the way...
...to campus today?
...HIS SLENDER, GENTLE FINGERTIPS...
...ARE WORRIED ABOUT ME.
SOMETIMES, IT EVEN FEELS LIKE...

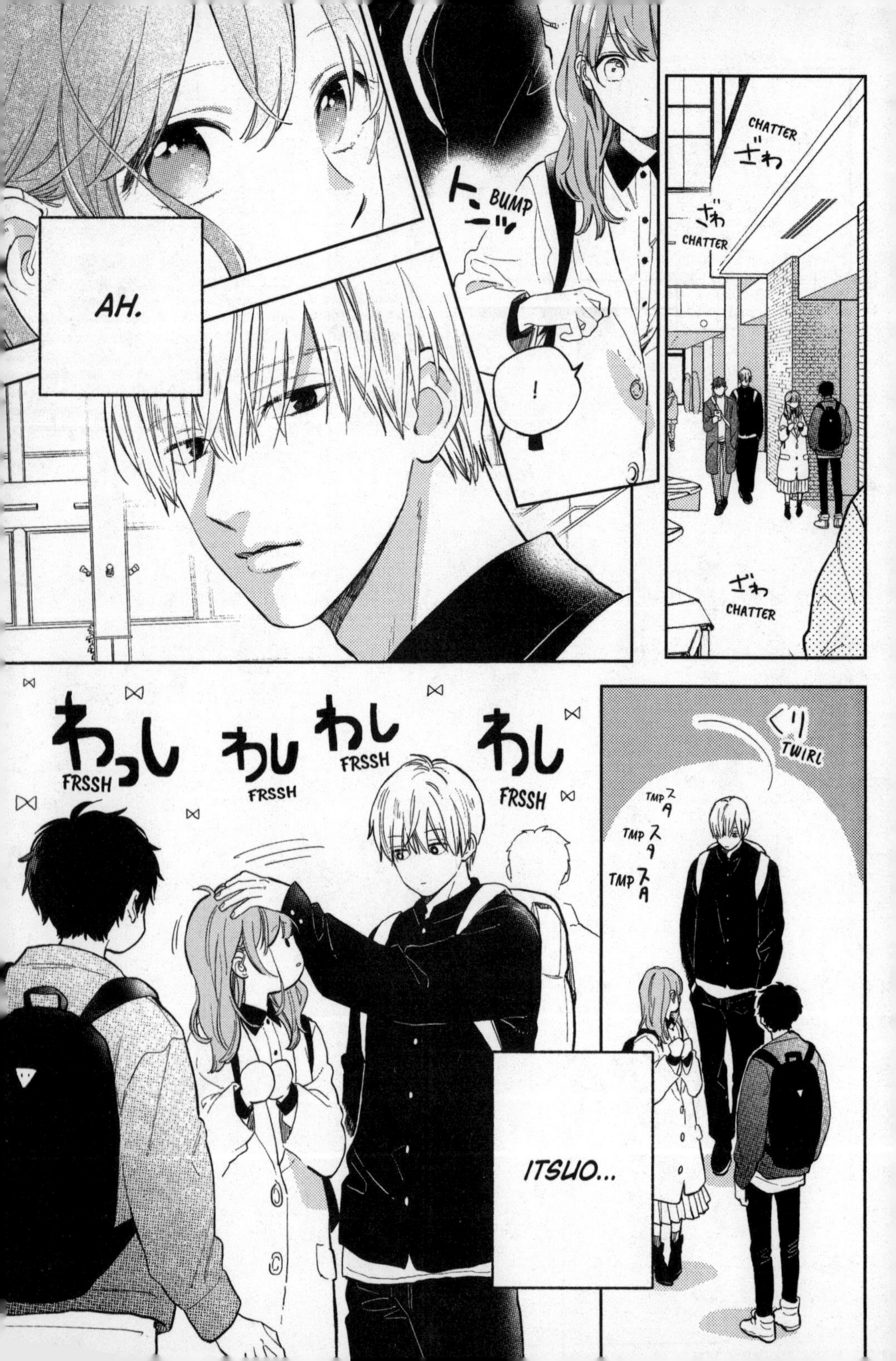
ざわ
CHATTER
ざわ
CHATTER
ざわ
CHATTER
トンッ
BUMP
!
AH.
くり
TWIRL
スタ
TMP
スタ
TMP
スタ
TMP
わし
FRSSH
わし
FRSSH
わし
FRSSH
わっし
FRSSH
ITSUO...

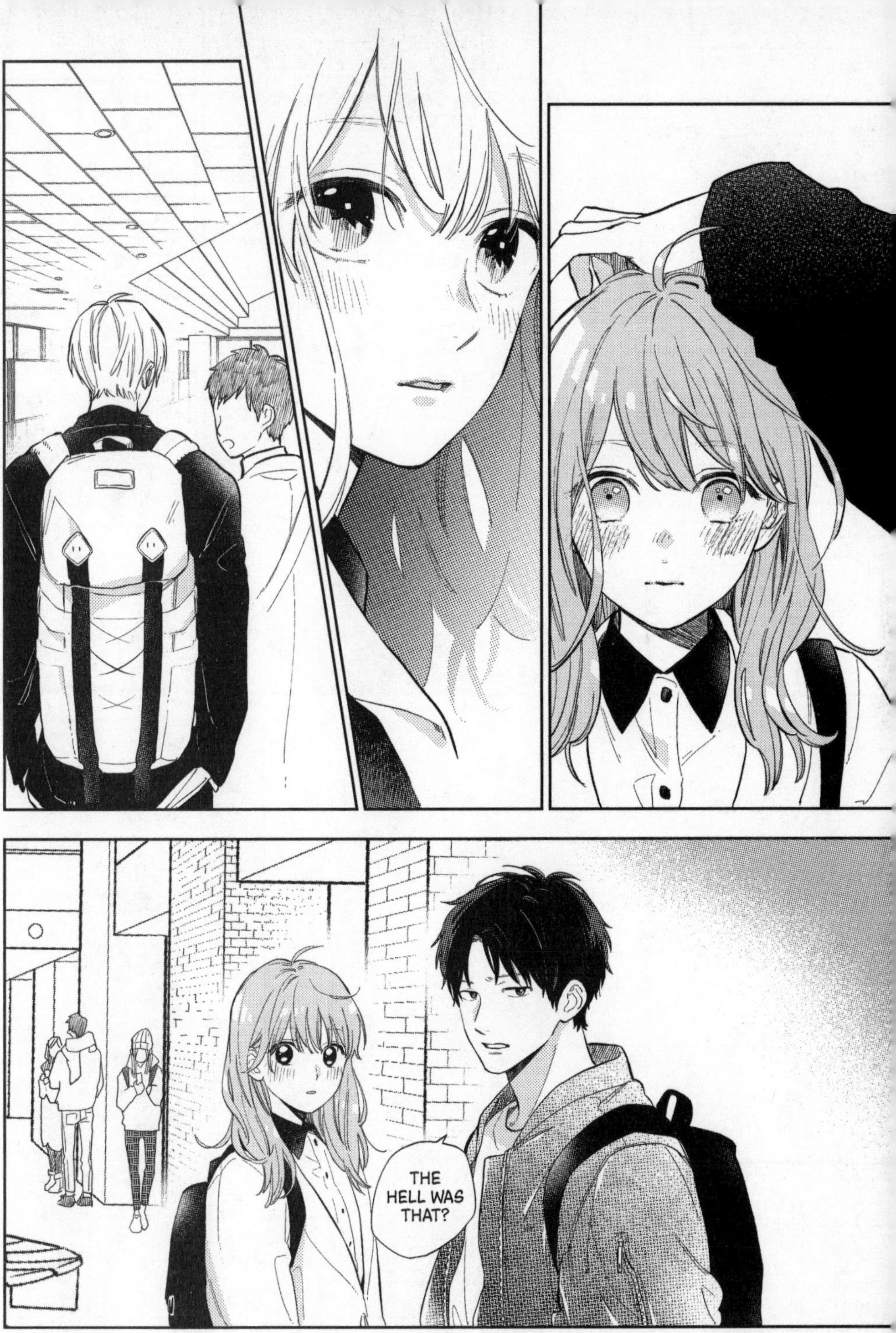
THE HELL WAS THAT?

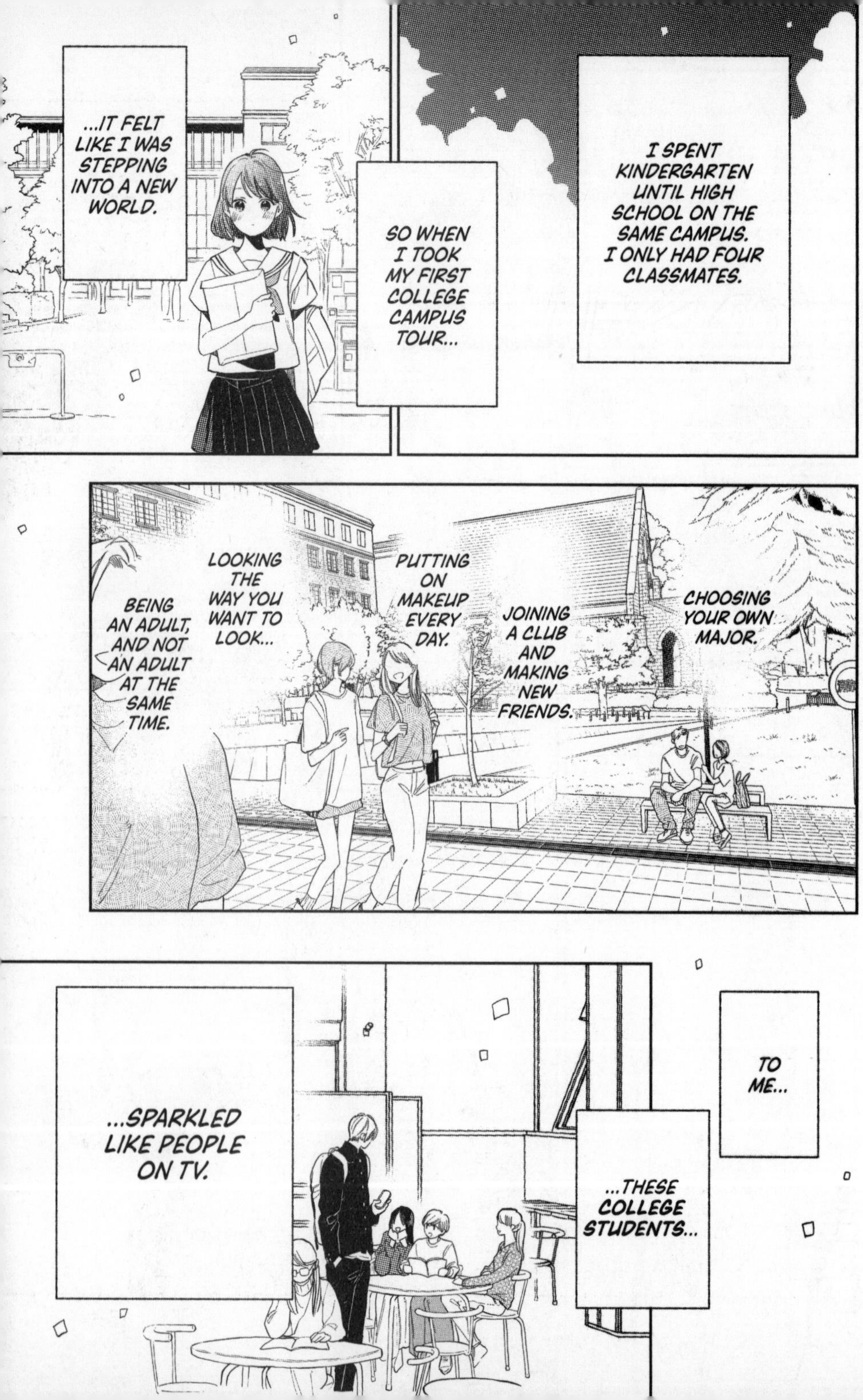
I SPENT KINDERGARTEN UNTIL HIGH SCHOOL ON THE SAME CAMPUS. I ONLY HAD FOUR CLASSMATES.
SO WHEN I TOOK MY FIRST COLLEGE CAMPUS TOUR...
...IT FELT LIKE I WAS STEPPING INTO A NEW WORLD.
CHOOSING YOUR OWN MAJOR.
JOINING A CLUB AND MAKING NEW FRIENDS.
PUTTING ON MAKEUP EVERY DAY.
LOOKING THE WAY YOU WANT TO LOOK...
BEING AN ADULT, AND NOT AN ADULT AT THE SAME TIME.
TO ME...
...THESE COLLEGE STUDENTS...
...SPARKLED LIKE PEOPLE ON TV.

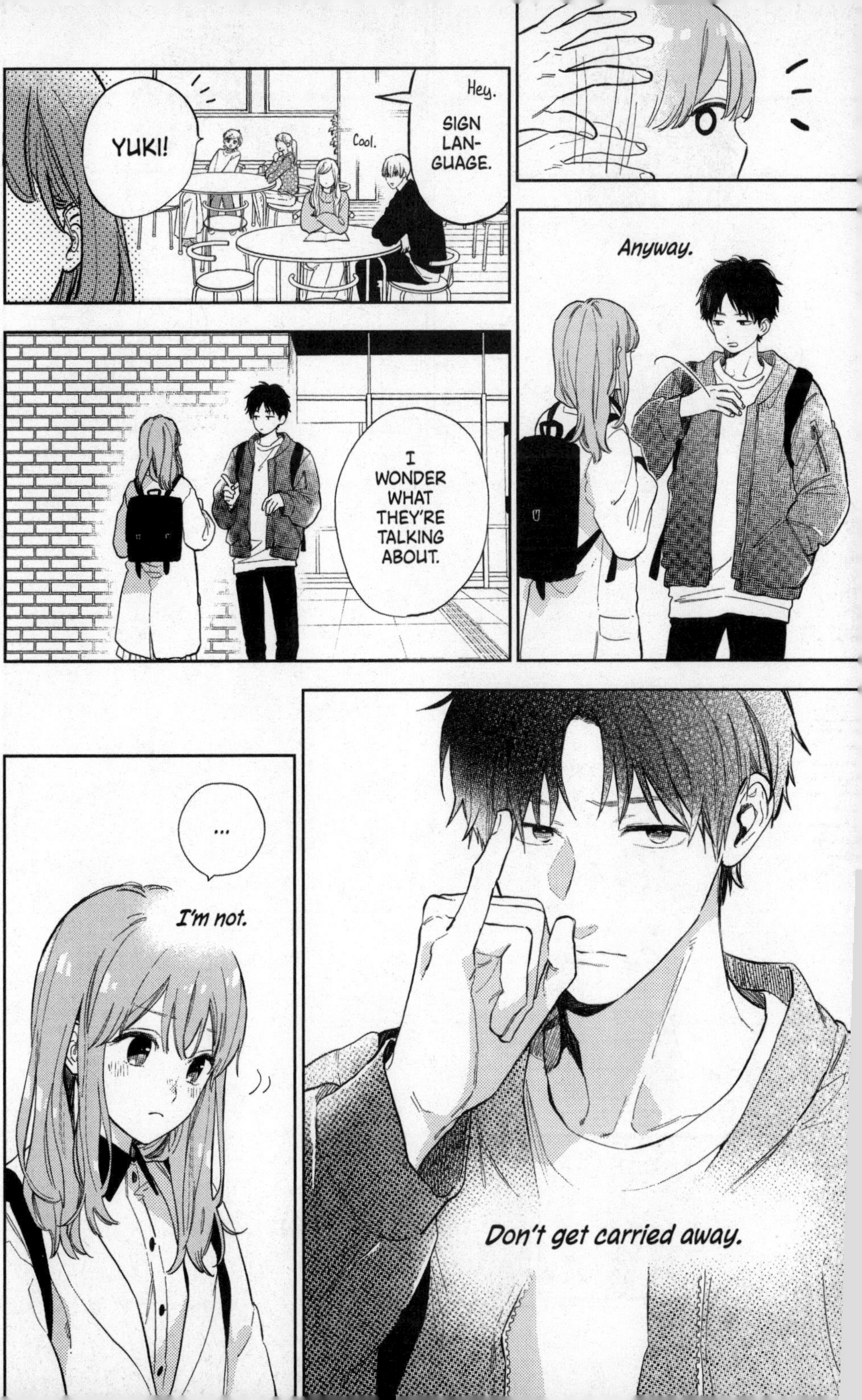
Hey.
SIGN LAN-GUAGE.
Cool.
YUKI!
Anyway.
I WONDER WHAT THEY'RE TALKING ABOUT.
Don't get carried away.
...
I'm not.

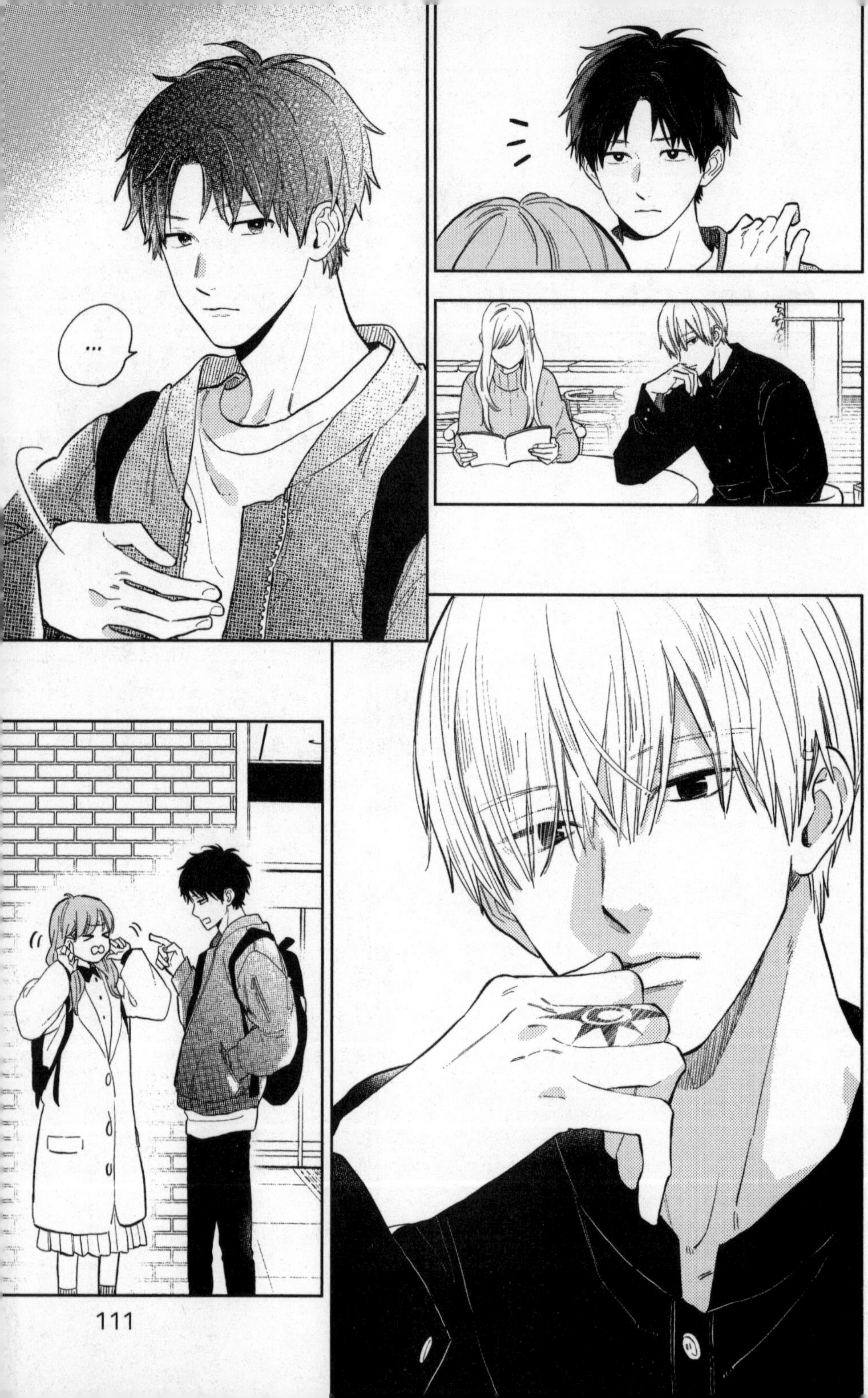
...

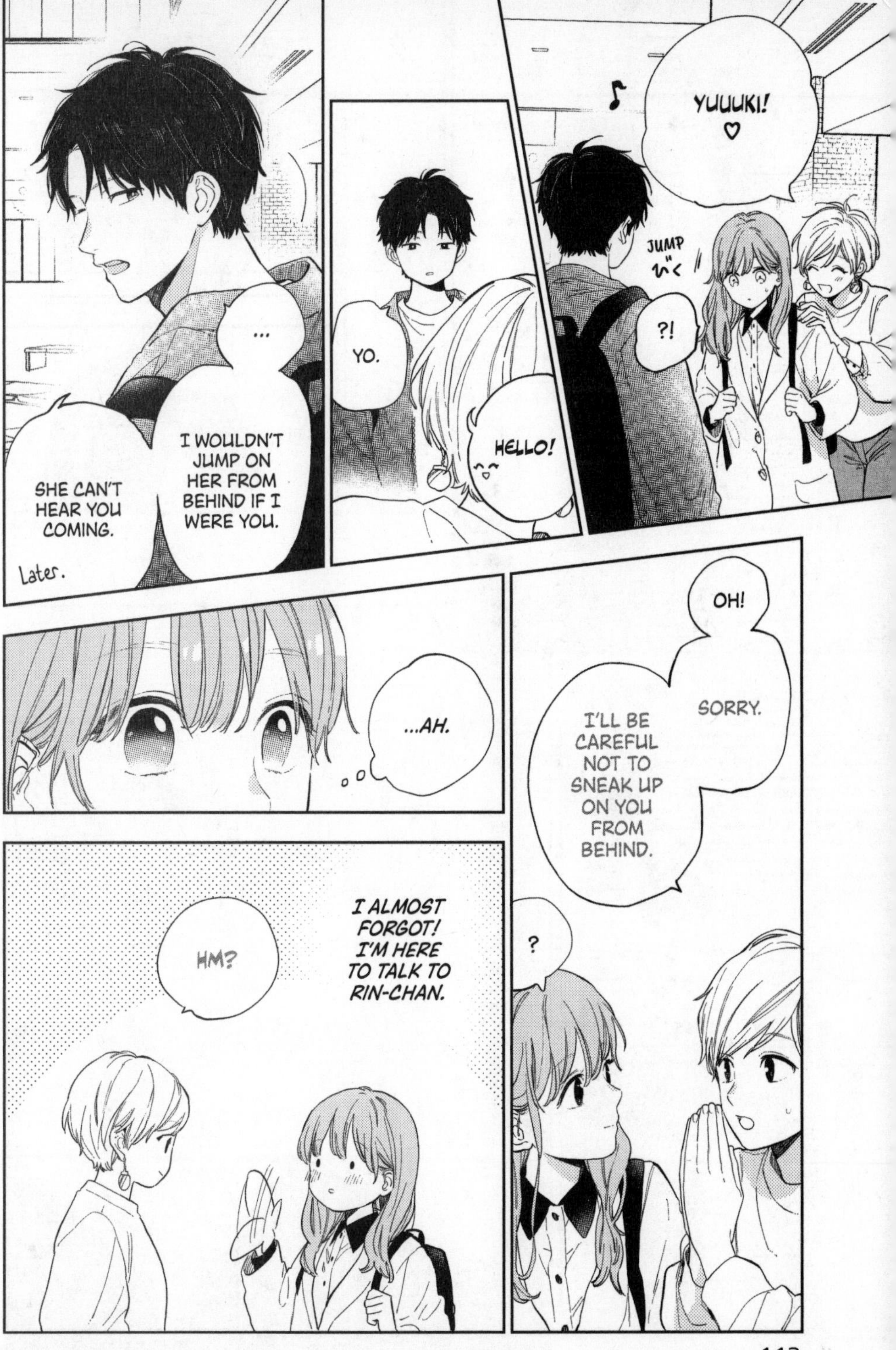
YUUUKI! ♡
JUMP
びく
?!
YO.
HELLO!
...
I WOULDN'T JUMP ON HER FROM BEHIND IF I WERE YOU.
SHE CAN'T HEAR YOU COMING.
Later.
OH!
SORRY.
I'LL BE CAREFUL NOT TO SNEAK UP ON YOU FROM BEHIND.
?
...AH.
I ALMOST FORGOT! I'M HERE TO TALK TO RIN-CHAN.
HM?

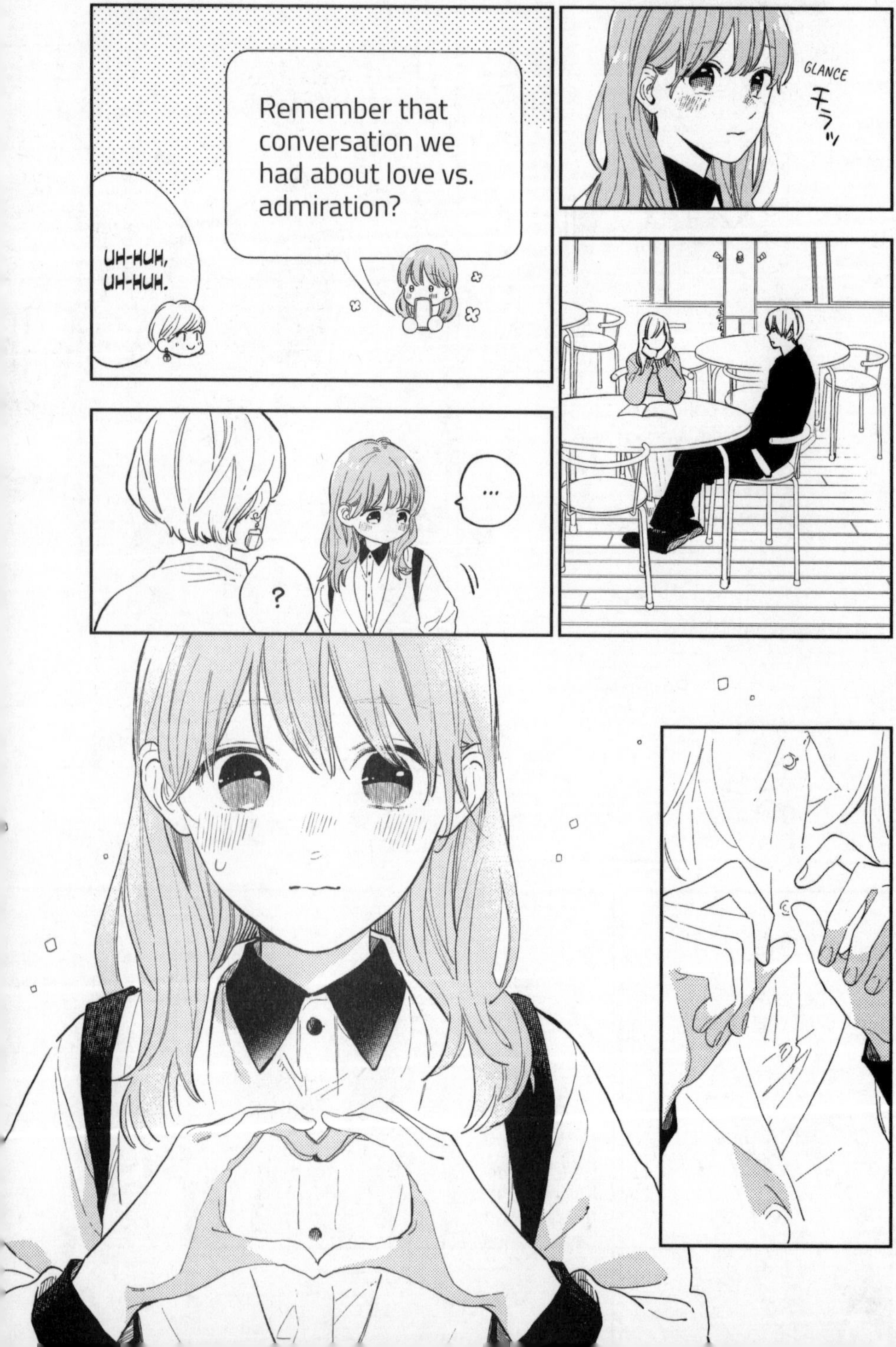
GLANCE
チラッ
Remember that conversation we had about love vs. admiration?
UH-HUH, UH-HUH.
...
?

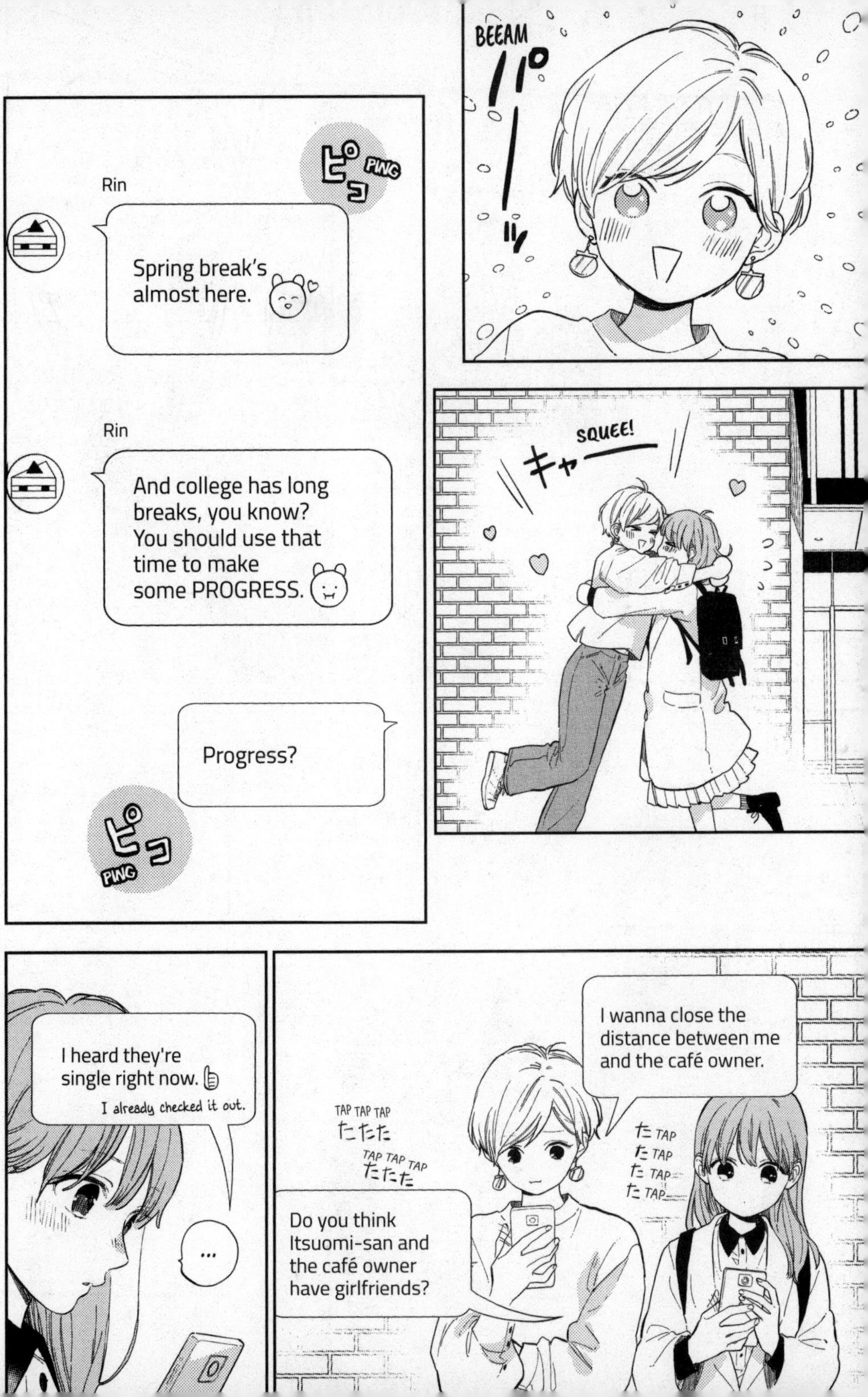
BEEAM
パーッ
SQUEE!
キャー
PING
ピコ
Rin
Spring break's almost here.
Rin
And college has long breaks, you know? You should use that time to make some PROGRESS.
Progress?
ピコ
PING
I wanna close the distance between me and the café owner.
た TAP
た TAP
た TAP
た TAP
TAP TAP TAP
たたた
TAP TAP TAP
たたた
Do you think Itsuomi-san and the café owner have girlfriends?
I heard they're single right now.
I already checked it out.
...

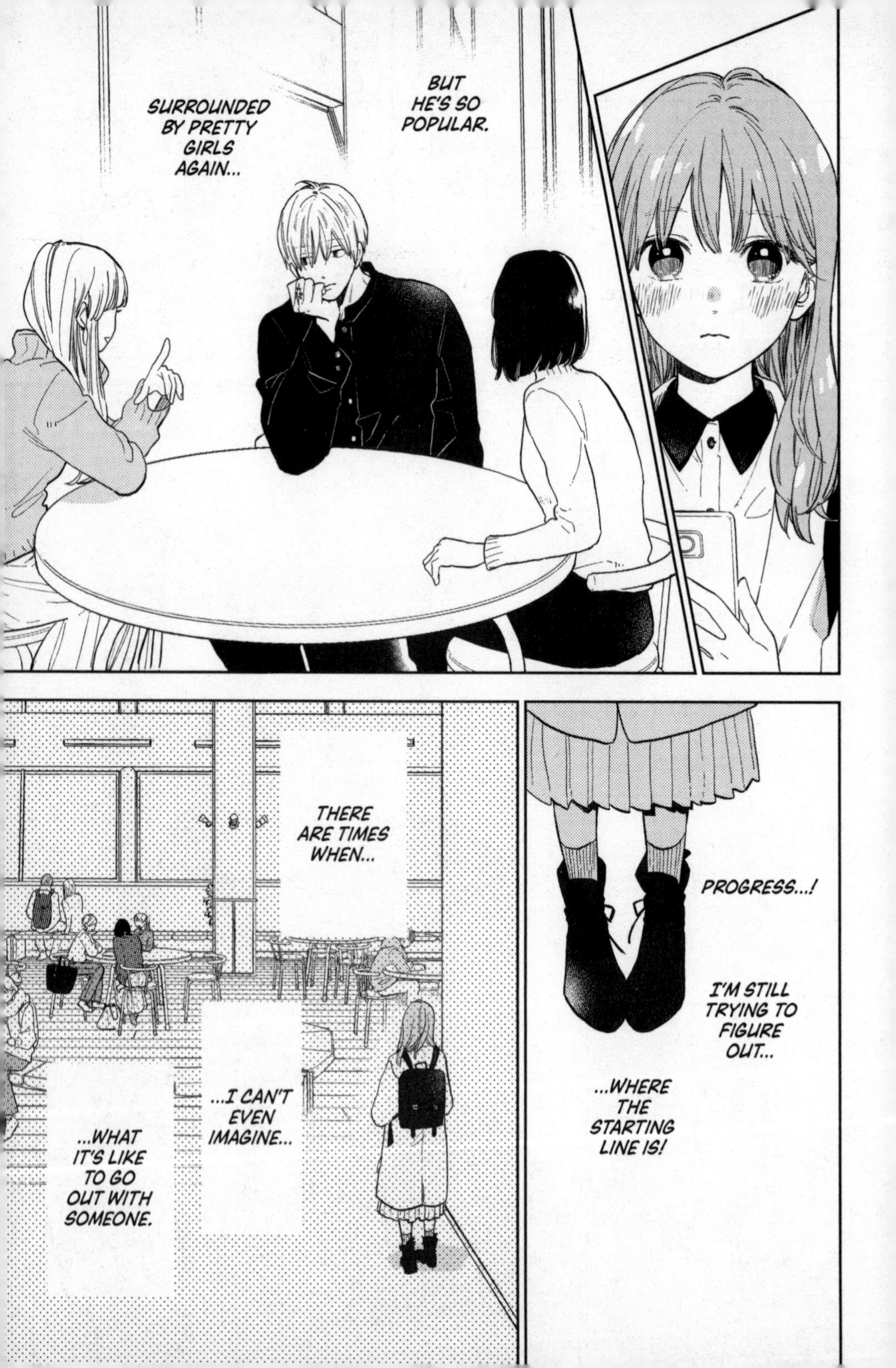
SURROUNDED BY PRETTY GIRLS AGAIN...
BUT HE'S SO POPULAR.
PROGRESS...!
I'M STILL TRYING TO FIGURE OUT...
...WHERE THE STARTING LINE IS!
THERE ARE TIMES WHEN...
...I CAN'T EVEN IMAGINE...
...WHAT IT'S LIKE TO GO OUT WITH SOMEONE.

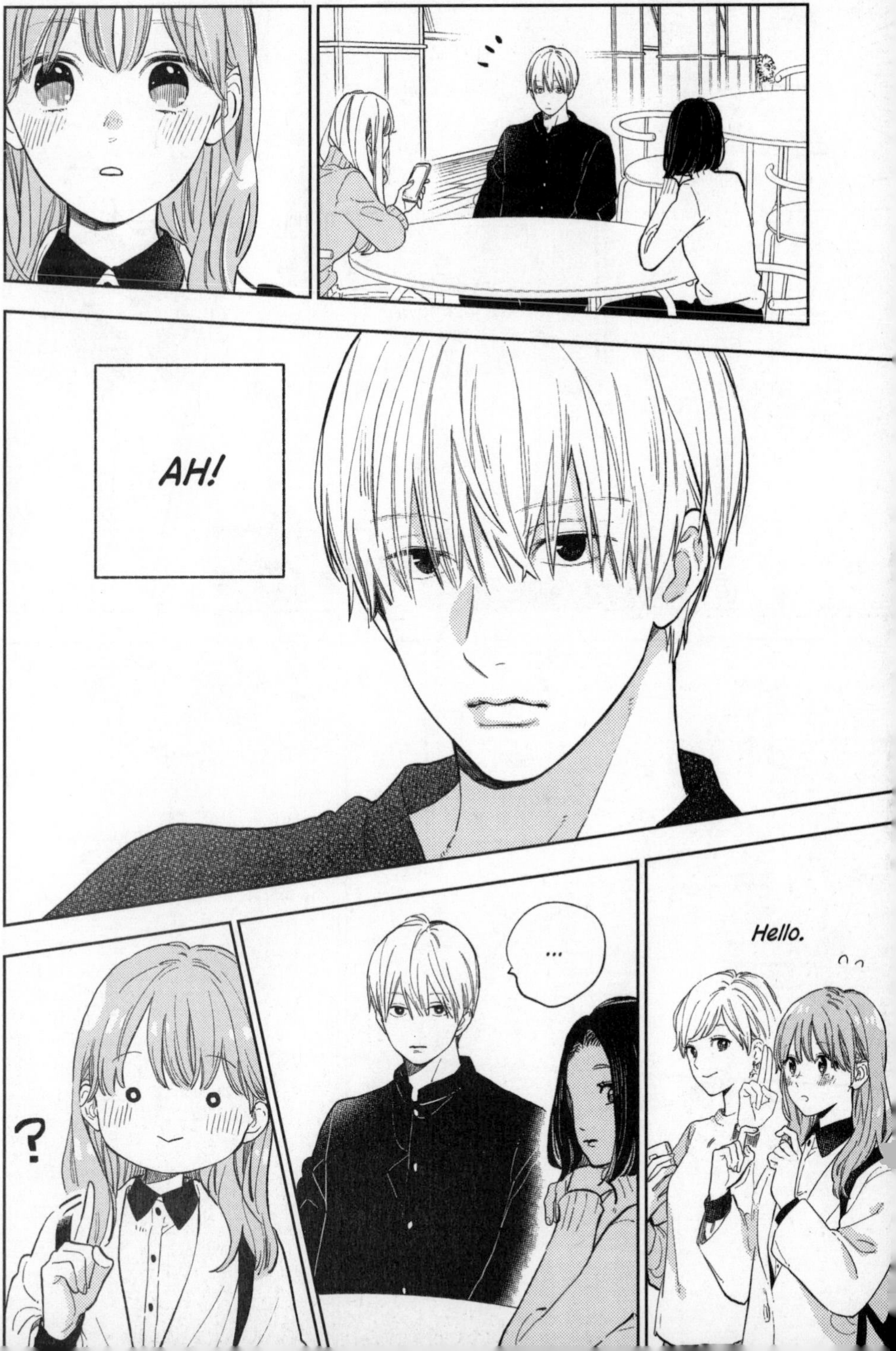
AH!
Hello.
...
?

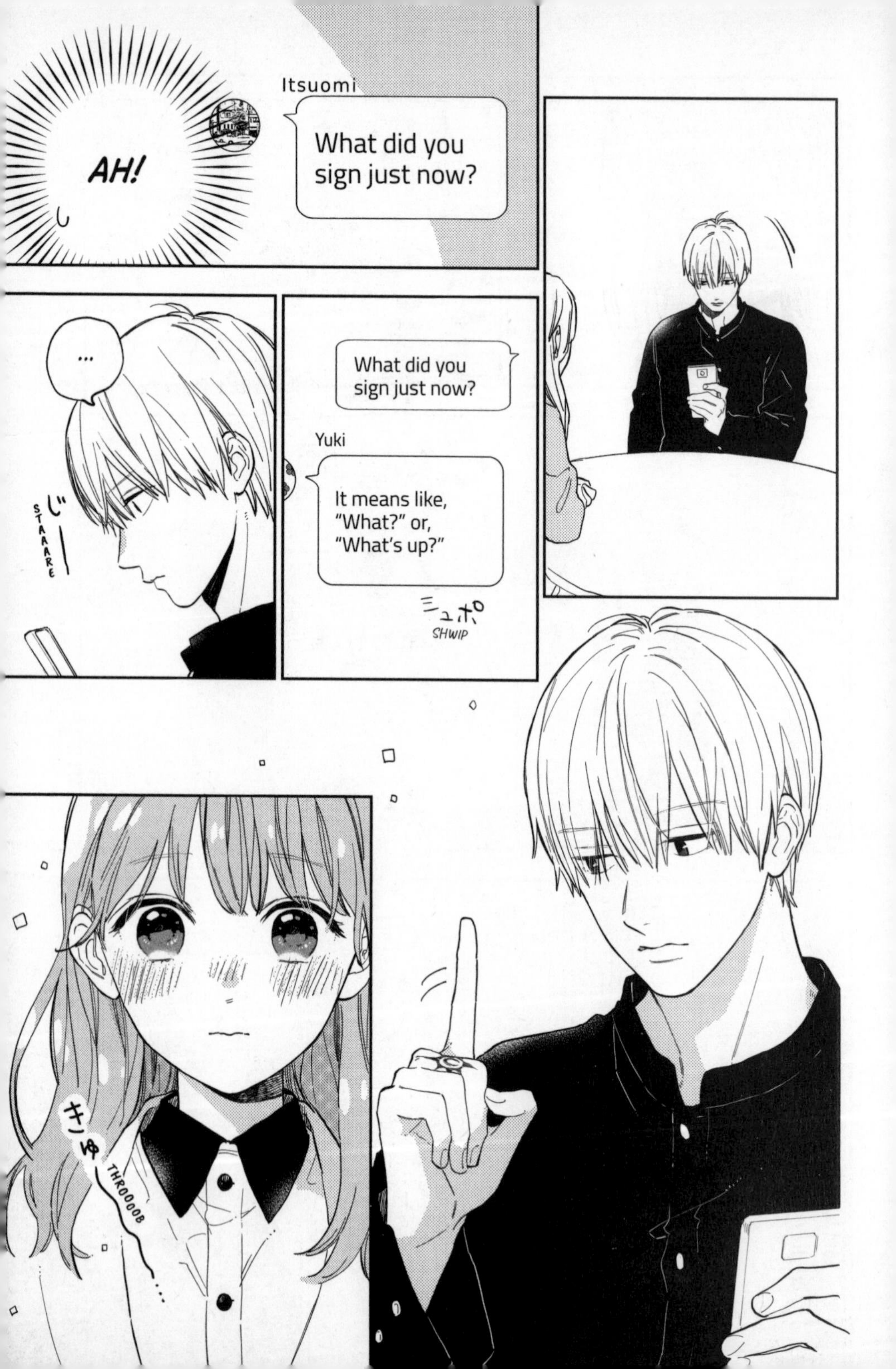
Itsuomi
What did you sign just now?
AH!
What did you sign just now?
Yuki
It means like, "What?" or, "What's up?"
ミュポ
SHWIP
...
じー
STAAARE
キュ
THROOOOB

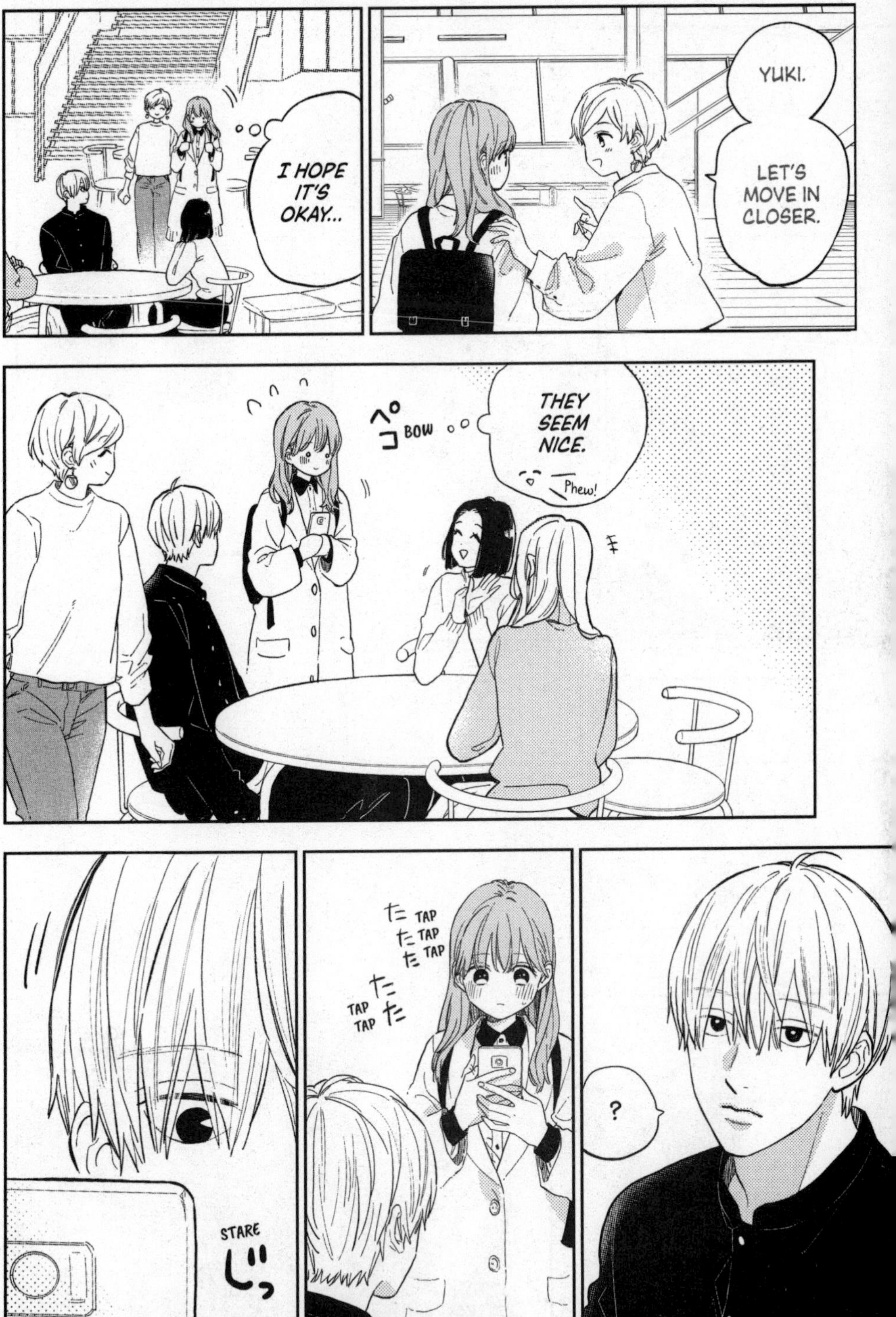
YUKI.
LET'S MOVE IN CLOSER.
I HOPE IT'S OKAY...
THEY SEEM NICE.
Phew!
ペコ BOW
?
た TAP た TAP た TAP
た た TAP TAP
STARE
じっ

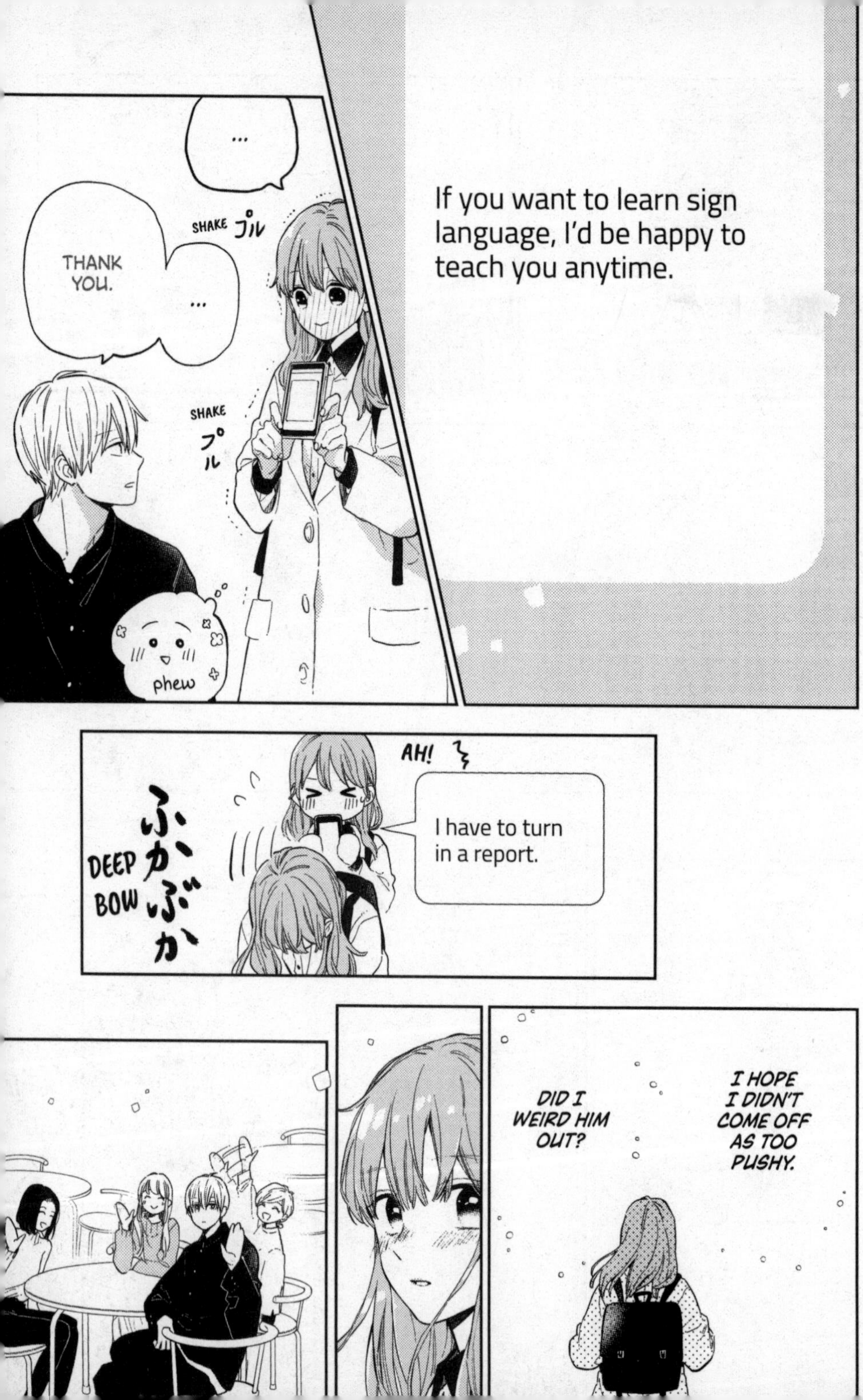
If you want to learn sign language, I'd be happy to teach you anytime.
...
SHAKE プル
THANK YOU.
...
SHAKE プル
phew
AH!
I have to turn in a report.
DEEP BOW ふかぶか
I HOPE I DIDN'T COME OFF AS TOO PUSHY.
DID I WEIRD HIM OUT?

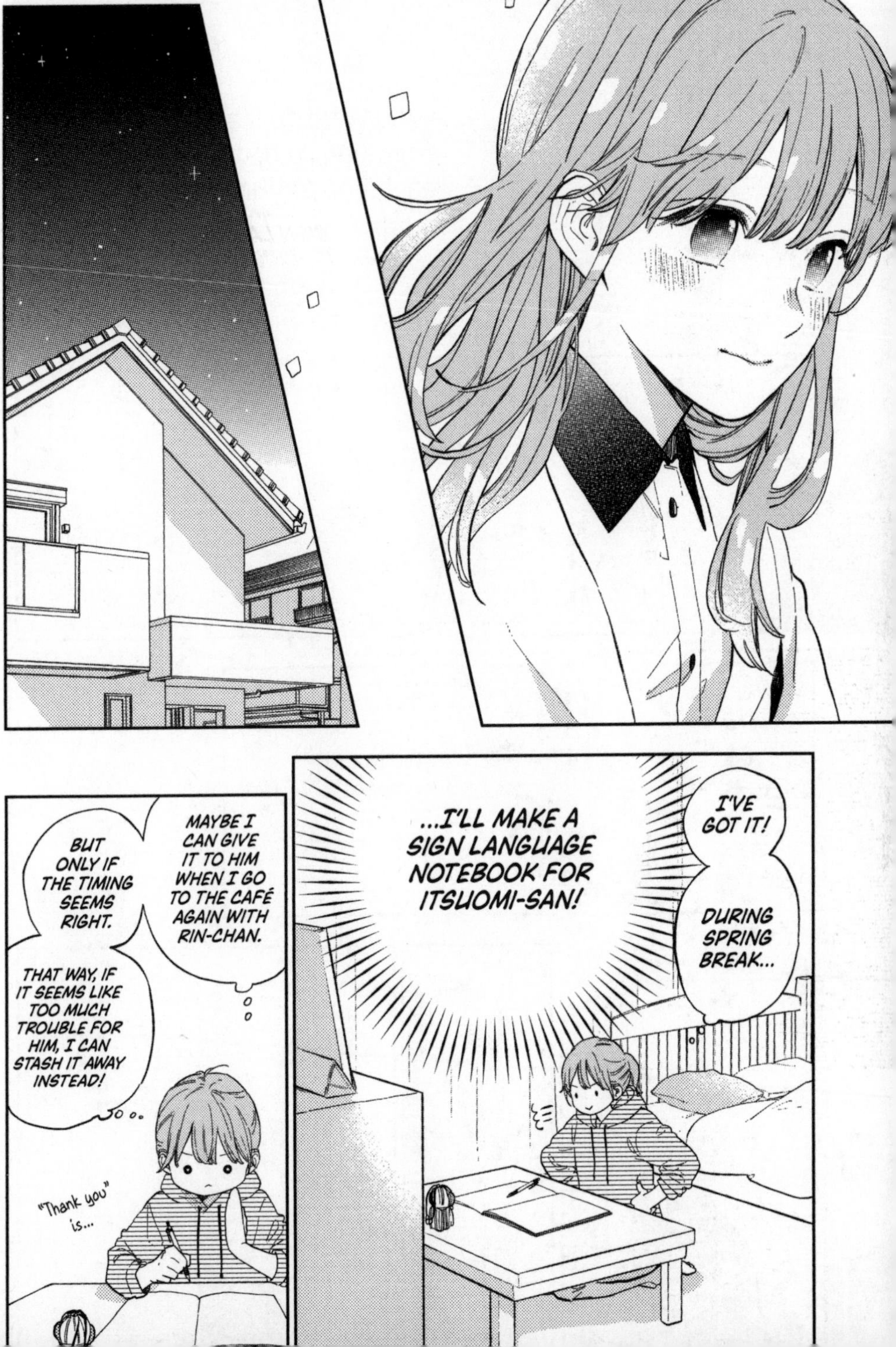
I'VE GOT IT!
DURING SPRING BREAK...
...I'LL MAKE A SIGN LANGUAGE NOTEBOOK FOR ITSUOMI-SAN!
MAYBE I CAN GIVE IT TO HIM WHEN I GO TO THE CAFÉ AGAIN WITH RIN-CHAN.
BUT ONLY IF THE TIMING SEEMS RIGHT.
THAT WAY, IF IT SEEMS LIKE TOO MUCH TROUBLE FOR HIM, I CAN STASH IT AWAY INSTEAD!
"Thank you" is...

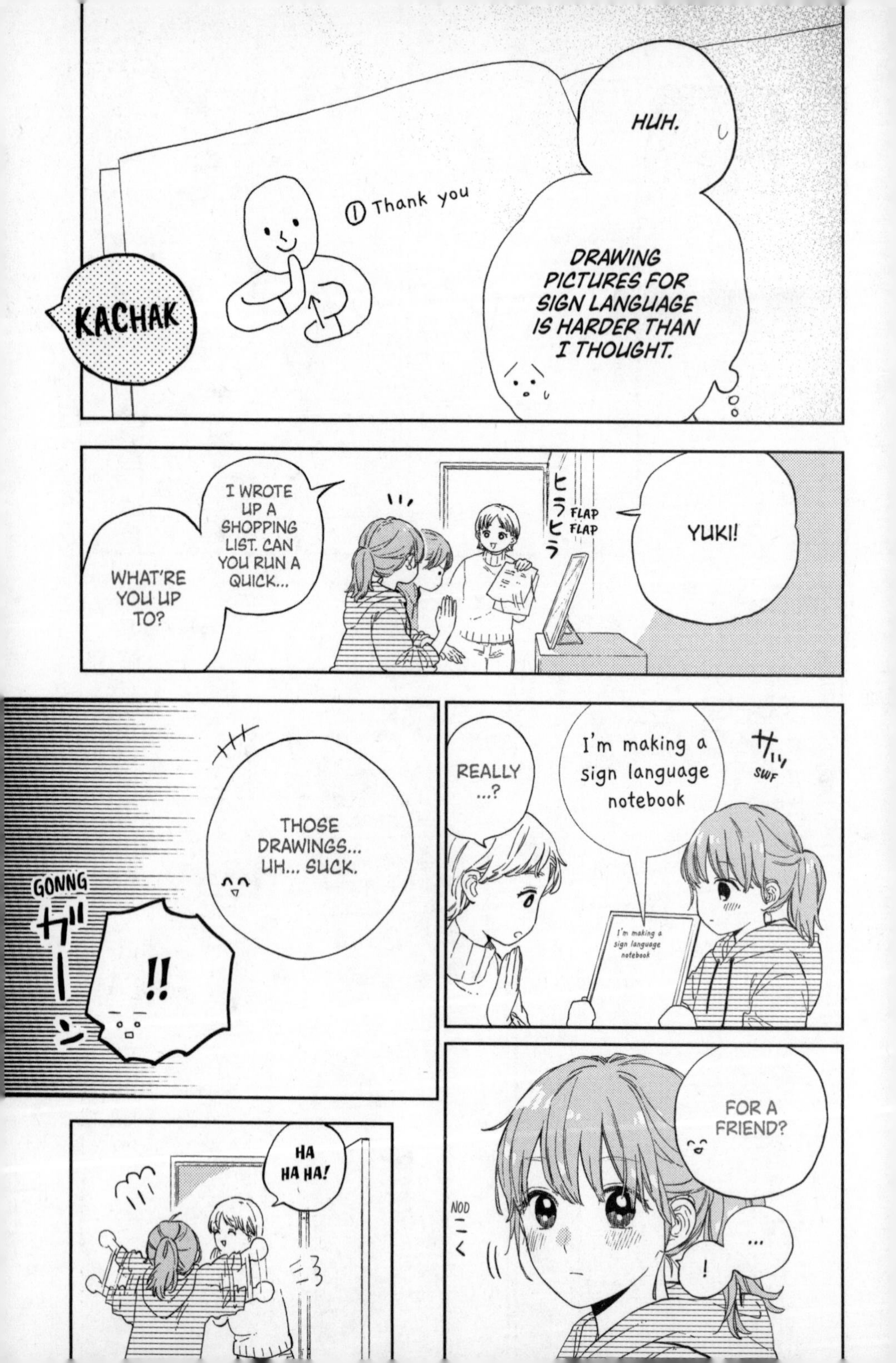
HUH.
DRAWING PICTURES FOR SIGN LANGUAGE IS HARDER THAN I THOUGHT.
① Thank you
KACHAK
YUKI!
ヒラヒラ FLAP FLAP
I WROTE UP A SHOPPING LIST. CAN YOU RUN A QUICK...
WHAT'RE YOU UP TO?
I'm making a sign language notebook
サッ SWF
REALLY ...?
I'm making a sign language notebook
FOR A FRIEND?
...
!
NOD こく
THOSE DRAWINGS... UH... SUCK.
GONNG ガーン
!!
HA HA HA!

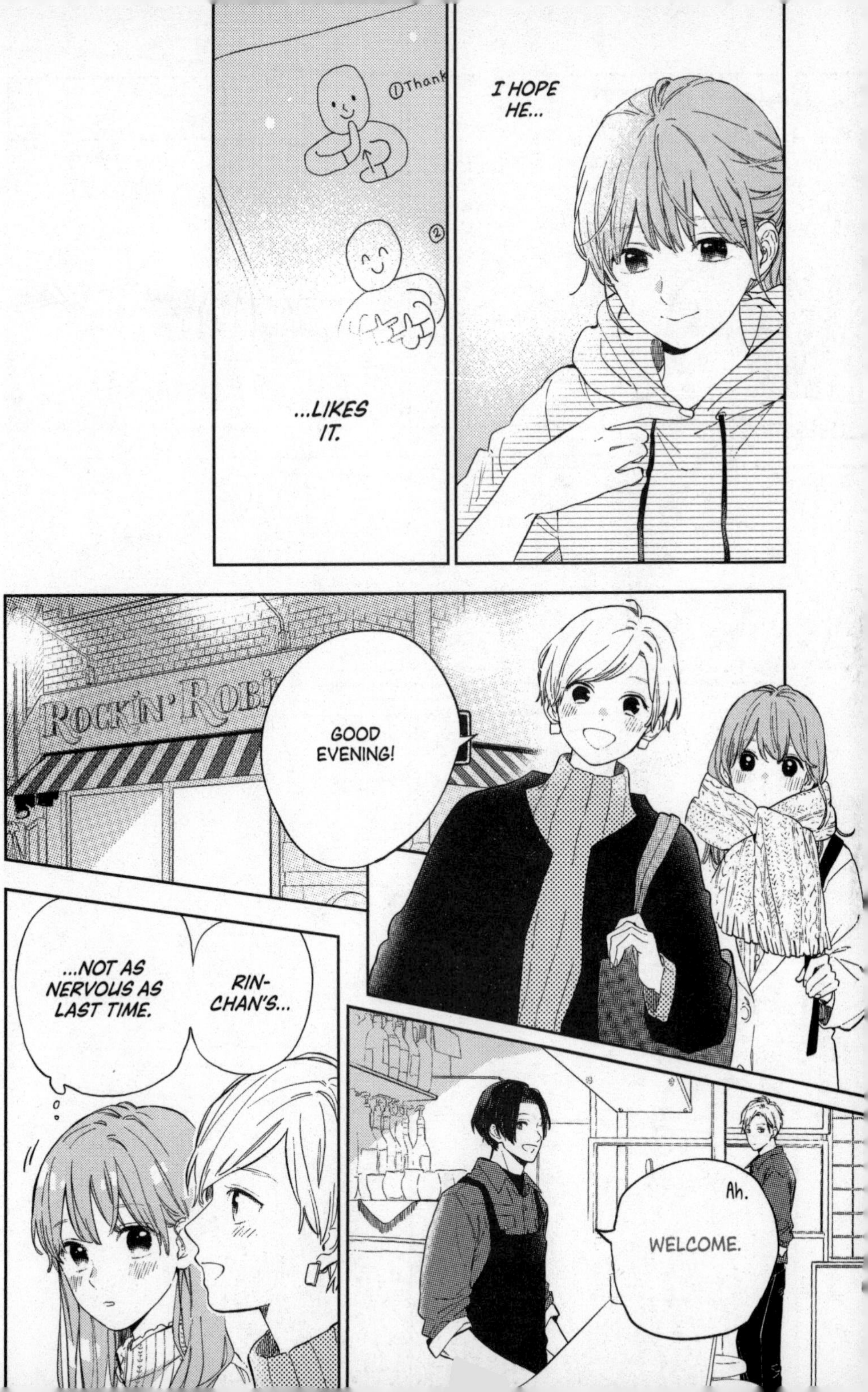
I HOPE HE...
①Thank
②
...LIKES IT.
GOOD EVENING!
RIN-CHAN'S...
...NOT AS NERVOUS AS LAST TIME.
Ah.
WELCOME.

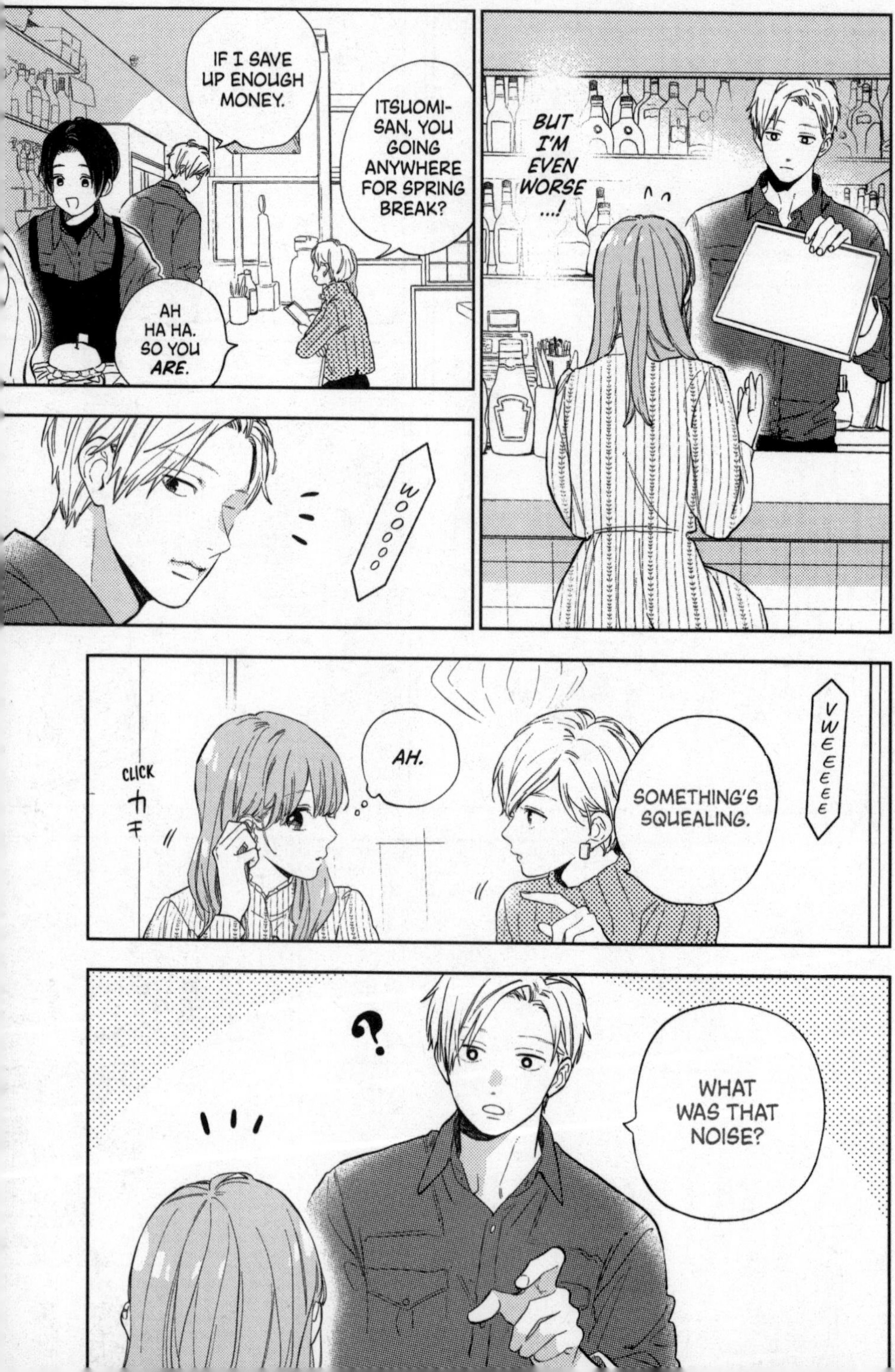
BUT I'M EVEN WORSE ...!
ITSUOMI-SAN, YOU GOING ANYWHERE FOR SPRING BREAK?
IF I SAVE UP ENOUGH MONEY.
AH HA HA. SO YOU *ARE*.
WOOOOOO
VWEEEEEE
SOMETHING'S SQUEALING.
AH.
CLICK
カチ
WHAT WAS THAT NOISE?
?

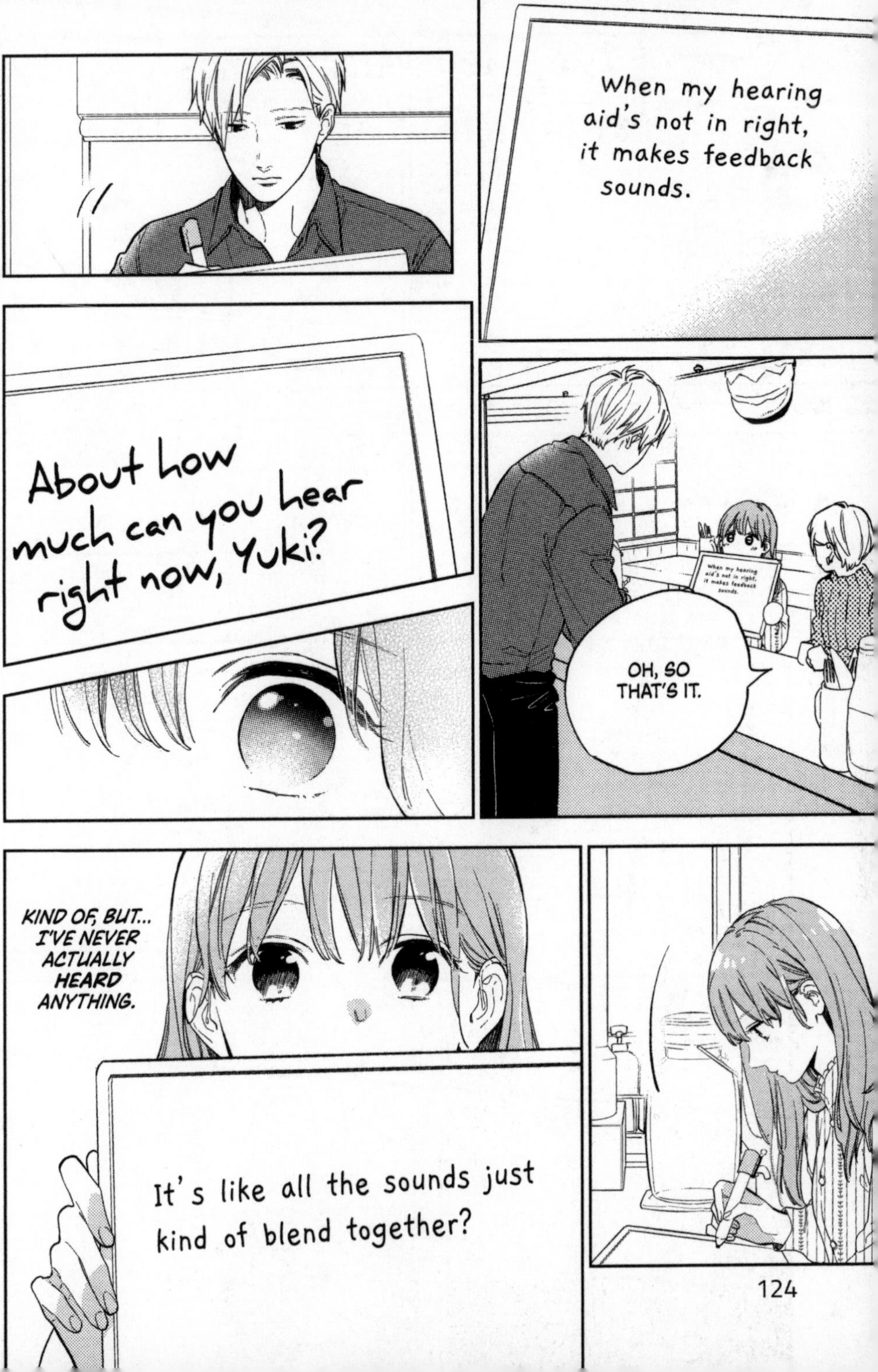
When my hearing aid's not in right, it makes feedback sounds.
OH, SO THAT'S IT.
About how much can you hear right now, Yuki?
KIND OF, BUT... I'VE NEVER ACTUALLY HEARD ANYTHING.
It's like all the sounds just kind of blend together?

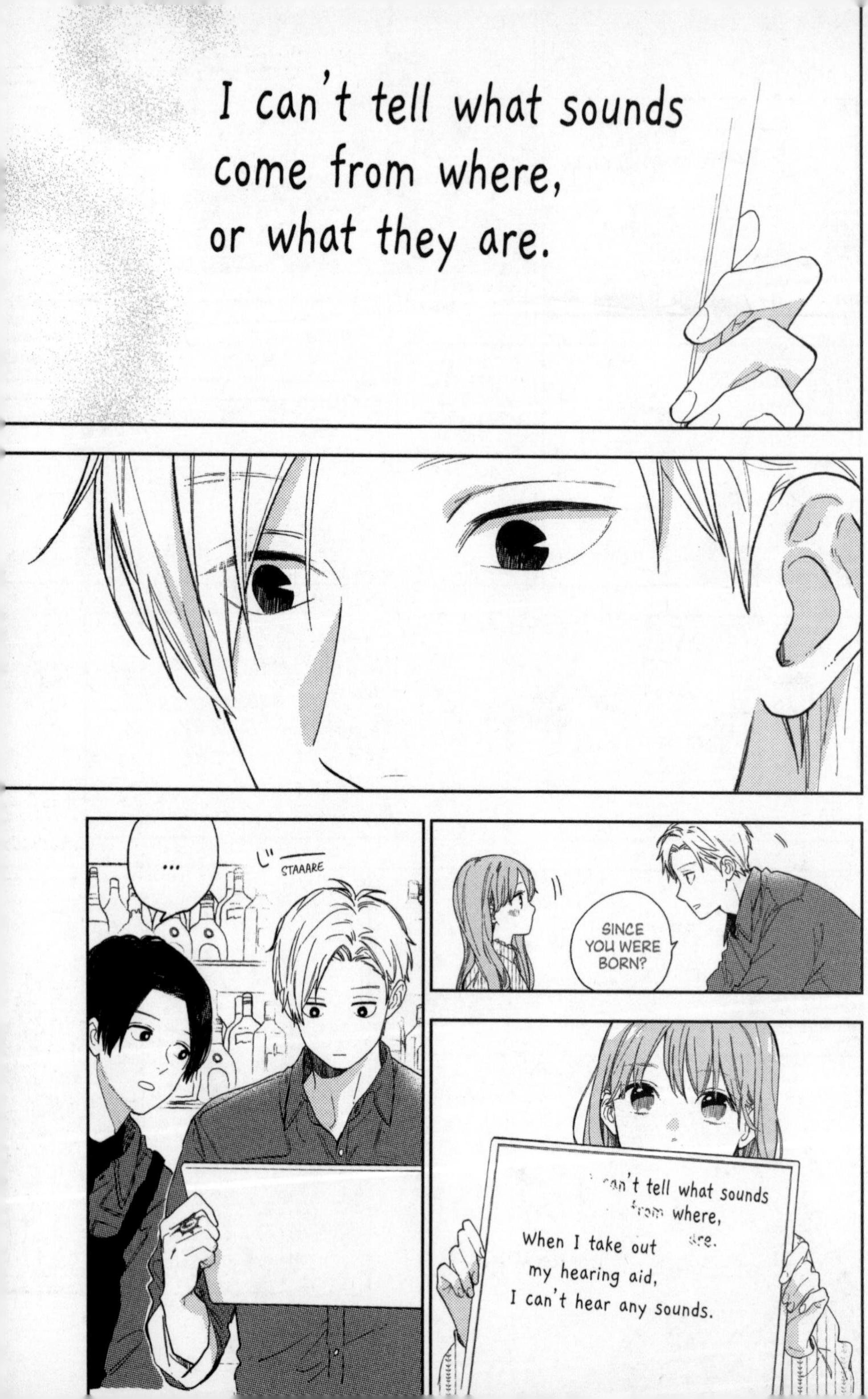
I can't tell what sounds come from where, or what they are.
SINCE YOU WERE BORN?
can't tell what sounds
from where,
When I take out my hearing aid, I can't hear any sounds.
...
じ
STAAARE

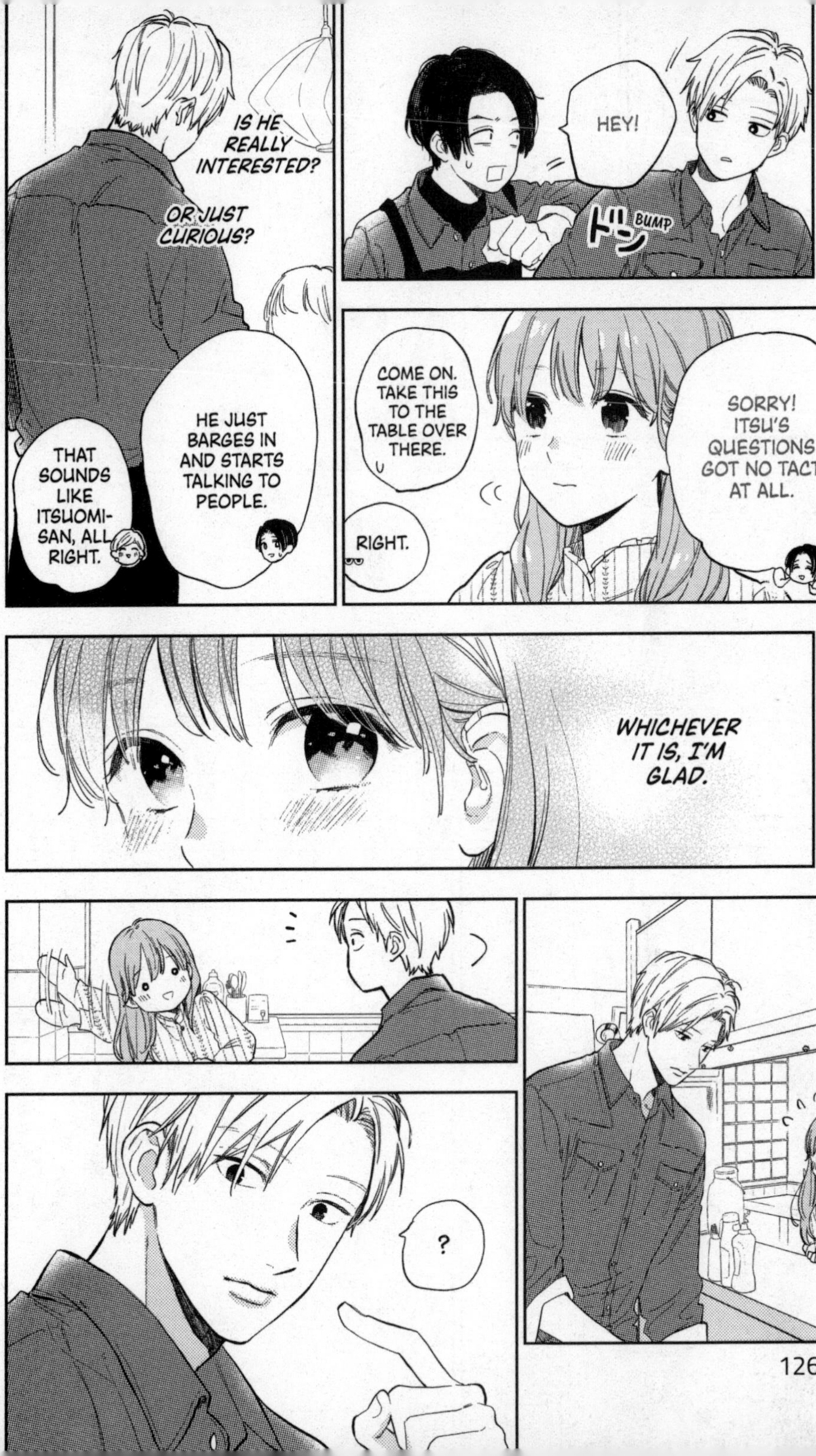
HEY!
ドン BUMP
SORRY! ITSU'S QUESTIONS GOT NO TACT AT ALL.
COME ON. TAKE THIS TO THE TABLE OVER THERE.
RIGHT.
IS HE REALLY INTERESTED?
OR JUST CURIOUS?
HE JUST BARGES IN AND STARTS TALKING TO PEOPLE.
THAT SOUNDS LIKE ITSUOMI-SAN, ALL RIGHT.
WHICHEVER IT IS, I'M GLAD.
?

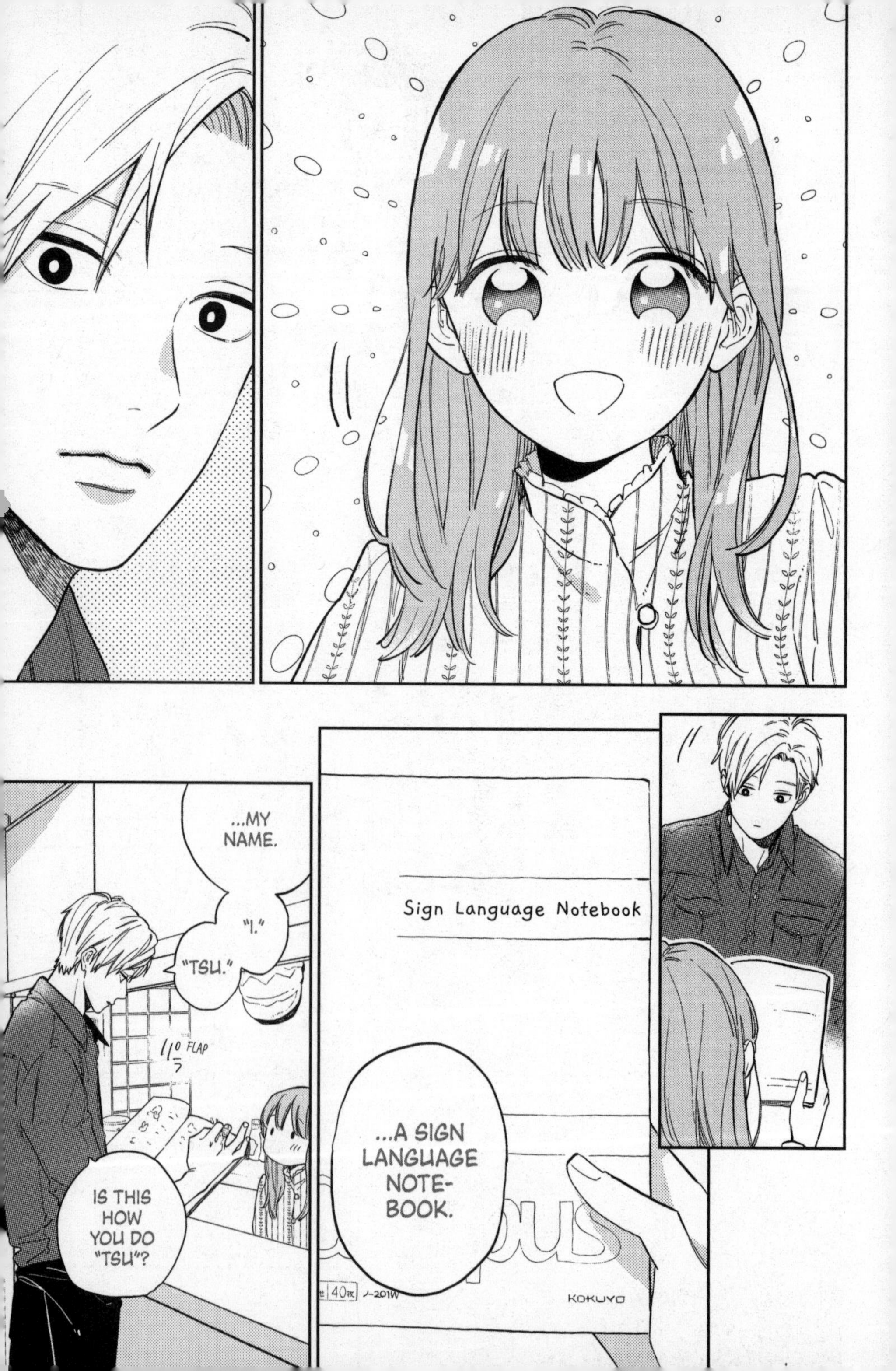
Sign Language Notebook
...A SIGN LANGUAGE NOTEBOOK.
KOKUYO
...MY NAME.
"I."
"TSU."
FLAP
IS THIS HOW YOU DO "TSU"?

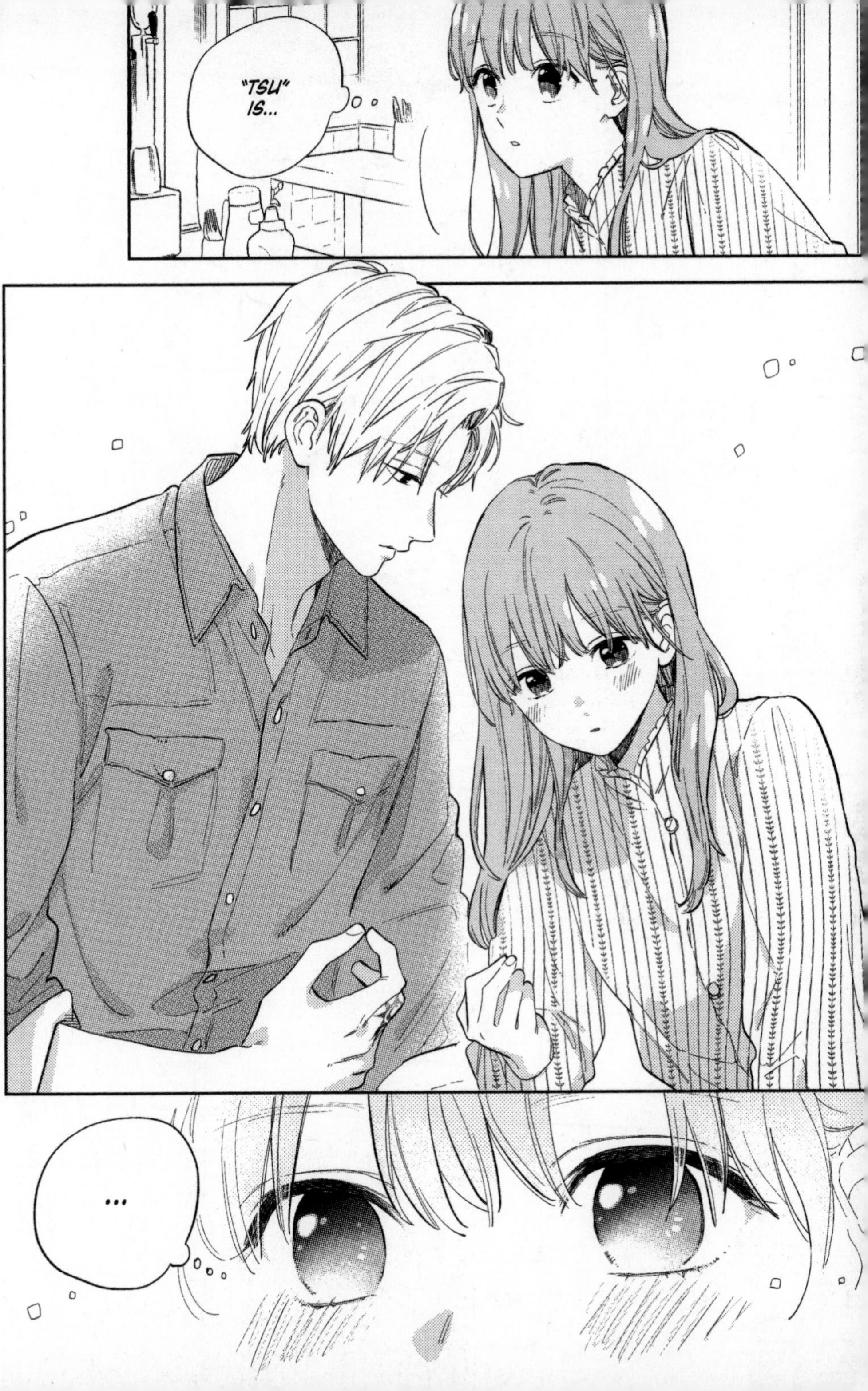
"TSU" IS...
...

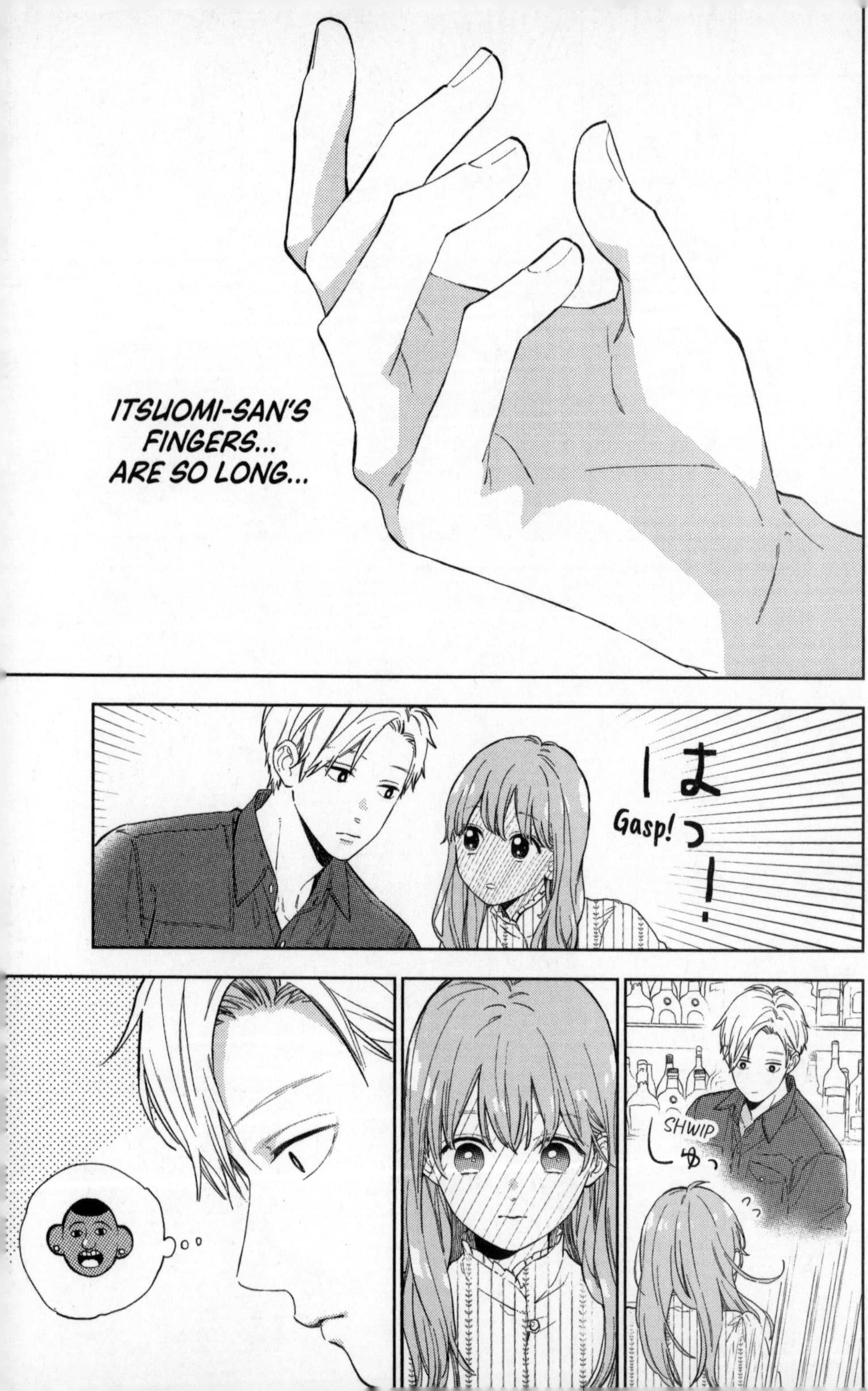
ITSUOMI-SAN'S FINGERS... ARE SO LONG...
はっ!
Gasp!
SHWIP
ゆっ

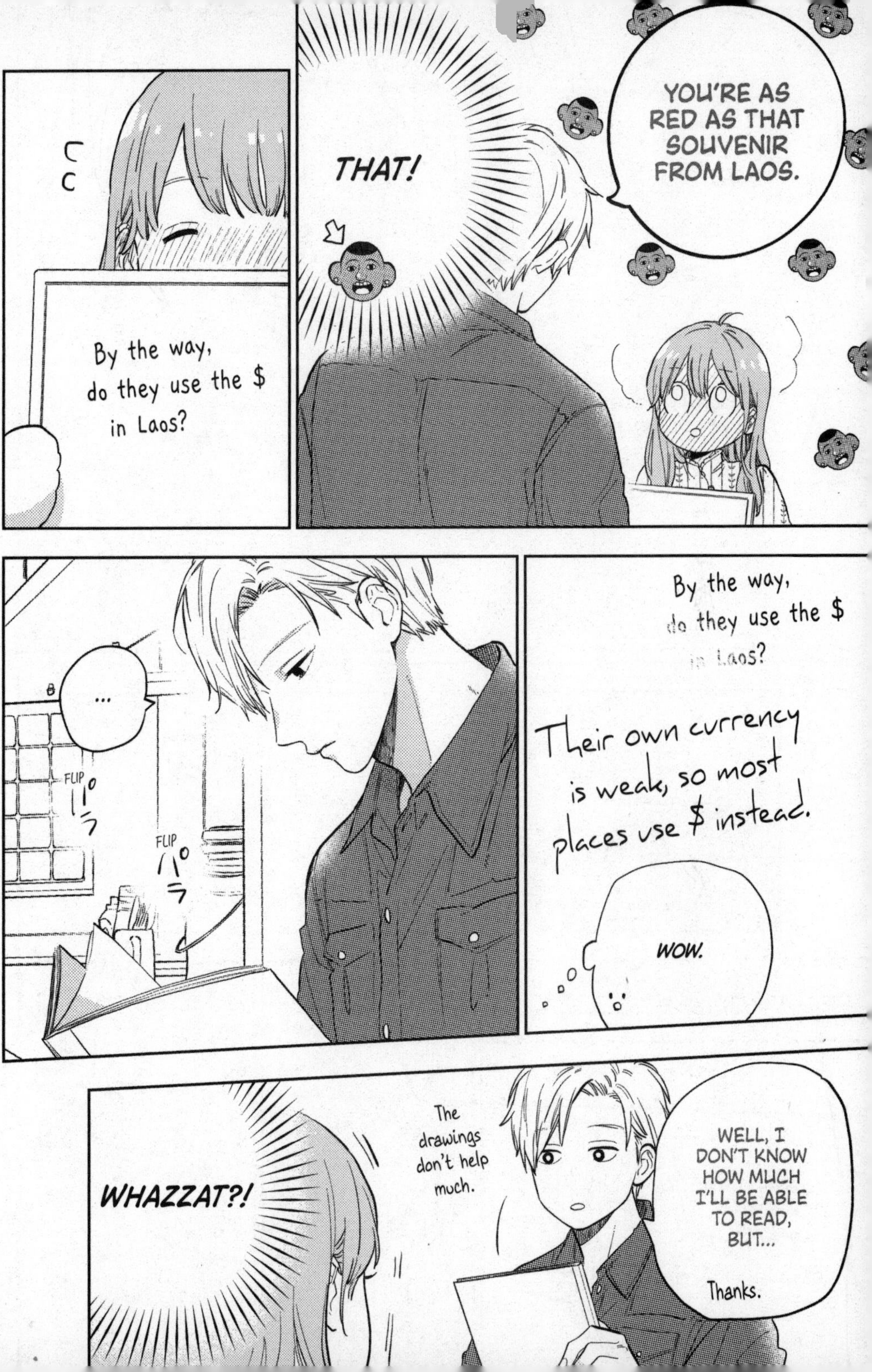
YOU'RE AS RED AS THAT SOUVENIR FROM LAOS.
THAT!
By the way, do they use the $ in Laos?
By the way, do they use the $ in Laos?
Their own currency is weak, so most places use $ instead.
WOW.
...
FLIP
FLIP
WELL, I DON'T KNOW HOW MUCH I'LL BE ABLE TO READ, BUT...
Thanks.
The drawings don't help much.
WHAZZAT?!

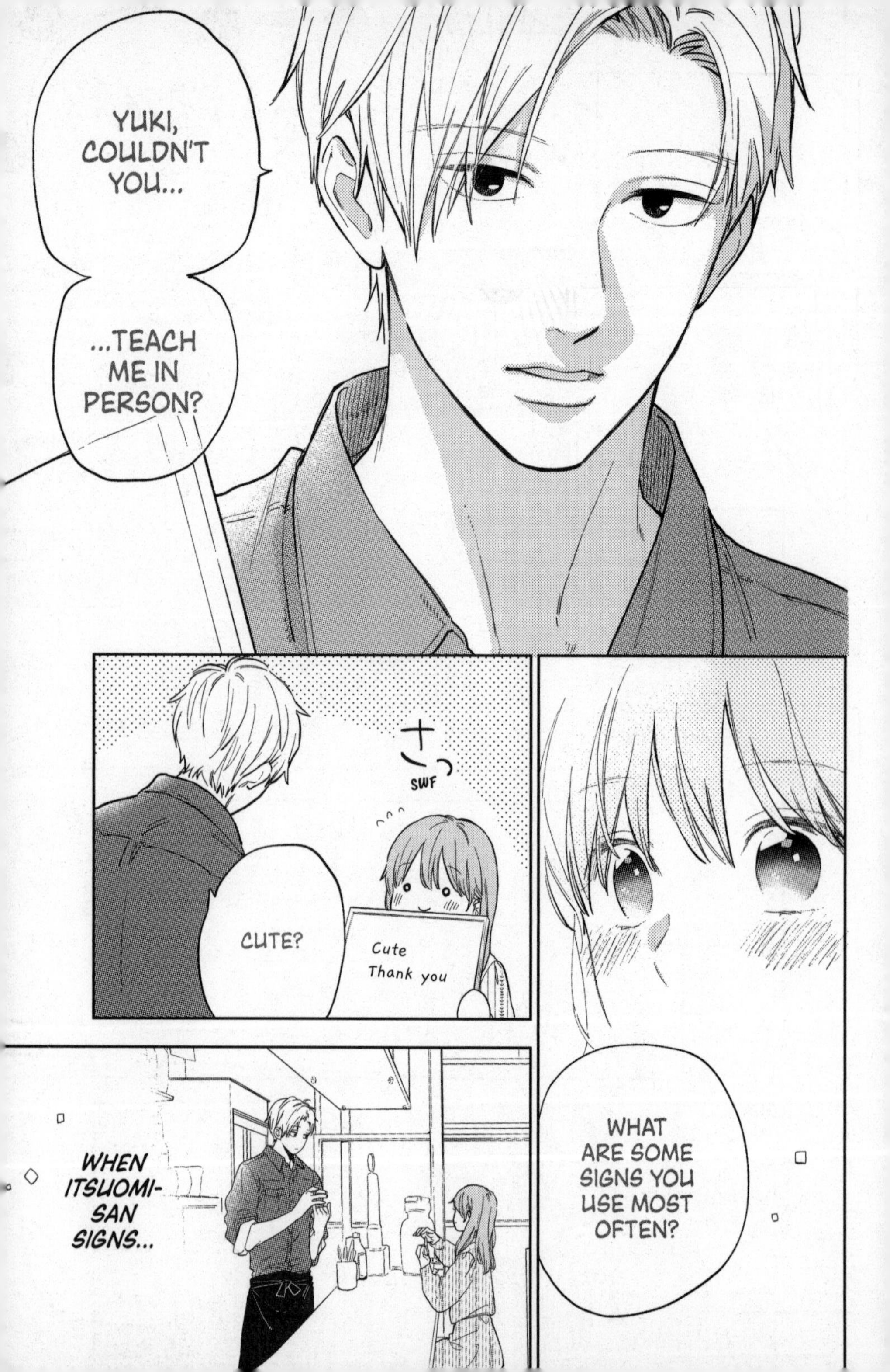
YUKI, COULDN'T YOU...
...TEACH ME IN PERSON?
WHAT ARE SOME SIGNS YOU USE MOST OFTEN?
さっ
SWF
Cute
Thank you
CUTE?
WHEN ITSUOMI-SAN SIGNS...

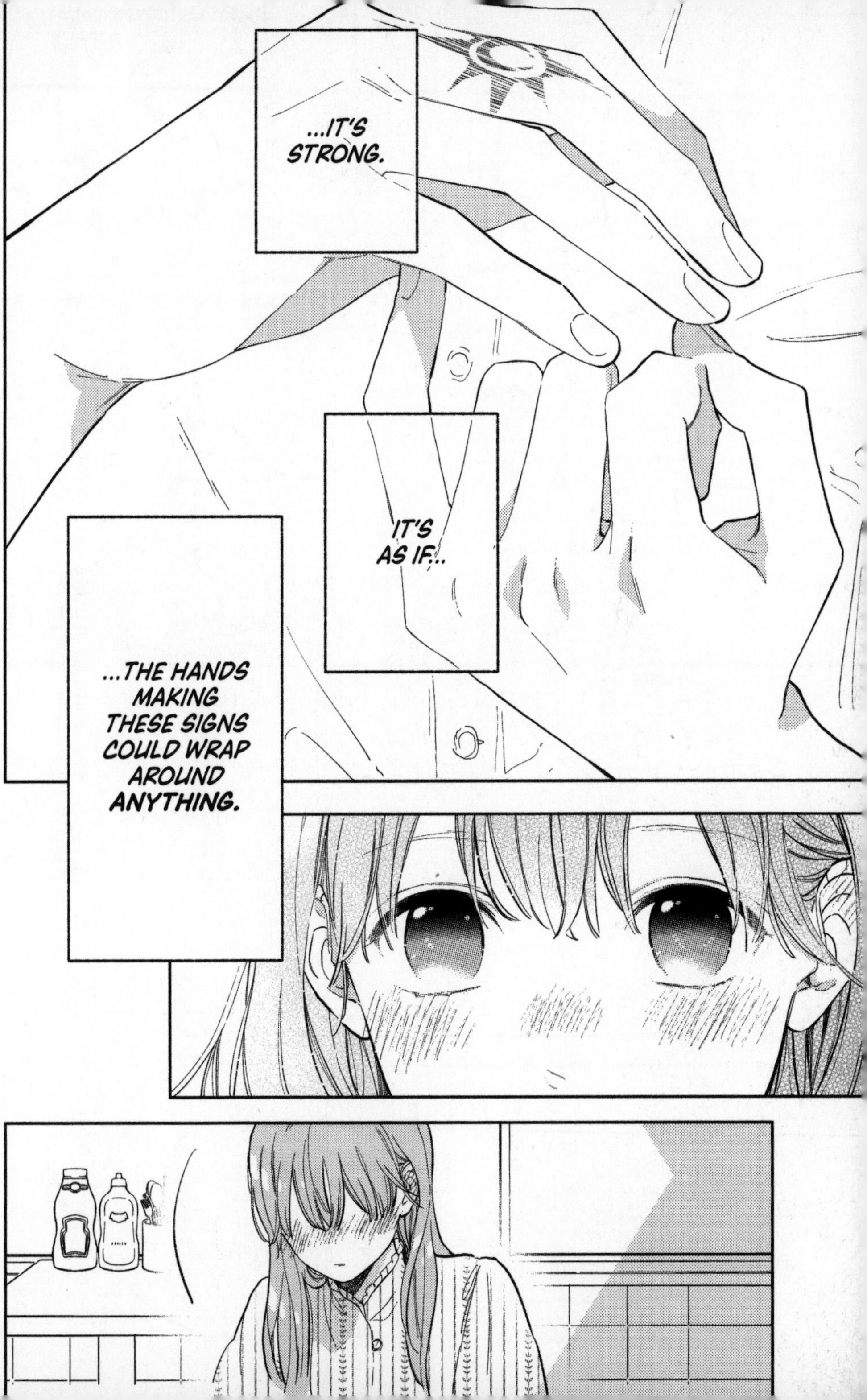
...IT'S STRONG.
IT'S AS IF...
...THE HANDS MAKING THESE SIGNS COULD WRAP AROUND ANYTHING.

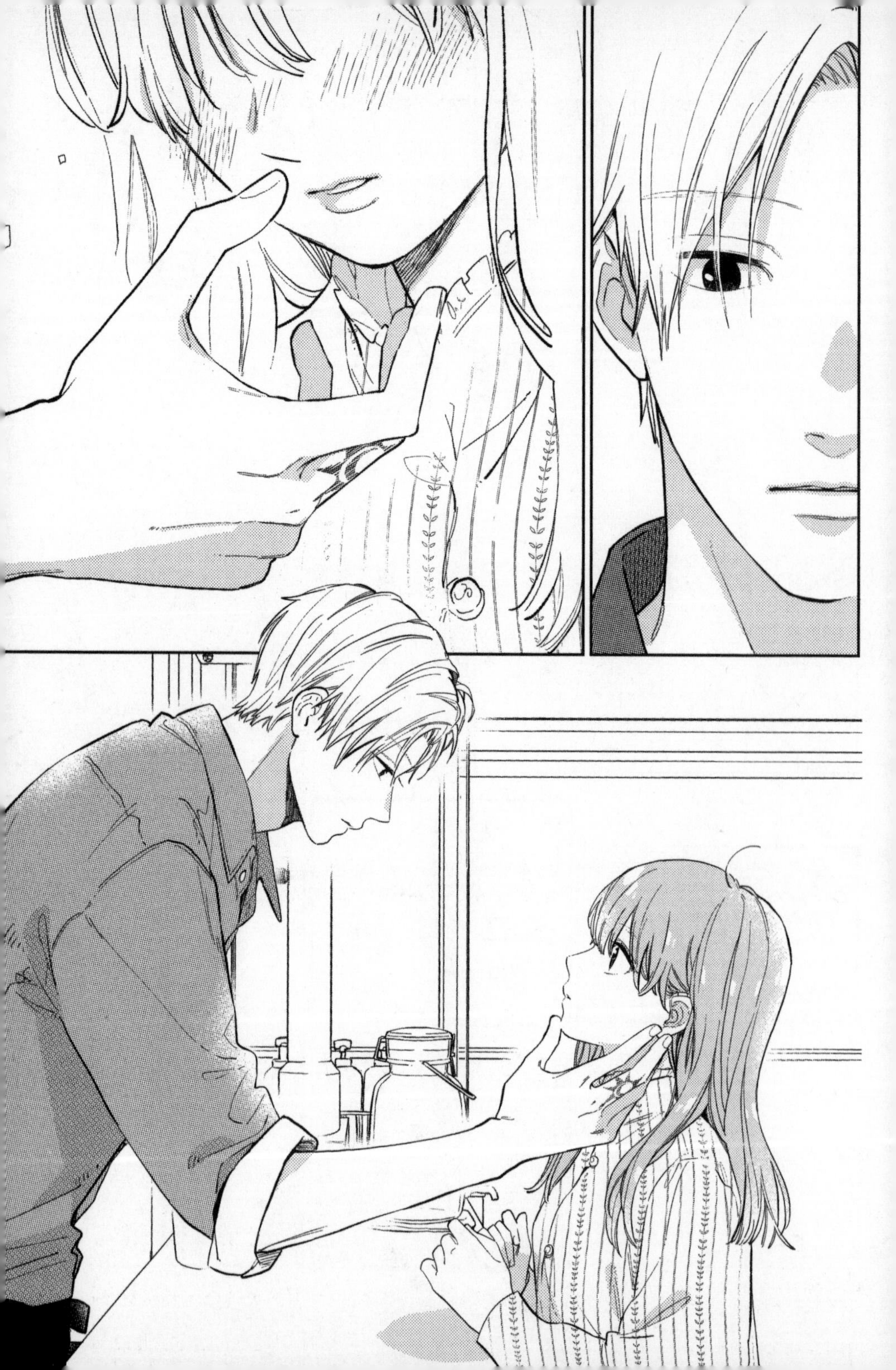

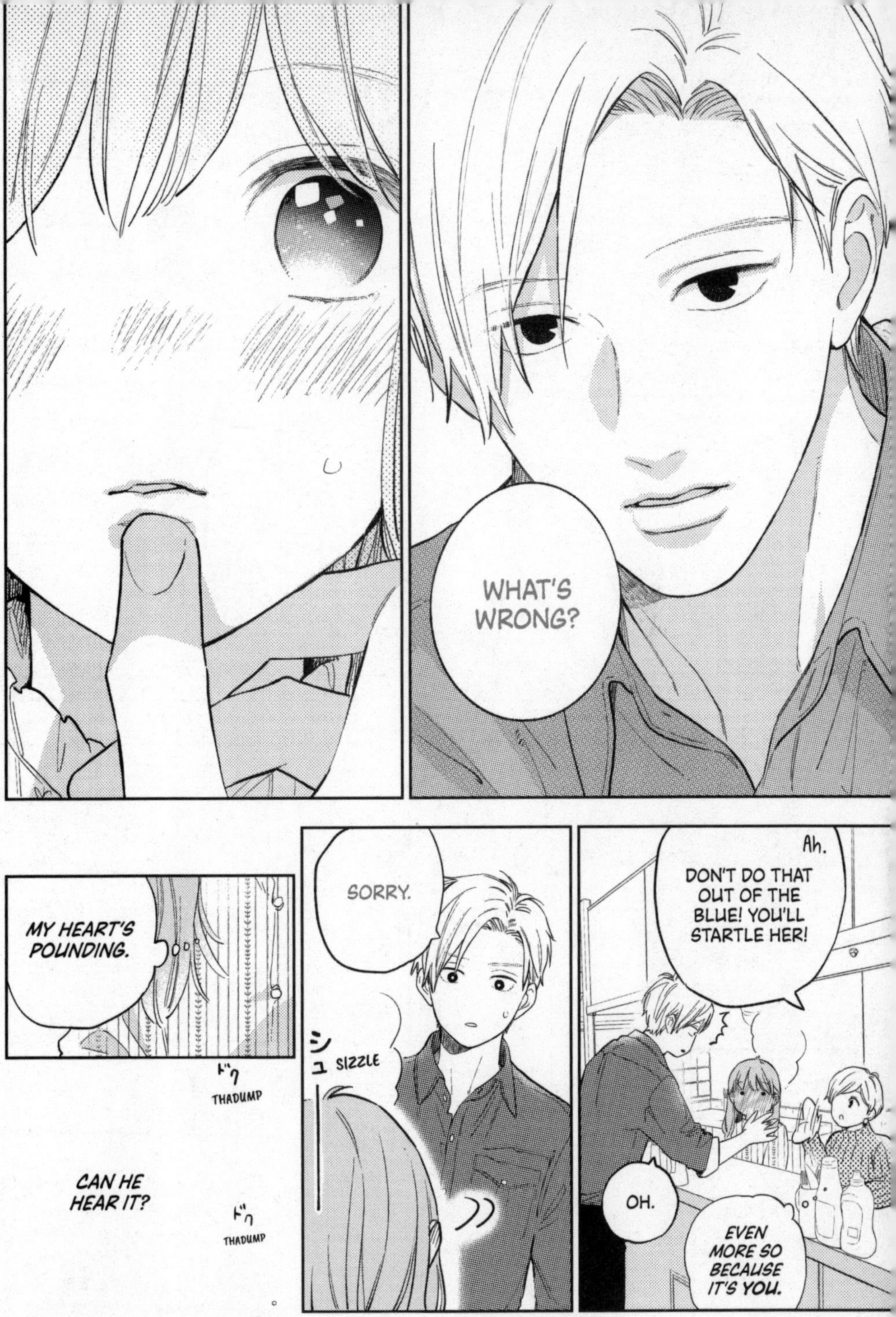
WHAT'S WRONG?
Ah.
DON'T DO THAT OUT OF THE BLUE! YOU'LL STARTLE HER!
OH.
EVEN MORE SO BECAUSE IT'S YOU.
SORRY.
シュ SIZZLE
MY HEART'S POUNDING.
ドク THADUMP
CAN HE HEAR IT?
ドク THADUMP

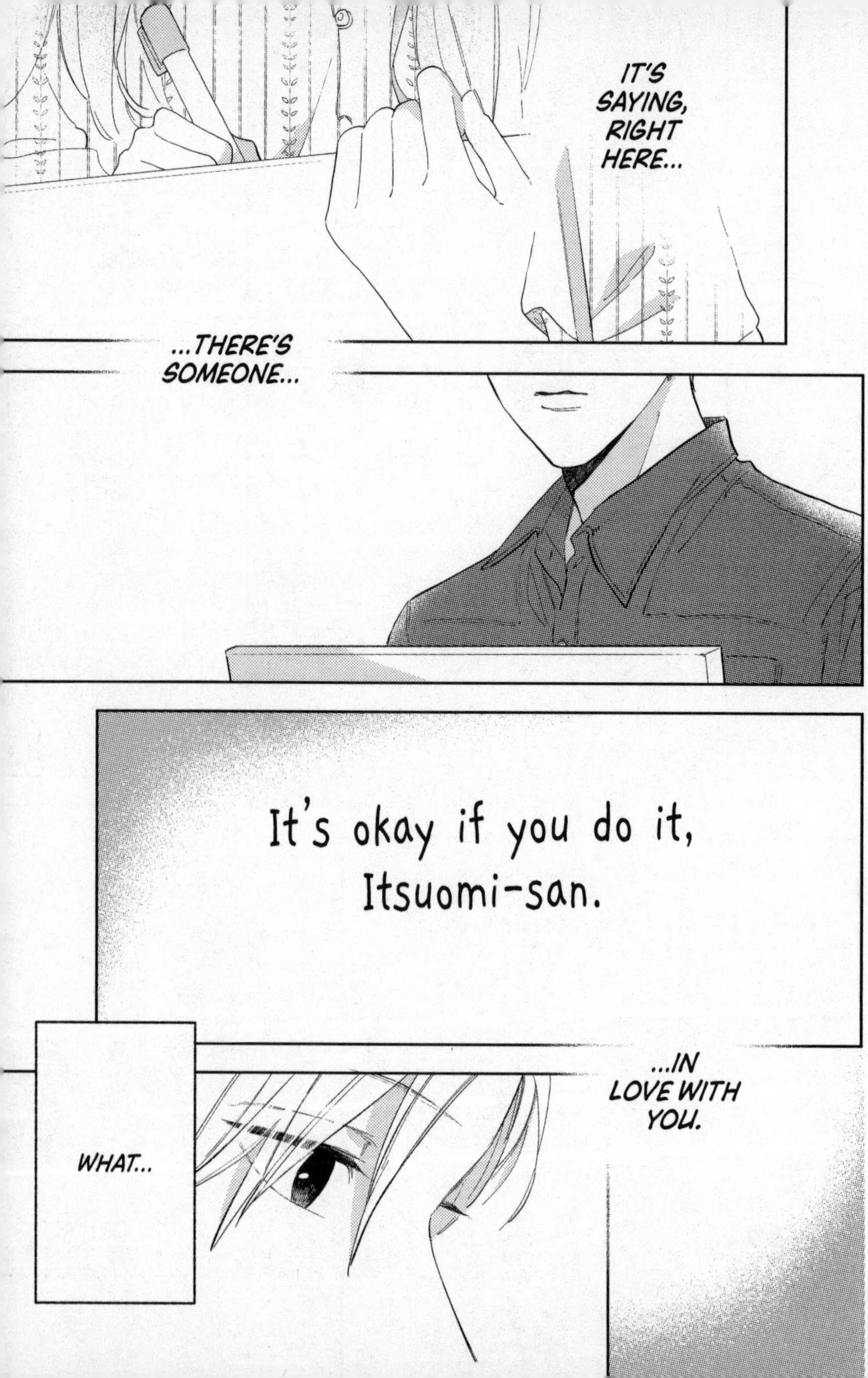
IT'S SAYING, RIGHT HERE...
...THERE'S SOMEONE...
It's okay if you do it, Itsuomi-san.
...IN LOVE WITH YOU.
WHAT...

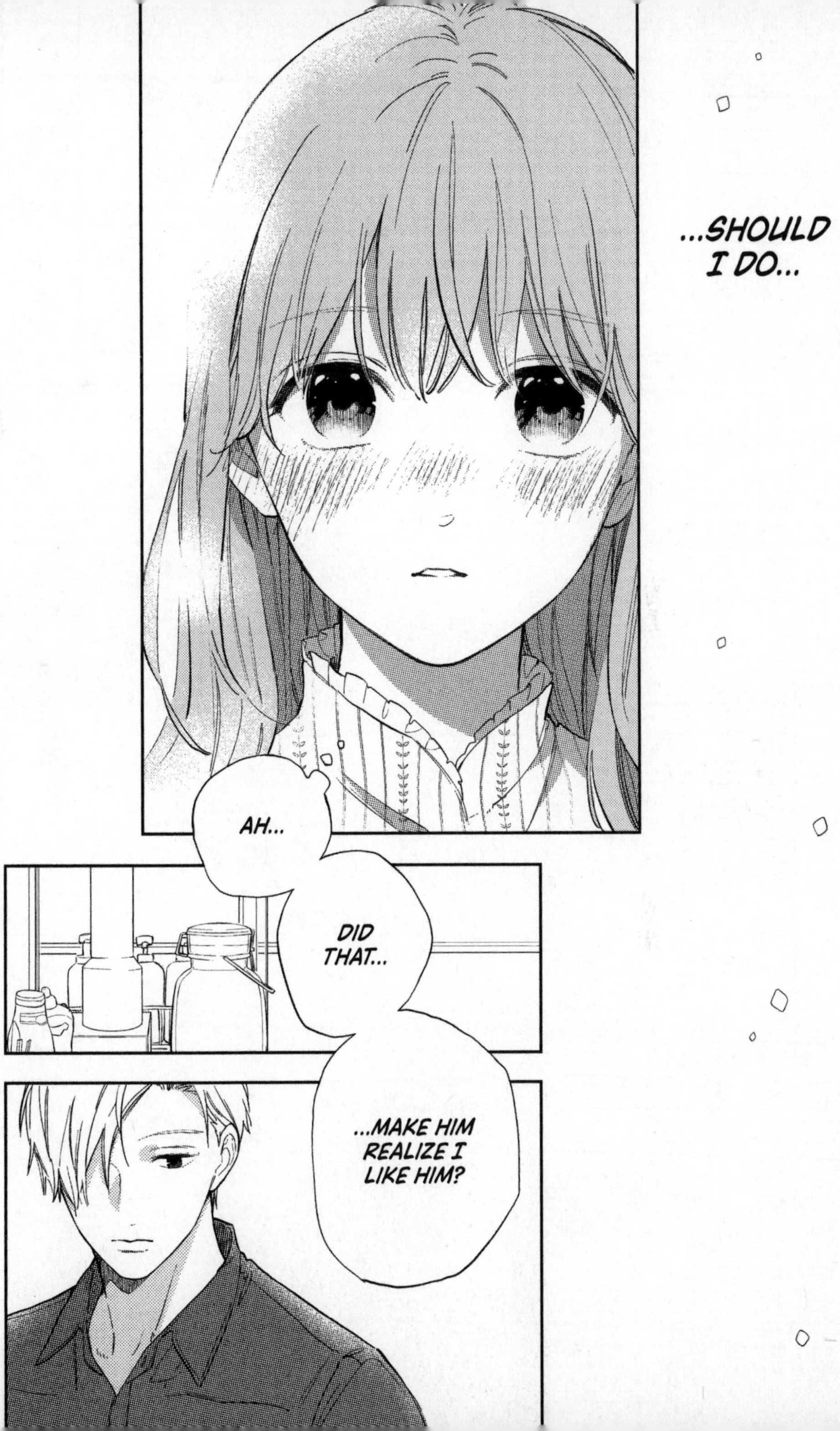
...SHOULD I DO...
AH...
DID THAT...
...MAKE HIM REALIZE I LIKE HIM?

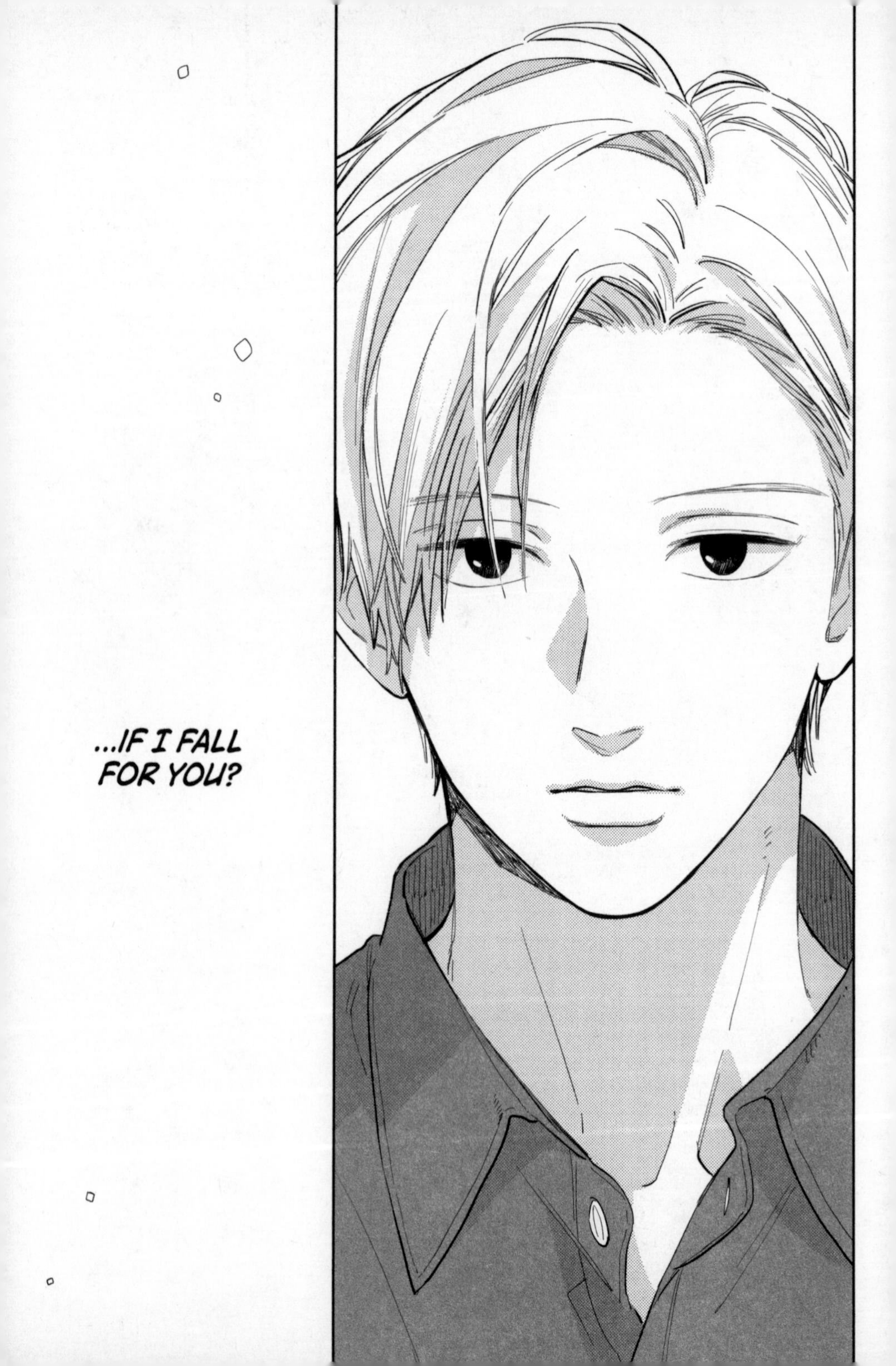
...IF I FALL FOR YOU?

Sign.4
More

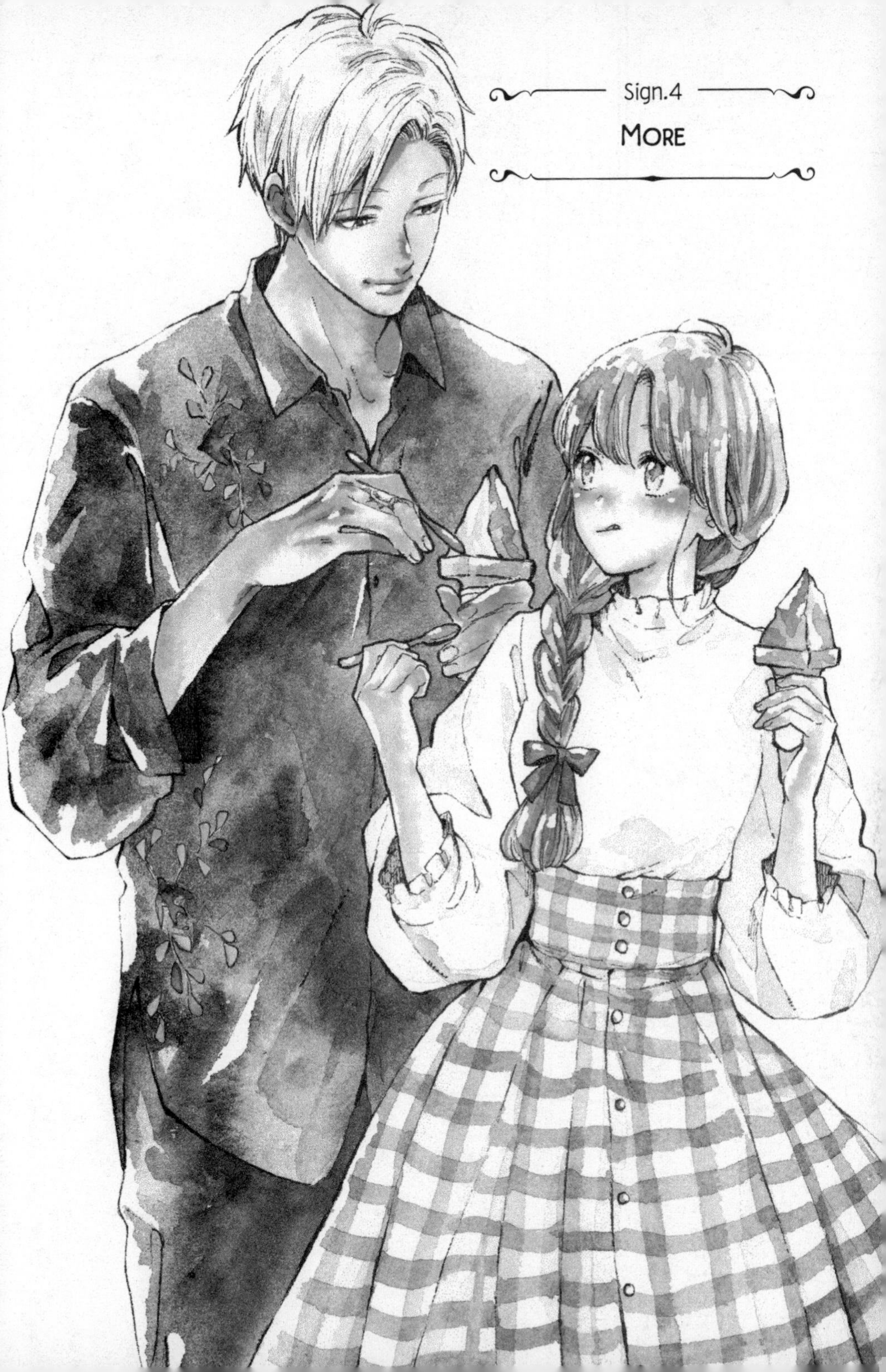

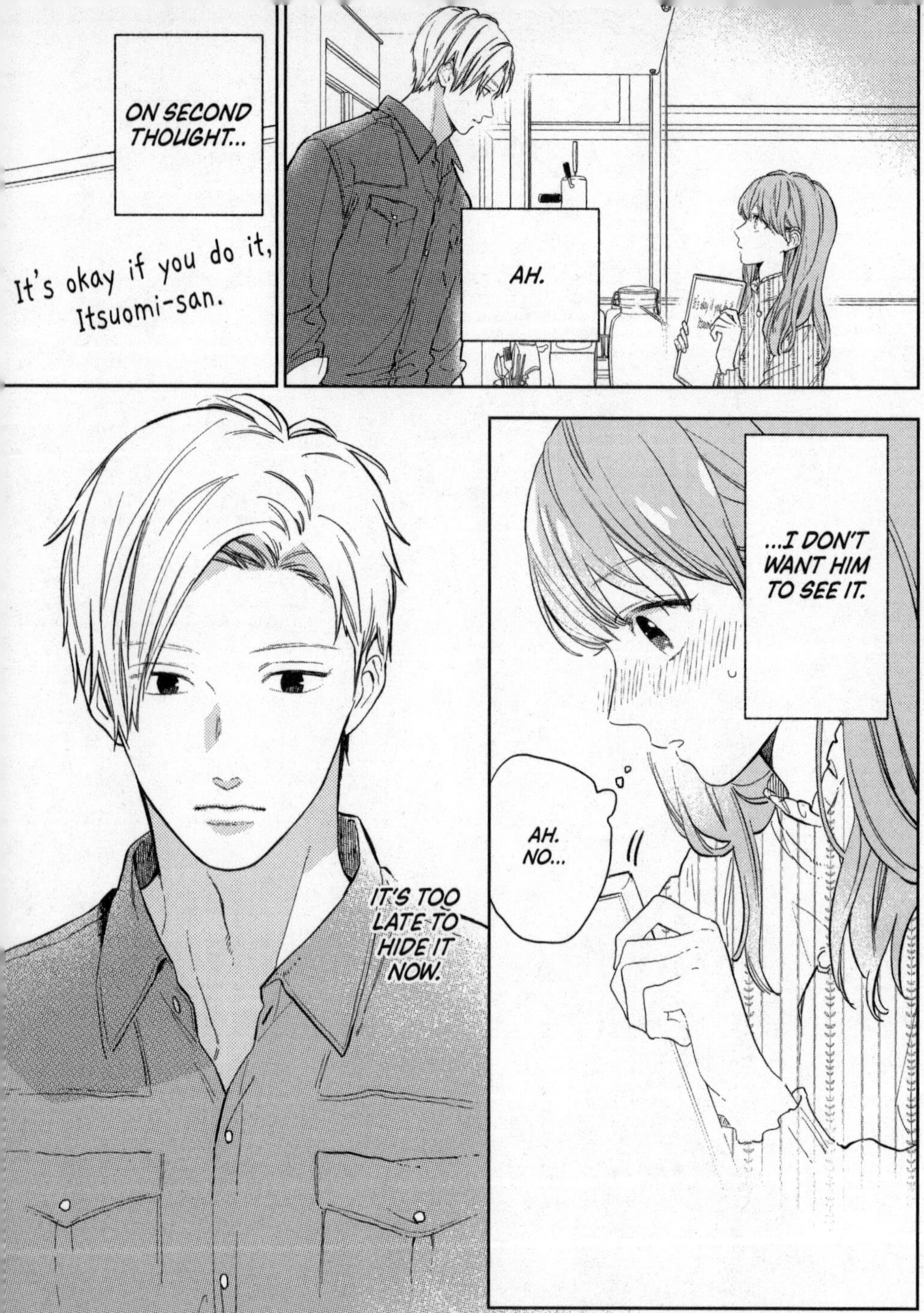
AH.
ON SECOND THOUGHT...
It's okay if you do it, Itsuomi-san.
...I DON'T WANT HIM TO SEE IT.
AH. NO...
IT'S TOO LATE TO HIDE IT NOW.

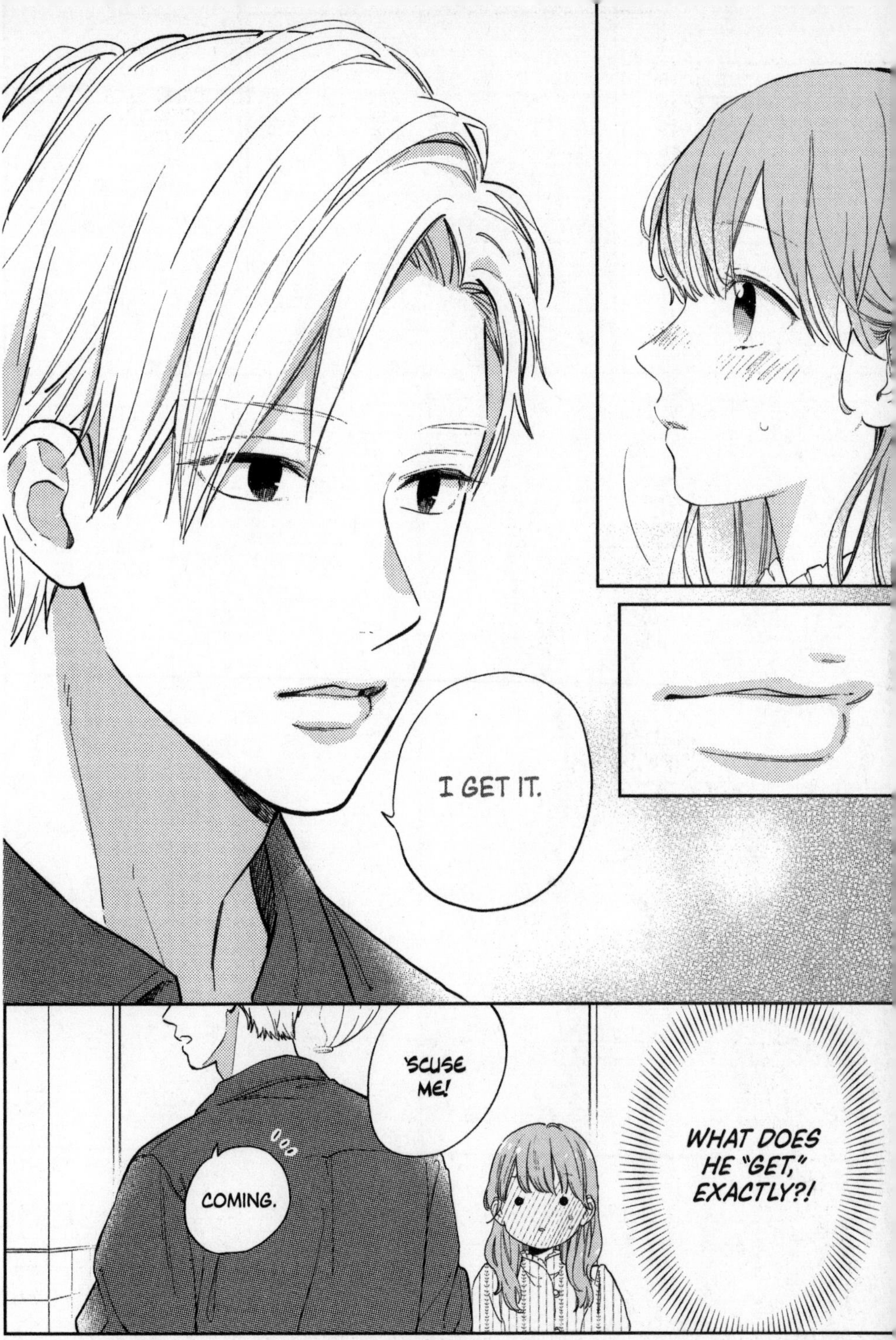
I GET IT.
WHAT DOES HE "GET," EXACTLY?!
'SCUSE ME!
COMING.

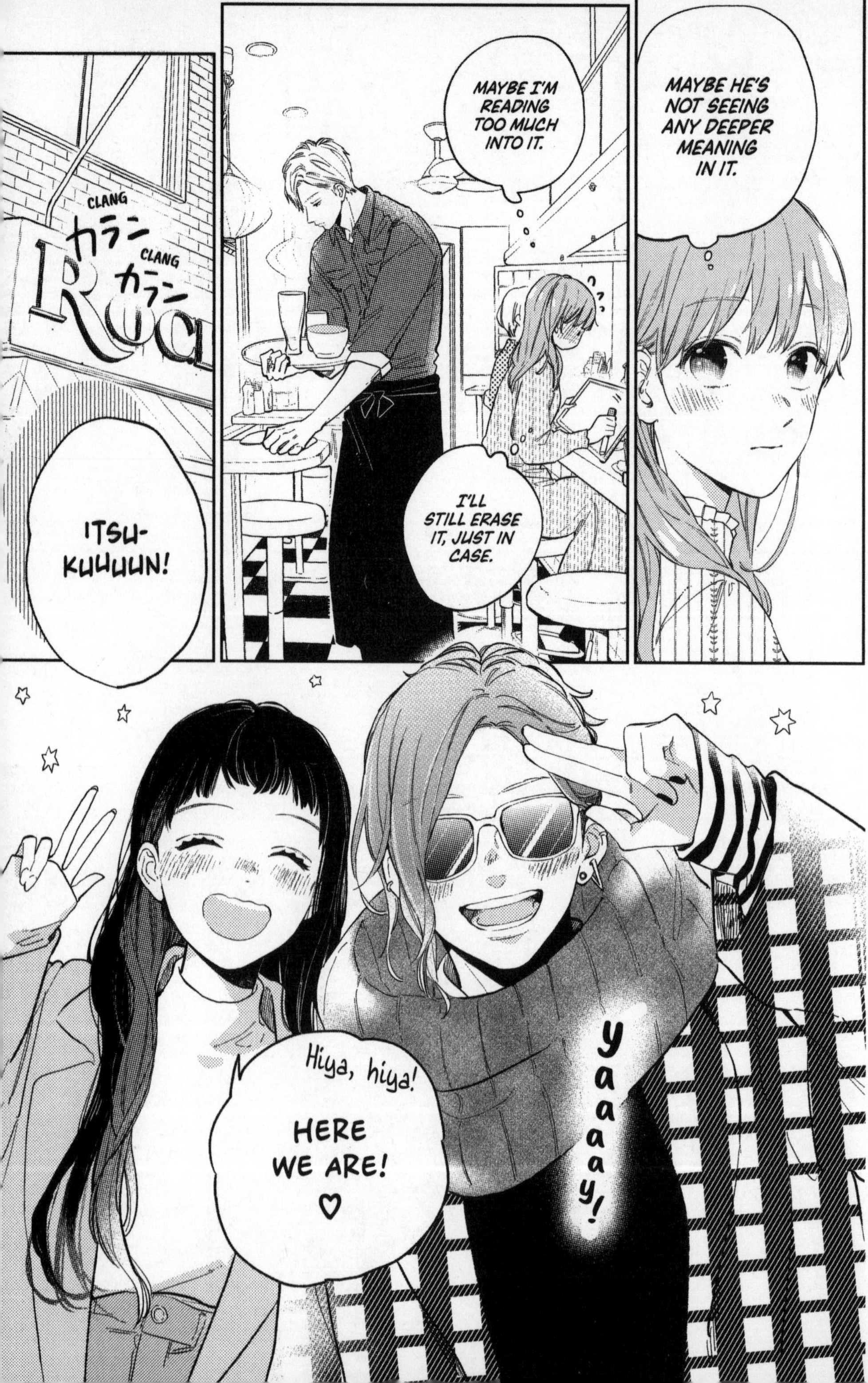
MAYBE HE'S NOT SEEING ANY DEEPER MEANING IN IT.
MAYBE I'M READING TOO MUCH INTO IT.
I'LL STILL ERASE IT, JUST IN CASE.
CLANG
カラン
CLANG
カラン
ITSU-KUUUUN!
Yaaaaay!
Hiya, hiya!
HERE WE ARE! ♡

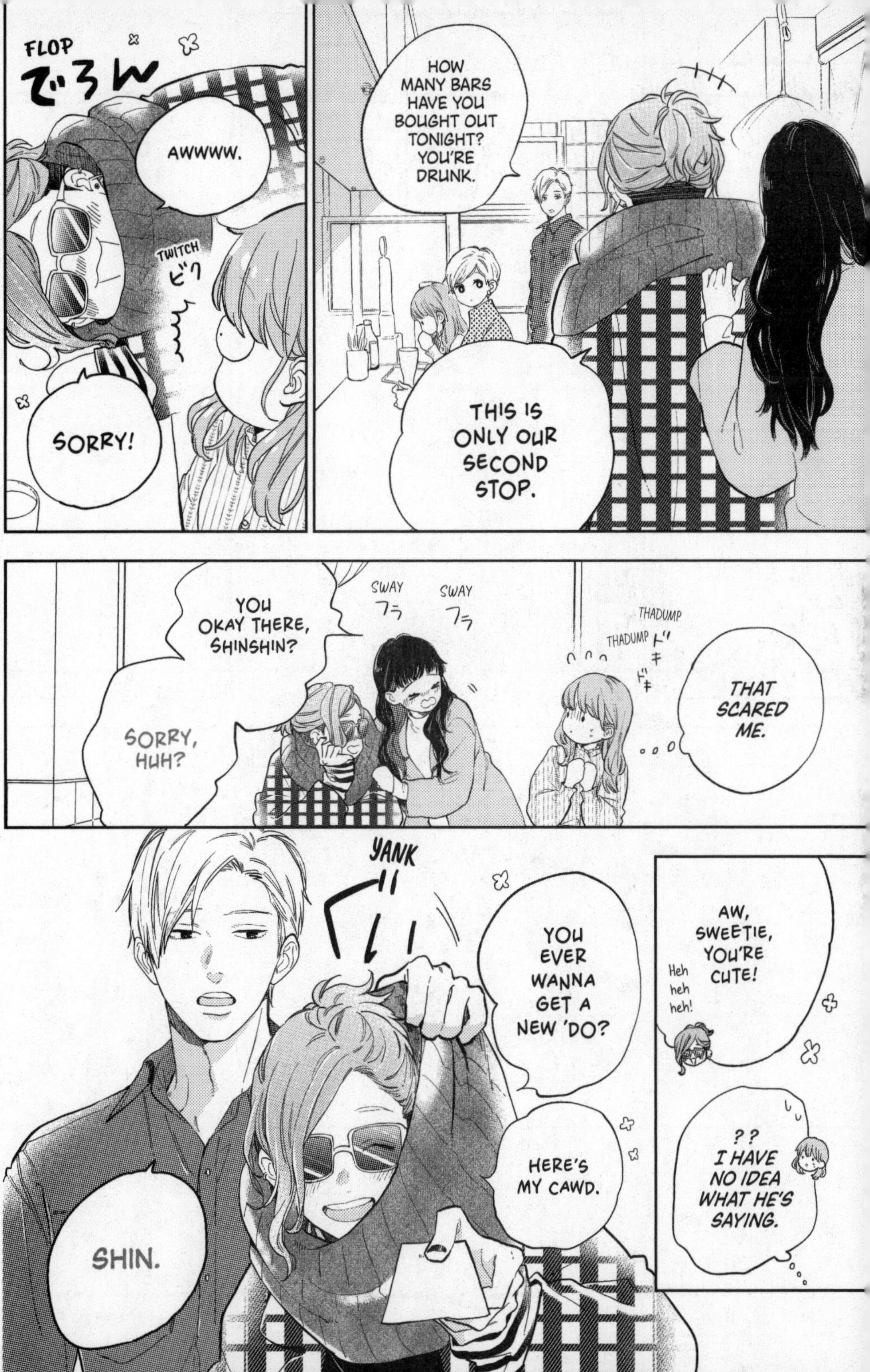
HOW MANY BARS HAVE YOU BOUGHT OUT TONIGHT? YOU'RE DRUNK.
THIS IS ONLY OUR SECOND STOP.
FLOP
でろん
AWWWW.
TWITCH
ビク
SORRY!
THADUMP
ドキ
THADUMP
ドキ
THAT SCARED ME.
SWAY
フラ
SWAY
フラ
YOU OKAY THERE, SHINSHIN?
SORRY, HUH?
AW, SWEETIE, YOU'RE CUTE!
Heh heh heh!
?? I HAVE NO IDEA WHAT HE'S SAYING.
YANK
YOU EVER WANNA GET A NEW 'DO?
HERE'S MY CAWD.
SHIN.

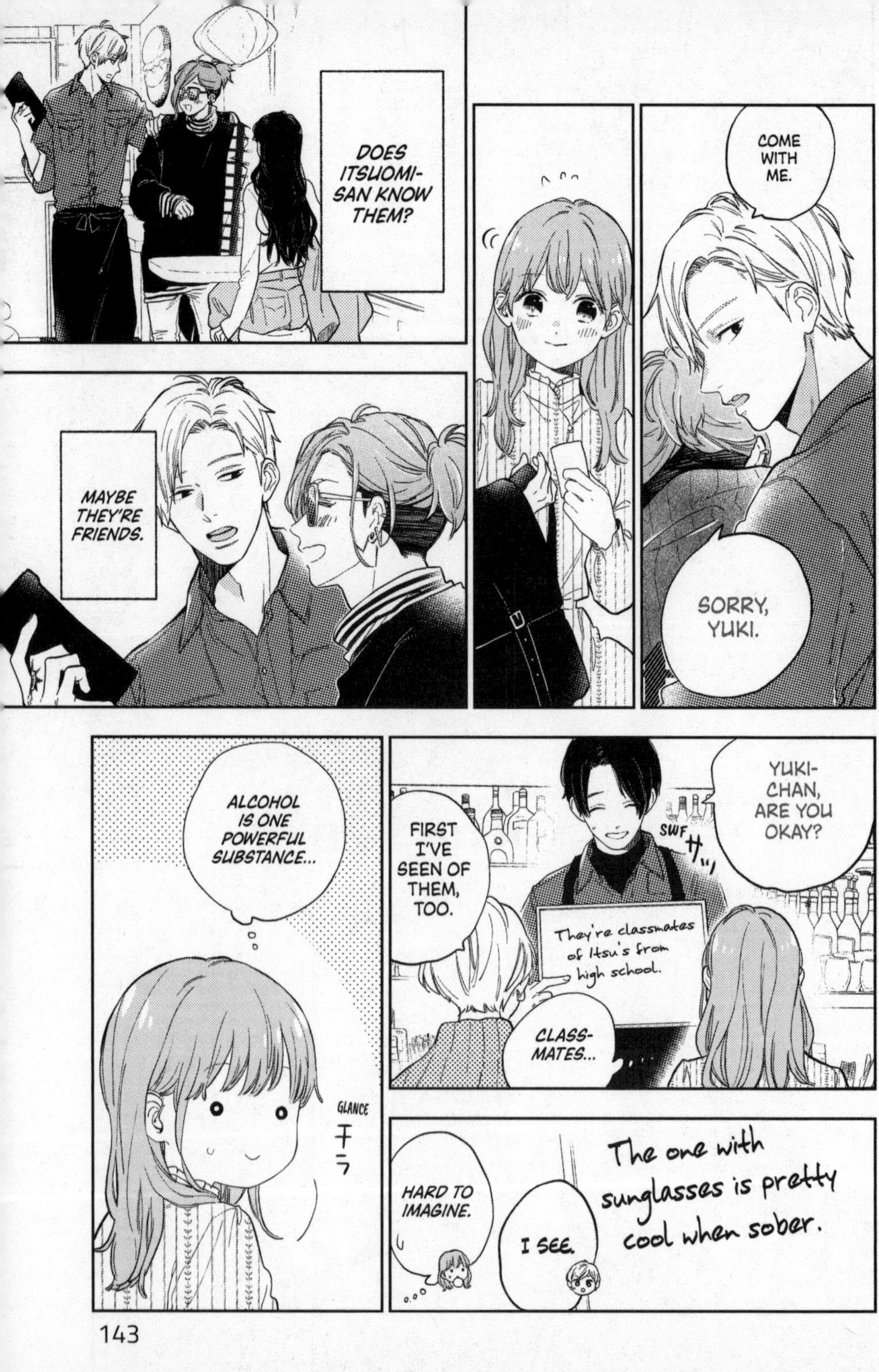
DOES ITSUOMI-SAN KNOW THEM?
MAYBE THEY'RE FRIENDS.
COME WITH ME.
SORRY, YUKI.
YUKI-CHAN, ARE YOU OKAY?
SWF
サッ
FIRST I'VE SEEN OF THEM, TOO.
They're classmates of Itsu's from high school.
CLASS-MATES...
The one with sunglasses is pretty cool when sober.
I SEE.
HARD TO IMAGINE.
ALCOHOL IS ONE POWERFUL SUBSTANCE...
GLANCE
チラ

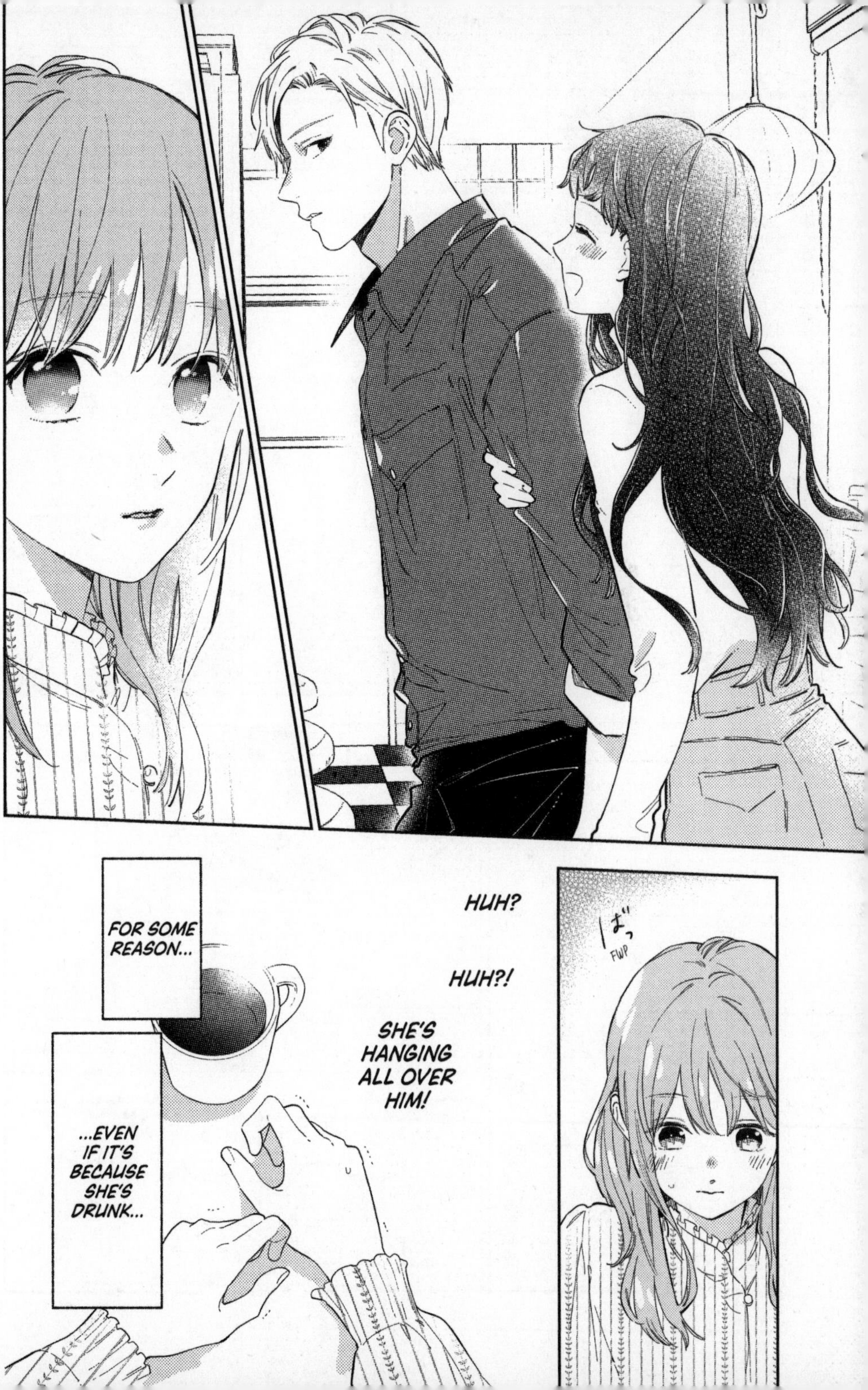
HUH?
ぱっ
FWP
HUH?!
SHE'S HANGING ALL OVER HIM!
FOR SOME REASON...
...EVEN IF IT'S BECAUSE SHE'S DRUNK...

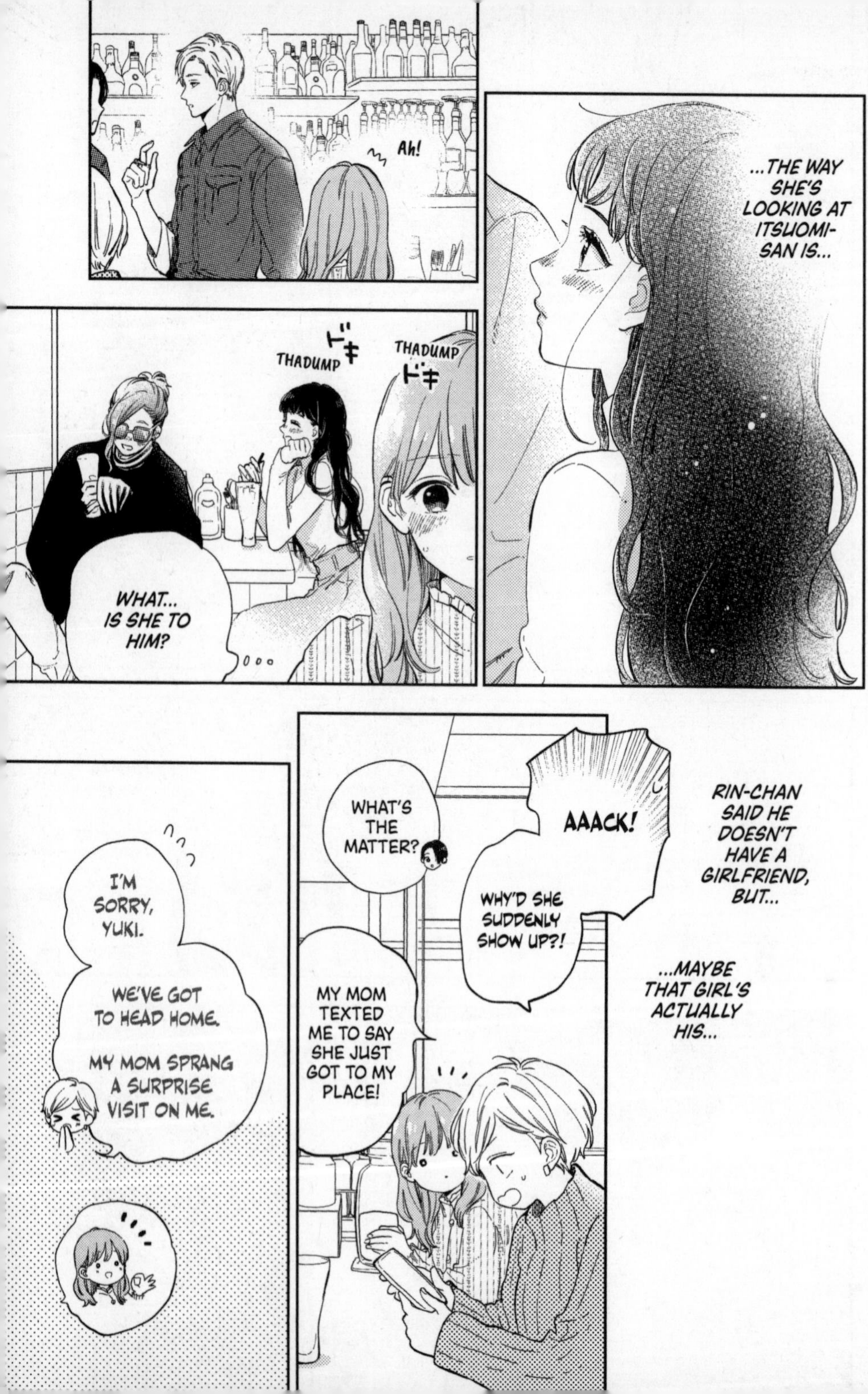
Ah!
...THE WAY SHE'S LOOKING AT ITSUOMI-SAN IS...
THADUMP
ドキ
THADUMP
ドキ
WHAT... IS SHE TO HIM?
RIN-CHAN SAID HE DOESN'T HAVE A GIRLFRIEND, BUT...
...MAYBE THAT GIRL'S ACTUALLY HIS...
AAACK!
WHY'D SHE SUDDENLY SHOW UP?!
WHAT'S THE MATTER?
MY MOM TEXTED ME TO SAY SHE JUST GOT TO MY PLACE!
I'M SORRY, YUKI.
WE'VE GOT TO HEAD HOME.
MY MOM SPRANG A SURPRISE VISIT ON ME.

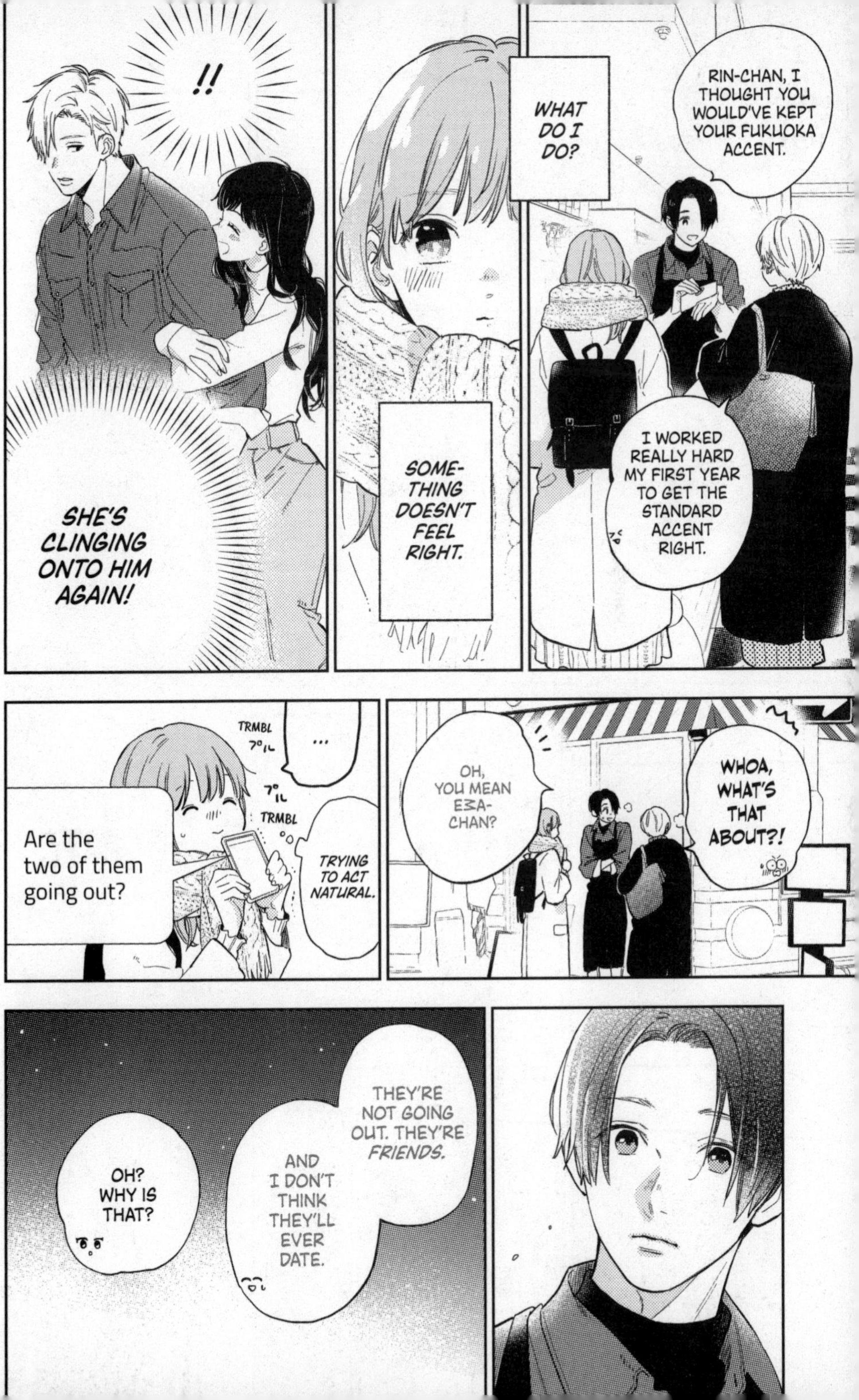
RIN-CHAN, I THOUGHT YOU WOULD'VE KEPT YOUR FUKUOKA ACCENT.
I WORKED REALLY HARD MY FIRST YEAR TO GET THE STANDARD ACCENT RIGHT.
WHAT DO I DO?
SOMETHING DOESN'T FEEL RIGHT.
!!
SHE'S CLINGING ONTO HIM AGAIN!
WHOA, WHAT'S THAT ABOUT?!
OH, YOU MEAN EMA-CHAN?
...
TRMBL
TRMBL
TRYING TO ACT NATURAL.
Are the two of them going out?
THEY'RE NOT GOING OUT. THEY'RE *FRIENDS.*
AND I DON'T THINK THEY'LL EVER DATE.
OH? WHY IS THAT?

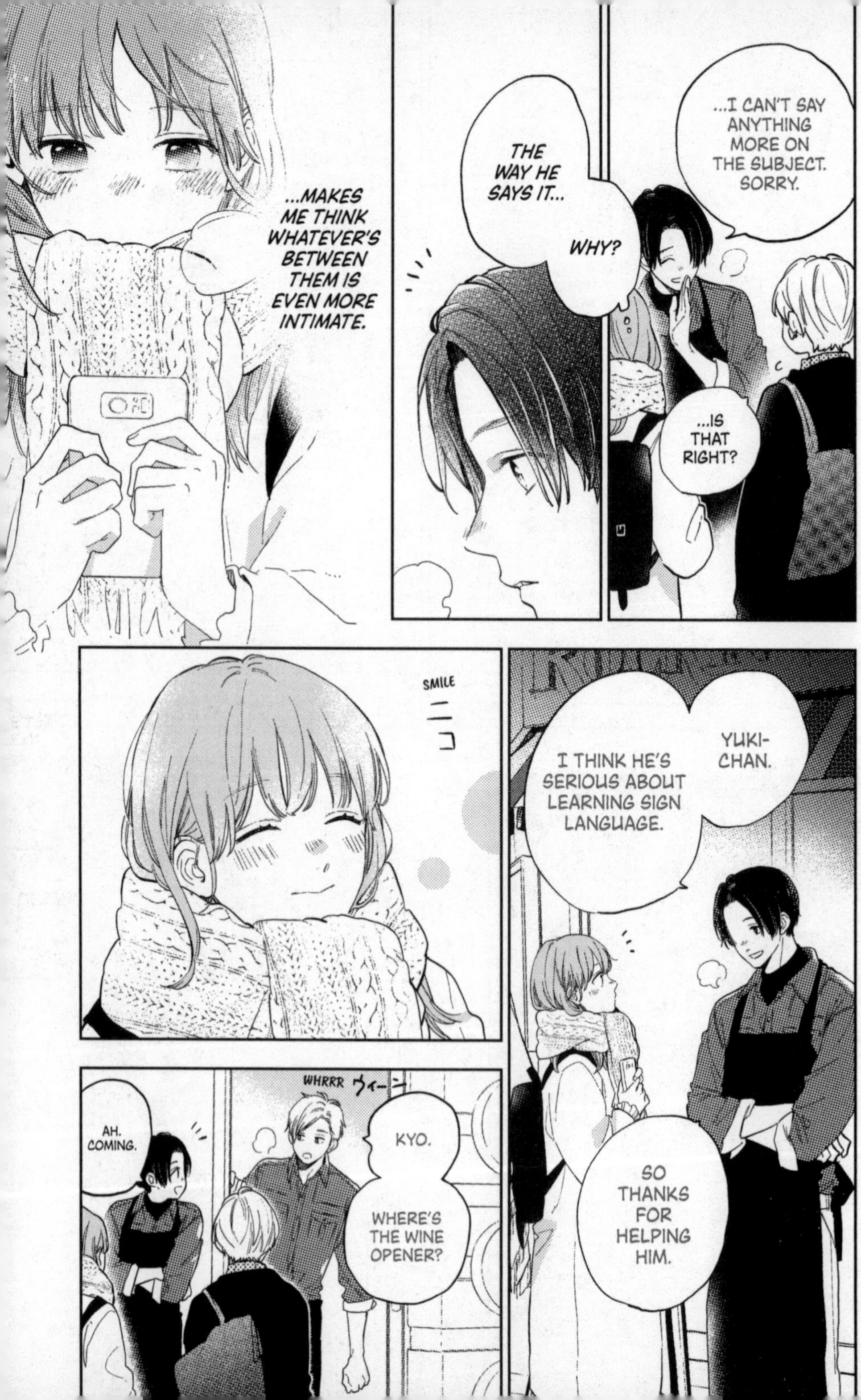
...I CAN'T SAY ANYTHING MORE ON THE SUBJECT. SORRY.
...IS THAT RIGHT?
THE WAY HE SAYS IT...
WHY?
...MAKES ME THINK WHATEVER'S BETWEEN THEM IS EVEN MORE INTIMATE.
YUKI-CHAN.
I THINK HE'S SERIOUS ABOUT LEARNING SIGN LANGUAGE.
SO THANKS FOR HELPING HIM.
SMILE
WHRRR
KYO.
WHERE'S THE WINE OPENER?
AH. COMING.

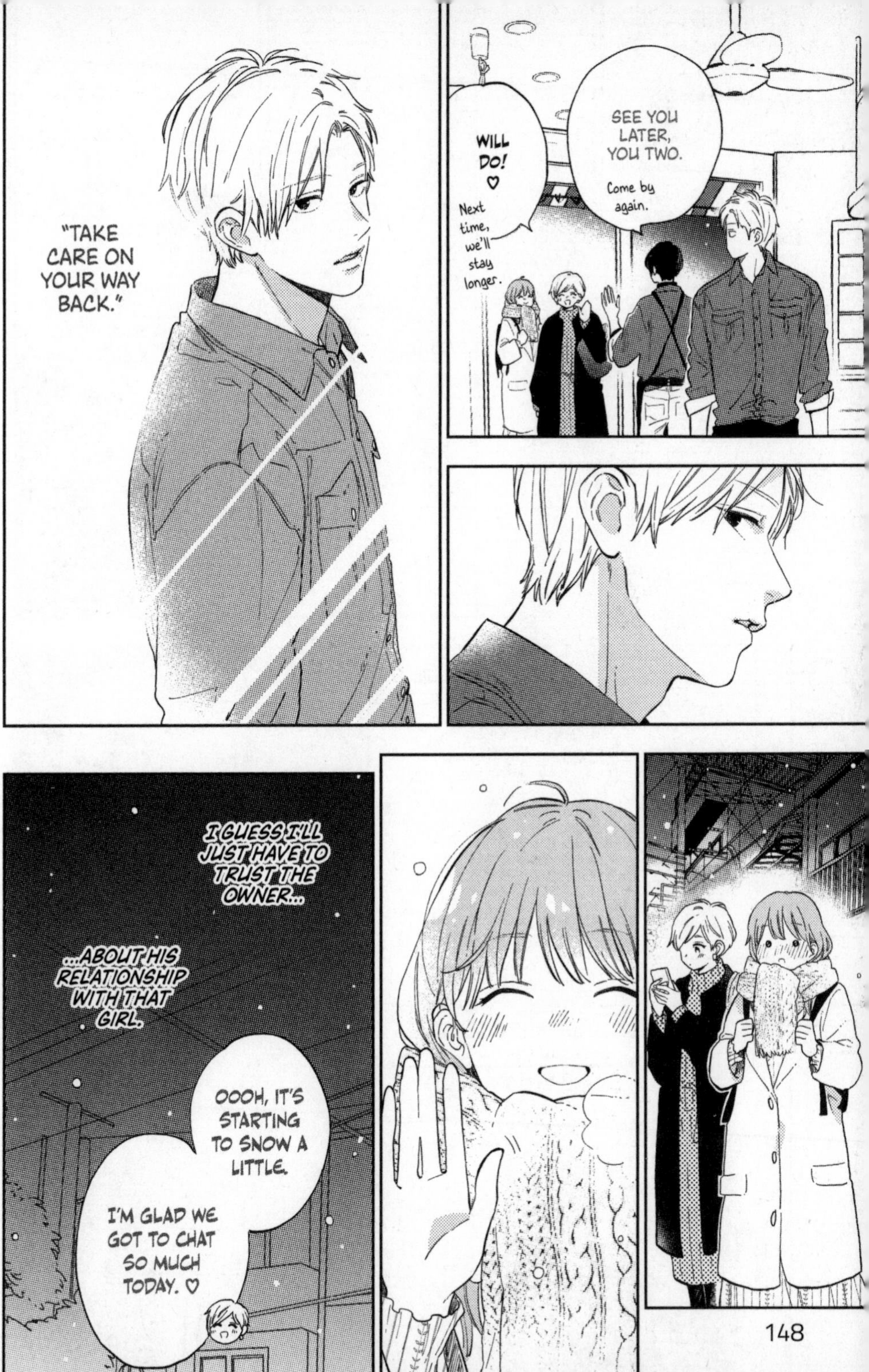

SEE YOU LATER, YOU TWO.
Come by again.
WILL DO! ♡
Next time, we'll stay longer.
"TAKE CARE ON YOUR WAY BACK."
I GUESS I'LL JUST HAVE TO TRUST THE OWNER...
...ABOUT HIS RELATIONSHIP WITH THAT GIRL.
OOOH, IT'S STARTING TO SNOW A LITTLE.
I'M GLAD WE GOT TO CHAT SO MUCH TODAY. ♡

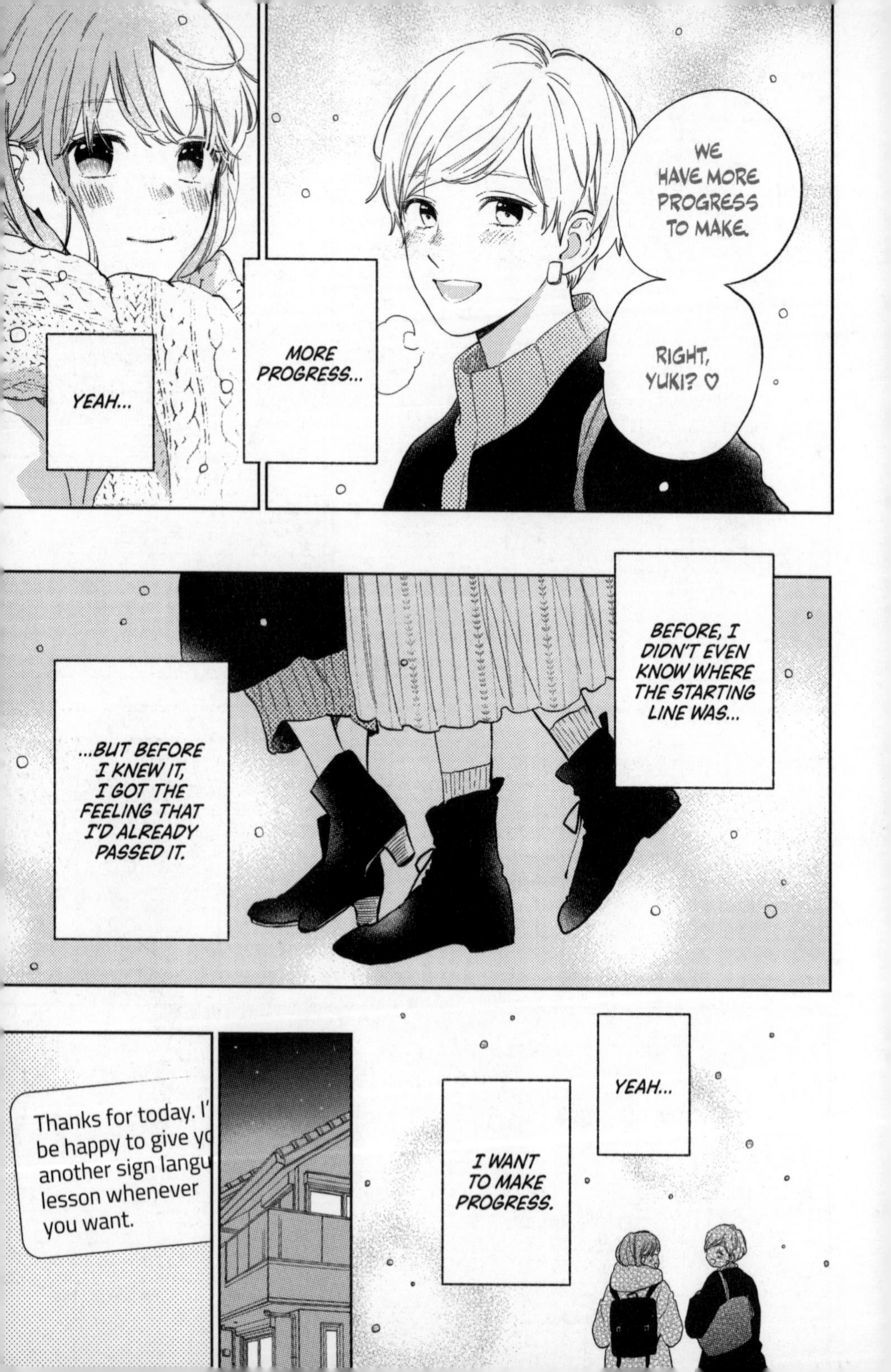
WE HAVE MORE PROGRESS TO MAKE.
RIGHT, YUKI? ♡
MORE PROGRESS...
YEAH...
BEFORE, I DIDN'T EVEN KNOW WHERE THE STARTING LINE WAS...
...BUT BEFORE I KNEW IT, I GOT THE FEELING THAT I'D ALREADY PASSED IT.
YEAH...
I WANT TO MAKE PROGRESS.
Thanks for today. I' be happy to give yo another sign langu lesson whenever you want.

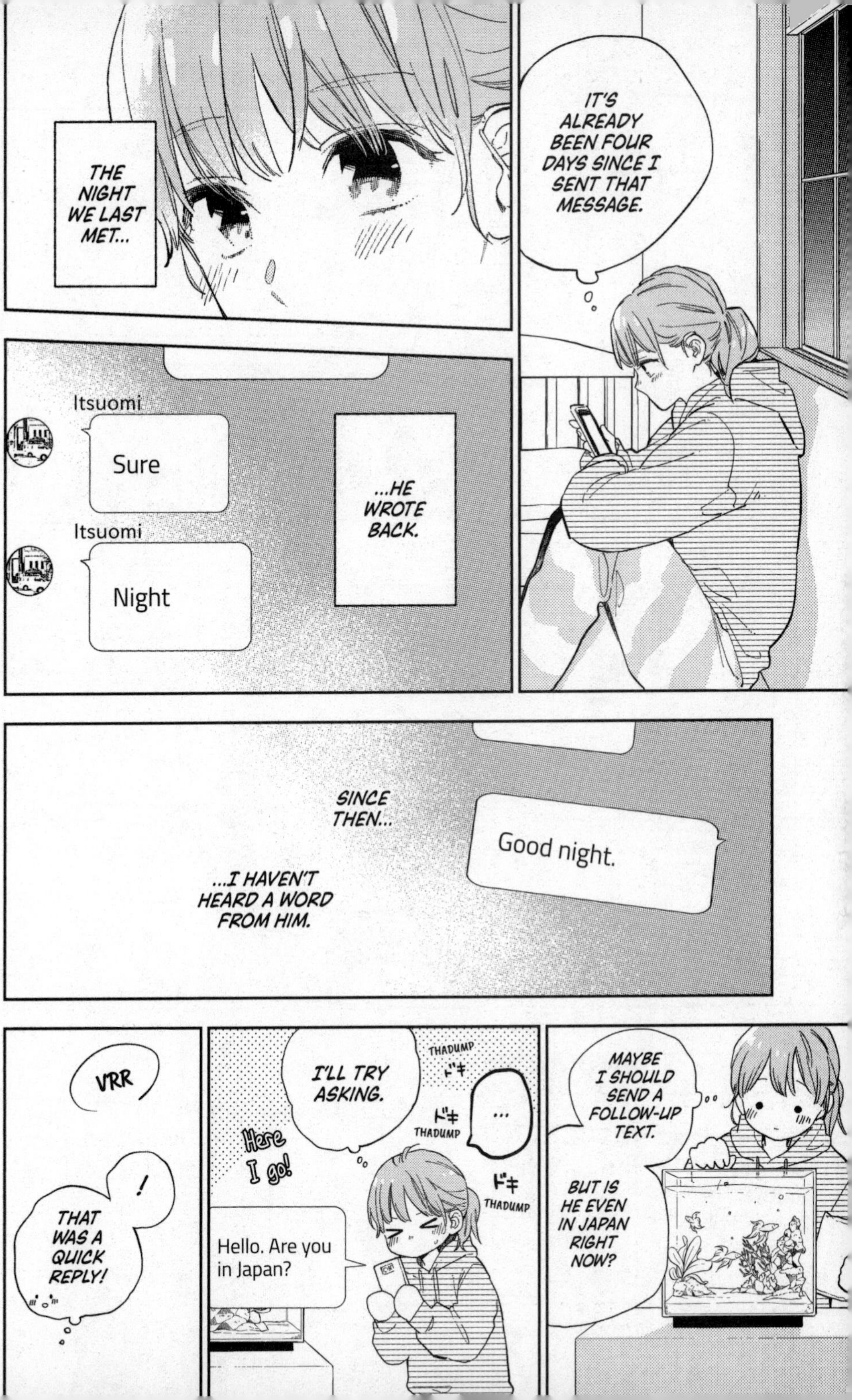
IT'S ALREADY BEEN FOUR DAYS SINCE I SENT THAT MESSAGE.
THE NIGHT WE LAST MET...
Itsuomi
Sure
Itsuomi
Night
...HE WROTE BACK.
Good night.
SINCE THEN...
...I HAVEN'T HEARD A WORD FROM HIM.
MAYBE I SHOULD SEND A FOLLOW-UP TEXT.
BUT IS HE EVEN IN JAPAN RIGHT NOW?
THADUMP
ドキ
...
I'LL TRY ASKING.
ドキ
THADUMP
Here I go!
ドキ
THADUMP
Hello. Are you in Japan?
VRR
!
THAT WAS A QUICK REPLY!

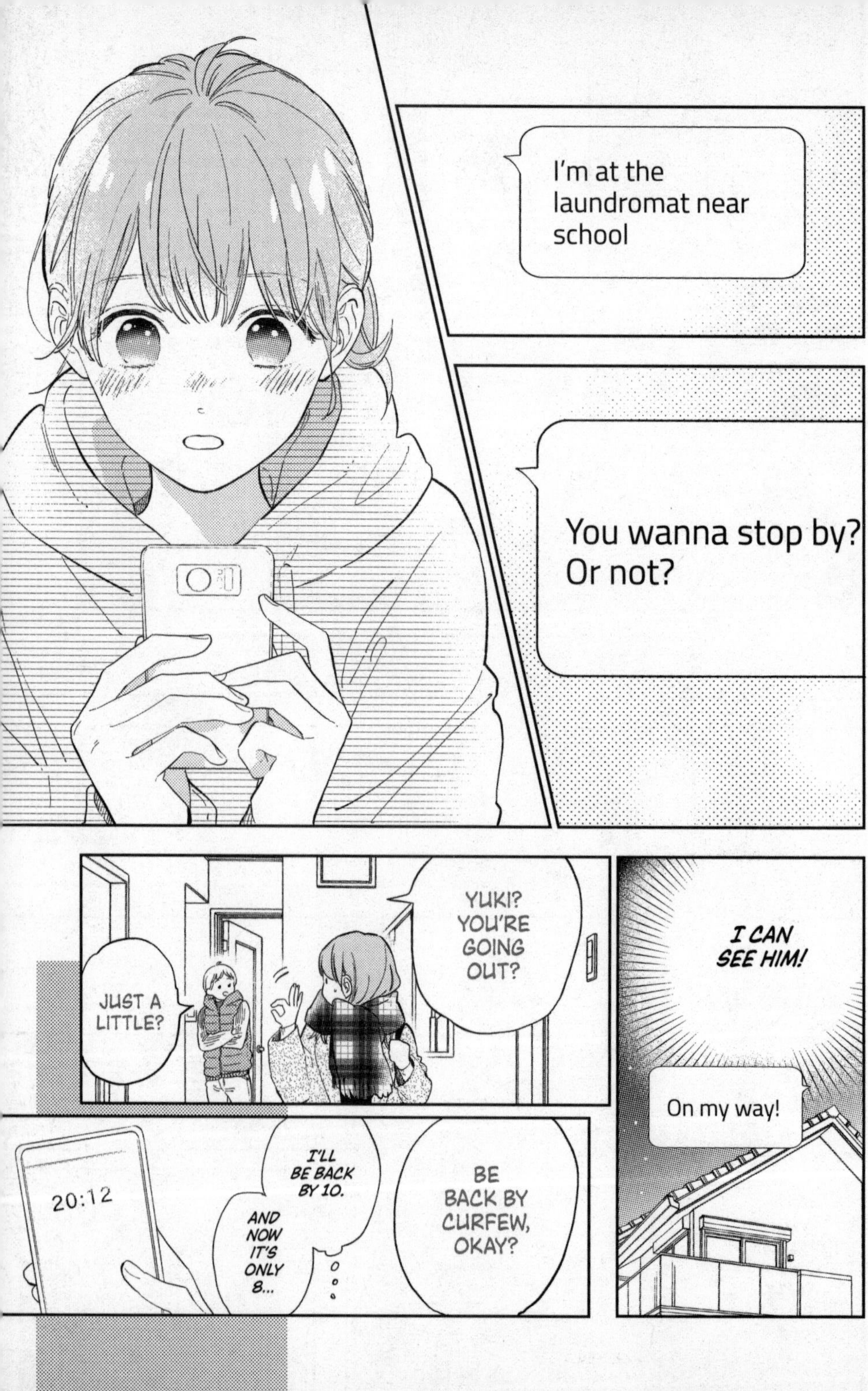
I'm at the laundromat near school
You wanna stop by? Or not?
I CAN SEE HIM!
On my way!
YUKI? YOU'RE GOING OUT?
JUST A LITTLE?
BE BACK BY CURFEW, OKAY?
I'LL BE BACK BY 10.
AND NOW IT'S ONLY 8...
20:12

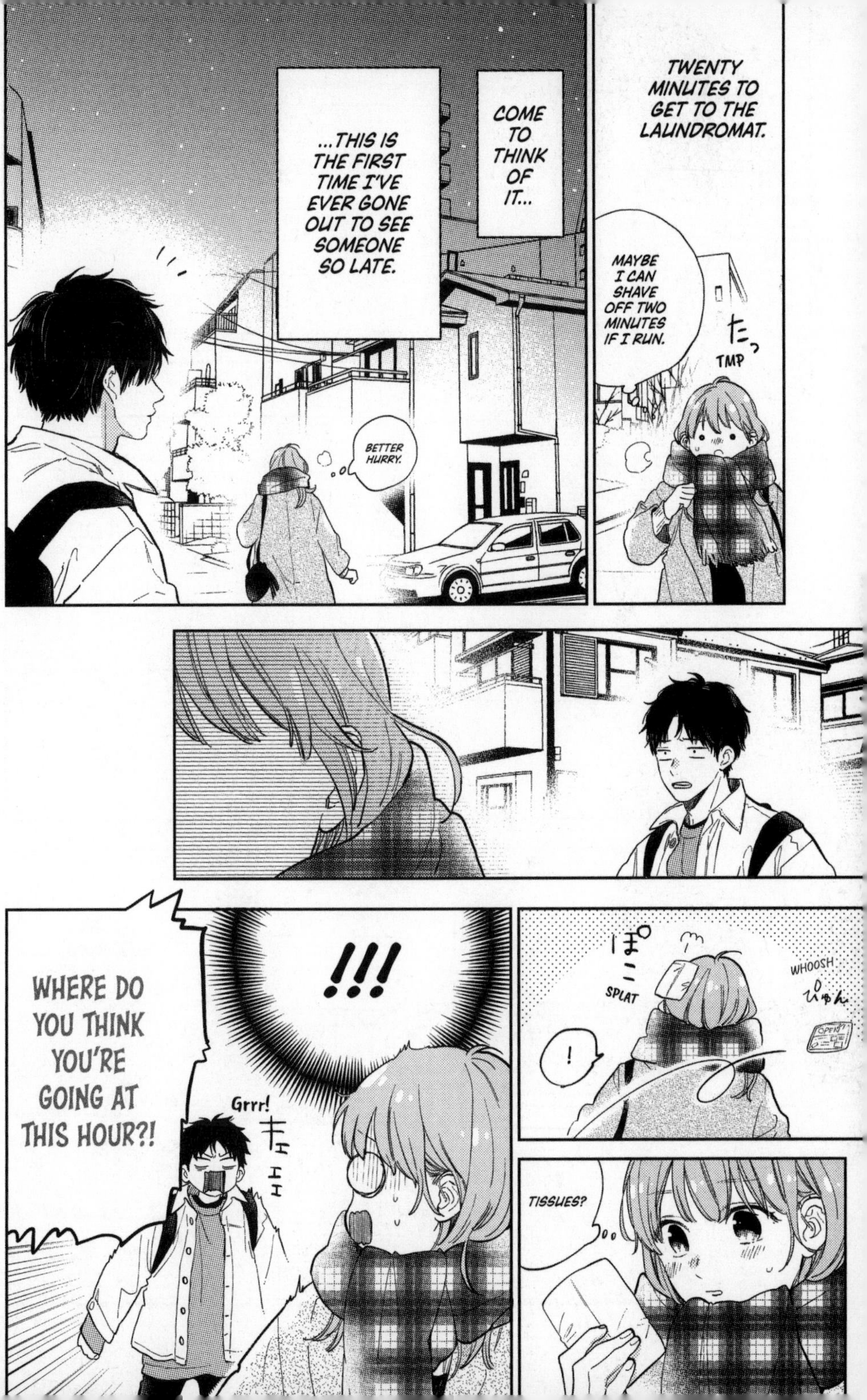
TWENTY MINUTES TO GET TO THE LAUNDROMAT.
MAYBE I CAN SHAVE OFF TWO MINUTES IF I RUN.
たっ
TMP
COME TO THINK OF IT...
...THIS IS THE FIRST TIME I'VE EVER GONE OUT TO SEE SOMEONE SO LATE.
BETTER HURRY.
WHOOSH
ぴゅん
ぽこ
SPLAT
!
TISSUES?
!!!
WHERE DO YOU THINK YOU'RE GOING AT THIS HOUR?!
Grrr!

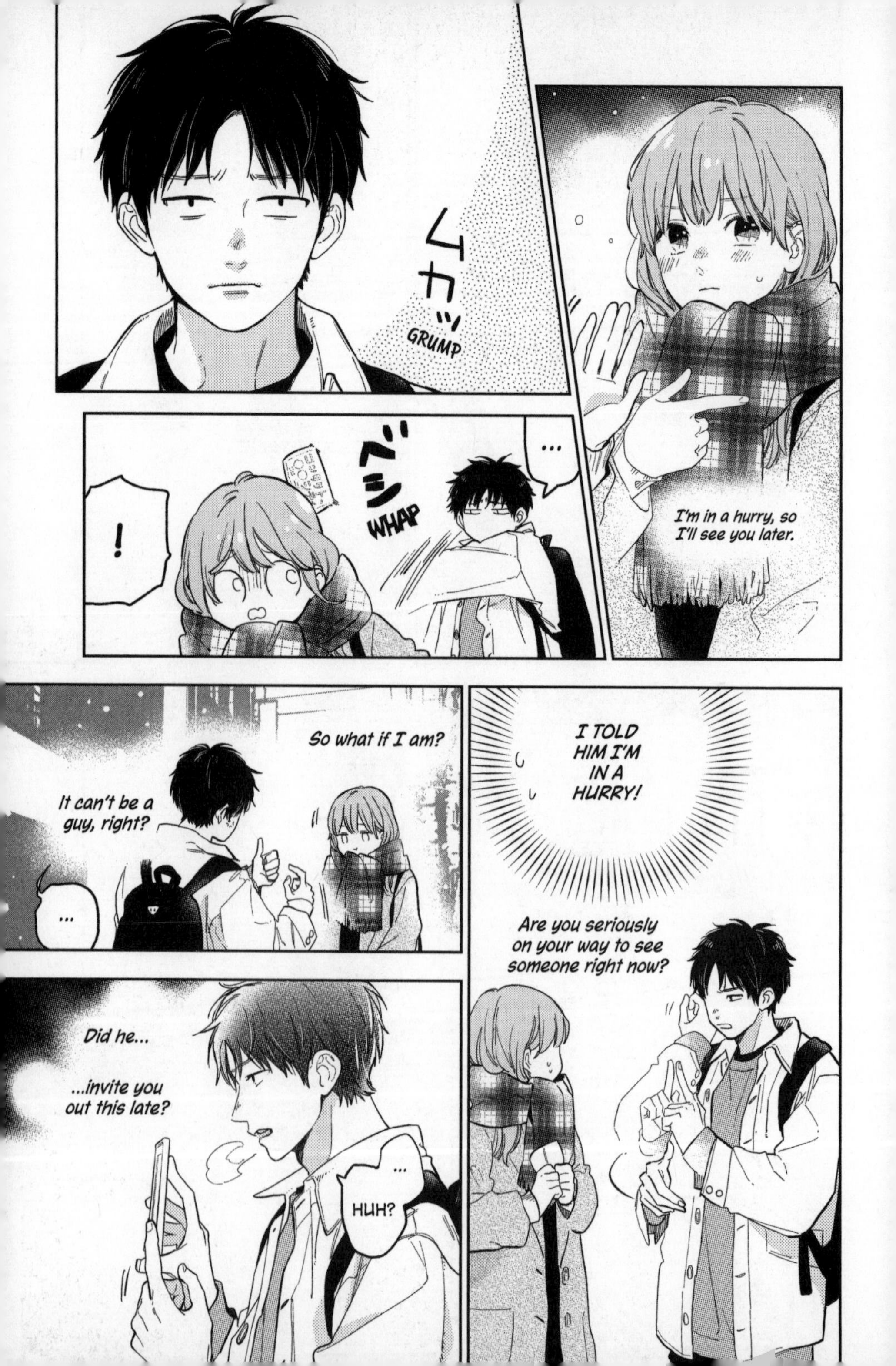
I'm in a hurry, so I'll see you later.
ムカッ
GRUMP
ベシ
WHAP
...
!
I TOLD HIM I'M IN A HURRY!
Are you seriously on your way to see someone right now?
So what if I am?
It can't be a guy, right?
...
Did he...
...invite you out this late?
...
HUH?

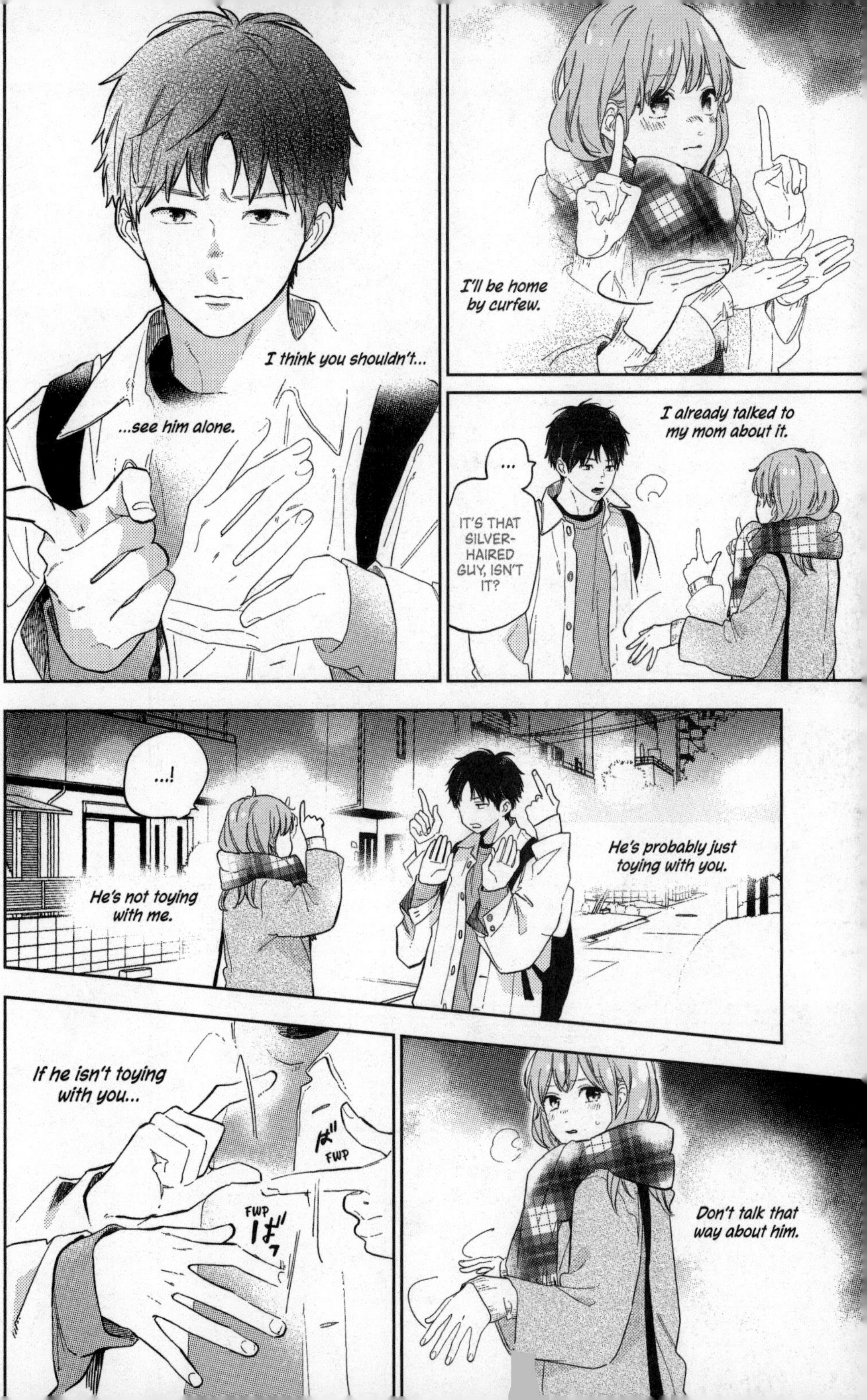
I'll be home by curfew.
I already talked to my mom about it.
...
IT'S THAT SILVER-HAIRED GUY, ISN'T IT?
I think you shouldn't...
...see him alone.
He's probably just toying with you.
...!
He's not toying with me.
Don't talk that way about him.
If he isn't toying with you...
ぱっ
FWP
ぱっ
FWP

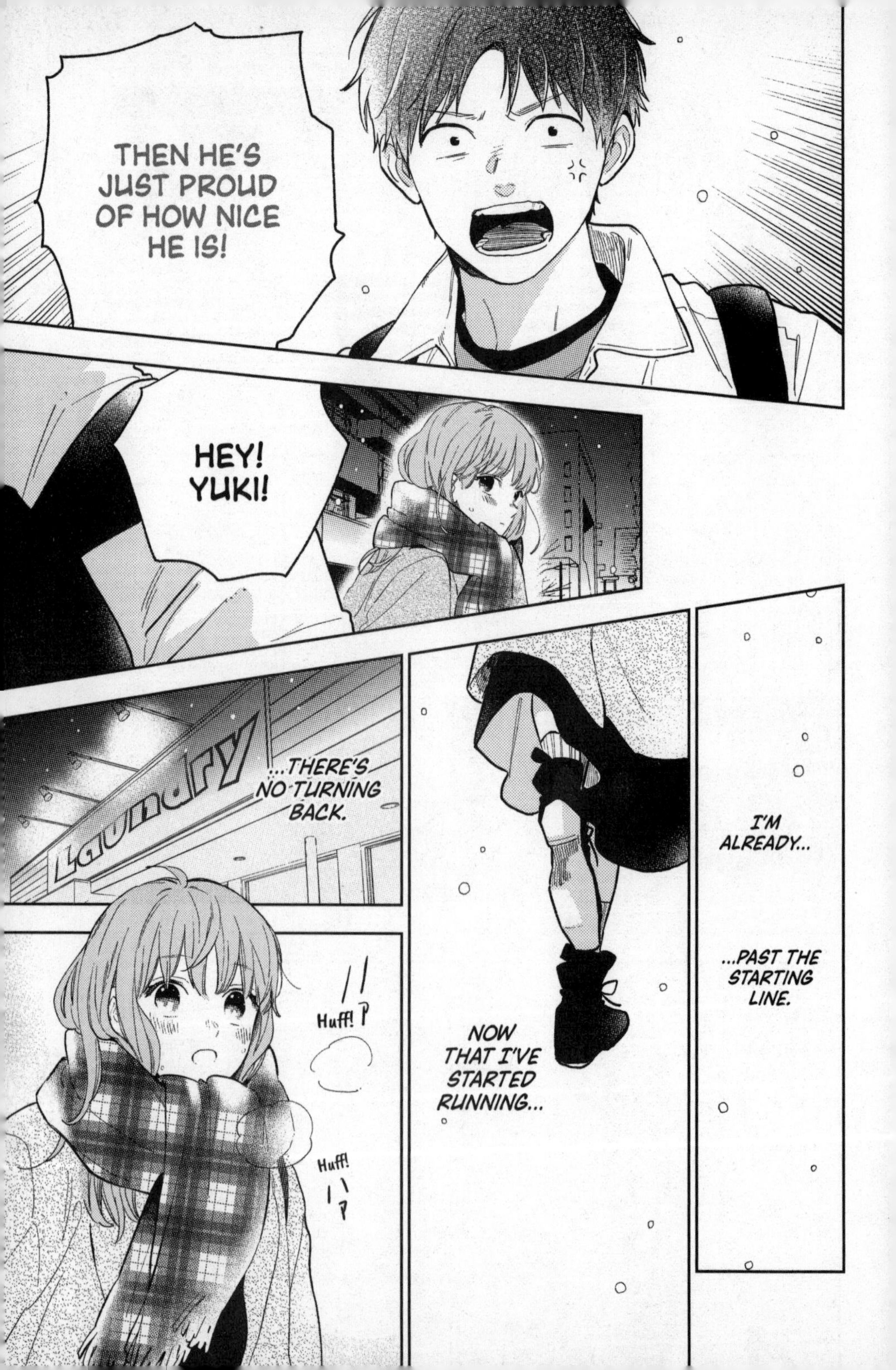
THEN HE'S JUST PROUD OF HOW NICE HE IS!
HEY! YUKI!
NOW THAT I'VE STARTED RUNNING...
Laundry
...THERE'S NO TURNING BACK.
Huff!
Huff!
I'M ALREADY...
...PAST THE STARTING LINE.

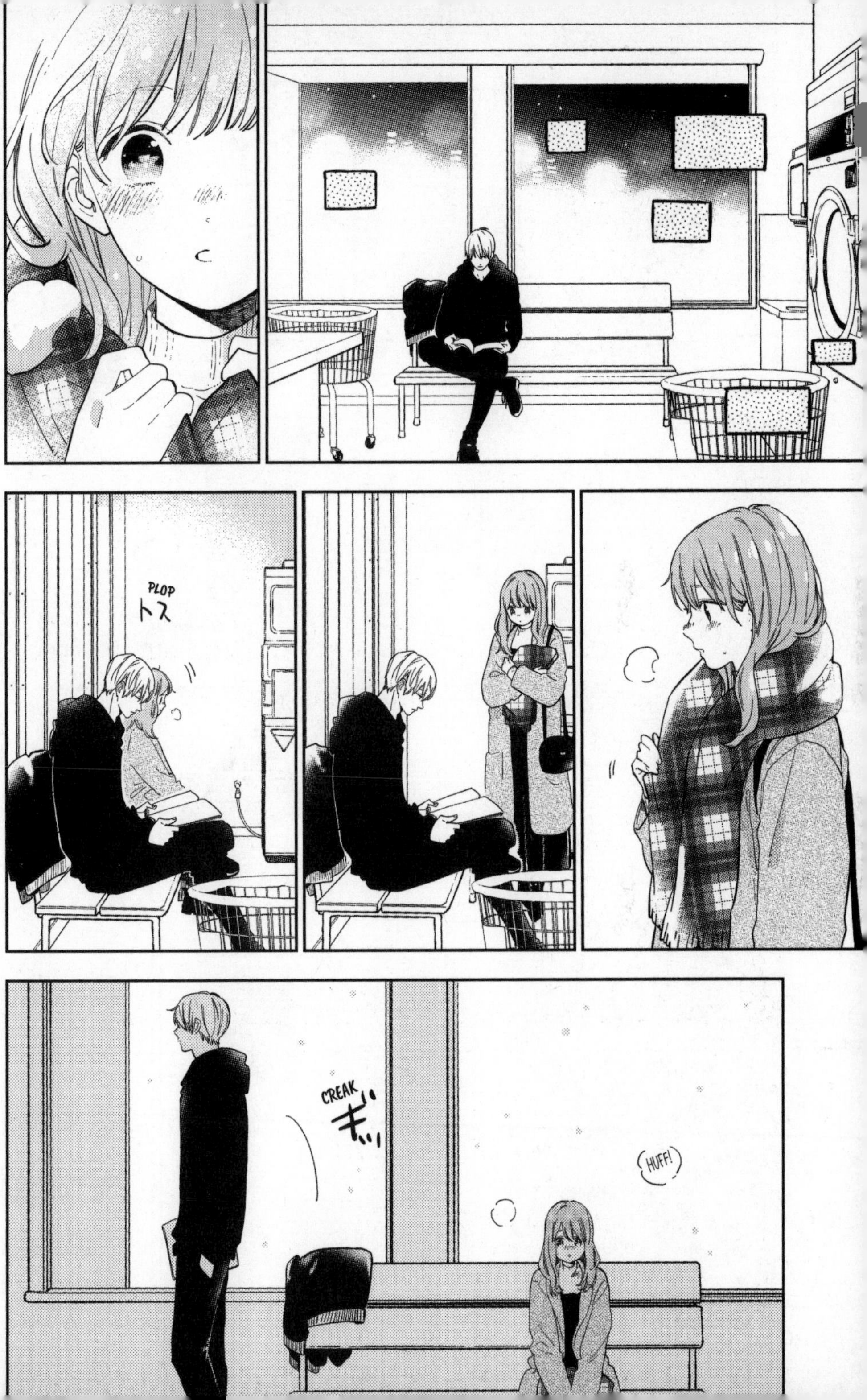
PLOP
トス
CREAK
ギッ
HUFF!

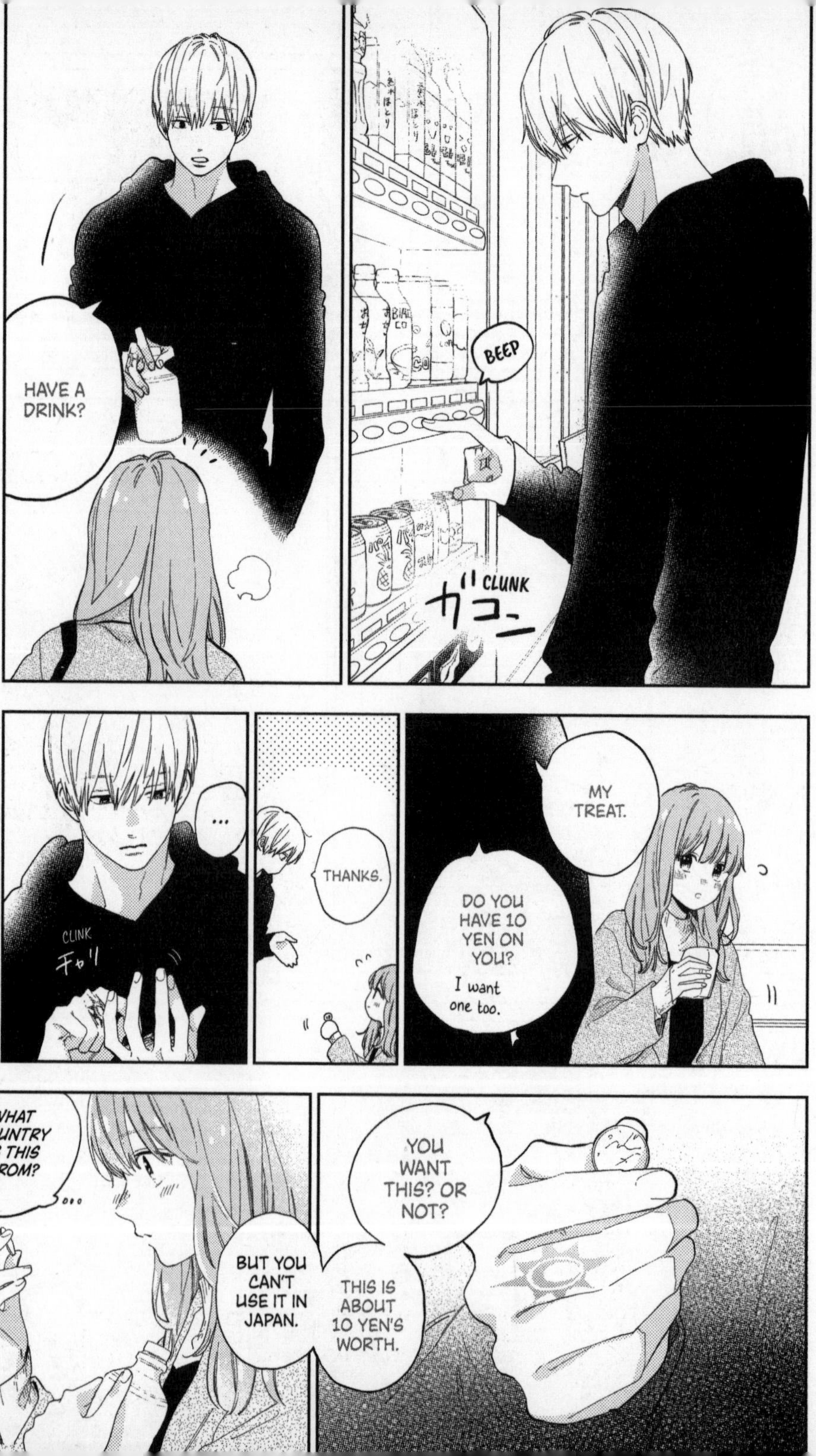
BEEP
CLINK ガコン
HAVE A DRINK?
MY TREAT.
DO YOU HAVE 10 YEN ON YOU? I want one too.
THANKS.
...
CLINK チャリ
YOU WANT THIS? OR NOT?
THIS IS ABOUT 10 YEN'S WORTH.
BUT YOU CAN'T USE IT IN JAPAN.
WHAT COUNTRY IS THIS FROM?

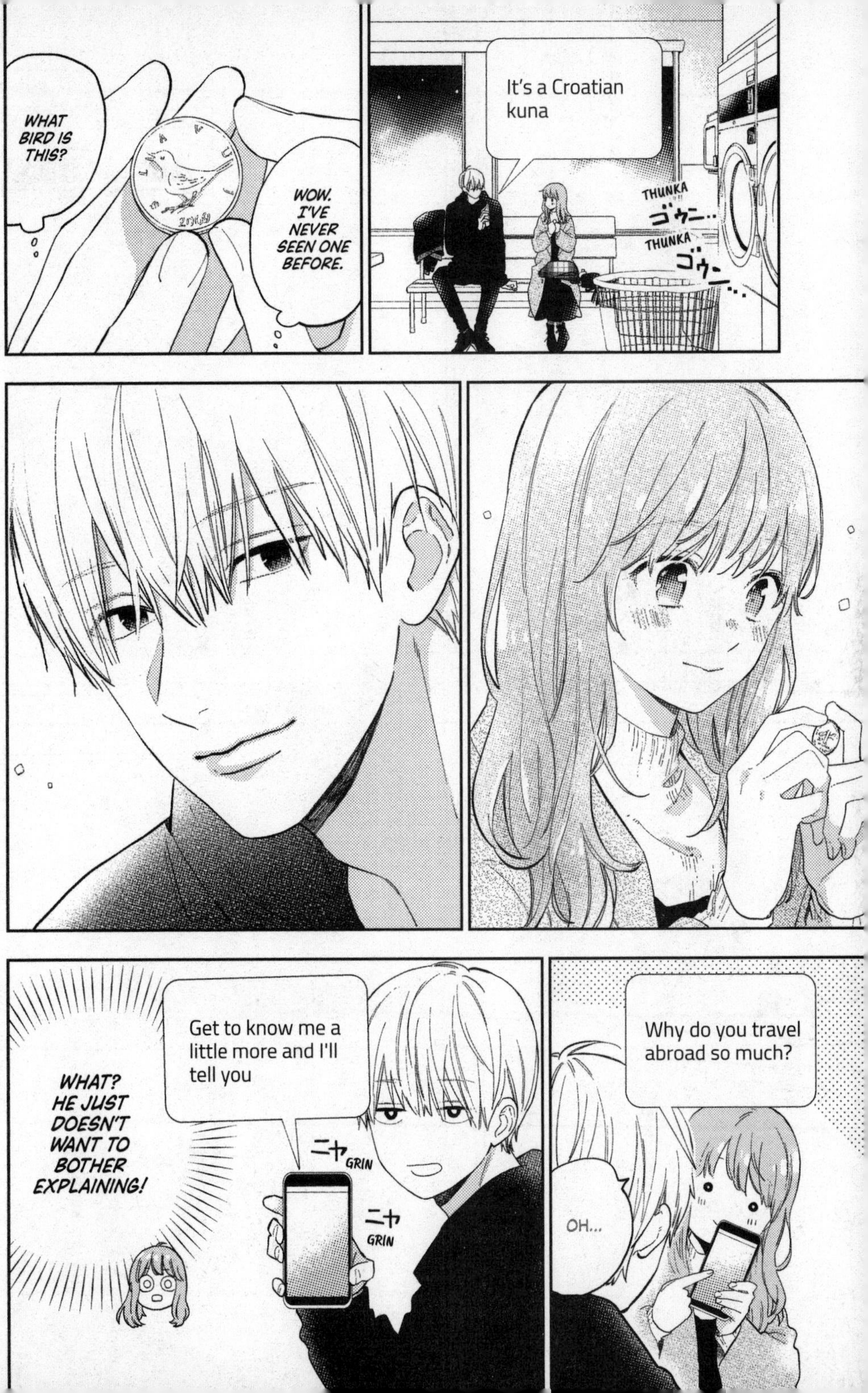
It's a Croatian kuna
THUNKA
ゴゥン…
THUNKA
ゴゥン…
WOW. I'VE NEVER SEEN ONE BEFORE.
WHAT BIRD IS THIS?
Why do you travel abroad so much?
OH...
Get to know me a little more and I'll tell you
ニヤ
GRIN
ニヤ
GRIN
WHAT? HE JUST DOESN'T WANT TO BOTHER EXPLAINING!

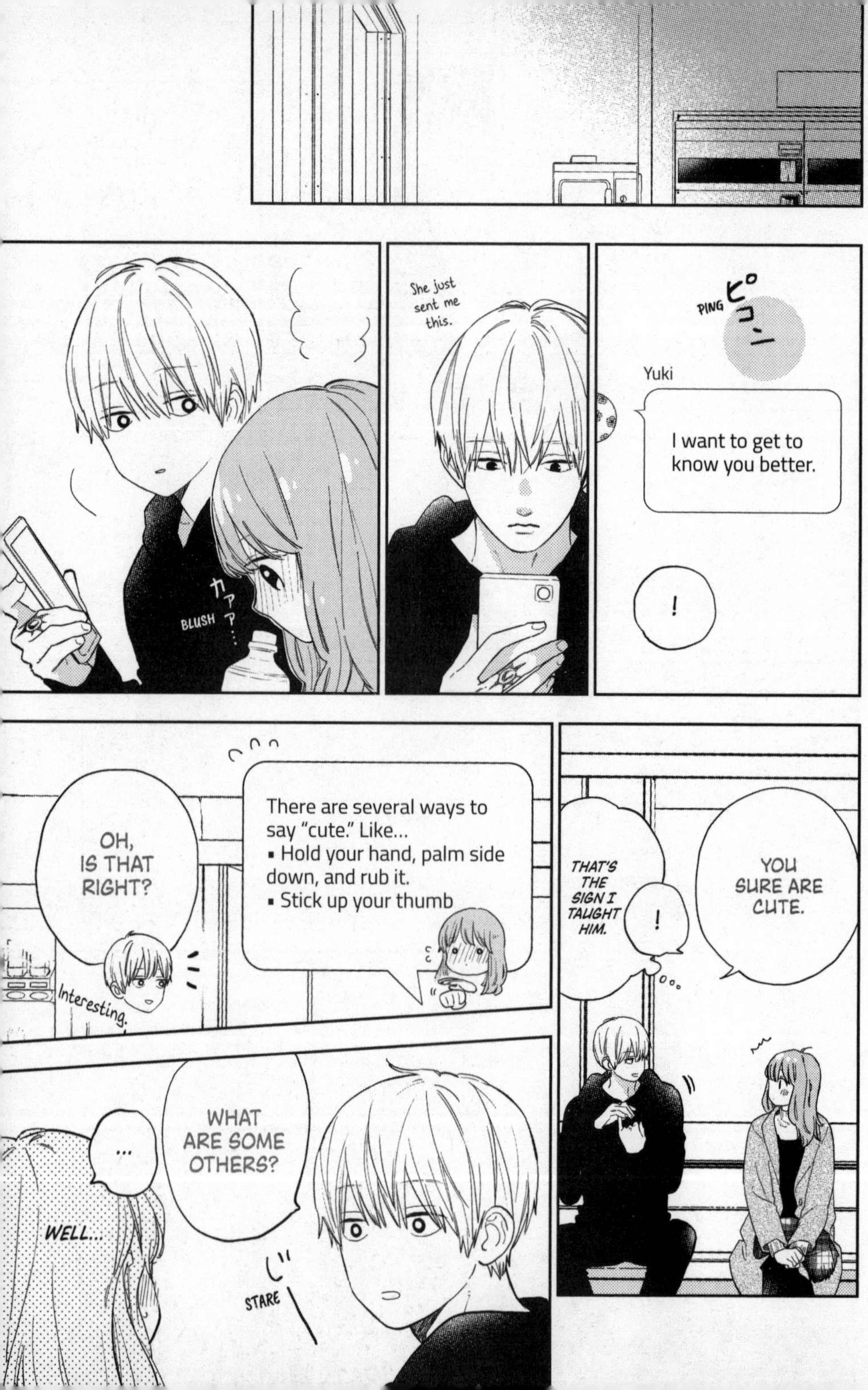
PING ピコーン
Yuki
I want to get to know you better.
!
She just sent me this.
カァァ…
BLUSH
YOU SURE ARE CUTE.
!
THAT'S THE SIGN I TAUGHT HIM.
There are several ways to say "cute." Like...
▪ Hold your hand, palm side down, and rub it.
▪ Stick up your thumb
OH, IS THAT RIGHT?
Interesting.
WHAT ARE SOME OTHERS?
...
WELL...
じー
STARE

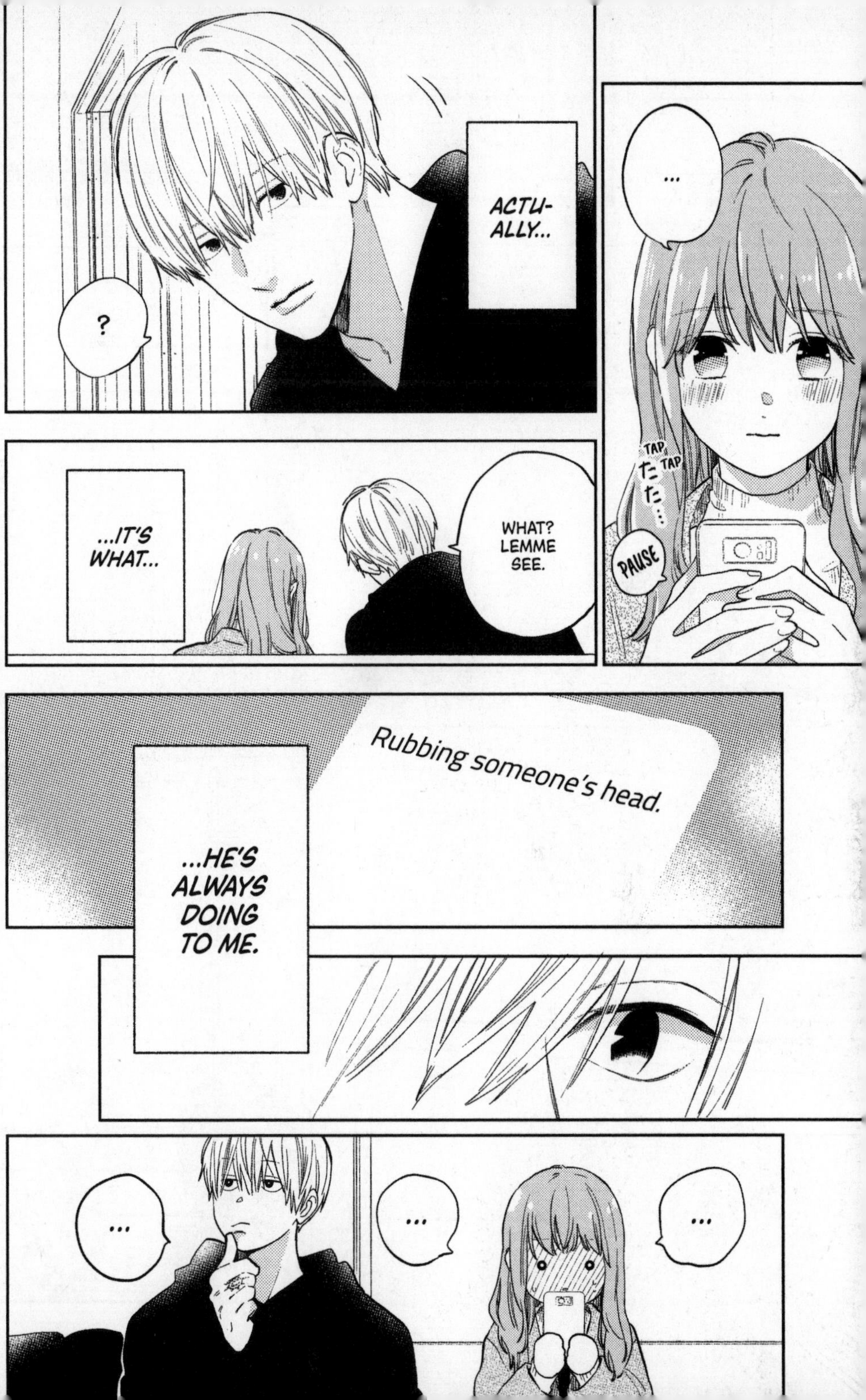
...
TAP TAP
たた…
PAUSE
ACTU-ALLY...
?
WHAT? LEMME SEE.
...IT'S WHAT...
Rubbing someone's head.
...HE'S ALWAYS DOING TO ME.
...
...
...

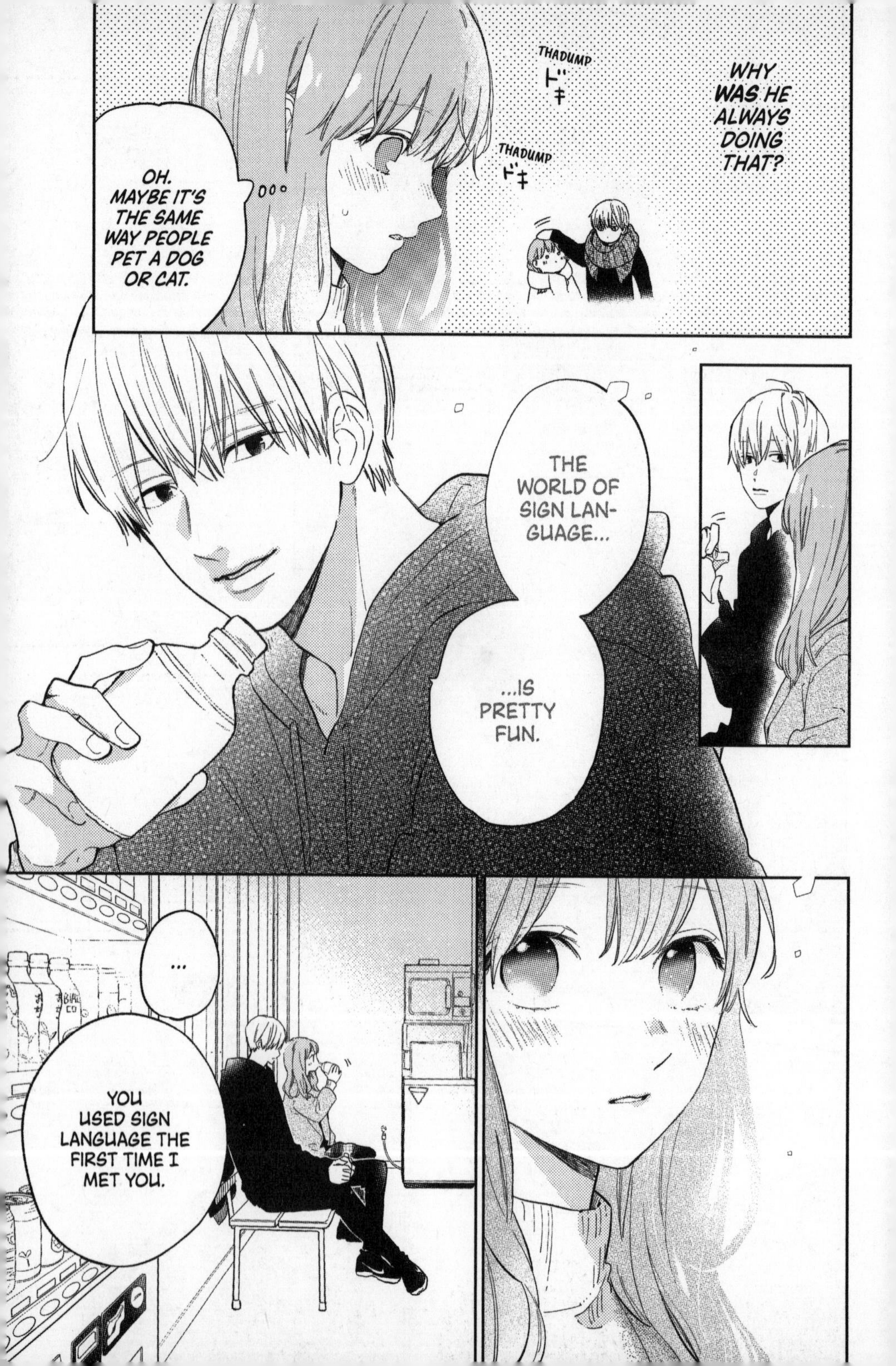
WHY WAS HE ALWAYS DOING THAT?
THADUMP ドキ
THADUMP ドキ
OH. MAYBE IT'S THE SAME WAY PEOPLE PET A DOG OR CAT.
THE WORLD OF SIGN LANGUAGE...
...IS PRETTY FUN.
...
YOU USED SIGN LANGUAGE THE FIRST TIME I MET YOU.

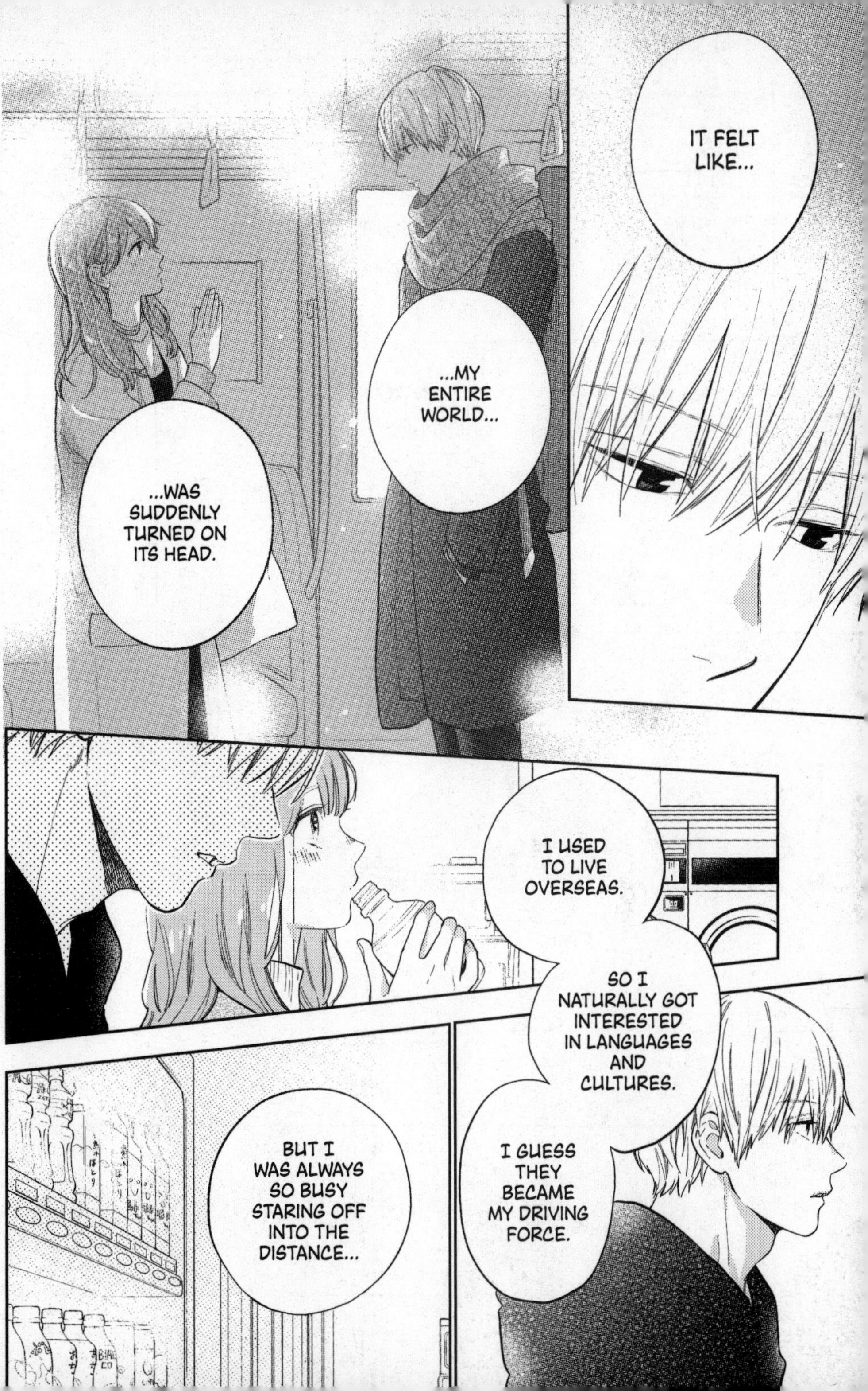
IT FELT LIKE...
...MY ENTIRE WORLD...
...WAS SUDDENLY TURNED ON ITS HEAD.
I USED TO LIVE OVERSEAS.
SO I NATURALLY GOT INTERESTED IN LANGUAGES AND CULTURES.
I GUESS THEY BECAME MY DRIVING FORCE.
BUT I WAS ALWAYS SO BUSY STARING OFF INTO THE DISTANCE...

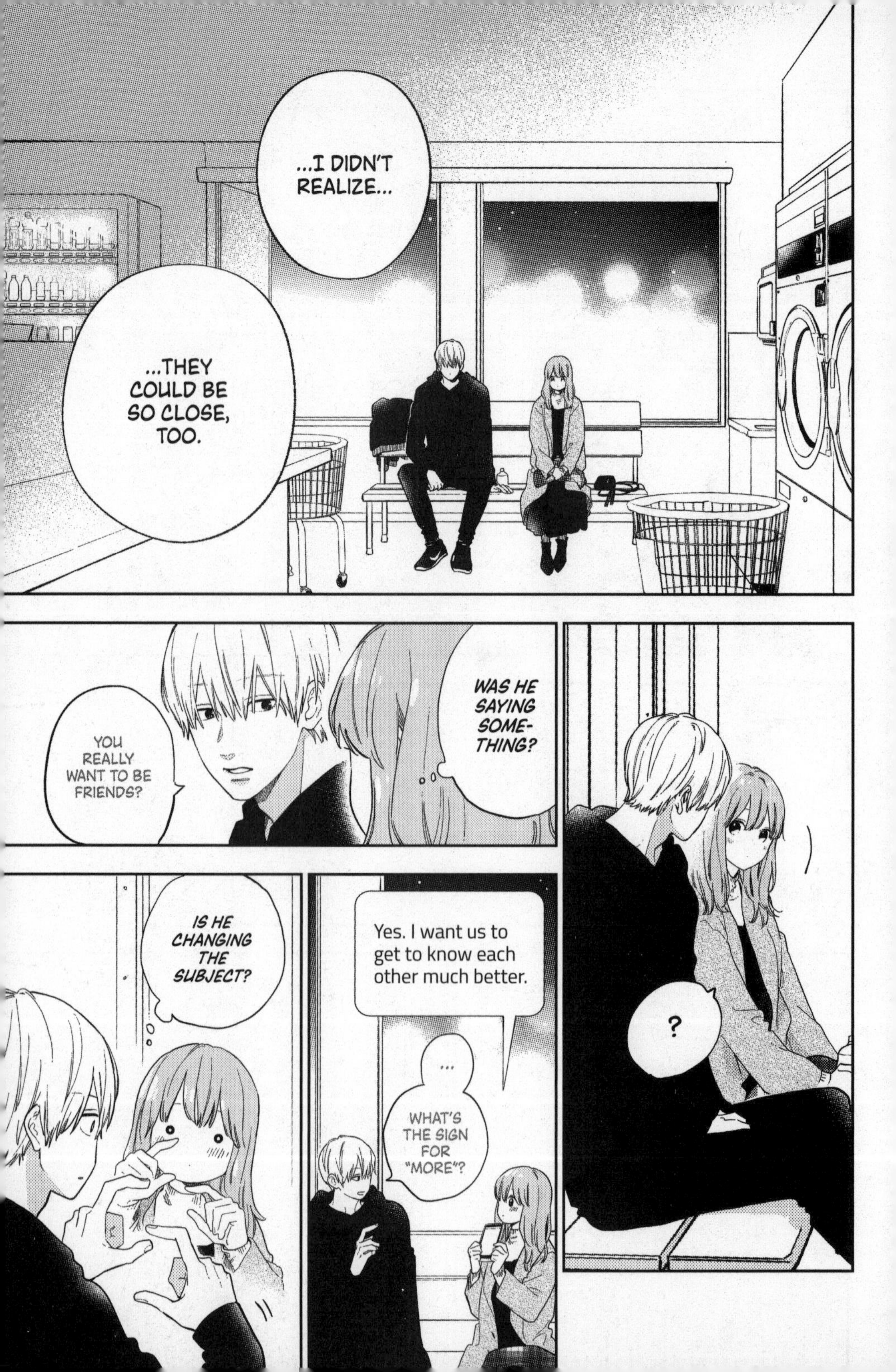
...I DIDN'T REALIZE...
...THEY COULD BE SO CLOSE, TOO.
?
WAS HE SAYING SOMETHING?
YOU REALLY WANT TO BE FRIENDS?
Yes. I want us to get to know each other much better.
...
WHAT'S THE SIGN FOR "MORE"?
IS HE CHANGING THE SUBJECT?

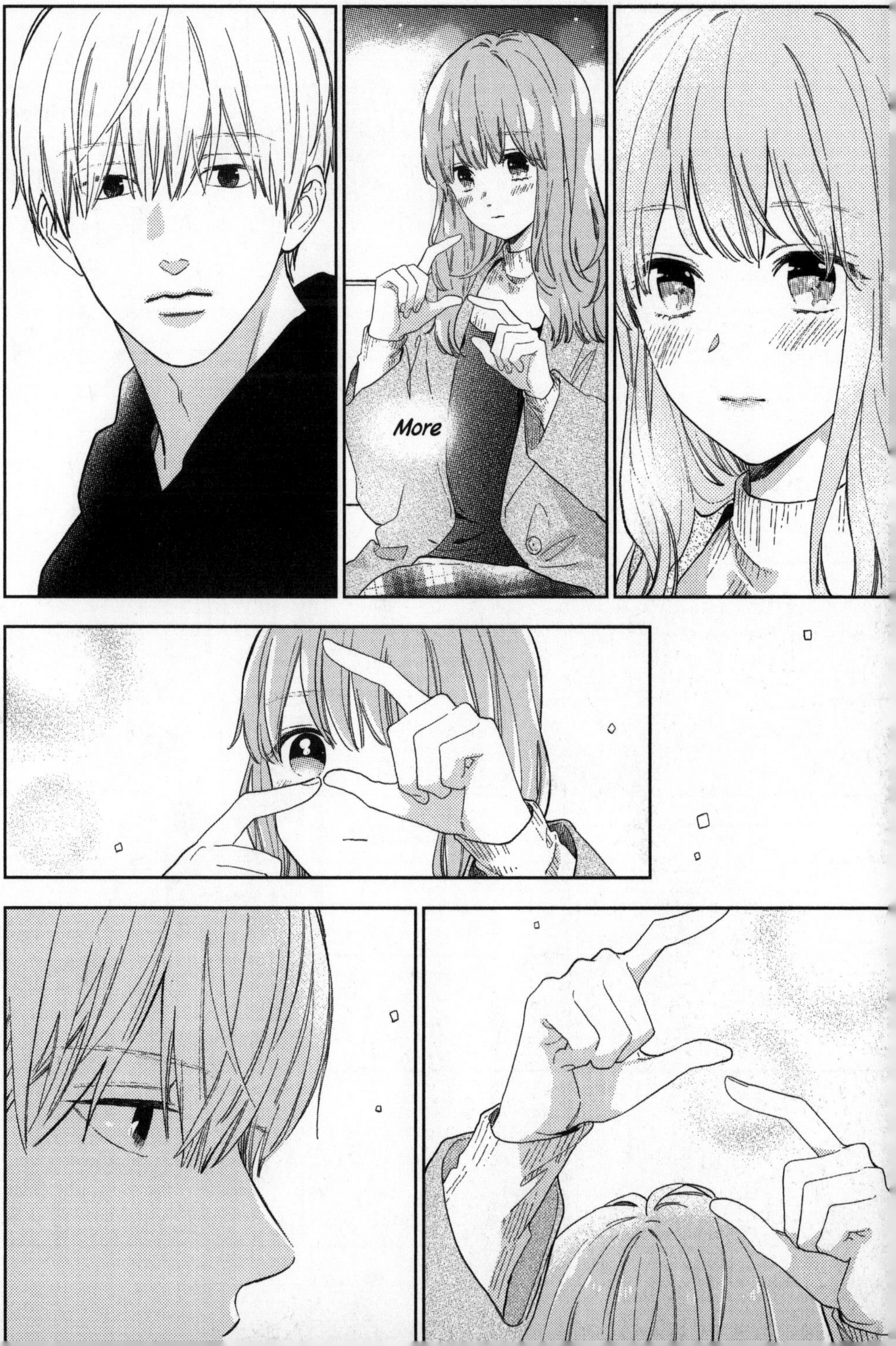
More

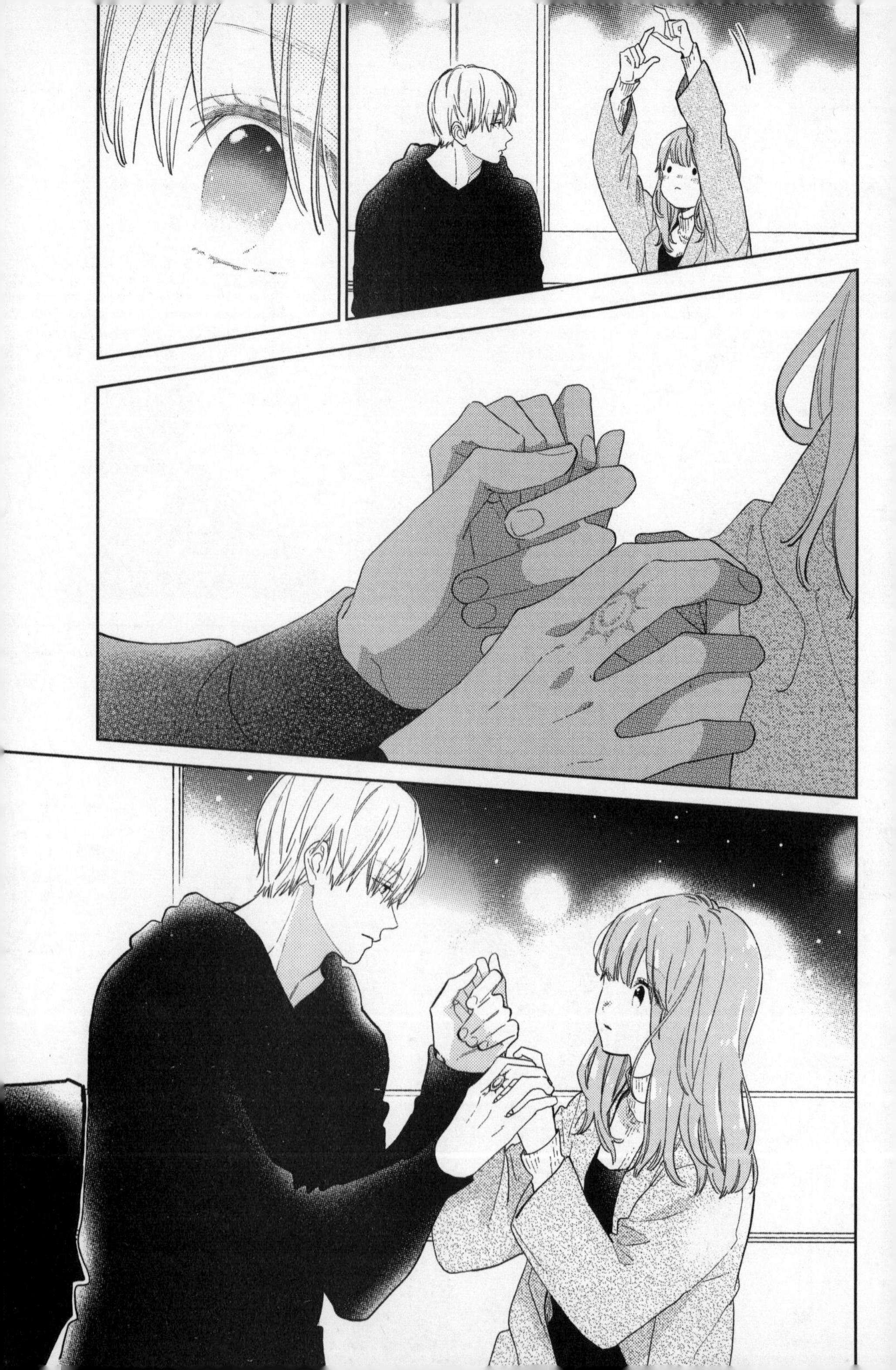

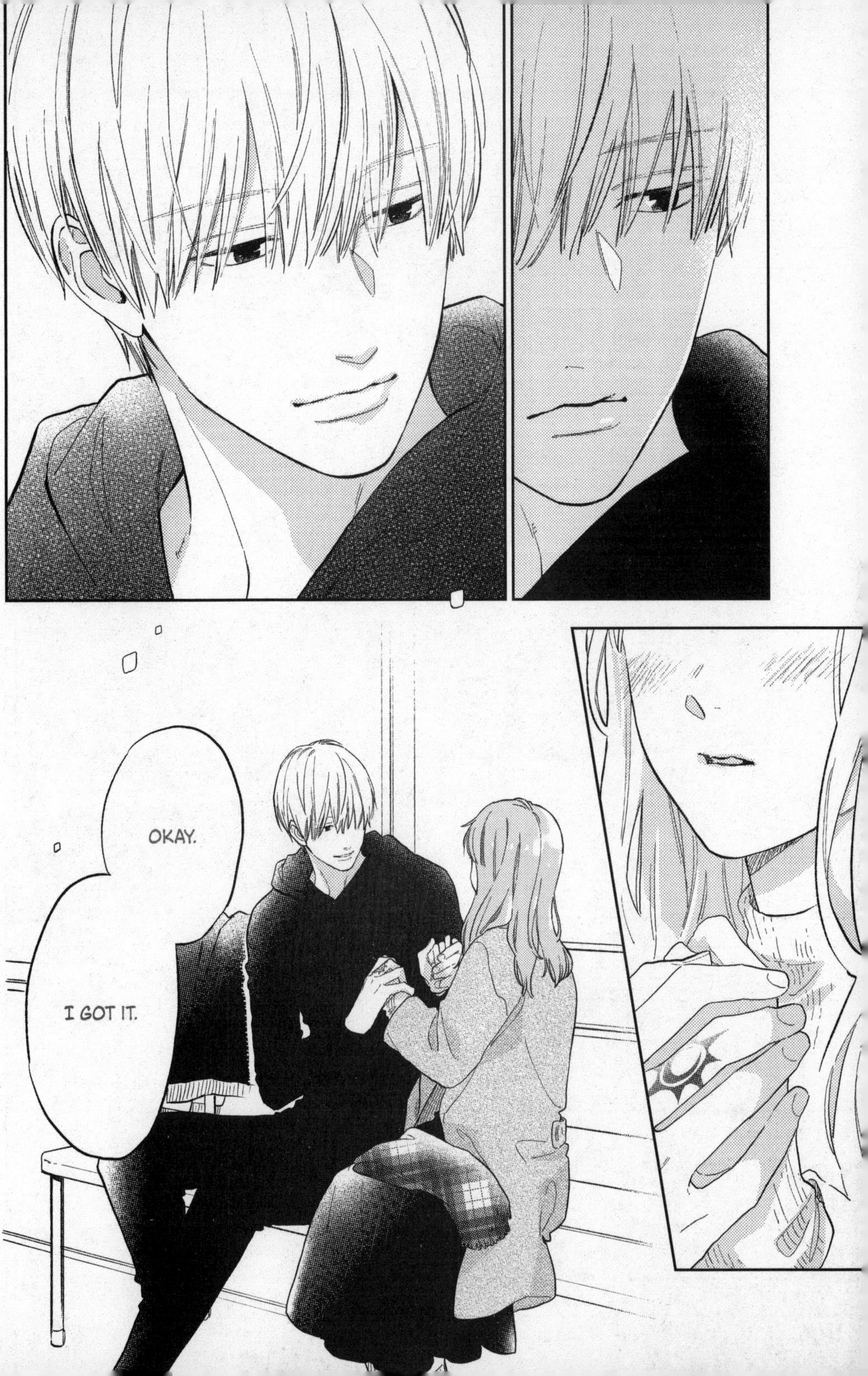
OKAY.
I GOT IT.

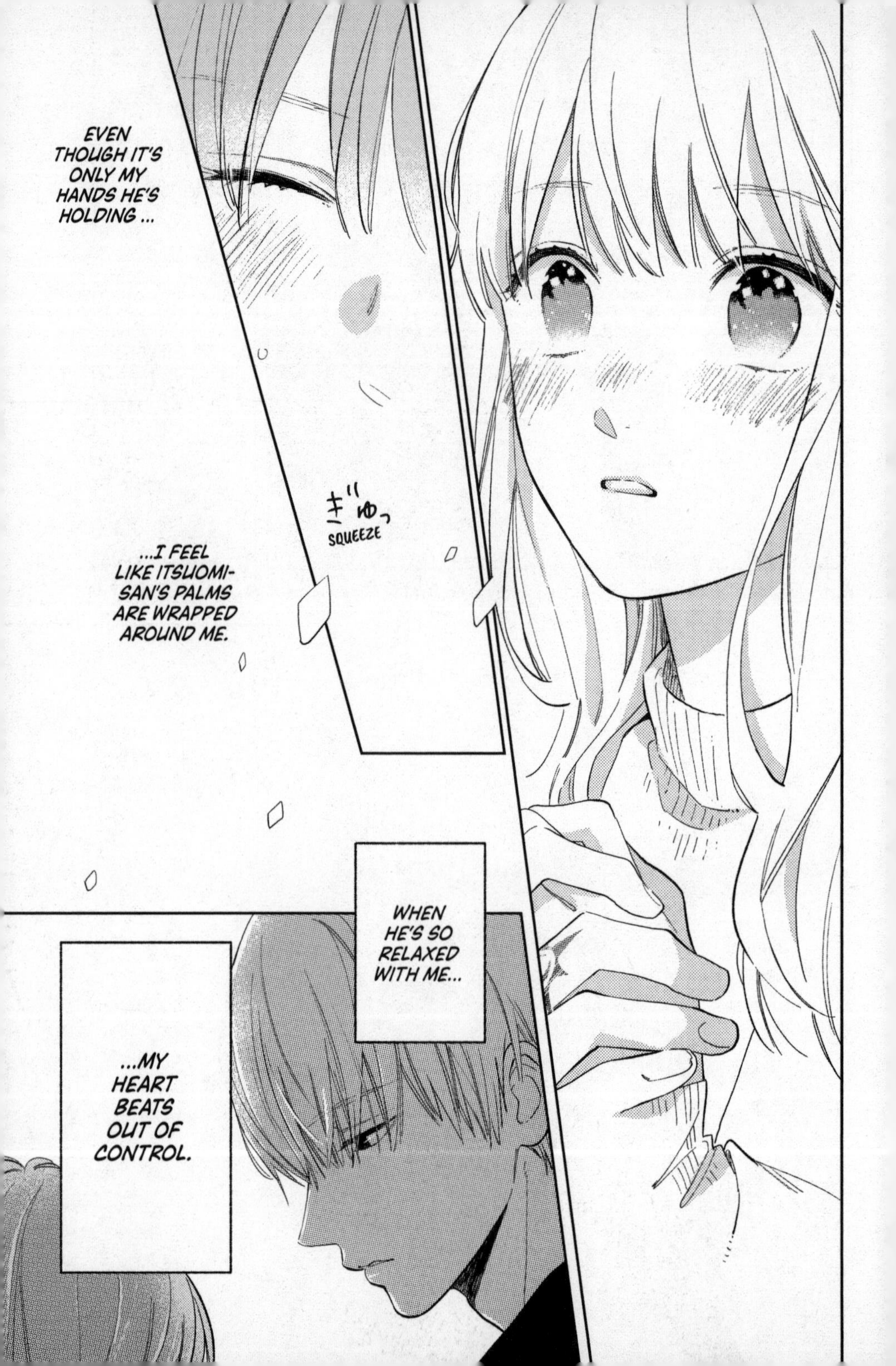
EVEN THOUGH IT'S ONLY MY HANDS HE'S HOLDING ...
ぎゅっ
SQUEEZE
...I FEEL LIKE ITSUOMI-SAN'S PALMS ARE WRAPPED AROUND ME.
WHEN HE'S SO RELAXED WITH ME...
...MY HEART BEATS OUT OF CONTROL.

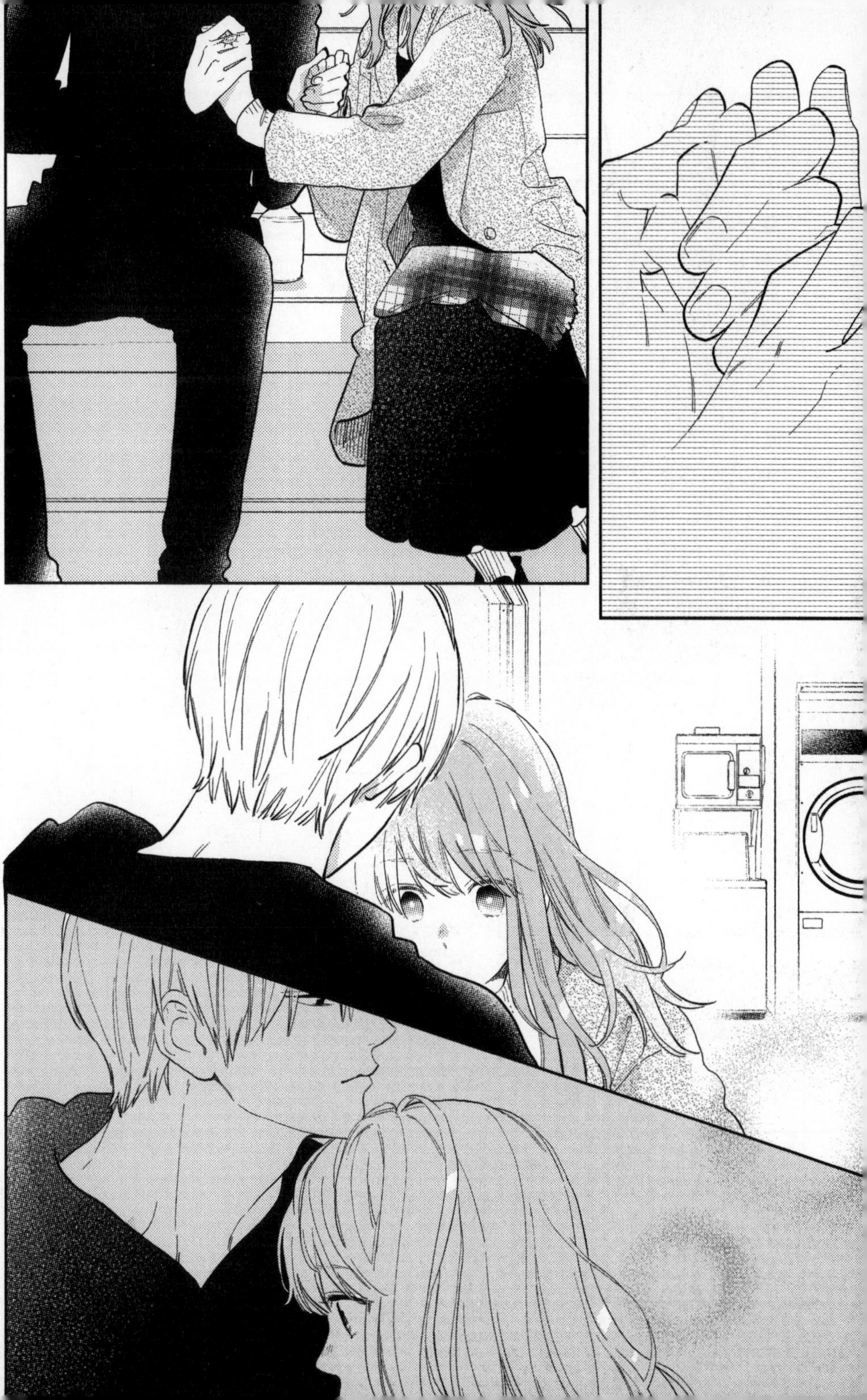

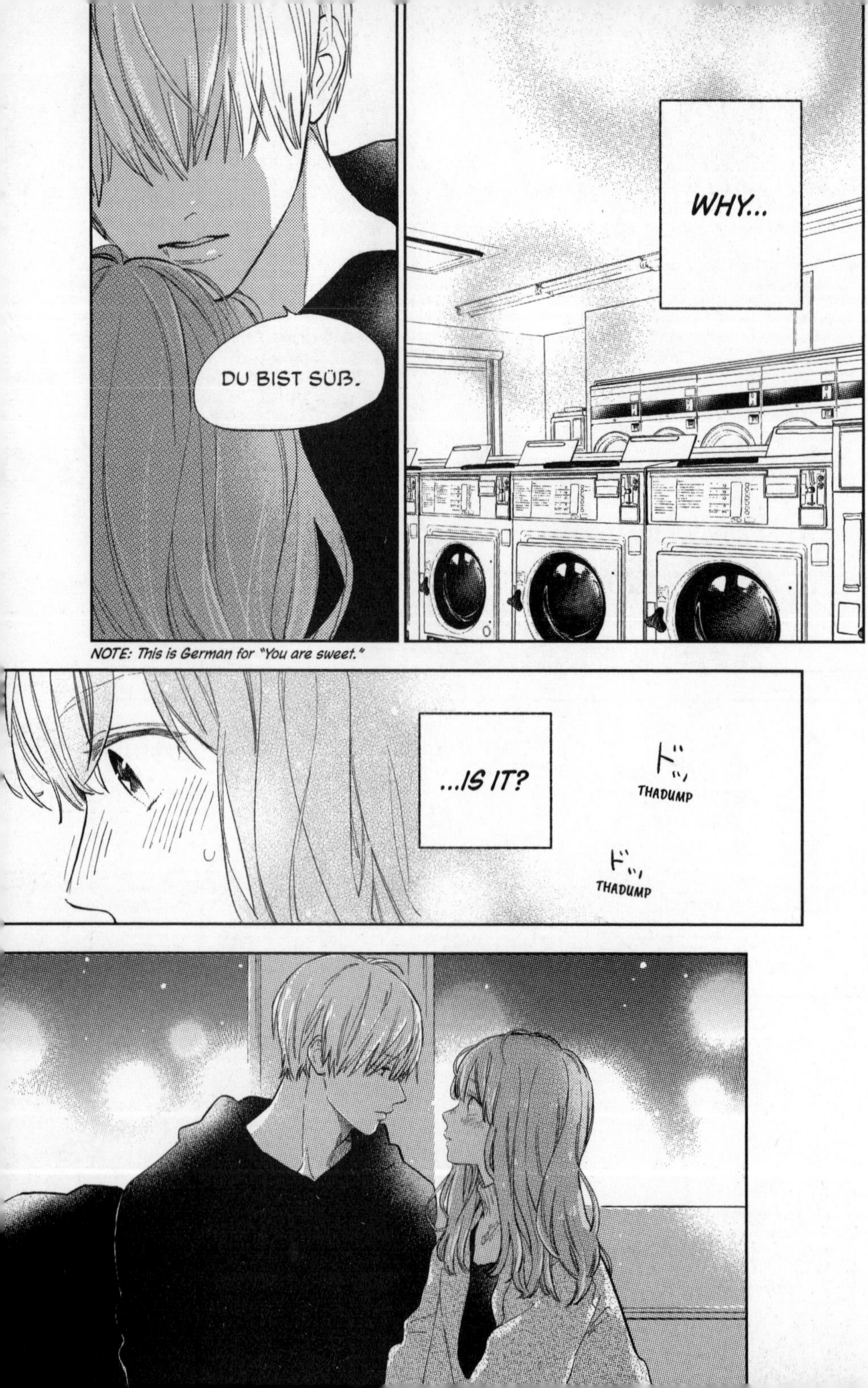
WHY...
DU BIST SÜß.
...IS IT?
ドッ
THADUMP
ドッ
THADUMP
NOTE: This is German for "You are sweet."

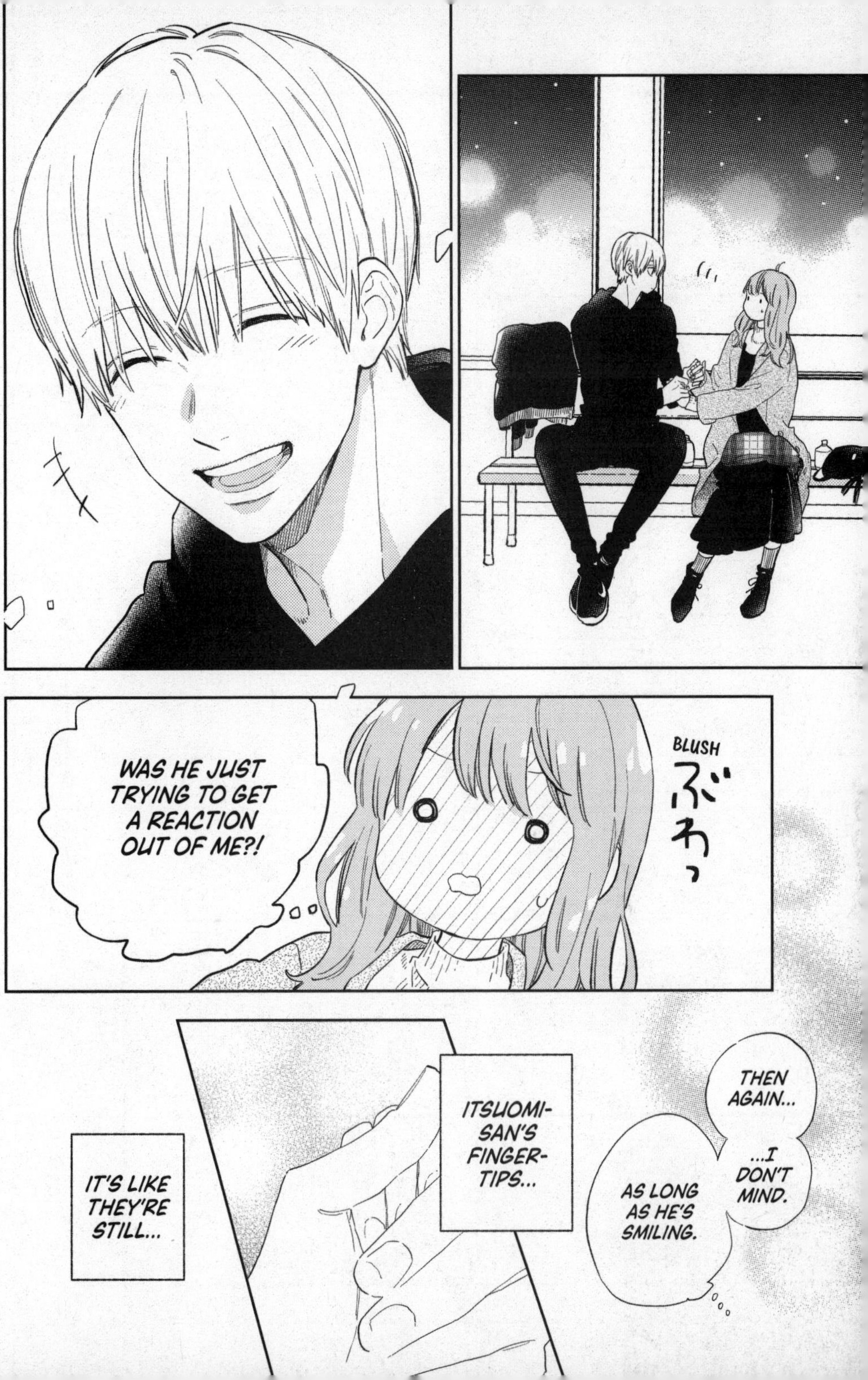
BLUSH
ぶわっ
WAS HE JUST TRYING TO GET A REACTION OUT OF ME?!
THEN AGAIN...
...I DON'T MIND.
AS LONG AS HE'S SMILING.
ITSUOMI-SAN'S FINGER-TIPS...
IT'S LIKE THEY'RE STILL...

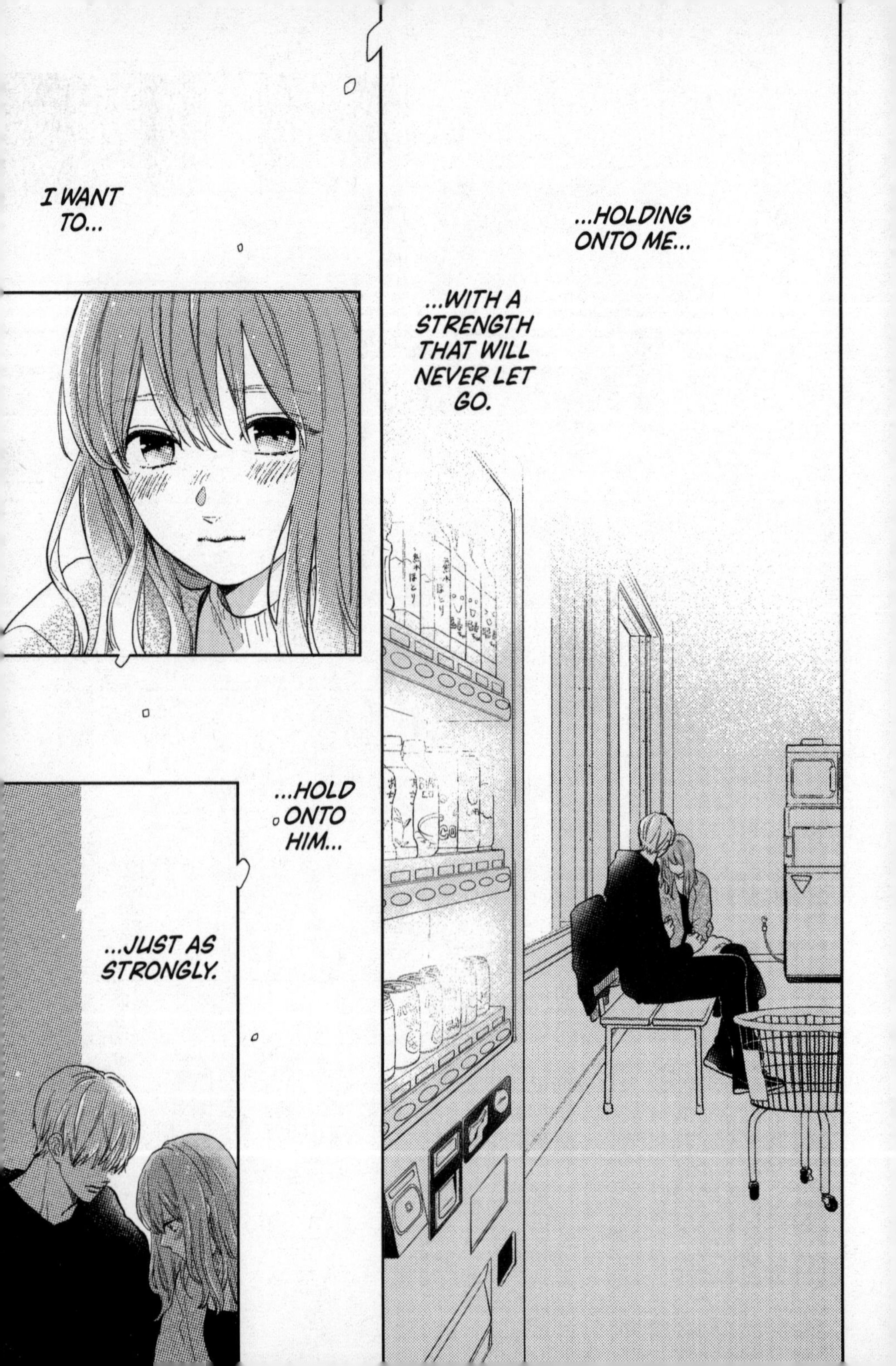
...HOLDING ONTO ME...
...WITH A STRENGTH THAT WILL NEVER LET GO.
I WANT TO...
...HOLD ONTO HIM...
...JUST AS STRONGLY.

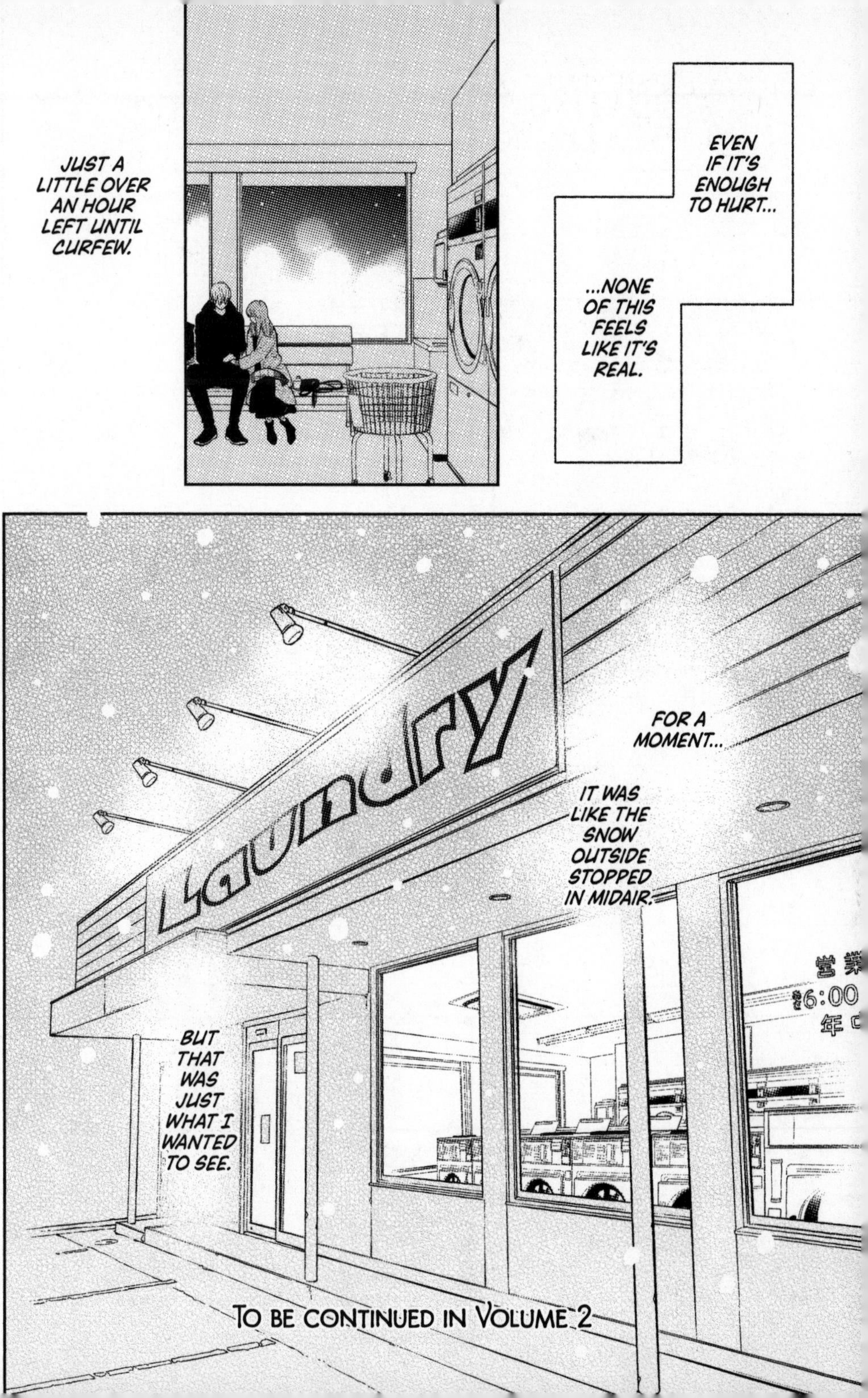
EVEN IF IT'S ENOUGH TO HURT...
...NONE OF THIS FEELS LIKE IT'S REAL.
JUST A LITTLE OVER AN HOUR LEFT UNTIL CURFEW.
Laundry
FOR A MOMENT...
IT WAS LIKE THE SNOW OUTSIDE STOPPED IN MIDAIR.
BUT THAT WAS JUST WHAT I WANTED TO SEE.
TO BE CONTINUED IN VOLUME 2

AFTERWORD

Thank you for reading volume 1 of *A Sign of Affection*!!

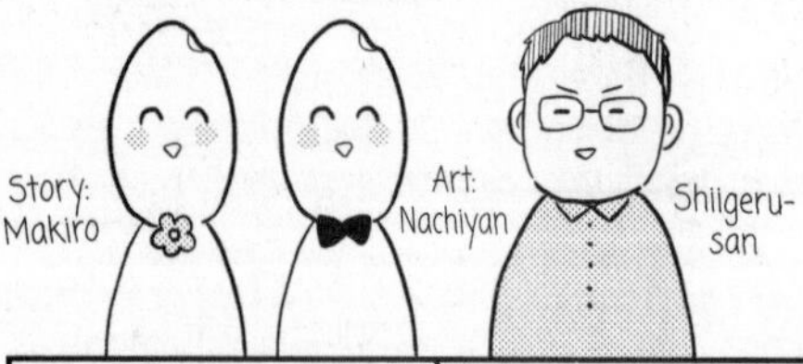

Story: Makiro
Art: Nachiyan
Shiigeru-san

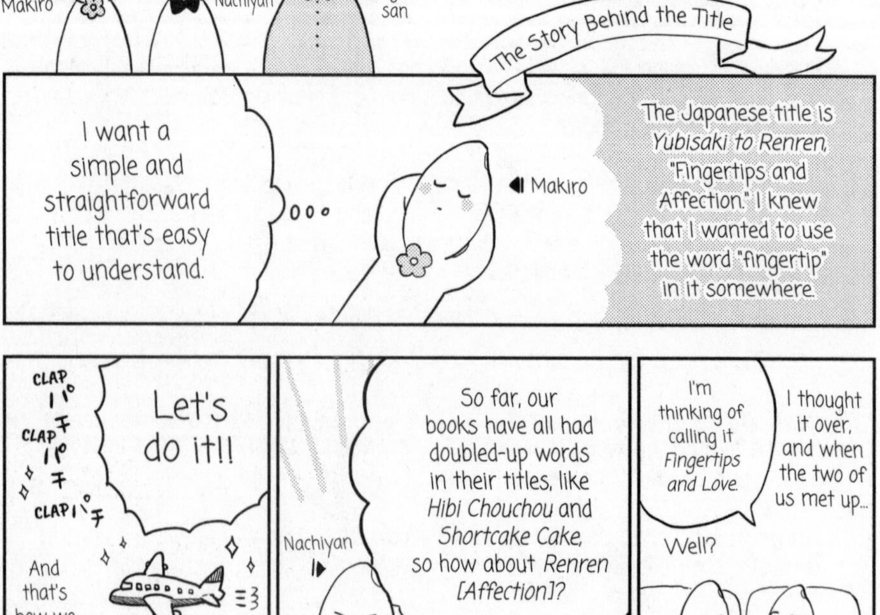

The Story Behind the Title
The Japanese title is *Yubisaki to Renren*, "Fingertips and Affection." I knew that I wanted to use the word "fingertip" in it somewhere.
Makiro
I want a simple and straightforward title that's easy to understand.
...
I thought it over, and when the two of us met up...
I'm thinking of calling it *Fingertips and Love*.
Well?
Nachiyan
So far, our books have all had doubled-up words in their titles, like *Hibi Chouchou* and *Shortcake Cake*, so how about *Renren* [*Affection*]?
It was during an international flight.
Let's do it!!
CLAP CLAP CLAP
And that's how we came up with it.

Special Thanks

- Editors: Shiigeru-san, Idenaga-san
- Balcolony's Takeuchi-san, Ichiki-san
- The editorial staff of *Dessert*
- Everyone at Spica Works
- The International Rights Department
- Sign language collaborator: Yuki Miyazaki-chan
- Backgrounds materials collaborator: Rockin' Robin, Osu branch
- Assistant: Nao Hamaguchi-chan
- Background help: Saya Aoi-san
- Everyone involved with the publishing

& all my readers!

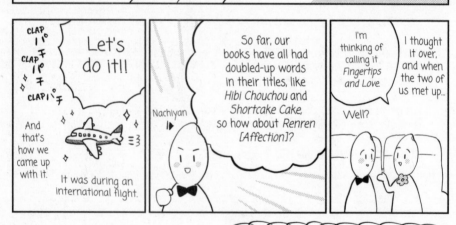

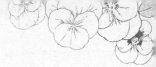

Interview with suu Morishita

This original interview between A Sign of Affection *creator suu Morishita and Kodansha Comics originally appeared on our website at kodanshacomics.com. Check it out for more peeks behind the scenes and insider videos!*

Kodansha Comics: I've heard that you are a two-person team making manga together. Could you tell us how you two met? How do you work together when you make a manga?

suu Morishita: We went to the same high school and were classmates. Makiro creates our storyboards/layouts, and Nachiyan illustrates the story. Along with our editor, the three of us discuss the series and check rough sketches together.

KC: Why do you draw yourselves as grains of rice in your self-portraits?

sM: The rice grain is a character called "Soboku-kun" that Nachiyan created when we were in high school. There's no specific reason why it's a rice grain, though (laughs).

We both liked that character, so when we debuted as manga artists and thought about our self-portrait, we decided to go with that. We also use it on our Twitter. *[Editor's note: Their handle is @morisita_suu, but, of course, their tweets are in Japanese.]*

KC: What inspired you to draw a manga focused on sign language and centered around a person with a hearing disability?

sM: When we were thinking about our next manga, Nachiyan suggested a story that involved sign language, and, coincidentally, that was a subject I wanted to personally try and figure out as a manga artist.

Sign language is difficult to express visually, and it's rare to see a Deaf protagonist in shojo manga. That's why we wanted to take up this challenge. Also, we felt that there were a lot of important elements that crossed over between both sign language and the shojo manga

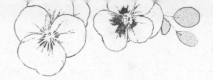

genre–both are full of expressions and emotions that aren't entirely stated, and exist beyond the spoken dialog. There's a feeling that in order to fully understand the emotions of the characters in shojo manga you need to pay attention to the entirety of the story, the expressions, the scenery, the reactions, and, yes, the dialog. Sign language is the same, in that you also have to pay attention to the signing, expressions, and more to fully understand what's being communicated.

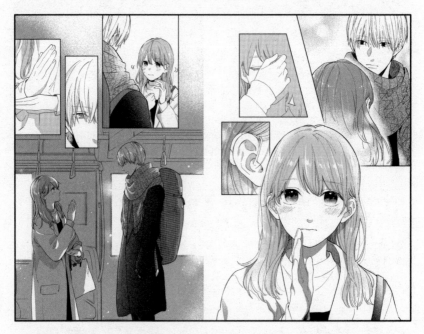

KC: Did you have firsthand experience using sign language before working on this manga? Or did you do a lot of research about the subject?

sM: I learned a little bit of sign language when I was in elementary school, but it was just singing a children's song in sign language. So we made sure to do some interviews before starting the series. We also read books, interviewed teachers at a school for the Deaf, and then, most importantly, we met Yuki Miyazaki, who supervised our use of sign language for this work. She also shares with us her world as a Deaf person and tells us about her daily life.

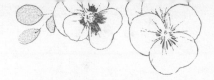

KC: When you started actually creating *A Sign of Affection*, **did you encounter any challenges? Or anything that went more smoothly than expected?**

Nachiyan-san: In shojo manga, it's important to show the faces and expressions of the characters in the story. But in this story, it's hard to keep panel composition from feeling stale, or, rather, all looking the same. Because if you try to draw only the facial expressions, you won't get to include the characters' hands doing sign language in the panel, or if you try to focus on the sign language, you won't get the facial expressions.

Makiro-san: I try to create Yuki's inner monologue and words carefully, since there are no speech balloons for her. I know it's a sensitive subject, so I'm careful of how I depict and represent this topic because I don't want people to get hurt by the way it's presented. Beyond Yuki, I also take care of the scenes, story arcs, and dialog. But the smoothest part is that Yuki is easy to portray as a character in terms of personality, moreso than the heroine characters we've had in our past works.

KC: What makes Yuki a unique person? What makes Itsuomi a unique person?

sM: In terms of personality, Yuki is more earnest and pure than our previous heroines. Also, I think her personality is more relatable and typical of a college girl. Itsuomi is someone who goes at his own pace and is not afraid of anything. But he's also very patient and empathetic.

KC: The color illustrations for *A Sign of Affection* **are very beautiful! Could you tell us a little bit about the tools that you use? I particularly love the use of warm color for the outline instead of solid black. Was this a stylistic choice for this series?**

Nachiyan-san: I use Copic Multiliner brown for the outlines, and Dr. Ph. Martin's color ink for coloring. In this manga, I'm trying to keep a soft and delicate art style.

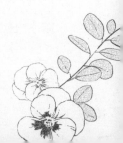

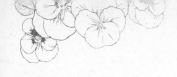

KC: Do you guys have a personal hobby? Do you think those hobbies help you to work on manga? Or not?

Nachiyan-san: My hobby is collecting the German toy PLAYMOBIL. It helps me to relax on a daily basis. Also, since I can't go out much these days, I've been playing *Animal Crossing*.

Makiro-san: I've also been playing *Animal Crossing* lately. Other than that, we like beauty blogs, beauty materials, and what's popular in beauty. Sometimes, we even use these beauty topics in our manga.

KC: What are some of the audience reactions on *A Sign of Affection* that you've seen so far?

sM: We often receive comments such as "it's きゅんきゅん (*kyun kyun*)*" and "it's 尊い (*toutoi*)*". We're happy to hear when people say that Yuki is a cute main character. Also, we feel we're getting more and more comments that fans read and reread this manga over and over again.

きゅんきゅん (kyun kyun): a kind of sparkling beauty
尊い (toutoi): too pure and should be treasured

WHAT?
HUH?
WHAT DO I SAY TO THAT?

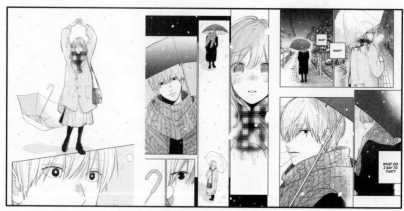

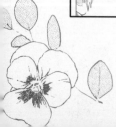

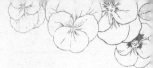

KC: *A Sign of Affection* is now available in English, and it's also going to be available as a simulpub. How does it make you feel to know that an overseas audience will be reading this manga at the same time as its release in Japan?

sM: It's so nice to be read by someone overseas in real time! There are many kinds of sign language in many countries, but I hope you can see that this is what Japanese sign language is like.

KC: Any last words to the fans of *A Sign of Affection*? What should the fans be looking forward to in this series in the near future?

sM: We're grateful that people are interested in our manga. We're getting more messages on Instagram from people abroad. We believe Itsuomi will learn sign language and use it more often in the future. Although sign language is a visual way to communicate, we hope that the emotions and sentiments that show up between the gaps in the fingers can be conveyed to the readers, as well, and that they take notice of what is left unsaid. We hope you will continue to read and enjoy this manga.

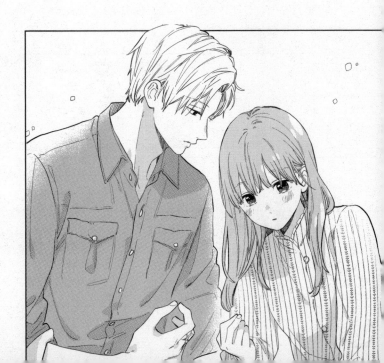

A SIGN OF AFFECTION

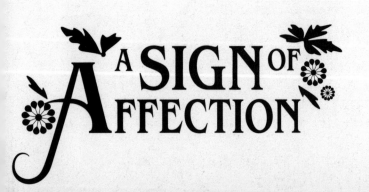

TRANSLATION NOTES

Yuki's Snowy World, page 3
Yuki's name is the Japanese word for snow. In Japanese, the title of this chapter is *yuki no sekai*, which means both "Yuki's world" and "world of snow." We decided to clue the reader into this double meaning by having her friend Rin-chan mention it on page 37.

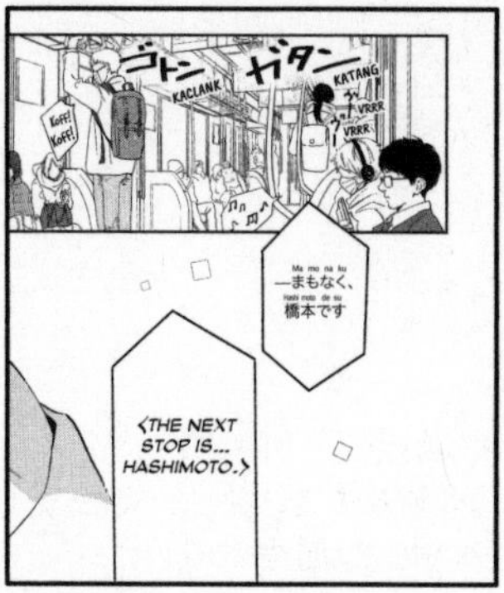
ゴトン
KACLANK
ガタン
KATANG
VRRR
VRRR
Koff! Koff!
—まもなく、橋本です
<THE NEXT STOP IS... HASHIMOTO.>

Train announcement, page 7
Like most train announcements in Japan, this one is bilingual, informing passengers of the next station first in Japanese, then in English.

College clubs, page 11
College activity clubs are called *saakuru* or "circles" in Japanese. They are important parts of a college student's social life, sometimes helping to nurture lifelong friendships.

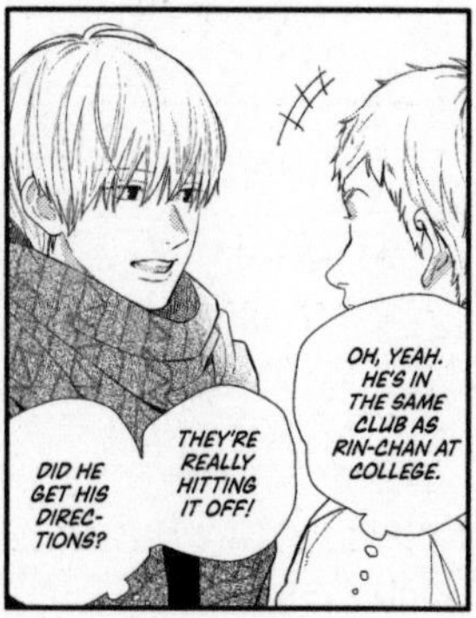
OH, YEAH. HE'S IN THE SAME CLUB AS RIN-CHAN AT COLLEGE.
THEY'RE REALLY HITTING IT OFF!
DID HE GET HIS DIREC-TIONS?

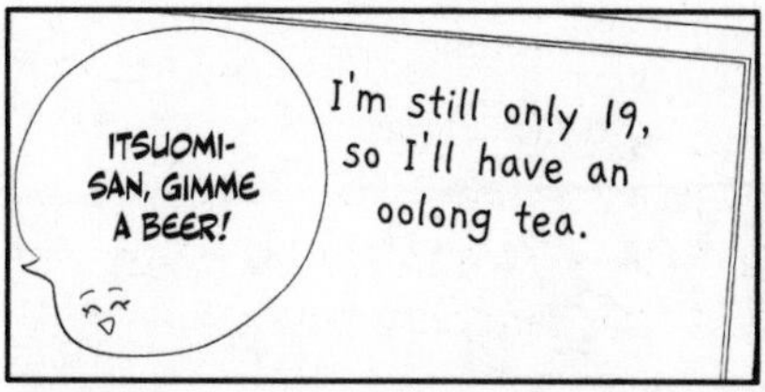
I'm still only 19, so I'll have an oolong tea.
ITSUOMI-SAN, GIMME A BEER!

Still only 19, page 30
In Japan, the drinking age is 20.

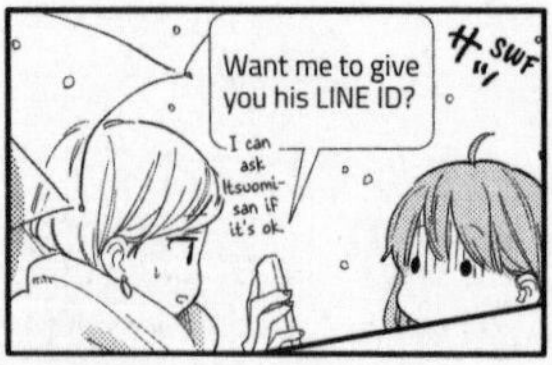
SWF
Want me to give you his LINE ID?
I can ask Itsuomi-san if it's ok.

LINE ID, page 36
LINE is a social network popular in Japan.

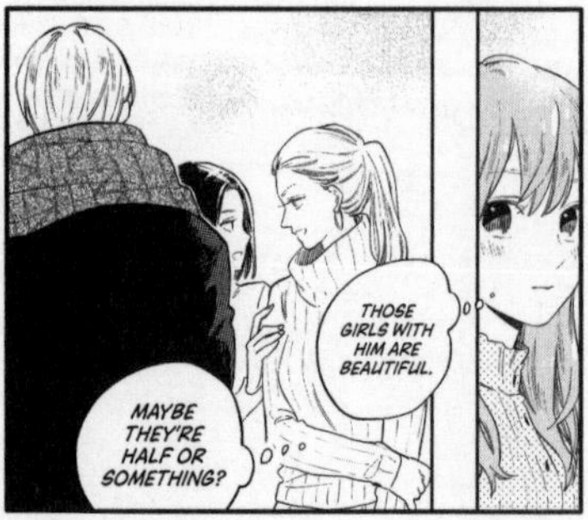
THOSE GIRLS WITH HIM ARE BEAUTIFUL.
MAYBE THEY'RE HALF OR SOMETHING?

Half or something, page 66
Yuki is wondering if the girls Itsuomi is talking with have one Japanese parent and one non-Japanese parent. The term for this in conversational Japanese is *haafu*, or "half."

20:12, page 151

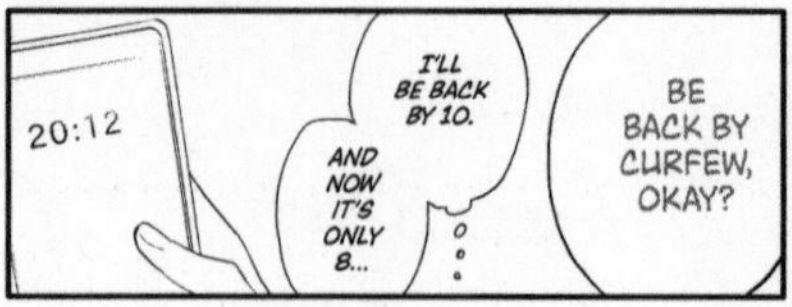
BE BACK BY CURFEW, OKAY?
I'LL BE BACK BY 10.
AND NOW IT'S ONLY 8...
20:12

In Japan, the 12-hour and 24-hour clock are both in common use. So one might say, "It's 8:12 pm" in conversation when their phone display reads "20:12."

Doubled-up words, page 173

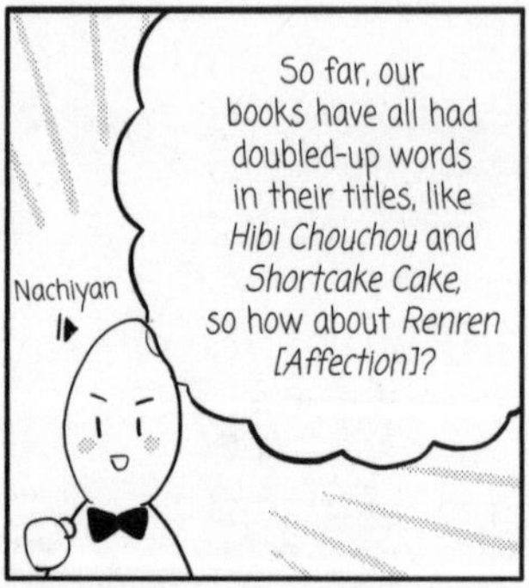
So far, our books have all had doubled-up words in their titles, like *Hibi Chouchou* and *Shortcake Cake*, so how about *Renren* [*Affection*]?
Nachiyan

The Japanese title of *A Sign of Affection* is ゆびさきと恋々 (*Yubisaki to renren*), or *Fingertips and Affection*. The character 々 usually has no set pronunciation associated with it in Japanese, instead indicating that the sound of the previous character should be repeated—in this case, *ren*, for love. suu Morishita's manga 日々蝶々 (*Hibi chouchou*) uses this character twice, to double up the characters for "day" and "butterfly," while, of course, *Shortcake Cake* doubles up the English word "cake."

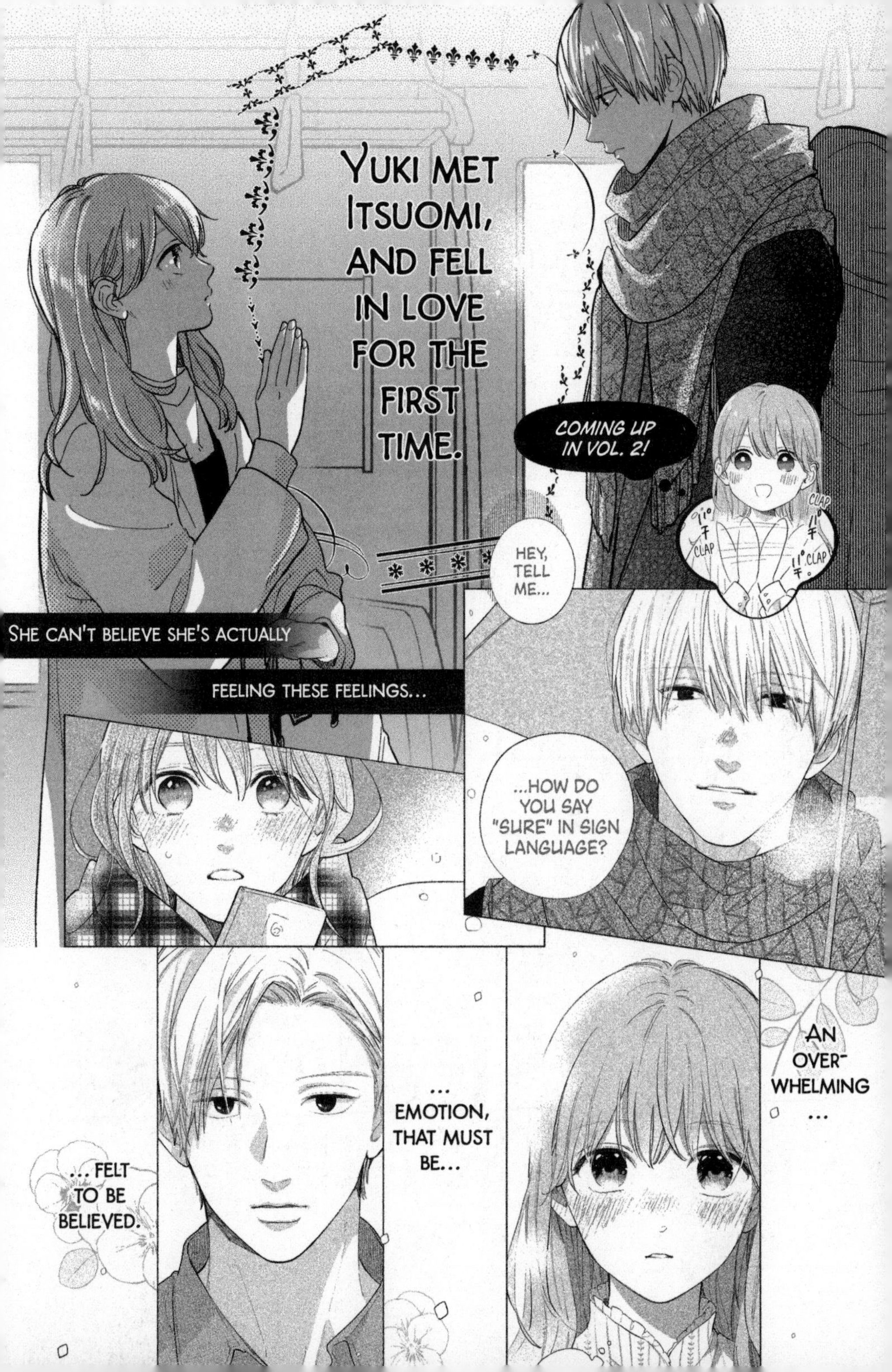

Yuki met Itsuomi, and fell in love for the first time.
Coming up in Vol. 2!
CLAP CLAP CLAP
Hey, tell me...
She can't believe she's actually
feeling these feelings...
...How do you say "sure" in sign language?
An over-whelming...
... emotion, that must be...
... felt to be believed.

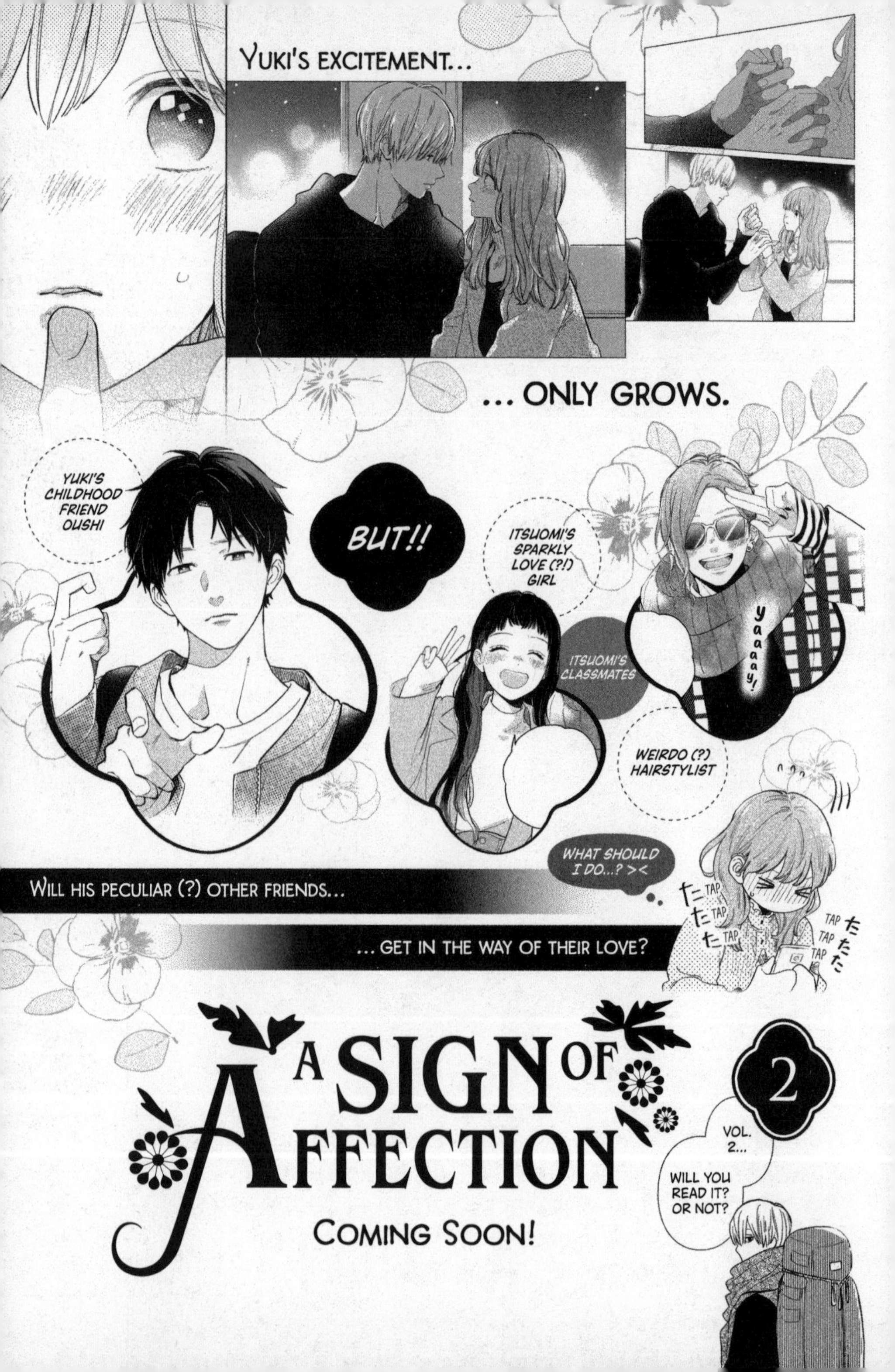
Yuki's excitement...
... only grows.
But!!
Yuki's childhood friend Oushi
Itsuomi's sparkly love (?!) girl
Itsuomi's classmates
Weirdo (?) hairstylist
Yaaaaay!
What should I do...? ><
TAP TAP TAP
たたた
TAP TAP TAP
たたた
Will his peculiar (?) other friends...
... get in the way of their love?
A Sign of Affection
2
Coming Soon!
Vol. 2...
Will you read it? Or not?

THE SWEET SCENT OF LOVE IS IN THE AIR! FOR FANS OF OFFBEAT ROMANCES LIKE *WOTAKOI*

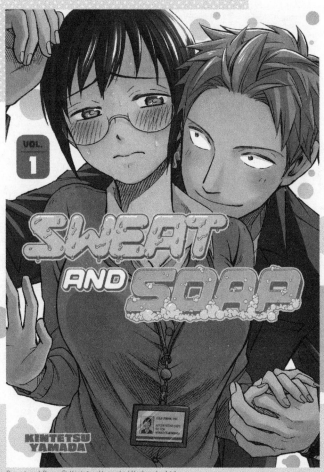

Sweat and Soap © Kintetsu Yamada / Kodansha Ltd.

In an office romance, there's a fine line between sexy and awkward... and that line is where Asako — a woman who sweats copiously — meets Koutarou — a perfume developer who can't get enough of Asako's, er, scent. Don't miss a romcom manga like no other!

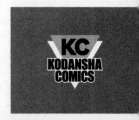

PERFECT WORLD

Rie Aruga

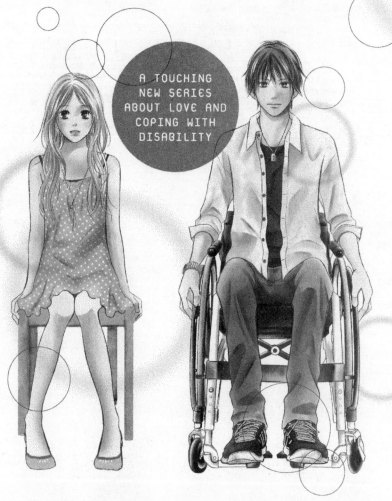

A TOUCHING NEW SERIES ABOUT LOVE AND COPING WITH DISABILITY

An office party reunites Tsugumi with her high school crush Itsuki. He's realized his dream of becoming an architect, but along the way, he experienced a spinal injury that put him in a wheelchair. Now Tsugumi's rekindled feelings will butt up against prejudices she never considered — and Itsuki will have to decide if he's ready to let someone into his heart...

"Depicts with great delicacy and courage the difficulties some with disabilities experience getting involved in romantic relationships... Rie Aruga refuses to romanticize, pushing her heroine to face the reality of disability. She invites her readers to the same tasks of empathy, knowledge and recognition."
—Slate.fr

"An important entry [in manga romance]... The emotional core of both plot and characters indicates thoughtfulness... [Aruga's] research is readily apparent in the text and artwork, making this feel like a real story."
—Anime News Network

KC
KODANSHA
COMICS

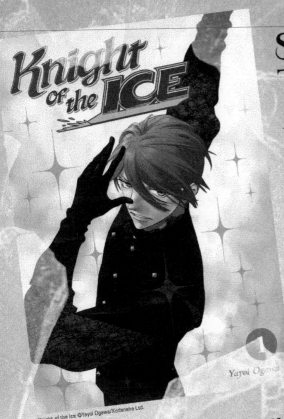

Knight of the ICE

Knight of the Ice ©Yayoi Ogawa/Kodansha Ltd.

Yayoi Ogawa

SKATING THRILLS AND ICY CHILLS WITH THIS NEW TINGLY ROMANCE SERIES!

A rom-com on ice, perfect for fans of *Princess Jellyfish* and *Wotakoi*. Kokoro is the talk of the figure-skating world, winning trophies and hearts. But little do they know... he's actually a huge nerd! From the beloved creator of *You're My Pet* (*Tramps Like Us*).

Chitose is a serious young woman, working for the health magazine *SASSO*. Or at least, she would be, if she wasn't constantly getting distracted by her childhood friend, international figure skating star Kokoro Kijinami! In the public eye and on the ice, Kokoro is a gallant, flawless knight, but behind his glittery costumes and breathtaking spins lies a secret: He's actually a hopelessly romantic otaku, who can only land his quad jumps when Chitose is on hand to recite a spell from his favorite magical girl anime!

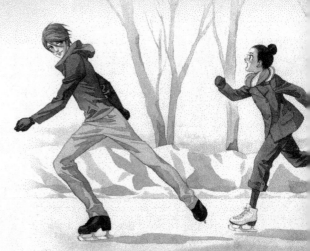

KC
KODANSHA
COMICS

SAINT ☆ YOUNG MEN

A LONG AWAITED ARRIVAL IN PREMIUM 2-IN-1 HARDCOVER

After centuries of hard work, Jesus and Buddha take a break from their heavenly duties to relax among the people of Japan, and their adventures in this lighthearted buddy comedy are sure to bring mirth and merriment to all!

"Brilliant…the physical comedy and facial expressions will make you literally LOL."
—Sam Humphries
(host of *DC Daily*; writer, *Green Lanterns, Legendary Star-Lord*)

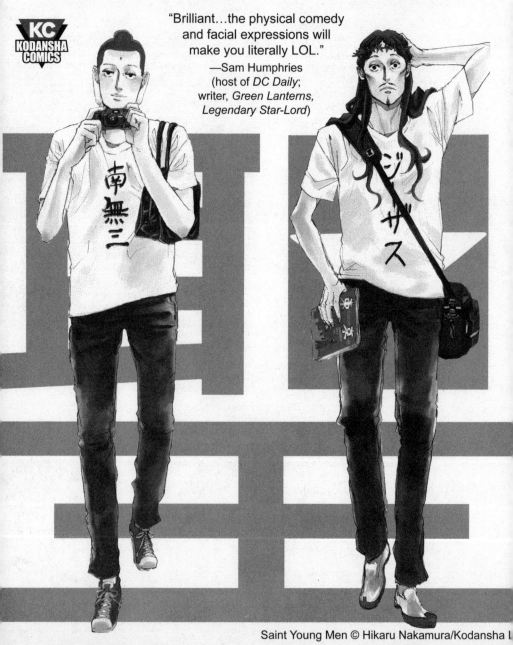

Saint Young Men © Hikaru Nakamura/Kodansha I

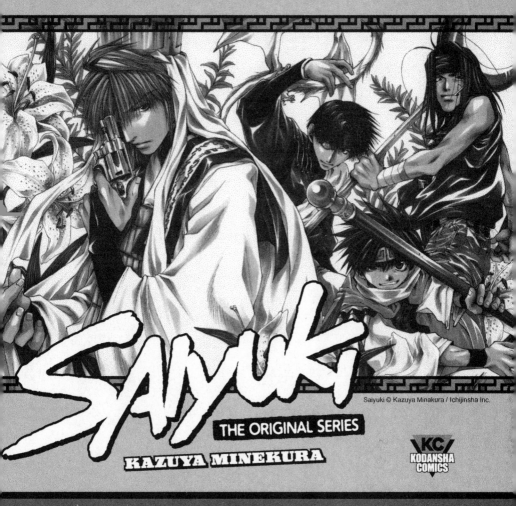

A SMART, NEW ROMANTIC COMEDY FOR FANS OF *SHORTCAKE CAKE* AND *TERRACE HOUSE*!

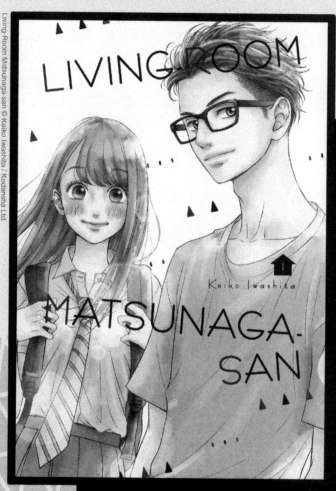

A romance manga starring high school girl Meeko, who learns to live on her own in a boarding house whose living room is home to the odd (but handsome) Matsunaga-san. She begins to adjust to her new life away from her parents, but Meeko soon learns that no matter how far away from home she is, she's still a young girl at heart — especially when she finds herself falling for Matsunaga-san.

Young characters and steampunk setting, like *Howl's Moving Castle* and *Battle Angel Alita*

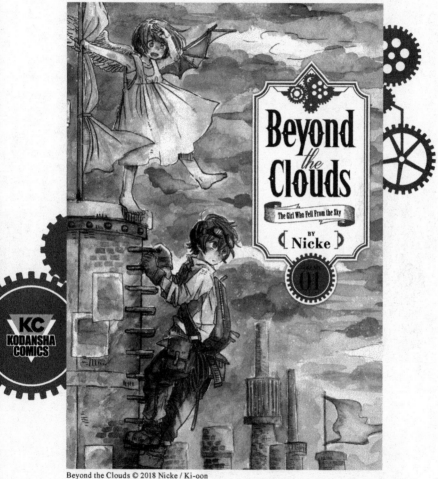

Beyond the Clouds © 2018 Nicke / Ki-oon

A boy with a talent for machines and a mysterious girl whose wings he's fixed will take you beyond the clouds! In the tradition of the high-flying, resonant adventure stories of Studio Ghibli comes a gorgeous tale about the longing of young hearts for adventure and friendship!

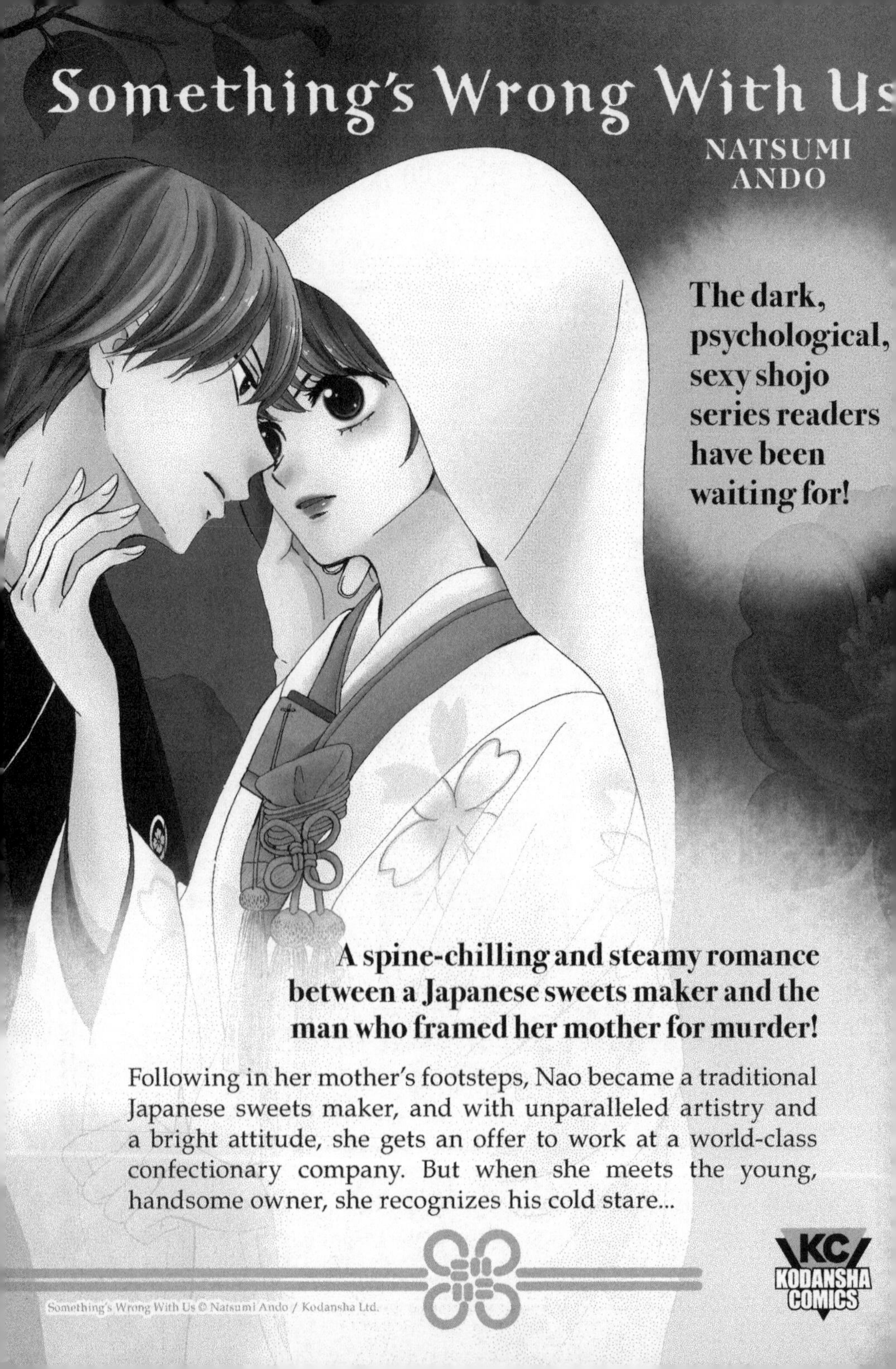
Something's Wrong With Us
NATSUMI ANDO
The dark, psychological, sexy shojo series readers have been waiting for!
A spine-chilling and steamy romance between a Japanese sweets maker and the man who framed her mother for murder!
Following in her mother's footsteps, Nao became a traditional Japanese sweets maker, and with unparalleled artistry and a bright attitude, she gets an offer to work at a world-class confectionary company. But when she meets the young, handsome owner, she recognizes his cold stare...
KC KODANSHA COMICS
Something's Wrong With Us © Natsumi Ando / Kodansha Ltd.

THE WORLD OF CLAMP!

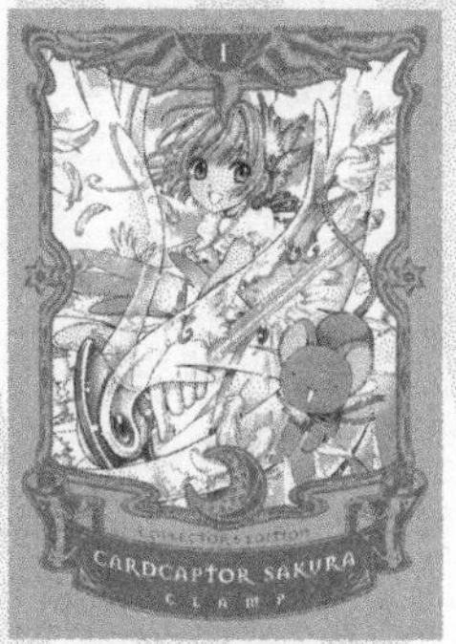
1
CARDCAPTOR SAKURA
CLAMP

Cardcaptor Sakura Collector's Edition

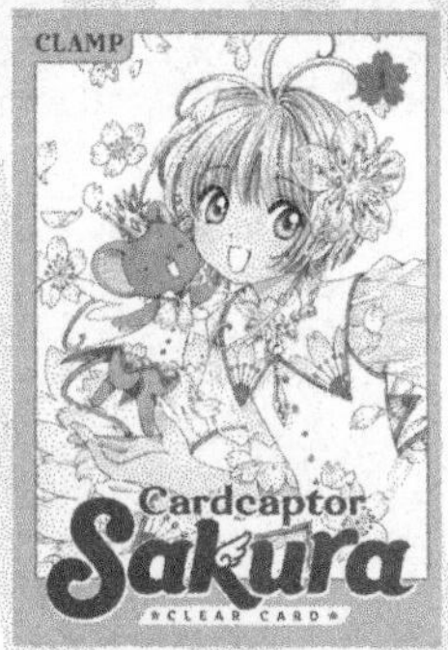
CLAMP
Cardcaptor Sakura
CLEAR CARD

Cardcaptor Sakura: Clear Card

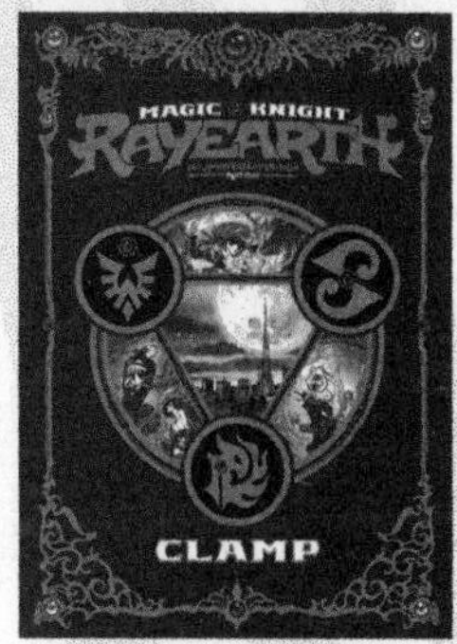
MAGIC KNIGHT
RAYEARTH
CLAMP

Magic Knight Rayearth 25th Anniversary Box Set

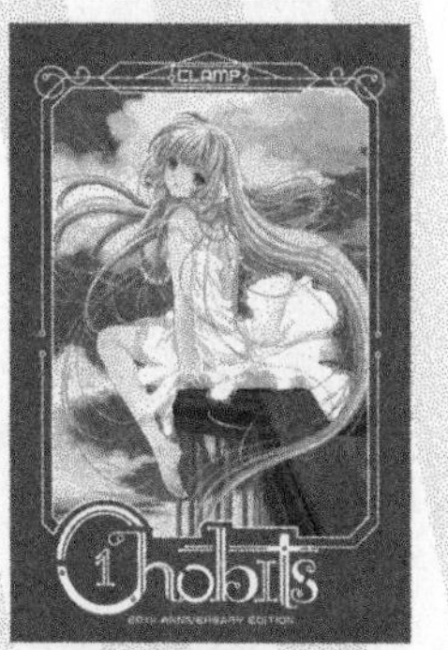
CLAMP
1 Chobits

Chobits

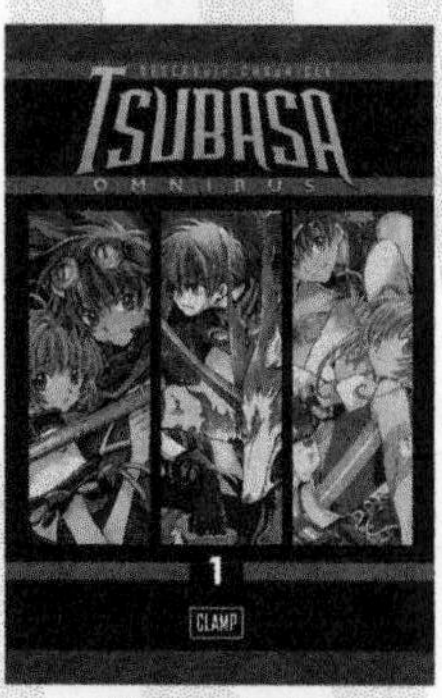
TSUBASA
OMNIBUS
1
CLAMP

TSUBASA Omnibus

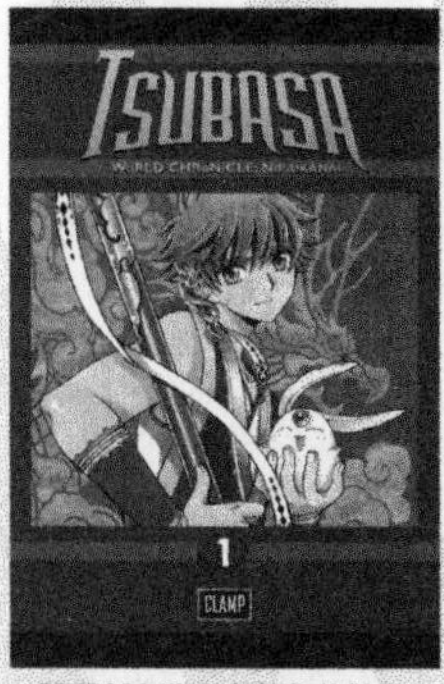
TSUBASA
1
CLAMP

TSUBASA WoRLD CHRoNiCLE

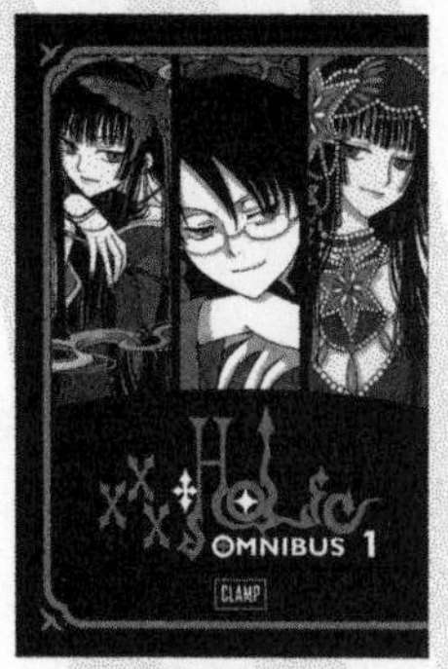
xxxHOLiC
OMNIBUS 1
CLAMP

xxxHOLiC Omnibus

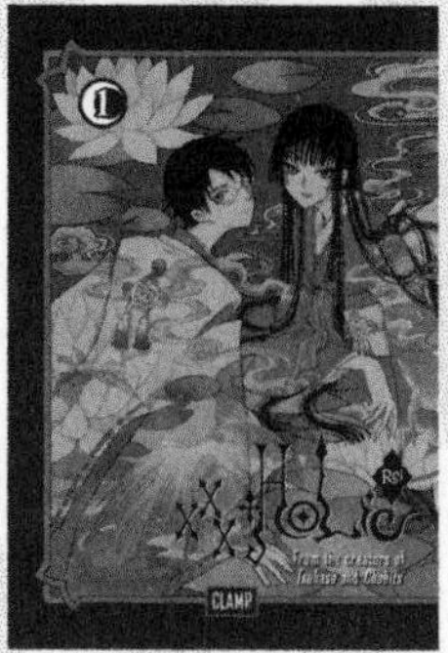
1
xxxHOLiC
Rei
CLAMP

xxxHOLiC Rei

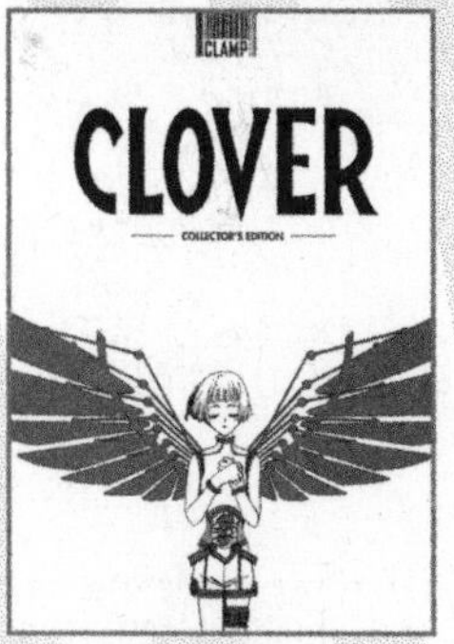
CLAMP
CLOVER
COLLECTOR'S EDITION

CLOVER Collector's Edition

Kodansha Comics welcomes you to explore the expansive world of CLAMP, the all-female artist collective that has produced some of the most acclaimed manga of the century. Our growing catalog includes icons like *Cardcaptor Sakura* and *Magic Knight Rayearth*, each crafted with CLAMP's one-of-a-kind style and characters!

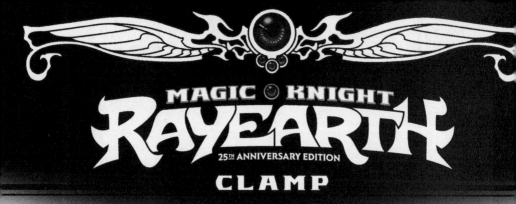

MAGIC ☆ KNIGHT RAYEARTH

25TH ANNIVERSARY EDITION

CLAMP

A BELOVED CLASSIC MAKES ITS STUNNING RETURN IN THIS GORGEOUS, LIMITED EDITION BOX SET!

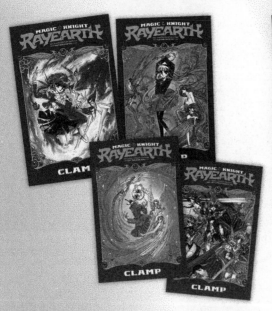

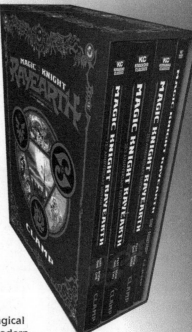

This tale of three Tokyo teenagers who cross through a magical portal and become the champions of another world is a modern manga classic. The box set includes three volumes of manga covering the entire first series of *Magic Knight Rayearth*, plus the series's super-rare full-color art book companion, all printed at a larger size than ever before on premium paper, featuring a newly-revised translation and lettering, and exquisite foil-stamped covers.

A strictly limited edition, this will be gone in a flash!

Magic Knight Rayearth 25th Anniversary Manga Box Set 1 © CLAMP ShigatsuTsuitachi CO.,LTD./Kodansha Ltd.

One of CLAMP's biggest hits returns in this definitive, premium, hardcover 20th anniversary collector's edition!

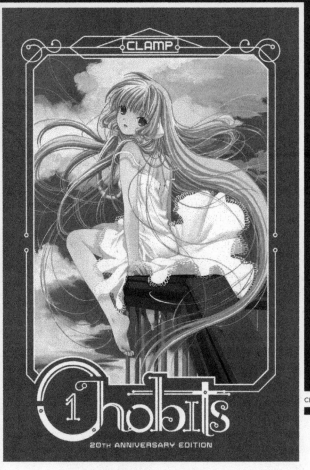

CLAMP

Chobits
20TH ANNIVERSARY EDITION

"A wonderfully entertaining story that would be a great installment in anybody's manga collection."
— Anime News Network

"CLAMP is an all-female manga-creating team whose feminine touch shows in this entertaining, sci-fi soap opera."
— Publishers Weekly

Poor college student Hideki is down on his luck. All he wants is a good job, a girlfriend, and his very own "persocom"—the latest and greatest in humanoid computer technology. Hideki's luck changes one night when he finds Chi—a persocom thrown out in a pile of trash. But Hideki soon discovers that there's much more to his cute new persocom than meets the eye.

**KC
KODANSHA
COMICS**

The art-deco cyberpunk classic from the creators of *xxxHOLiC* and *Cardcaptor Sakura*!

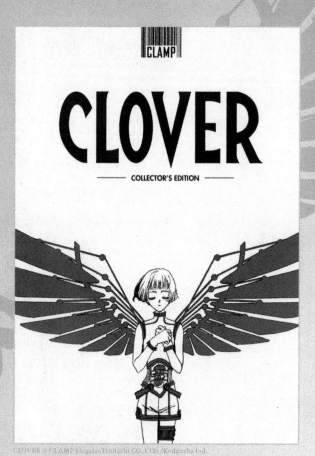

CLAMP
CLOVER
COLLECTOR'S EDITION

"Starred Review. This experimental sci-fi work from CLAMP reads like a romantic version of *AKIRA*."
—Publishers Weekly

Su was born into a bleak future, where the government keeps tight control over children with magical powers—codenamed "Clovers." With Su being the only "four-leaf" Clover in the world, she has been kept isolated nearly her whole life. Can ex-military agent Kazuhiko deliver her to the happiness she seeks? Experience the complete series in this hardcover edition, which also includes over twenty pages of ravishing color art!

KC KODANSHA COMICS

A Kodansha Comics Trade Paperback Original
A *Sign of Affection* 1 copyright © 2019 suu Morishita
English translation copyright © 2021 suu Morishita

Published in the United States by Kodansha Comics, an imprint of Kodansha USA Publishing, LLC, New York.

Publication rights for this English edition arranged through Kodansha Ltd., Tokyo.

First published in Japan in 2019 by Kodansha Ltd., Tokyo.

ISBN 978-1-64651-184-6

Original cover design by Sari Ichiki (Balcolony)

Printed in Mexico.

www.kodansha.us

W9-CKD-081

9 8 7 6 5 4
Translation: Christine Dashiell
Lettering: Carl Vanstiphout
Additional Lettering: Lys Blakeslee
Editing: Ben Applegate, William Flanagan
Kodansha Comics edition cover design by Adam Del Re

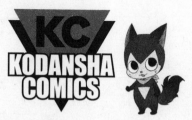

Publisher: Kiichiro Sugawara

Director of publishing services: Ben Applegate
Associate director of operations: Stephen Pakula
Publishing services managing editor: Noelle Webster
Assistant production manager: Emi Lotto, Angela Zurlo
Logo and character art ©Kodansha USA Publishing, LLC